A SMALL TOWN NEAR AUSCHWITZ

ORDINARY NAZIS AND THE HOLOCAUST

MARY FULBROOK

OXFORD
UNIVERSITY PRESS

Great Clarendon Street, Oxford, OX2 6DP,
United Kingdom

Oxford University Press is a department of the University of Oxford.
It furthers the University's objective of excellence in research, scholarship,
and education by publishing worldwide. Oxford is a registered trade mark of
Oxford University Press in the UK and in certain other countries

First Edition published in 2012
First published in paperback 2013

Impression: 1

Published in the United States of America by Oxford University Press
198 Madison Avenue, New York, NY 10016, United States of America

British Library Cataloguing in Publication Data
Data available

ISBN 978-0-19-960330-5 (Hbk.)
ISBN 978-0-19-967925-6 (Pbk.)

Printed in Great Britain by
Ashford Colour Press Ltd, Gosport, Hampshire

A SMALL TOWN NEAR AUSCHWITZ

Mary Fulbrook is Professor of German History at University College London (UCL). She has written widely on modern German history, including *A Concise History of Germany* (1990), *Anatomy of a Dictatorship: Inside the GDR* (1995, also published by Oxford University Press), *German National Identity after the Holocaust* (1999), *The People's State: East German Society from Hitler to Honecker* (2005), and *A History of Germany 1918–2008* (2008). Her most recent book is *Dissonant Lives: Generations and Violence through the German Dictatorships* (Oxford University Press, 2011). A Fellow of the British Academy, she is former Chair of the German History Society and a member of the Academic Advisory Board of the Foundation for the former Concentration Camps at Buchenwald and Mittelbau-Dora.

Preface

This book explores the overlapping stories of individuals and groups in the *Landkreis* or county of Będzin, an area annexed by the German Reich following the Nazi invasion of Poland in 1939. In particular, it focuses on the role of the principal civilian administrator or chief executive of the county, the *Landrat*, and the experiences of the tens of thousands of Jews in the area for which he held responsibility—an area a mere 25 miles from Auschwitz. It also confronts the ambiguous legacies, memories, and representations of this past with the historical realities, as far as these can be reconstructed, on the basis of a wide array of sources.

There are innumerable narratives and eyewitness accounts on which this book draws; only a tiny fraction of this rich material could be included or discussed here, and even after working on this project intensively over many years I am all too aware of its shortcomings. This book addresses a topic that, for so many reasons that scarcely need spelling out, is intrinsically beyond the capacity of any one person to address in any manner adequate to the questions that it raises.

But it is nevertheless a book that I felt compelled to write. For it is not merely about the history and memory of the Holocaust as experienced in one small town in Poland: embedded in this exploration are unsettling personal uncertainties as I seek to confront an emergent historical view of the *Landrat* with his own later version of his past, in which he claims he knew very little and did nothing wrong, but did not want 'innocently to become guilty'. For there are close personal connections between his family and mine that troubled me deeply, once I realized both what his wartime role had been, and how little I had realized anything at all about this past during the many decades when I knew him personally. I have sought to respect the rights to privacy of those who were not 'persons of contemporary history', as German archival guidelines call those who were not acting in official or prominent historical roles. But inevitably both my interest in and my wider understanding of the story were informed and driven by personal connections, and these interests have in part structured my account.

Should a professional historian undertake research on a topic with such close personal implications? At first, I did not think so. But it increasingly became clear to me that the questions raised and the implications suggested by this case are of wider significance than the personal aspects that initially drew me towards it. Furthermore, the sense of an acute personal interest must be shared by so many 'second- and third-generation' Europeans concerned about the ways in which members of their families and others they knew well had been involved in the horrendous history of the mid-twentieth century. This is, therefore, also in part a book about ambivalence and ambiguity in history, about the personal meanings and interpretation of historical accounts, and about the differences between what people may have thought or felt, and the ways in which they actually behaved. Unfortunately it was the latter that had historical consequences.

This case study also inevitably raises questions of far wider historical significance. It became clear to me, in trying to make sense of the *Landrat*'s role at the time, his actions, inner doubts, and later self-justifications, that his story is in many ways paradigmatic of ways in which the Holocaust was made possible even and perhaps especially because of the actions of those who would never explicitly have supported or implemented policies of mass murder; and also paradigmatic of ways in which it was possible to live with the knowledge of these events afterwards, by selective silences and by constructing an acceptable life story couched in terms of widely prevalent patterns of self-exculpation. This particular *Landrat* is in some senses, then, merely posthumously unlucky in being singled out for such extensive exploration; his case could be replicated endlessly, with variations across different roles and areas in the Third Reich.

And there are other more general lessons to be learned from this case. Here, I have sought particularly to highlight the unintended longer-term consequences of action when people have been mobilized to behave in certain ways and within certain roles in a dynamically developing system, whatever their inner attitudes and values at the time may have been. Ultimately in this case, as in so many others, it is behaviour as constrained by a system, and not the purity of inner convictions, that actually matters in determining what historical outcomes are possible and which are precluded. Even so, exploring inner ambivalence can help to provide some sort of guide as to where the difficulties lay in keeping an eye open to injustices, or in taking action to refuse to cooperate further with a fundamentally immoral system.

This is a story neither of a committed 'perpetrator', nor of someone engaged in active resistance; it may perhaps therefore contribute, equally significantly, to our knowledge of some of the reasons why so many who held themselves to be 'decent' people went along with the Nazi regime for so long, and what some of the ultimately murderous consequences of their behaviour actually were, however horrific this may have appeared in retrospect. It is relatively rare to be able to lay contemporary sources alongside later self-representations in quite such detail. There are, however, some things that can be known, and others that cannot. I am sure that, as in other areas and even where the facts are incontrovertible, the interpretations and conclusions I reach will be contested; but that is inevitable in history, and particularly so in relation to a topic so contentious and so significant as the Holocaust.

Not least, I want here also to give some voice to those who were the victims, and whose own stories too are often only partial. Limited by their particular worm's-eye view within a system of terror, where they had constantly to second guess unpredictable moves by the authorities and scrabble for survival against all the odds; on the receiving end of Nazi policies and practices that affected them in devastating ways; partially buffered but also, by virtue of its role, repeatedly betrayed by the Central Office of the Jewish Councils, which was coerced into unwilling collaboration with the Nazi authorities; and on the receiving end of violence in the persons, among others, not only of members of the 'gendarmerie' or local constabulary, the regular and criminal police forces, the Gestapo and the SS (*Schutzstaffel*), but also of the Jewish militia; in this context of raging violence and uncertainty, of progressive degradation and humiliation, of exploitation and expropriation, of maltreatment and starvation, most Jews never explicitly identified or grasped the roles of civilian administrators, the consequences of whose actions they most certainly had to bear. And nor did the *Landrat* seem ever to register fully the consequences of the policies he implemented on those who were subjected to them; this lack of insight or empathy on his part was perhaps a key factor in his being able to play the role that he did at the time. Although he did not live with an entirely easy conscience after the war, continually reassessing the past and the ways he had got caught up in Nazism, he never entirely registered the consequences of his behaviour for the Jews.

This is a scholarly work, but it is not only that; it is not what might be called a purely academic account of the fate of the Jews of Będzin. If there are personal interests connected with my exploration of the role of the *Landrat*, I have then to admit also to a sense of personal obligation towards remembrance of the victims. For all sorts of reasons, it is not possible to write about this period and place without some degree of emotional involvement.

Mary Fulbrook

London
14 September 2011

Acknowledgements

I would like to thank the Leverhulme Trust for awarding me a three-year Major Research Fellowship to work on a monograph, *Dissonant Lives: Generations and Violence through the German Dictatorships* (OUP, 2011), out of which this book also, inadvertently, grew. I had initially intended to use some family papers only as a small case study within the context of that already rather long book; but the concerns raised by this case appeared so significant that I soon felt it had to be explored separately, in its own right, led by different questions and pursued in a very different manner. My thanks are due to Christopher Wheeler of Oxford University Press for his characteristic perceptiveness and acuity when I talked this through with him and clarified the distinctions between the projects, and to Matthew Cotton for bearing with my repeatedly amended timetables for completing not one but two books.

Many archivists assisted me with my research. I was fortunate to be able to undertake research in the following: the Archive of the Rhineland Regional Council (*Landschaftsverband Rheinland*) in Pulheim-Brauweiler, near Cologne; the Central Office of the Judicial Authorities for the Investigation of National Socialist Crimes (*Zentrale Stelle der Landesjustizverwaltungen zur Aufklärung nationalsozialistischer Verbrechen*) in Ludwigsburg; the Federal Archive of Germany (*Bundesarchiv*) in Berlin; the Secret State Archive of Prussian Cultural Heritage (*Geheimes Staatsarchiv Preussischer Kulturbesitz*) in Berlin; the Katowice State Archive (*Archiwum Państwowe w Katowicach*) in Katowice; and the Archive of the Institute of Jewish History (*Archiwum Żydowskiego Instytutu Historycznego*) in Warsaw. I am very grateful to Judith Cohen for access to the photographic collection of the United States Holocaust Memorial Museum (USHMM) in Washington, DC. Lara Silberklang kindly provided me with copies of testimonies from the Yad Vashem archive in Israel. I also benefited from the tremendous resources of the interviews carried out by Steven Spielberg's Survivors of the Shoah Visual History

Foundation, now collected and preserved as the Visual History Archive of the University of Southern California Shoah Foundation Institute; I accessed these interviews both in the Free University Berlin, and in Columbia University, New York.

My thanks are especially due to Dr Ekkehard Klausa for so generously making his family archive available to me, including his mother's wartime letters; for sharing with me over many discussions and in writing the results of his own researches into his father's actions and thoughts; and for reading through and commenting in detail on a complete draft of this book. If ever there were a moment for the standard comment about the author taking all responsibility for the failings that remain, this is it; Ekkehard Klausa and I will probably never completely agree on how best to interpret his father's role, but I hope I have given his views an adequate hearing and adjusted my presentation accordingly, as well as presenting my own interpretation of this ambiguous past. I am deeply impressed by Ekkehard Klausa's willingness to face and determination to understand his parents' past with such honesty. He knows that in the course of long-running legal investigations his father was never brought to prosecution or found to have done anything wrong in the terms of the West German criminal law; but nor did his father ever claim to be a hero of the resistance. Udo Klausa's private papers and his wife's letters of the time show him to have been troubled, but he continued to act as a loyal servant of the Reich; whatever his private feelings may have been, in his conformist behaviour—so similar to countless others at the time—lies part of the explanation of the unfolding tragedy of the Holocaust. While respecting his father for his determination to return to military service rather than remain on the home front, Ekkehard Klausa has dedicated his own life, not only in his career but even as a volunteer in retirement, to opening up this awful past to students and the general public, with a particular emphasis on the experiences of the victims and the possibility and desirability of resistance. In a sense, Ekkehard Klausa's approach is illustrative of just how courageously many Germans of the 'second generation' have faced up to the actions and also the failures to act of their parents' generation.

Eyewitnesses, survivors, and members of the 'second' and subsequent generations have been immensely helpful in this research. My particular thanks are due to Arno Lustiger, who gave so much of his time and expertise in telling me about his own experiences and sharing his professional knowledge of the wider history of the area; I would also like to thank his daughter

Gila Lustiger for speaking from her perspective. Many people in Będzin and surrounding villages were extremely helpful: we were able to talk both with key eyewitnesses and also with people with a professional interest in history and memorialization. Polish perspectives on the history of the area only really began to come alive for me through such discussions.

I am very grateful to Marta Szymska for help with the oral history interviews conducted in Polish, and to Conrad Fulbrook and Lara Silberklang for assistance with filming these interviews and the surrounding memorial culture in the wider Będzin and Auschwitz area. My thanks are due to my Polish teachers at both UCL-SSEES and the City Lit for their valiant efforts to imbue me with sufficient Polish to be able at least to identify which sources in Polish archives might be relevant—but, even with the aid of good teachers and a dictionary, Polish proved to be not as easy as I would have liked. I am also grateful to Kinga Bloch for assistance with translation into English of quotations from the Polish interviews; I alone am responsible for reading and translating the Polish testimonies from the Institute of Jewish History in Warsaw, and, unless otherwise indicated, for translations from German sources throughout. As always, UCL continued to provide a highly congenial and supportive environment for my work; and I benefited from discussions with students and colleagues not only at UCL but also in numerous seminars and conferences across continents.

Finally, my thanks are most of all due to my family. Julian accompanied me on all trips to Poland, read through and commented in detail on successive drafts of this book, and constantly sustained me in so many ways while I worked through the difficult personal questions at the heart of this research; he has had to live with it too. My eldest brother, Hanno, was an interested discussion partner and a highly supportive sounding board, reading through a whole draft of the manuscript. Conrad and Lara played a key role in exploring the Będzin area, filming and talking to local people. Carl, Erica, and now also John continually reminded me that there is far more to life than an obsession with the past, however significant the legacies of that past may still seem to be so many decades later.

Contents

A Note on Terms, Polish Place Names, and Other Conventions

Given the overwhelming significance of the topic and the need to concentrate on essentials here, I do not follow the current practice of trying to avoid use of the very widely used term 'Holocaust', however inappropriate some of its assumed associations may be. The term Holocaust, derived from the Greek words meaning 'totally burnt', is alleged to imply associations with a 'burnt offering' or 'sacrifice', which certainly has nothing to do with the policies of extermination referred to by the Nazis as the 'final solution of the Jewish question'—but I see no particular benefits in always trying to use variants of that Nazi phrase either. I shall therefore deploy whichever term comes most easily in any given context, in the interests of focusing on the central questions rather than distracting attention unnecessarily.

Place names have posed some difficulty, given the changes back and forth between a number of spellings and particularly between German and Polish versions, which also changed at different times and are sometimes spelled phonetically in a number of inconsistent ways. The Polish Będzin was referred to as Bendin by the Jewish population, and renamed Bendsburg by the Germans on 21 May 1941. Among other variations, it is frequently spelled Bendzin to reflect the Polish pronunciation, where the 'ę' letter is pronounced nasally, almost as 'en' or 'eng', and the 'dz' is pronounced somewhat like the 'j' in 'jeans'; the emphasis is on the first syllable, hence for Anglophones phonetically perhaps pronounced as 'Benjin', rhyming with 'engine'. Other features of Polish pronunciation are occasionally footnoted where a place name first occurs. As far as general principles are concerned, I have sought to retain clarity while not further embedding Nazi neologisms into contemporary usage, and have generally desisted from perpetuating particularly innovative Nazi 'Germanizations' of Polish names; but in quotations the original spellings within the source are retained. Where there is a question of balance, I have generally used the Polish spelling in preference to other versions (as in

Sosnowiec rather than Sosnowitz), but have used the German version in cases where there was a long-standing German name for a particular place that had formerly been part of the state of Prussia, or where there is a good reason for using the German version of the name (for example, in distinguishing the concentration camp of Auschwitz from the town of the same name, for which I use the Polish Oświęcim). I have sometimes used the Polish version when referring to the location after 1945 (Katowice) and the German version for the place at the time of Nazi occupation (Kattowitz).

Some paragraphs, sections, and quotations in this book have also been used in other publications, including two articles on closely related themes. I have on occasion retranslated quotations, so the wording may not always be identical across publications.

'Persons of contemporary history' by virtue of the public roles they played in this highly significant historical context have been named in full. I have also not sought to anonymize the names of people who gave testimonies or oral history interviews for explicitly public, legal, or educational purposes (witness testimonies for war crimes trials, the filmed USC Shoah Foundation interviews, and some of my own oral history interviews); but I have sought to preserve the anonymity of those individuals who do not come under the category of 'persons of contemporary history' by virtue of their historical roles. The one significant exception to this is the *Landrat*'s wife, who might perhaps not be considered a 'person of contemporary history' in her own right—but it is in large part because of her observations in her letters of the time that I became interested in this case in the first place. I have therefore, with Dr Ekkehard Klausa's permission, quoted quite extensively from her letters to her mother and to a family friend at the time. These letters are not only crucial in trying to understand the state of mind and the movements of the *Landrat*, his inner ambivalence and outer behaviour; they also provide revealing insights into the lives of German women of her class in this area of annexed Poland. It is also worth remembering that this book need not have been written if the occupying Germans had at that time had more respect for the privacy and family lives of the Będzin Jews; German attitudes in everyday life are an integral part of the story of how the deportation and murder of the Jews were possible, and 'privacy' is itself a historical concept. I have nevertheless sought as best I could to respect the privacy of the *Landrat*'s family life in areas not directly related to the *Landrat*'s role and the extermination of the Jews of Będzin.

List of Maps and Figures

List of maps

List of figures

I

Legacies of Violence

Every September, at the beginning of the school year, the brass band of the renowned Jewish High School of Będzin, the Fürstenberg Grammar School, would march at the head of a procession of the students and teachers to the Great Synagogue, situated on the hillside below the ancient and dominating castle of Będzin.[1] There, in a ceremony directed by the Rabbi, the school would receive its blessing for the coming year.

But not so in September 1939. Following the German invasion of Poland and the rapid conquest of this border region, the school was closed down. Within days, the Great Synagogue was set on fire, and, locked inside it and the surrounding houses, several hundred Jews were burnt alive, or shot dead as they jumped out of windows and sought to flee their burning homes. Local Polish people could hear the screams as Jews plunged into the water of the nearby river, in a vain effort to put out the flames, but were shot at if their heads popped up to get some air. Others were luckier, and found sanctuary in the nearby Catholic church. For days, the river ran red with blood; and people had to step over dead bodies in the streets between the ruins of the burnt-out houses.[2]

This mass murder of civilians, at the beginning of September 1939, was one of the very first atrocities in a spiralling sequence of violence that later became known as the Holocaust. Będzin was located in a strip of land, Eastern Upper Silesia, that was soon incorporated into the Greater German Reich. Over the following two years, the Jews of the area were forced out of their homes and made to live within increasingly overcrowded areas, robbed of their livelihoods and possessions, exploited as forced labour or sent away to work camps, and made to live under ever more restricted conditions, on ever reduced rations, under a regime of terror. The pattern of ghettoization here differed from that in other places, but the various stages of the Jews' progressive concentration and effective incarceration tell us much about the role of local initiatives in the meandering policies that ultimately led to Auschwitz. Eventually, even the labour of Jews appeared less important to some Nazis than their removal entirely from German-dominated Europe; physical extermination, mass murder, ultimately became the Nazis' 'final solution' to their self-imposed 'Jewish problem'. In the course of 1942–3, the vast majority of the Jews who had remained in Będzin were taken, in three major deportations and innumerable smaller round-ups, to their deaths—most of them gassed in the extermination camp of Auschwitz–Birkenau, a mere 25 miles away down the railway tracks.

Within less than fours years after the German invasion, virtually half the population of the town of Będzin—the Jewish half—including nearly all the children and teachers of the Fürstenberg High School, were dead. Not only the Great Synagogue, but the entire culture and society that it represented, were erased.

How was the murder of half the citizens of this town made possible? We know a great deal about the roles of those at the front lines of violence—the SS, the Gestapo, and the police forces under Heinrich Himmler—as well as about policy formation and decision-making processes at the very top of Hitler's state. We also know about the ways in which members of the German Army were drawn into or facilitated the killing of civilians on the eastern front, the ways in which people of a variety of ethnic and national backgrounds collaborated in the perpetration of atrocities committed in areas conquered by Germany across Eastern Europe, and the implementation of ghettoization and extermination policies in some of the occupied territories, particularly the General Government, the rump Polish state under Hans Frank. Victim and survivor accounts are increasingly giving us a sense of the experiences of those on the receiving end of these policies—yet they generally record or remember only those perpetrators who directly beat and bludgeoned them, who chased them into or out of cattle trucks, who coerced them in slave labour or killed and hurt people for no reason other than their 'race'. But the testimonies of victims and survivors tell us little about the everyday civilian administration that lay behind their experiences of being thrown out of their own homes, forced into ghettos, deprived of their liberty and their livelihoods. Moreover, the details emerging from archival evidence can tell us about policy formation and implementation, but little about how those carrying out this administration saw their roles. Only recently have there been developments in researching the mentalities and personalities involved.[3]

Figure 1. Fürstenberg high school classroom, 1938
Pictured (in alphabetical order) are Hanka Barenblatt, Dobka Birenbaum, Karola Bojm, Szyja Brodkiewicz, Hala Buchwajc, Cesia Czarnes, Sala Czarnocha, Abram Dafner, Lolek (?) Danciger, Naftali Feder, Ksylek Golenzer, Tusia Graubart, Salka Gutman, Kuba Heller, Schewa Ingster, Prof. Jozef Kleinfeld, Alek Koninski, Dudka Lipszyc, Jadzia Liwer, Lola Majerczyk, Ada Neufeld, Marys Ptasznik, Minek Rappaport, Cwi Rozencwajg, Esta Strochlic, Roza Strochlic, Rozia Szenker, and Hanka Tintpulwer.
United States Holocaust Memorial Museum, courtesy of Joan Liwer Wren. From Kersten Brandt, Hanno Loewy, and Krystyna Olesky, Before They Perished: Photographs found in Auschwitz *(Oświęcim: Auschwitz–Birkenau State Museum, 2001), ii. 61.*

This book tries to bring several sides of the story together, focusing not only on how the exploitation and eventual murder of the Jews of the area unfolded, but also on the diversity of ways in which it was later remembered, exploring particularly the self-representations of the principal civilian administrator, the *Landrat* or Chief Executive of the *Landkreis* or County of Będzin.[4] The *Landrat* of Będzin at this time was one Udo Klausa, who provided his own account both in his memoirs and in defence statements to legal investigations; his wife also wrote frequent letters to her mother at the time, providing insights into her day-to-day experiences and perceptions. It is therefore possible to explore the period and place in some detail, juxtaposing archival evidence and subjective testimonies.

This enquiry poses many questions, not least arising from the former *Landrat*'s own account of his time in Będzin. Was the *Landrat* essentially powerless in the face of the brute force of the Gestapo (secret state police) and the SS (*Schutzstaffel*, Hitler's elite 'protection squad', which expanded massively under Heinrich Himmler)? Did he protest in subtle ways that have barely left a residue in the archival debris, and then offer himself silently for potential self-sacrifice at the front? Or were his later self-representations something of a camouflage, a way of dealing with a more disturbing truth? Was he, like so many others in Nazi Germany, acquiescent and effectively complicit in the rule of terror, turning a blind eye to the policies of murder carried out by his colleagues, and barely registering the consequences of his own actions? Did he even play an active role in the unfolding tragedy of the Jews of Upper Silesia? What can we learn from a case where the outcomes of actions were out of line with the individual motives and intentions of those charged with the implementation of Nazi policies? And how typical was this particular *Landrat*? How far do his actions and his apparent ambivalence help us to understand those Germans who played along at the time and later professed to be shocked at what Hitler's Third Reich had unleashed? What were the long-term legacies for those involved in this area, whether as victims, perpetrators, bystanders, or facilitators of the Holocaust, as well as for those of later generations, and what light does this case throw on memory and memorialization?

Answers to these questions are intended not as an attempt at either exoneration or indictment of this particular individual, but rather as a contribution to understanding how the Holocaust was possible. Klausa's career path, his underlying assumptions and unthinking racism, and even his distaste for aspects of Nazi brutality and eventual unwillingness to be associated with acts of outright murder while earlier turning a blind eye to the causation of innumerable deaths by starvation and disease, were typical of many Nazi functionaries and facilitators. Klausa's experiences and perceptions, and the ways in which his career and the lives of the Jews of Będzin came together, can help us better understand the functioning of the Nazi system, the development of the preconditions for mass murder, and the lingering consequences of Hitler's rule.

The fate of the Jews of Będzin

The rough outlines of the story of Będzin echo those of so many other places in Poland that had, until the German invasion of September 1939, enjoyed just a couple of decades of national independence after the First

World War. With the benefit of hindsight we now know how the always brutal racism of the Nazis turned eventually into a policy of extermination, but it must be remembered that at the time it was by no means clear at each stage how matters would develop.

The conquest of Poland by the Germans, who carved it up in conjunction with the Soviet Union, was a short, ruthless, business. Following a mere matter of weeks of *Blitzkrieg* or 'lightning war', western areas of Poland—Eastern Upper Silesia, in which Będzin was located, the Wartheland directly to the north, and parts of East Prussia and West Prussia—were incorporated into an enlarged 'Greater German Reich'; in the east, the Soviet Union took possession of territories agreed under the Hitler–Stalin pact that had been stitched up in August 1939; and the remaining rump state in the centre became the Polish 'General Government', under the German Governor, Hans Frank, with his headquarters in Kraków.

Although Będzin was now annexed as part of the expanded Greater German Reich, conditions in this frontier area—the 'wild east', with its predominantly Polish population and significant Jewish communities—were very different from those in what Germans called the 'Old Reich', Germany in the pre-expansion borders of 1937. Once the immediate violence of the invasion was past, new forms of 'legalized' violence were introduced, as the Jewish population was progressively stigmatized, exploited, degraded—and eventually murdered.[5]

During the first three years after the German occupation of Będzin, Jews were moved out of their homes and crammed into poorer quarters of town; their businesses and possessions were seized and taken over into German hands; they were either exploited as slave labour within the locality, or transported to labour camps further afield; they were humiliated, beaten, randomly shot at, increasingly restricted in what they could do and where they could go; they had to live on radically reduced rations, and could be hanged, in public, for minor infringements of the newly imposed rules, such as dealing on the black market in a futile attempt to have enough to eat to survive; and eventually they were constrained in the linked ghettos of the Kamionka/Środula area between Będzin and the neighbouring town of Sosnowiec, prior to what the Nazis called the final 'cleansing' of Będzin of Jews. Throughout this period, the Jewish community was riven with debates over whether to comply with the Nazi authorities—as encouraged by the Jewish Council, under the controversial leadership of Moniek (also called Moses or Moshe) Merin—or to engage in underground resistance, or to seek to escape before it was too late.

The nearby concentration camp of Auschwitz was for much of this time not even an 'open secret': it was widely used by the German authorities as an explicit threat and a reality of punishment, including for local Polish people. But at first, despite everyday experiences of horrendous brutality, shootings, hangings, and imprisonment, no one thought that the murder of the entire Jewish population would be seen by the Nazis as preferable to the systematic exploitation of slave labour, which appeared seemingly vital, in this highly industrialized area, to the Nazi war effort.

Yet the unthinkable became reality.[6] Following the invasion of the Soviet Union in the summer of 1941, there were widespread killings of Jewish civilians in Eastern Europe, often by shooting into mass graves dug especially for the purpose, sometimes also by burning or hanging or more random shooting. From September 1941 experiments took place on Soviet prisoners of war in Auschwitz with the use of Zyklon B gas for killing, and in December 1941 murder by exhaust fumes piped back into the inside of trucks filled with Jews started at Chełmno, some 40 miles from the ghetto of Łódź.[7] By the spring and summer of 1942, as part of the Nazi effort to make Będzin, along with the rest of the Greater German Reich, 'cleansed of Jews' (*judenrein*), those Będzin Jews considered to be too old, too young, or too weak to be useful as slave labour were also sent down the railway track to nearby Auschwitz. Here, they were among the first groups to be murdered in their entirety by the use of Zyklon B gas; they were also the first to fall victim to early improvisations in Nazi attempts at psychological camouflage of what was to take place. The initial 'transports' of Jews were taken to the gas chamber in the original camp of Auschwitz I; later groups were murdered in the improvised 'farmhouse' redesigned for gassing in the new camp, established less than 2 miles away, of Auschwitz II (Auschwitz–Birkenau); and those who had managed to remain in the ghetto until the summer of 1943 were murdered in the four specially designed gas chambers and crematoria that had by then been constructed in Birkenau. The final, bloody clearance of the ghetto of Będzin/Sosnowiec in the summer of 1943 was accompanied by fierce resistance, prolonging the 'clearance', as Jews refused to go passively to their deaths: a small but by no means insignificant uprising, which has to date received far less publicity than that of the Warsaw uprising a few weeks earlier. Given the extent of the fighting in Będzin, one entire trainload was even shot dead immediately on arrival at the Auschwitz siding, or *Judenrampe* (Jewish platform), since the SS was unwilling to risk unloading people for 'selection'. Last splutterings of resistance were evidenced when some of the few surviving Jews from Będzin participated in the unique *Sonderkommando* revolt in Auschwitz–Birkenau in October 1944, a courageous action that succeeded in blowing up one of the gas chambers and crematoria. Two young women from Będzin were among the four hanged for their part in this, watched by one of their friends, whose brother, a member of the *Sonderkommando*, was put to death in the gas chambers for his part in the attempt to destroy the machinery of death.

In all, according to Hans Dreier, the Gestapo official most involved in the deportations through the ghetto of Będzin/Sosnowiec, some 15,000 predominantly young Jews were taken to labour camps, and a total of around 85,000 Jews 'resettled' to extermination in Auschwitz—more than the figure of some 77,000 deported from the whole of France during this time.[8]

The case of Będzin can reveal much about the various improvisations of policy and stages of violence that eventually culminated in the 'final solution'. For all the courage displayed, Jewish attempts at resistance were ultimately doomed to failure—and this not only as a result of the superior physical force commanded by the Germans, but also, in the case of resistance to deportation from the ghetto, because of the constrained and degraded conditions in which Jews found themselves as a direct result of policies implemented by local government functionaries. Strategies of resistance or escape were also made more difficult because of the coerced collaboration of the Central Office of the Jewish Councils, and the somewhat more willing collaboration of many Poles with the Nazis, as well as the terrorization by the Nazis of others, and the sheer difficulty of mounting any effective opposition under these conditions. Although there is plenty of evidence of local antisemitism, there is also considerable evidence of individual Poles helping Jews to escape or hiding Jews, despite risks not only to themselves but also to their whole families.[9] The picture is highly diverse and more complex than any easy stereotyping might suggest—and it is only through a multifaceted exploration of many sides of the story that a more adequate composite picture can begin to emerge. To focus primarily on the experiences of the victims, or primarily on questions about physical perpetrators at the final stages of violence, is to miss the many shades of participation and the complex processes that ultimately brought the two together.

Hitler's willing functionaries and witting beneficiaries

Perhaps most importantly in the current context, and certainly least well explored to date: the case of Będzin illustrates how this outcome was also made possible by Hitler's civilian functionaries, facilitators, and beneficiaries—even when they may have had quite different intentions and were perhaps, or so it would seem, personally unsettled and belatedly horrified at the ultimate outcomes of policies to which they had themselves been party.

Not all Nazis were similar. Some were radical, fanatic, energetic; others played the game for reasons of opportunism, careerism, ambition, fear. Some took initiatives; others simply stumbled along, barely querying their role in the system. Some may have 'worked towards the Führer'; others simply did their job in a routine way.[10] Some were explicitly driven by ideological motives; for others, background assumptions simply provided a latent framework allowing them to ignore the human consequences of inhumane policies. Mobilized rather than motivated, they acted in ways that were predicated on 'not seeing' how people were affected, 'not knowing' what the outcomes of their actions really were. Some had individual priorities that conflicted with the priorities of others at certain times: the files are riddled with personal animosities, professional rivalries, competing concerns, as the situation became ever more complex and the self-made problems mounted, making people ever more open to considerations of an ever more radical 'final solution'. The archival material does not always allow us much insight into people's minds, into the thoughts they repressed or dared not express; but the files do reveal the difficulty of reaching simple, monocausal explanations about those whose outward behaviour was certainly in service of the Nazi cause, but often in diverse ways.

With respect to the *Landrat* of Będzin in particular, Udo Klausa, there appears to have been a curious combination of a sense of innocence combined with a sense of unease, encapsulated in a phrase he repeatedly used after the war to describe his position: that he did not want 'innocently to become guilty' (*unschuldig schuldig werden*). Klausa went along with his role until, and arguably well beyond, the point where he must have realized where Nazi racism was leading; his implementation of Hitler's policies—along with the actions of many others—eventually had murderous consequences way beyond what might have appeared acceptable to him or to many other civilian administrators at the time. We may be shocked and horrified by the ways in which people could go along with such a system at any time, let alone right up until the point where Hitler's ideas became genocidal reality; but, unless we try to understand how those who considered themselves to be fundamentally 'decent' could get caught up in this system, and how they saw their options for resistance or escape, it will be impossible to acquire a better understanding of how the Holocaust was possible.

The Holocaust was not merely a result of the actions of those perpetrators directly involved in policy formation at the top and in the provinces, or in the actual physical implementation of policies of mass murder; nor did it take place primarily because of the failures and omissions of those accused of insufficient opposition; nor even—worst of all to target as a culprit in this context—because of the constrained and enforced complicity of the Jewish Councils, or the alleged weaknesses of the Jewish victims of Nazi brutality and superior force. Taken together these are all significant in terms of historical causation, although accusations of 'guilt' should be reserved for perpetrators rather than for those whose resistance was insufficient in the face of overwhelming force. But, even taken together, they do not constitute a sufficient explanation of genocide on this scale.

The Holocaust was also, centrally, made possible by the attitudes and actions of those Germans who, after the war, would successfully cast themselves in the role of innocent 'bystanders', even claiming they 'had never known anything about it': those Germans who were the facilitators, the functionaries, and the beneficiaries of Nazi rule.

These people have almost entirely escaped the familiar net of 'perpetrators, victims and bystanders'; yet they were functionally crucial to the eventual possibility of implementing policies of mass murder. They may not have intended or wanted to contribute to this outcome; but, without their attitudes, mentalities, and actions, it would have been virtually impossible for murder on this scale to have taken place in the way that it did. The concepts of perpetrator and bystander need to be amended, expanded, rendered more complex, as our attention and focus shifts to those involved in upholding an ultimately murderous system.

Here we have one of the major clues as to how the Holocaust was possible: it was not always a matter of individual motives or personal intentions but rather a question of the conditions under which people could be mobilized to behave in certain ways, whatever their inner qualms; and of the tragic consequences of their behaviour.

Who, then, were the civilian facilitators of Nazi rule in this area and what was their role? The *Landkreis* of Będzin was the equivalent of a large county, covering the three neighbouring towns of Będzin, Czeladź, and Dąbrowa as well as sixty-three rural communities or parishes, organized in ten administrative units under local functionaries (*Amtskommissare*), with a total population of nearly one quarter of a million people (241,261 in the census of 1939).[11] Senior members of the civilian administration of the territory, particularly the *Landrat*, remained at one remove from the front line of physical brutality, while implementing, monitoring, and authorizing the Nazi policies of 'Germanization'. Removing Jews from areas to be occupied by Germans, and displacing and exploiting Poles, were, for anyone working under the direction of the Ministry of the Interior at the time, included under what was meant by 'purely administration'. The civil service was intrinsically political, inescapably caught up in and compromised by the aims of the Third Reich and its Führer, Adolf Hitler.

Like so many other Nazi functionaries who had held this sort of position, after 1945 the former *Landrat*, Udo Klausa, first went into hiding and evaded the automatic internment that would have come his way if he had been captured during or right after the war, and then pulled 'connections' to make his way through the denazification procedures once the Allies had turned this over into German hands. Despite later legal investigations into crimes committed in the area for which he was responsible—investigations that dragged on for some thirty years from the early 1960s until the late 1980s—Klausa himself was never brought to court. A significant part of his own defence rested on his claims to have been frequently, indeed largely, absent from the area over which he held formal responsibility, and certainly never present at the times of particular incidents that were under criminal investigation; and a significant part of his private story was that his departures to the army were a form of silent protest, an escape or 'disappearance' to the last remaining realm of decency in the Nazi state when he could have opted for the softer but morally compromised life on the home front. But the records make it clear that such 'disappearances' were neither quite as Klausa later represented them, nor entirely under his control: he was caught up in the power struggles between the army and the Ministry of the Interior in terms of respective needs for manpower during the war. Klausa's first spell on military service was in the summer of 1940, before the army's needs were prioritized over those of civilian administration, but at a time when Klausa himself was keen not to miss out entirely on the glory of participation in military victory when it looked as if the war might be over very soon. Subsequent absences were of a rather different nature. Having been in charge of his *Landkreis* during the autumn and winter of 1940–1, and despite attempts to gain 'indispensable' status, in the spring of 1941 Klausa was called up against the wishes of his superiors in regional government and participated in the invasion of the Soviet Union in the summer, before being invalided out and eventually returning to his *Landkreis* again in the autumn of 1941. Now on extended sick leave, he remained in Będzin virtually throughout 1942, finally returning to the army on 1 December 1942, and he spent the rest of the war in military service or in medical care for wounds suffered at the front. The dates of his absences, as recorded in the archival files, do not accord with the somewhat variable dating in his own recollections in different places; these discrepancies are, as we shall see, of considerable interest in his story.

The *Landrat* of Będzin is in many ways typical of Germans who sustained the Nazi system; and Klausa's memoirs present standard ways in which many former Nazis sought to disassociate themselves from ever having 'really' been a Nazi, or ever having known anything about what 'really' went on in Auschwitz. Klausa's life course and changing perceptions—his early commitment to the Nazi cause, the areas of agreement and growing tension, and the ways in which he later addressed his Nazi past—are highly revealing.

Born in Allenstein in 1910, Klausa was brought up in Leobschütz (now Głubczyce), in a traditionally Prussian area of Silesia to the west of Kattowitz, an area that had remained part of Germany even during the interwar years. Further back in the nineteenth century, the Klausa family had deep roots in the area around Kattowitz, with both connections and property ownership in Tarnowitz and Myslowitz, the latter in the predominantly Polish region in which Będzin was situated. Udo Klausa's father had been *Landrat* of Leobschütz, and his own long-term career ambition was to follow in his father's footsteps in the German civil service.

Like so many of his generation, reaching adulthood as Hitler came to power, Klausa found the pursuit of his career goals was inevitably affected by the character of the Nazi regime. Yet, despite his Catholic upbringing and distaste for any anti-Christian policies, Klausa had in practice to make very few compromises. Socialized in the troubled Silesian borderlands, he had already as a schoolboy engaged in extensive paramilitary training from the mid-1920s onwards, and had already applied to join the SA (*Sturmabteilung* or 'stormtroopers', a Nazi paramilitary organization) while a student in 1932. Imbued with nationalist ideals, but also with a pragmatic eye on career opportunities and eager to seize the moment before it was too late, Klausa applied to join the National Socialist Party (*National Sozialistische Deutsche Arbeiter Partei* (*NSDAP*)) in February 1933, on a tip-off from a friend, just three weeks after Hitler's accession to power. The bourgeois Catholic milieu in which Klausa had been raised might well have caused him some difficulties in his otherwise smooth and rapid upward career as a civil servant in the Nazi state (as well as apparently ruffling some family feathers when he proposed marriage to a Protestant woman of aristocratic background; these confessional differences still played a significant role in the circles of the German upper classes at the time). But *NSDAP* membership was not merely pragmatically helpful; it also corresponded closely to his own views of the need for an economic turnaround, a return to national greatness, and what he saw as the reintroduction of law and order on the streets.

Again, like many others of his generation, in the course of the 1930s Klausa pursued a dual path in both administrative and military tracks. He compensated for any passing difficulties occasioned by his Catholic background by more than demonstrating his commitment to the Nazi cause, as in his authorship in 1936 of a racist tract entitled 'Race and Military Law' ('Rasse und Wehrrecht').[12] Despite his considerable examination successes and practical experience along the way, Klausa also hedged his bets about an administrative career. Always keen on military activities, he became a reservist in the Potsdam Infantry Regiment Number 9—a source of influential contacts providing access to significant social networks and people in positions of power, later also distinguished for the role some of its officers played, along with others, in the 1944 July Plot against Hitler. But Klausa's health was apparently not adequate to contemplate a long-term military career, and he settled again into the career path of civilian administration.

Intelligent, hard-working, ambitious, articulate, and charming in manner, conventionally handsome and with appropriate social connections, Klausa had all the attributes required to train as a lawyer and make a successful career in the civil service. He was in some senses paradigmatic of many who considered themselves to be 'decent Germans' and who sustained the Nazi regime, while distinguishing themselves from those they saw as the 'real' or 'fanatic' Nazis, and then realized only too late just what depths of criminality this regime actually entailed.

And, like so many other former Nazis, after the war Klausa managed to make the transition to a successful post-war career in the Federal Republic of Germany, rapidly adapting and conforming to the demands of the new democracy. His former *NSDAP* membership and experiences in a significant administrative post so close to Auschwitz did not hold him back from a career in the West German civil service. In 1954 Klausa became Director of the recently established Rhineland Regional Council (*Landschaftsverband*) in North-Rhine Westphalia, a weighty administrative post in regional government with a staff of some 12,000 employees. His post carried wide organizational responsibilities, including for psychiatric institutions, community organizations, youth work, and care for people with disabilities. The irony of having someone in this position of responsibility who had in the Third Reich served a regime that had initiated the 'euthanasia' programme, murdering people in institutions for those with mental and physical disabilities, was a cause of some contention; vociferous critiques by '1968ers' of alleged abuse and maltreatment of psychiatric patients in North-Rhine Westphalia began in the 1970s, and remained a source of controversy and public debate more than a decade after Klausa's death.[13] Here too, Klausa's case—while with individual twists and specificities—is typical of that of many former Nazis.

Klausa's career and the fate of the Jews of Będzin came together for just a short period. Klausa was not an independent initiator of Nazi policies, but he faithfully implemented directives passed on to him by his superiors in the administrative and political hierarchy. Similarly, although not personally fired by what has controversially been called 'exterminationist antisemitism', Klausa had underlying assumptions about the essential reality of 'racial' distinctions, and these, together with his unexamined belief in the intrinsic superiority of Germans over Poles and Jews, partially explain his failure of empathy and willingness to subordinate and discriminate against those he considered 'racially' inferior. These 'racial' assumptions were widespread at the time, and were not sufficient on their own to cause murder in the limited criminal sense of an individually motivated act of brutality. But they played an essential role in the path that led the way to the systematic deaths of millions of Jews in the ghettos, labour camps, local killing sites, and dedicated extermination centres of the Third Reich.

Finally, Klausa's post-war stories about his time under Nazism betray many features that are typical among former Nazis in West Germany. He managed, like so many others, to massage the indisputable contours of his former life, bringing them into line with the morals and values of post-war society; to recast key facts, omit others, and weave the remnants into a new chronology, bound together not by the logic of those times but by that of the new era. Interspersing with anecdotes and periodic commentaries, Klausa's memoirs say much about both the persistence of certain Nazi modes of thinking and the ways in which a rejected and discredited past can be made compatible with a later framework of self-interpretation. He clearly was forced into some rethinking, and was sufficiently troubled by the past to engage actively in reassessing both this period of history and the ways in which he was 'tangled up' in it; but he was never quite able to square the circle of his life.

The former *Landrat* was clearly uncomfortable about his past, and claimed that, at the time, he had not liked what he saw developing all around him. His major claim was that, despite being officially classified as 'indispensable' to civilian administration, he chose to return to military service at the front than remain party to what he sensed, allegedly without full knowledge, to be mounting criminality at home. As a summary of his life produced by the Rhineland Association archive holding his papers later put it, at this time repeating fairly faithfully the account Klausa gave in his memoirs:

> According to his own account, when in 1942 the deportation of the Jewish inhabitants of his county began, Udo Klausa did not want to be party to this crime, the true dimensions of which he was at that time unaware. Even though as Landrat he was registered as 'indispensable', he arranged to be called up in the army, and with this was sent to various fronts until the end of the war.[14]

This was the version passed down in the family also, and expressed in rather more detail in Klausa's memoirs.

What then were the *Landrat*'s strategies of self-representation, against which we have to explore the past? There are several key aspects of his memoirs, some already mentioned and others that will be clarified in more detail in the following chapters.[15] He claims he was frequently absent from his area of responsibility, away on stints of military service, and thus when challenged on specific incidents he often claimed that it was his deputy or others who held primary responsibility for what went on in the area. He makes distinctions between significant numbers of his colleagues, whom he portrays as fundamentally 'decent' people, and others who were the 'real Nazis', including certain—but not all—members of the *NSDAP* and the SS. He emphasizes the fact that he was engaged 'only' in administration, portrayed as entirely anodyne, and with little power to develop his own initiatives. He highlights his commitment to his religious faith as a devout Catholic, something that was not well liked by senior members of the Nazi hierarchy, including one of his earlier immediate superiors, August Jäger, for whom he worked as Personal Assistant in the Warthegau before being transferred to Będzin. He relates a selected number of incidents and individual stories that cast his own actions and motives in a good light. The converse of selectivity—a feature common to any account of the past, including the narratives of professional historians—is omission; certain aspects are passed over unnoticed in the later account, and were perhaps even relatively unnoticed at the time. Striking omissions relate specifically to policies towards the Jews. He neither accepts any responsibility for Nazi policies towards Jews, nor does he even register much of what went on among Jewish communities in his area during the time he was responsible for it. He emphasizes further his inner distance from the period and practices of the Third Reich, highlighting a sense of inner resistance, although it would have been—as he repeatedly makes clear—too dangerous to act openly in ways that would have betrayed his inner feelings. Nevertheless, he still on occasion deploys essentially Nazi turns of phrase, even decades after the end of the Third Reich, and even, extraordinarily, sometimes supplies Nazi justifications for particular actions or developments.

It would be quite easy to be cynical about this kind of account, seeing it more as a form of self-justification and camouflage for having gone along with the tide, along with so many others, accompanied by a degree of disquiet held in check by cowardice—perhaps well justified in the circumstances—than as a convincing demonstration of genuine distance from the Nazi project, let alone of inner resistance. Yet there is some evidence of a rising degree of disquiet and unease: for all his later protestations of ignorance as well as innocence, Klausa was clearly increasingly disturbed by the role in which he found himself, in ways that are hard to identify precisely but are encapsulated in his frequently used expression that he did not want 'innocently to become guilty'. And he does appear to have sought some means of escape from a situation that he may have been finding increasingly unbearable, although—as we shall see—his later accounts of his absences and final exit from Będzin do not fully accord with the evidence of the time.

This is, then, a more complex position than that often portrayed with respect to those at the front line of physical violence; and Klausa's post-war memoirs betray a quite complex pattern of silences, reinterpretations, and (mis-)representations. In both its ambiguity and psychological complexity, as well as in its typicality and deployment of standard formulae, the manner in which the former *Landrat* of Będzin later represented himself provides many clues to the condition of post-war Germans, upright citizens of a democratic state who frequently felt, by virtue of a sensed inner distance, that they bore little personal guilt for a terrible past that they had themselves, by their attitudes, their actions, and their failures to act, in practice helped to bring about. Having 'not seen' at the time quite what the consequences of their own actions were in terms of causing suffering to others, they found it only too easy later to claim that they had 'never known anything about it' with respect to the mass murder of the Jews.

In this sense, this case may not only serve to complicate our conception of 'perpetrators', but it may also, by focusing attention on those who were, irrespective of their intentions, effectively facilitators of the preconditions for mass murder, help to make the apparently inexplicable somewhat easier to comprehend. It may, too, help us to understand the complexity of the longer-term legacies for those involved.

Reconfiguring the past

This book is not only about the past, but also about its lingering legacies for later generations. And here, it rapidly becomes only too apparent that there is no such thing as a single 'collective memory', but, rather, many conflicting interpretations, as well as inchoate legacies and burdens beyond narrative or commemoration.

The Holocaust had a horrendous aftermath for all those victims of Nazi policies who managed to escape from death at the time, but who subsequently had to learn to live with the wounds, the losses, and the scars, and for whom 'survival' often was deeply traumatic. The accounts of Będzin survivors in very different post-war contexts—whether in earlier or later decades, whether in Israel, the USA, or different areas of Europe, including Poland, Germany, and France—present in microcosm some of the common issues haunting those who lived through Nazi oppression and the varying responses to the challenge of constructing new lives and reconstructing or repressing the past under changing later circumstances. What one might have thought would be communities sharing common memories were often rent with conflicts and tensions over different constructions and interpretations of the past, even among former victims who later cast themselves as 'survivors' or 'resistance fighters'. And, of course, their stories stand in remarkable contrast to the 'memories' of those who were, at the time, on the other side of the Nazi fence—often quite literally. The former functionaries and facilitators of Nazi racism often did not suffer from the much-vaunted 'collective amnesia' frequently attributed to post-war Germans, but rather reshaped and reconfigured quite explicit accounts of their own lives in such a way as to hang a supposedly acceptable narrative framework around their actions of the time: to cloak the undeniable basic 'facts' in a shroud of later explanations, self-justifications, and evasions, often spliced with convenient absences, thus appearing quite open about their roles in the past, while yet evading any attribution of responsibility. This case, then, with the density of both contemporary and later documentation that is possible through an in-depth study, also sheds much light on the contested and highly problematic notion of 'collective memory'.

The case of Będzin is interesting, not only for the long shadows it has cast over those who lived through it, and survived to tell, recast, and reframe, or to suppress, their own stories; but also over the descendants, the 'second generation', the children both of survivors and of the perpetrators and facilitators of Nazi racial policies.

This is the inchoate legacy experienced by many of what has often been called the 'second generation' of 'war children' in Germany—both wanting to confront the past in principle, yet also fearing what might be revealed in the case of members of their own families. Many Germans born during or shortly after the war did not have the time, experience, or opportunity, or did not want or dare to take the trouble, to investigate their parents' involvement in the Third Reich in any depth; many were ultimately unable to draw the full circle, and either ignored the legacies entirely or fell back into comfortable distinctions between the truly guilty and the innocently implicated, distinctions already developed by their parents' generation. For some of this 'second generation', it was possible politically to rage against the Third Reich and all it stood for, while still exonerating their own parents; to remain complicit in comfortable family stories, or simply to evade any personal confrontations; and to honour their parents while condemning some generic notion of 'fascism'. It took a long time, in both West and East Germany, to begin to explore the ways in which Nazism was enacted at the grass roots, by the everyday actions of innumerable—but by no means all—Germans. By the time of the grandchildren's generation, while historical knowledge of the Third Reich had become ever sharper and more detailed, emotionally acceptable images of kindly grandfathers—often themselves cast in part as victims of the times—could sit quite happily within the only vaguely shaped contours of an increasingly misty family past.[16]

The former *Landrat*, Udo Klausa, had apparently spoken quite openly to members of his own family about his role—although all memories and accounts of a personal past are in large part a product of later periods, values, and priorities, and the precise shaping, interpretation, omissions, and emphases of his narrative remain to be explored.

By contrast, and with far greater difficulty, the children of some of the very few Jewish survivors of Będzin have also had to face the ghosts of the past in the ways in which their parents brought them up and told them, or failed to tell them, about a past that would not go away but that was often far too painful to revisit in the telling. The scars of this past often produced far more difficult legacies, and troubled them to a far higher degree. This was particularly so because so many of the survivors had—unlike the vast majority of their former Nazi oppressors—immense physical and psychological difficulties in re-entering the world of the living, as virtually the sole members of their former families to remain alive; because so many of them had to begin radically new lives, emigrating from their former homeland and having to master new cultures, new languages, new professions; because those who survived and were still able to bear children were relatively young, and had often lost not only their own parents and siblings at a sensitive age but also, in some cases, their own first partners and very young children about whom they could not or did not want to speak, and had all manner of difficulties in starting an entirely new family in wholly new circumstances; or because they were, in so many ways, deeply troubled and unable to 'parent' and comfort their post-war offspring in ways similar to non-traumatized families in the still unfamiliar environments in which they sought to make new lives. The pressures on the next generation to be successful as individuals, to identify as Jewish, to secure the 'biological future' of 'their people', were often unbearable for those who came after; and, for members of the second generation, their own troubles as children and teenagers or young adults would always pale in comparison with what their parents had suffered, doubly adding to the burden of a sense of worthlessness or pressures for unattainable achievements, or pervasive and partly enforced happiness accompanied by inadequately suppressed sadness, that characterized so many of these homes.

The past of Będzin troubled many of its Polish inhabitants too, whose own complex history of suffering and victimization at the hands of the Germans had been overlain by a degree of complicity and collaboration, and to some considerable extent also a sense of unacknowledged (or stubbornly ignored, or rapidly denied) discomfort about later profits derived from the removal of the Jewish community of the area; a twisting tale further complicated by the repression and rewriting of history during the long period of communist rule in Poland during the cold war. But the past did not go away during this time, and the collapse of the Iron Curtain began to open up space for renewed interest and exploration as well as memorialization in the late twentieth and early twenty-first century. More than sixty years after the end of the war, older Polish people began to talk openly about their own experiences under Nazi occupation, and to show proudly to visitors such as myself the sites of Polish suffering, such as the spot in Celiny, in the north of the county, where thirty-two entirely innocent people were killed in 'reprisal' for the death of one German gendarme. The role of the Catholic Church in assisting resistance to Nazi rule was also prominently memorialized, as with the plaque on the church commemorating the prelate who had allegedly opened the gate and provided sanctuary to Jews fleeing from the flames in September 1939. Yet until recently the Będzin area displayed remarkably little, given the scale of the tragedy, by way of remembrance of its former Jewish population and their sites of suffering, bravery, resistance, and death—except, or so it seemed to me, where connected with or partially prompted by commemoration of simultaneous Catholic and Polish resistance and suffering. Questions of memorialization also occasioned considerable controversy between local personalities: a troubling past that still played a role in a far later present, in the capitalist, democratic Będzin, now even part of the European Union, in the early twenty-first century.

I might myself never have thought much, if at all, about this particular small town in Poland, one of so many in a country that had lost some six million of its population—three million of them Jews—at the hands of the Nazis. But this past troubled me greatly too, once I had stumbled across this case, such that I felt a compelling need to explore it in far greater depth, to understand it as comprehensively as I could. For, in early 1930s Berlin, the teenage girl who was to become the *Landrat*'s wife had been the closest schoolfriend of my own mother; in due course, the former *Landrat*'s wife became my own godmother, and indeed, in one of my middle names, Alexandra, I am even partly named after her. So I knew Klausa personally, and all my life have been connected to the Klausa family in ways that, once I discovered Udo Klausa's former role, made me acutely uncomfortable.

Personal entanglements

My mother and her schoolfriend Alexandra were both born in Berlin; close friends as young teenagers, they parted company during the 1930s and lost touch during the war. My mother left Nazi Germany for both political and 'racial' reasons: an active socialist and a committed Christian, she was also of Jewish descent and was made to realize very early on that, as so many people told her, she had 'no future' in Nazi Germany. Having married a practising Jew, she first lived in Spain and, following a brief return to Germany, left again and settled in Britain. The friendship had already been somewhat rocky for political reasons in the early years of Hitler's rule. The first big argument was, my mother told me, about the burning of the books on 10 May 1933; later there were emotionally fraught debates about 'race' and further political disagreements, including over Hitler's Nuremberg Rally speech in September 1935. But by effectively agreeing not to discuss politics, they ensured a continuing emotional bond despite physical separation, with exchanges of photographs while living in different countries in the later 1930s. All this of course changed with the war, and the two lost touch with each other entirely. In the later 1940s they made contact again, and the friendship was maintained, as a sort of special relationship, for the rest of their lives; when my mother's best friend became my godmother, she fulfilled this social role in exemplary fashion.

As far as I am aware, my godmother never spoke in any depth, if at all, with my mother about her experiences during the war, or the role her husband had played as *Landrat* in Będzin. Even if his wartime experiences were discussed openly within his own family, they were simply not a topic of conversation with my mother (nor with myself, once I was old enough, or indeed even after I had become a professional historian of Germany and was occasionally asking questions). A precondition of the renewed friendship after the war seems to have been a continuing avoidance of potentially sensitive topics. So, however open the former *Landrat* seems to have been about his past within his own family, and probably also among friends, relatives, and colleagues in Germany, this was not something that crossed the multiple borders to my family in quite the same way, however emotionally attached my mother remained to her former best friend, a friend who—despite an acute awareness of social and political differences—remained very special to her throughout her life.

I realized that my godmother and her husband had actually been involved in any way in the machinery of the Nazi system only following the death of my godmother, when a small memorial booklet was produced by one of their sons, including extracts of letters she had written to her own mother during the war years.[17] Even then, the significance of the extracts simply did not dawn on me until many years later, following the deaths of both my own parents. But one day I did begin to get beyond merely savouring my godmother's sense of humour and reflecting on the Prussian values characteristic of her class and generation, and suddenly wondered, on reading through an extract in which she had described witnessing the violent deportation of some 15,000 Jews, where on earth she might have been living at the time.[18] The name of the town in her address, 'Bendsburg', was not familiar to me. And when I googled this name, and within a matter of minutes found not only that it was the Polish town of Będzin, but also that my godmother's husband had held the role of *Landrat*—a position clearly of considerable authority and responsibility—I was utterly amazed; shocked. I do not think that this information had ever been withheld in any way by my godmother's family; she had even mentioned it, if slightly belatedly, in a post-war letter to my mother; but it had also certainly never been openly on the agenda for detailed discussion, and it had never come explicitly to my attention, even when I was an adult and a professional historian of Germany. Yet now, for the first time, I sensed that, in this context, at the front line of the Nazi state, and so close to the major extermination centre of Auschwitz, it must inevitably have implied something very different from routine local authority administration under democratic circumstances.

The questions about the *Landrat*'s role therefore have, for me, far more than what is often called 'purely academic interest'. I have sought here to understand the extraordinary setting and historical context in which someone whom I knew, as I thought, relatively well could have acted in ways that I find incomprehensible; and I have reflected on the ways in which he sought to represent this period afterwards, juxtaposing his own account in his memoirs and elsewhere with the archival evidence of the time. I have also sought to give voice, as best I can, to at least a few of the tens of thousands of people who lived and died in the area under his administration, in order to gain some deeper understanding, however limited, of the sheer scope of the perceptions, struggles, and suffering of the people of this area under Nazi rule, and the impact on their lives of the policies implemented by the *Landrat*.

Because of these personal connections, I have sought hard (and I hope successfully) to avoid the multiple perils of, on the one hand, falling into the trap of accusing the former *Landrat* of more than he deserved, born of a sense of outrage that he could in any way have 'supped with the devil'; or, on the other, engaging in the kind of exoneration exercises towards which family and friends might be tempted, even accepting at face value his own account and effectively becoming complicit in the self-exculpation efforts of a former Nazi. There is also a sense of slight unease about allowing one particular 'ordinary Nazi' to come under the historical spotlight in this way; this case is arguably very typical of many, and it is not very comfortable for those close to him to see this particular story analysed in any detail, in place of many others that were similar. Seeking to arrive at an objective balance of the historical evidence has thus proved particularly demanding, not least because of my own emotional engagement in the case; but I hope that the resulting account has in fact been rendered not only more robust but also more insightful by virtue of a heightened awareness of the emotional sensitivity and broader contemporary implications of any historical interpretation.

This book is, then, about the fate of the Jews of Będzin, exploring in particular the involvement of the *Landrat* in that fate; it is not about my mother or her best friend, the former *Landrat*'s wife. This book could, in principle, have been written by any other historian with access to the relevant archival materials, family papers, and oral history interviews. But, because of my personal links with the *Landrat*'s family, it is important to make the distinctive character of my own involvement clear.

This is not the kind of 'second-generation literature' that is now quite familiar, written by the offspring of either 'victims' or 'perpetrators'; nor is it a personal 'coming to terms with the past' with respect to skeletons rattling about in a family cupboard. Rather, it is slightly more complicated and perhaps unusual: an account by a professional historian of a topic in which there is a deep personal, but not directly familial, interest; an account driven, not only by the usual curiosity about the past that turns one into a historian in the first place, but also by a personal 'need to know', and a greater emotional investment in trying to arrive at an adequate interpretation.

There often seems to be a yawning gap between what we know as 'history', and what those who lived through certain periods tell us about their own past. This is even more the case in this instance. I had an immediate sense of shock and indeed horror that anyone I knew, and to whom my mother was emotionally very close, could have been so personally involved in the story on what would seem to virtually anyone after the Holocaust as having been so self-evidently the 'wrong side' of history—and which had already even self-evidently been the 'wrong side' to my mother and to so many others on the receiving end of Nazi racism and political violence from the spring of 1933 onwards. Moreover, I still feel—despite years of professional engagement with these questions—that what became known to the world as the Holocaust is, even when one seeks to explain every constituent part of the unfolding tragedy, cumulatively almost inexplicable. To attempt to solve the conundrum of how people I knew as family friends and upright citizens of the Federal Republic of Germany had nevertheless played a role in the Nazi system of rule so close to Auschwitz would seem—whatever my personal views on the matter—to provide some clues as to how the implementation of the Holocaust was actually possible. It is, in a sense, an extreme case study of the widespread claim of many Germans after the war that they 'never knew anything about it'. This detailed exploration may therefore help to shed light on how those who thought of themselves both before and afterwards as fundamentally decent people could be involved in making Hitler's Germany what it was; and on the lingering, multiple, and contested legacies of this period throughout and even well beyond the events themselves.

2

Będzin before 1939

Walking around the dilapidated streets of the town of Będzin today—in virtually any weather—is a dispiriting experience. Over the course of my research, I have visited it in all seasons: in the almost unbearable dry heat and blazing sun of a central European summer; in incessant driving rain, which leaves one perpetually sodden to the core and running for shelter; in deep, white-out blizzards of snow, when one is skidding on ice and feeling existentially frozen after a mere few moments of exposure to a biting wind. I have also been there when it is temperate, grey, mild, and drizzling or with a thin watery springtime sunshine. On different visits, various members of my family accompanied me; on some, we had an interpreter along with us too, and were able to get to know some of the local people and explore differing memories of Będzin's past. But, despite the warmth and incredible helpfulness of the people to whom we talked, and the pride some of the citizens take in protecting their landmark heritages, such as the castle and 'palace', Będzin always looks miserable to me. And this is not only because of its now virtually invisible past.

It of course appears miserable in part because the economy did not thrive under nearly half a century of communism; and because, unlike Warsaw or Kraków, Będzin has not yet benefited massively from the advent of capitalism and incorporation of the new Poland into the European Union. There are barely any tourists, business travellers, or international corporations with an interest in Będzin. Even the one fairly pleasant pub that we frequented on many occasions, with an extremely hospitable woman tending the bar—concerned to facilitate my research as much as she could, having herself had an aunt who was incarcerated in Auschwitz—had, on the occasion of our last visit, closed down.[1] Będzin has made gestures towards modernity and tourist attractions: the castle still dominates the landscape and has a respectable collection of medieval armoury as well as a gruesomely atmospheric bar serving hot sweet mead in its cellars, the former dungeon; there is a local history museum in the nearby 'palace' (on a tiny scale) suggesting the high society splendours of former centuries, but skipping over the five years of Będzin under Nazi occupation; and a large Lidl supermarket is strategically located just off the main highway, next to a modern sports complex and the public library, as well as some nondescript-looking municipal offices. But, if anyone from outside the area were to be attracted by these features, it would essentially be a matter of stopping off the motorway for a brief break, and staying no longer than necessary to refuel, mentally and physically. Będzin does not give the impression of being a place where one would want to stay for any length of time, if one did not happen to live there already. Nor, despite these gestures towards 'historic' status, does it immediately reveal much about its past. It took me a great deal of detective work, using old maps as well as local knowledge, to find out where things had been, and what the topography of the Nazi period might have been.

Even the neighbouring Katowice (formerly Kattowitz), and the industrial area sprawling all around through the seemingly unending conurbation of the Dąbrowa mining region, looks on the whole dilapidated and shabby,

Figure 2. View of Będzin from a distance, 1939–43
United States Holocaust Memorial Museum, courtesy of Beit Lohamei Haghetaot.

if punctuated by landmark civic buildings and statues, a central market place or Rynek (in Katowice actually a traffic island with a tangle of tram lines through an absurdly complicated one-way system), and a series of old and new hotels and places to eat, as befits a serious university town as well as hub of local transport links and capital of Upper Silesia. But driving from Katowice through Bytom (formerly Beuthen) evokes a depressing sense of *déja vu*: there are shades of late-1980s communism about the crumbling façades, the blocked-up windows, and the dispirited and ashen faces of people standing around listlessly on street corners with bottles of alcohol—although many of those we saw on our visits to the area were presumably unemployed, a status officially unknown under communism.

Even if dusty sooty air and a sense of post-industrial depression pervades much of the extensive conurbation surrounding Katowice—including Sosnowiec, Czeladź, Będzin, and Dąbrowa Górnicza to the north-east—there are also wide swathes of countryside punctuated by small villages and more isolated farms, as well as the occasional former Prussian estate or aristocratic castle, particularly around the former Tarnowitz (now Tarnowski Góry), seat of the immensely rich Henckel von Donnersmarck family in the nineteenth and early twentieth centuries, with minor castles in Naklo and Repty (Repten), now partially destroyed or adapted for other purposes.[2] The appearance of the more purely agricultural areas has probably changed little since the early 1940s, although the area is already sliced through by the motorway heading northwards towards Częstochowa, and a new super highway is being cut through previously quiet hamlets, linking Katowice to its airport situated many miles to the north.

As one drives around, it is possible to gain some sense of the sheer size and scope of the area over which the *Landrat* was responsible, and also of the contrasts between the industrial and agricultural, as well as between the formerly German/Prussian and the predominantly Polish areas in what had historically been a highly contested border region. It is also possible—although with considerable effort—to imagine what it must have been like before and when the Germans arrived in the area in 1939.

The topography matters hugely. It was important to me to try to imagine, in my mind's eye, what a thriving multicultural town and centre of industrial as well as cultural life would have looked like before the Nazi invasion; just where the Nazis located themselves; when and how, over a period of three years, they moved Jews out of their former homes and into worse accommodation, then banned them completely from entering certain streets and areas, then squeezed them into an ever more closely guarded and overcrowded ghetto area before their final deportation, in order to make this area *judenrein*—literally 'cleansed of Jews', a phrase still echoing in survivors' accounts half a century later. It was important to imagine just how rapidly the appearance of these streets would have changed; how visible would have been the shifting, uprooting, and progressive concentration of peoples, how evident the progressive 'culling' of the very young and the old; and how easy it would have been to have witnessed—or, rather, how difficult it would have been to ignore—not merely the everyday racism of segregation and degradation, but also the mass selections, the shootings and rounding up and filing to waiting trucks and railway carriages. Without a sense of the scope of the place in which Nazi policies were put into effect, one cannot even begin to try to understand the sensibilities of those who not merely witnessed these developments, but effectively allowed them to happen: either by passive unwillingness to register the criminality involved, or by more active involvement in facilitating such policies. Understanding the apparently hermetically sealed mental worlds of the 'bystanders' who later claimed they 'knew nothing about it' becomes both more problematic and more urgent when one realizes just what kind of blinkers and blindfolds would be required to have failed to see what was going on all around. And—for all the indisputable difficulties of any kind of approximation of imagination—this can only begin with some sense of place and proximity.

This was a complex community of real, living people, with tens of thousands of Poles and Jews who were dramatically affected by Nazi policies, as a result of which so many were killed. Although there can, for many reasons, be no way of adequately reconstructing the world of Będzin before the Nazi invasion, there can also be no real understanding of the process of its destruction if our knowledge of the victims remains a matter purely of the numbers of corpses to which the overwhelming majority of Jewish residents were reduced. We have to try to understand the world that was before, as well as the ways in which people experienced the Nazi invasion, and the ways in which they sought to escape or survive the machinery of destruction.

Będzin before the Nazi invasion

The area around Katowice had long been an important industrial and mining centre, rich in natural materials, and economically advanced already in the early nineteenth century. The Henckel von Donnersmarck family, owning land, mines, ironworks, and agricultural estates across a wide area just north of Katowice, was among the richest families in Imperial Germany: in 1901 Count Guido Henckel von Donnersmarck was promoted by Emperor Wilhelm II to the status of prince in recognition of his significance. After the Versailles Treaty, the western part of the region remained in German hands, but the industrially crucial strip of mining and manufacturing territory to the south-west, south, and east of Katowice was awarded to Poland in the territorial settlement of 1922.

The changing territorial boundaries were complex. To the west, parts of this ethnically mixed border area of interwar Poland had formerly been part of Prussia/Germany, whereas eastern parts had previously been Austrian, or under Russian domination in Congress Poland.[3] The Nazi interest in conquest, 'Germanization', and exploitation of this area after 1939 was not simply a matter of regaining 'lost territory' after Versailles: the boundaries of the area annexed by Germany in 1939 extended eastwards well beyond formerly German territory, precisely because of the economic significance of this industrial area. In the process, the expanded Greater German Reich took in territories in which there were relatively few people claiming German descent.

Before the arrival of the Germans in 1939, Będzin was a flourishing town, at the centre of industry and trade even in the nineteenth century. The county included a high percentage of Jewish inhabitants, but the highest concentration was in the town of Będzin itself: nearly one-half (some 24,495 or more) of the town's 54,000 inhabitants at the start of the war were Jewish.[4] On some estimates, over two-thirds of the population living in the centre of the town were Jewish, while many of the Catholic Polish residents lived in poorer areas a little away from the town centre. Yetta Kleiner, resident in Będzin as a young girl, remembers that by late Friday afternoon, with the onset of Shabbat, Będzin was 'like a ghost town', with everything closed. But elsewhere, in the more rural parts of the county or *Landkreis* of Będzin, Jews lived as small minorities among a predominantly Polish Catholic population. Across the county as a whole, there were an estimated 33,286 Jews, some living scattered in small communities and villages, with more significant numbers in the two other towns of the county, Czeladź and Dąbrowa Górnicza.

The Jewish community in Będzin itself was socially mixed, with different communities and classes living close together within a relatively small area.[5] The Great Synagogue was located alongside the principal Catholic church, on the hill by the castle, complementing the small synagogue as well as a number of prayer houses in nearby streets. The area below and around the Great Synagogue was relatively poor, particularly in the run-down streets around the Rynek or marketplace. Slightly to the east of the marketplace were the better main streets of the town, forming an elongated triangle with one major thoroughfare running along the side of the hill, below the castle, the Great Synagogue, and the Catholic church, towards the Jewish Fürstenberg High School, and two major roads completing the triangle by running southwards and south-east towards the railway station, where they converged. Beyond the railway tracks lay areas of much poorer housing, predominantly inhabited by Polish people but with the occasional large civic building, such as the Jewish orphanage just opposite the railway station.

It requires an effort of the imagination now to see these streets as they may have been in the 1920s and 1930s. It is hard to get beyond the images of deportation and death so prevalent in Holocaust literature. Yet, however hard, it is not impossible to gain some sense of the wider society at this time, both through visual sources and from the memories of survivors.

The rich variety of life in the Jewish communities of the Będzin area, prior to the Nazi invasion, has been captured visually in an extraordinary collection of photographs saved from the piles of victims' clothing and possessions after their deaths in the gas chambers of Auschwitz.[6] These photographs of pre-war life must first of all have been illicitly smuggled in by individuals selected for deportation to death: some photos were folded into smaller and smaller squares, some were torn, some had been hidden in shoes, in hems of clothing, even behind back teeth. Discovered by Jewish prisoners who were on duty in 'Canada'—the part of Auschwitz-Birkenau devoted to sorting out the clothing and possessions of Jews who had been gassed, saving valuables, good clothes, hidden money, gold and jewellery, and casting aside 'worthless' papers for burning—these photographs were recognized as perhaps being the last testimonies to the life of Jewish communities in this area of Poland. Under conditions of considerable risk, the photos were collected together in an old suitcase, smuggled out of Canada, and hidden elsewhere in the camp until after liberation. Only in the late 1980s was a systematic attempt made to piece together the broken lives of a small fraction of those whose experiences had been captured by the camera before they ever had any inkling that this was a world that would soon, unimaginably, be destroyed for ever.

In these photos—the most important traces and visual mementos of their lives, that which they wished to be able to remember, chosen as prized

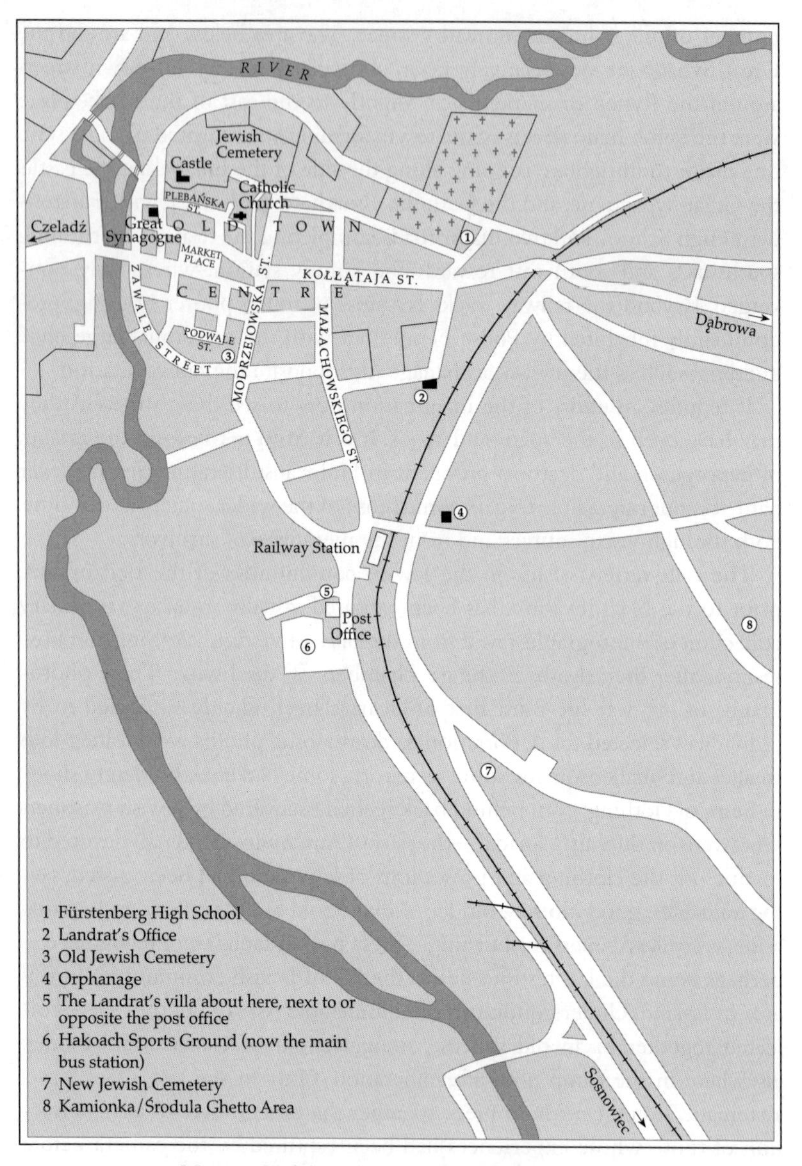
RIVER
Jewish Cemetery
Castle
Catholic Church
PLEBAŃSKA ST.
Czeladź
Great Synagogue
OLD TOWN
MARKET PLACE
KOŁŁĄTAJA ST.
CENTRE
MODRZEJOWSKA ST.
MAŁACHOWSKIEGO ST.
ZAWALE STREET
PODWALE ST.
Dąbrowa
Railway Station
Post Office
Sosnowiec
1 Fürstenberg High School
2 Landrat's Office
3 Old Jewish Cemetery
4 Orphanage
5 The Landrat's villa about here, next to or opposite the post office
6 Hakoach Sports Ground (now the main bus station)
7 New Jewish Cemetery
8 Kamionka / Środula Ghetto Area

Map 1. Będzin town centre and ghetto areas

possessions to be hidden and taken even on deportation; and therefore perhaps that which they should primarily be remembered by—we see Będzin families both well-to-do and poor, we gain impressions of moments of fun, of vacations in the nearby mountains or further away, of loved ones, of family members playing in the Rappaport Orchestra, practising on musical instruments at home, playing pianos and violins, we see weddings, eating and drinking at social gatherings and family events, sporting activities, hiking in the mountains, skiing and sledging in Zakopane, posing outside clothing stores, tram rides, boating, swimming, young men in Polish army uniform, pictures of newborn babies and toddlers, proud fathers and mothers, showing off gymnastics, new dresses, bicycles, strolling around town, relaxing in parks or the garden, children playing, formal posed group photographs and informal activities with youth groups and school classmates, institutions such as the orphanage or the hospital, the new school building of the Fürstenberg Gymnasium built in 1928–9, the bakery and pastry shop at 18 Kołłątaja Street, activities of the sports group 'Ha Koach' ('The Strength', often spelt Hakoach, occasionally Hakoah), snapshots from the activities of movements such as Hasidism and the Zionist group Hashomer Hatzair.[7] We gain, from the arduously reconstructed life stories of some of those whose faces appear in these photographs, just some small sense of the friendships and complex networks of social interaction: the multiplicity of stories, aspirations, and achievements of people's individual lives. Most of those depicted in the photographs—including parents proudly showing off their young babies and toddlers, small girls wearing the characteristic large white ribbons in their hair, young people making jokes at the camera, older people with families or strolling on the streets—did not survive to write their memoirs or reminisce onto video tapes. Their world was wiped out instantly and for ever. But the memories of the few who did survive can help us to understand the broad contours of this world.

The Jewish community was socially diverse, reflecting wider patterns of employment and wealth in a thriving industrial area that was also a centre of Jewish intellectual and cultural activities. In Arno Lustiger's words, 'Będzin was, before the Second World War, the most significant spiritual, cultural and economic centre of Jewish life in western Poland'.[8] Emanual Wajnblum emphasized the diversity of professions: alongside 'devoted Talmudic scholars, engaged in intense prayers and studying the Torah and Talmud day and night' there were 'Jewish craftsmen, joiners, cabinet makers, glaziers, metal workers, plumbers, goldsmiths, locksmiths and saddlers . . . blacksmiths who were hammering out steel horse shoes on anvils from red hot iron... cart drivers... and people... working in all kinds of sweat shops'. Będzin had 'a fair share of middle class people by today's standards and even a couple of Jewish millionaires' as well as those who 'were impoverished and barely managed to make a living... [and] a fair share of professional beggars and thieves as well as highly skilled pickpockets'.[9] Leah Melnik, interviewed in Israel at the age of 90, similarly recalls the social diversity of her home town, from the 'very wealthy' to the many small traders and wide variety of craftsmen: 'Everything was made in that place.'[10]

As in any major industrial conurbation, there was not only great wealth but also considerable poverty; and here, the Jewish community played a major role. Care of the poor traditionally relied on philanthropy and a sense of community responsibility.[11] In Będzin, the prosperous Schein family (sometimes spelt as Szayn or Schayn) endowed an orphanage, a substantial multi-storey building with a pleasant garden a little away from the town centre.[12] The benefactress Cyrele Schein also, somewhat unusually for a woman, served on the Town Council, and took a personal interest in the activities and welfare of the children of this orphanage, which enjoyed a wide reputation. More informally, many families ensured, every Friday, that the poorer Jewish families of the town would have the appropriate food for the Sabbath. Leah Melnik remembered that 'every Friday we went with fish, with a challah and so, or if somebody was sick'.[13] She also recalled the 'blue box' in their household: 'Every Friday Mother, when she would light the candles, we put the coins in this and then somebody came to pick this up... for poor Jews.'[14] Like many others, Melnik emphasized the significance of the community: 'everything was bound up with "Geminde" [*Gemeinde*, community]'.[15] In the novelistic account of Będzin life by Minka Pradelski, there are similar descriptions of community care efforts, including Friday night charity distribution of food for the Sabbath.[16] David Kane emphasizes the way the *Gemeinde* provided help right through to the grave, assisting even with payments for funerals for the poor: it was 'a beautiful Jewish community, we had our own cemetery, Jewish cemetery, after about 1938... a new cemetery was begun'.[17]

Będzin was a multicultural society divided on lines of class as well as communities of religious and cultural belonging. Close friendships often developed between Jews and Poles from similar social backgrounds, irrespective of whether or not they were Jewish. Maintenance of religious and cultural boundaries was, of course, crucial, particularly in choice of marriage partners; but class often cross-cut these boundaries in other respects. Zofie Kosobowicz-Rydel, for example, came from a distinguished Catholic family with connections to many of the early twentieth-century Polish intelligentsia. Her mother was a member of the Town Council, serving alongside a substantial contingent of Jewish Town Councillors, including Cyrele Schein. Kosobowicz-Rydel's father was the Director of Będzin Hospital; he suffered incarceration in a number of concentration camps during the Nazi period, later receiving the Yad Vashem accolade of 'Righteous among Nations' for the assistance he had given to Jewish friends and neighbours, as well as for helping a Polish officer to forge papers and hiding him from arrest by the Nazis.[18] Arno Lustiger, too, came from a distinguished Będzin family, in this case Jewish: his father was an elected member of the Town Council, and his grandfather was the president (*Obermeister*) of the Jewish Baker's Guild of the town. Photographs of the Town Council including Kosobowicz-Rydel's Catholic mother and Lustiger's Jewish father show a group of Będzin citizens, of whom a substantial number were Jewish, and the majority Catholic, but all relatively weighty members of the local political community.

In the neighbouring and larger city of Sosnowiec, Jews were more assimilated, but, as Melnik put it, 'in Bedzin a Jew is a Jew'. Yet with industrialization things were beginning to change. Younger members of the Jewish community were somewhat more adventurous than their parents, exploring beyond the confines of a strictly Jewish life. They frequently travelled to the neighbouring city of Katowice, sometimes for what appeared to their parents to be legitimate purposes—Leah Melnik's sister 'went to the school for music in Katowice'—but sometimes for less acceptable social pursuits, since they were, as Melnik put it, 'with the times, progressive'.[19] Melnik nevertheless was highly aware of parental authority: 'Sometimes I was afraid of my father because he could be very mad when I did something what he didn't like.'[20] In her view, the poorer Jews of Będzin tended to be more assimilated, attending public schools alongside Polish children rather than the segregated Jewish schools, and having difficulties maintaining Jewish customs.[21]

Others recall that even their fathers were already more 'modern', at least in appearance, although this did not affect their observance of Jewish religion, traditions, and community life. Marion Landau's father 'was rather progressive as far as religion was concerned; he already shaved and that was quite unusual at the time'. This 'modernity' was related to his profession: Landau's father owned a wholesale textile business, some twenty minutes from the

German border by train or car; he spoke fluent German, and visited many establishments in Silesia and the border area in order to make sales of his textiles. As Landau recalls, it was 'expedient not to go in these places in a beard and Jewish outfit': his 'father had to shave, that was necessary already for business purposes. Otherwise a lot of Jews wore these kaftans, these long kaftans and certain Jewish little hats.'[22] Marion Landau grew up in a relatively privileged environment, and Polish Jews from this sort of social background might well—had the Nazis not intervened—have become assimilated in a manner similar to German Jews over the preceding century. The Landau family lived in a comfortable home in a large building with many tenants, where his father was a part owner of the building: 'We had a very comfortable apartment in that building and that's where [my sister's] wedding took place', which was, Landau recalls, 'a glorious wedding'. More generally, 'we had a rather pampered youth, because even though it was depression at the time when I was a young boy... my father was making a good living at the time, he was known as a fine businessman and he was doing very well'.[23] Marion Landau too became central to the work of the family business as he grew up. By the age of 18 he was entrusted with a trip to visit textile factories in Łódź when his father was unable to travel to buy the necessary merchandise; he also visited customers in Upper Silesia, across the border in Germany, even while still in school, on behalf of the business. Such expertise and connections were later to prove very helpful in his survival.

David Kane similarly recalls that before the war 'we had a very nice life'.[24] His father was an administrator in Będzin, working in the accounting office of a large iron business owned by a Mr Gutman, who was 'one of the richest Jews in Będzin', employing a large number of people and manufacturing iron products. Kane's mother was a midwife. Kane came from a large and very religious family; while most of his relatives lived in Będzin, some lived in Sosnowiec. Kane claims that he 'mingled with the non-Jews as well', but mainly with Jews, because he attended a Jewish school from the age of 3 until he was 12, and outside school there was little free time 'because study was very important, and learning was very important, so you got out of the day school, you went to the cheder, you went to religious school, to Hebrew school'.[25] From the age of 6, Kane also sang with some of the cantorial choirs. At home Kane's family spoke Polish, Yiddish, Hebrew, and also some German; his mother also spoke English, and taught him some. But the default language was mainly Yiddish when the family was together. Family life was very much structured around festivals, rituals, and celebrations from the Jewish calendar: Hanukkah,

Pesach, Rosh Hashanah, Yom Kippur; Kane describes this as an 'active religious life as well as a secular life'. The family would get together for the Seder at Pesach (Passover), at which time they would often have new clothes. Despite what appears to have been a remarkably settled, successful, and pleasant existence, the Kane family had already sensed the change in the international climate before 1939, and, having relatives in the USA and Britain, as well as friends in Palestine, Kane's father tried to arrange visas to emigrate—but in the event this proved to be too late.

Educational, leisure, and cultural life was very largely organized within community borders, with many specifically Jewish sporting, theatrical, and musical associations. A range of youth groups—Zionist, left wing, traditional, and conservative—were significant in Jewish community life. Sports pitches included the Hakoach football stadium, behind the imposing modern post office near the railway station. Many survivors mention the highly regarded co-educational Jewish grammar school, the Fürstenberg Gymnasium, which at the time enjoyed a reputation for miles around, and which forged a sense of identity and close bonds among former students. For Marion Landau and many others who had attended this school, the most important aspect 'was that we had a school that was Zionist-minded . . . with Polish and Hebrew the two main languages, and boys and girls would come to that school from all surrounding cities and villages'.[26] The school offered an excellent education in the widest sense, with graduates from the Fürstenberg school often going on to professional careers; but some former pupils nevertheless still found difficulties because of wider conditions restricting Jewish careers in Poland. Landau's brother graduated from the Fürstenberg school and wanted to study medicine, but, despite progress since the era of pre-war Russian domination, a *numerus clausus* or restriction on the number of Jews who could enter higher education still existed at this time, so he had to study medicine abroad. Będzin was, in Landau's summary, 'quite a progressive city'; even with the wider restrictions, conditions for Jews had greatly improved over the preceding decades, and Będzin was, as he put it, 'not one of the shtetls from eastern Poland or Ukraine'.[27]

Even for those Jews from less privileged social backgrounds, who attended Polish schools and mingled on a daily basis with Polish people, Jewish traditions and practices generally remained central. Much leisure time was spent with members of the family and in informal social activities. Josef Baumgarten, who came from a typically numerous Jewish family with six siblings, was the son of a tailor. He recalled that they lived in a 'nice apartment' but that money was always scarce and the family 'tried just to survive'.[28] His 'dad was strict with us, my mother also . . . my dad used to get up in the mornings, used to pray'. They attended 'schul' at the synagogue on the Sabbath. Otherwise, as a boy, he had considerable freedom and 'used to run all over the city' when he was 9 or 10 years old. He attended a Polish school, played football, had fun with his friends, helped out at home, and also worked with his father at home. Their family adhered to traditional Judaism, but belonged to no organizations; they met up with relatives on Sundays, went to his aunt's house, played cards, dominoes, or went to a movie. The house in which they lived was owned by a Polish woman who was very friendly with them. She was a midwife, and had delivered all the children in his family; Baumgarten recalled that she and her family were always very nice to them, they used to have a grocery store, and used to help them out: 'they always gave us for the holidays, stuff to eat.'

Yetta Kleiner recalls a happy childhood, playing, doing homework, 'like any ordinary child', until the war started; the period before the war she describes as 'peaceful days', growing up in a close-knit family. Her father had a store that supplied leather for cobblers to make shoes; her mother stayed at home. On weekdays, after school, Yetta Kleiner went to a Hebrew school. She had a number of aunts and uncles living around the corner, and they would celebrate Shabbat and holidays together. She belonged to the Hanoah Hatzioni organization, which she describes as 'like being a scout', singing Hebrew songs, and talking about the promised land, Israel.[29]

Elias Burstyn's father was 'in the painting business'. Burstyn started to work with his father when he was 15. He had been born a twin, but his twin sister had not survived. He attended the Rapaport school, which was, as he put it, a 'regular school' that nevertheless had 'maybe 75 per cent Jewish kids', located as it was in a highly Jewish residential area. Burstyn described Będzin as a 'very very nice city, they even have a castle there in this city, that's why the name became Będzin, because "Będzin" means "we're going to stay here"'. As a child, he spent a lot of time playing football, or picking cherries and blueberries in the summer. In 1936 the family moved into a new apartment on the fourth floor of a building on the corner of two of the most elegant streets, Malachowskiego and Piłsudksiego streets. Much of his free time was spent with his extended family: he recalls having had many uncles and aunts, as well as a grandmother living nearby.[30]

Housing conditions varied according to class. While the large apartment buildings on the main streets had spacious rooms and good sanitary facilities, many poorer Jews (and Poles) lived in very basic conditions, in small and overcrowded apartments with no running water or indoor toilet facilities. Memories of childhoods often emphasize the fact that, despite the often severe hardships of everyday life, the scarcity of food, the difficulty in making ends meet—particularly in large families, with many children and a precarious income—and the frequency of significant illnesses, the close ties of family and communal life provided a warm and secure environment. But not all memories of times before the war were so rosy.

Jewish–Polish relations in memories of childhood

How antisemitic—or otherwise—were the local Poles? Often accounts emphasizing their role in the deportation and murder of the Jews of Poland suggest an intrinsic hostility, overlooking the changing character of Jewish–Polish relations over centuries in which they had cohabited relatively peacefully. It is worth remembering that one of the reasons why Poland had such a large Jewish population by the twentieth century was precisely because of a long history of relative tolerance, if punctuated by periodic outbreaks of violence and inter-community tensions, in contrast to other areas of Europe.

Relations within and between the Jewish and Christian communities in Będzin were changing both with processes of economic and cultural modernization, and with the political unrest that characterized the area in the interwar period. There were periodic flare-ups of antisemitism, such as in the economically and politically unstable years right after the First World War. But those Będzin Jews who survived and were interviewed decades later were generally from a generation born into a period a relative calm. Survivors' stories differ in many details, but a general picture nevertheless emerges from a wide range of accounts. They generally portray a picture of partially peaceful coexistence in relatively self-contained communities, with flashpoints of tension that erupted more in some locations than others, and were significantly exacerbated by the changing political climate of the later 1930s, even before the German invasion.

Relations between Polish Catholics and members of the Jewish community should be neither idealized nor demonized. Survivors who were young children or teenagers in the 1930s have mixed memories of childhood friendships and fights. Most can recall experiencing a degree of antisemitism, but this seems to have been worse in areas where the Jewish community was in a minority, and less virulent where there was a critical mass of fellow Jews or the community was well insulated and relatively self-contained, although even here there was a perpetual risk of scuffles. But many can also recall relatively friendly and even symbiotic relationships with Poles. The existence of separate, Jewish and Christian Polish milieus did not necessarily make for tensions.

Things changed in the course of the 1930s. There were increasingly frequent incidents of antisemitism, perhaps whipped up by the agitation of ethnic Germans encouraged by Hitler's rise to power in the neighbouring German Reich, just a few miles away. Josef Baumgarten, for example, recalls that 'before the war people used to get along pretty good', but in the later 1930s, when there was increasing talk of war, antisemitism grew and 'that's when things started getting really bad'. Baumgarten could remember many unpleasant incidents, including Poles throwing a dead cat or pigeon into the garden where they sometimes ate on summer evenings, so that they decided to eat only indoors, even if the weather was very hot. Poles started 'picking fights', pulling Jewish beards and hair; but Baumgarten's response was typical of many: 'What could you do, start fights . . . ? Just tried to protect yourselves as best as you could and just stay away from them.'[31]

Elias Burstyn too remembers rising antisemitism before the war: 'They used to come and make pogroms from the outskirts of Będzin'; Poles tried to rob and kill Jews. In Burstyn's view, there was a strong element of religious motivation or at least legitimation for these incidents, 'because they say the Jews killed Jesus Christ'. Although Burstyn was convinced that antisemitism was strong throughout Poland at this time, he was himself fortunate in that nothing serious ever happened to him or his parents, nor to his friends, before the German invasion.[32] When the war broke out, however, he felt that he already knew what would happen: the Germans 'would round us up and take us to camps' because he had already heard before the war what Nazis were doing.

David Kane remembers that 'even before the war antisemitism was known to me personally'. As a child, however, it was largely a matter of short-lived and unpleasant but not life-threatening incidents between children: Polish children would call out '*Żyd* . . . "lousy Jew" and name calling, stone throwing . . . I was abused by kids my age, when I was a child'. But things became far worse after the German invasion: 'the Polish people would say "*on jest Żyd*", he is a Jew, they would point out to the German people that there is a Jew etc. . . . They were afraid to do it before that, our town was predominantly Jewish . . . the people would make a living from the Jews . . . but after of course, in 1939, that was a different story.'[33]

Yetta Kleiner attended what she calls a 'normal Polish school' in Będzin, although the pupils were predominantly Jewish. On the way home, older Polish children would call them 'dirty Jews'; Kleiner comments that 'it was a sport for them to throw a rock and see a Jewish child bleeding', so the Jewish mothers would often come to collect their children from school. But 'we felt it all the way through our childhood, growing up, it was "Jew go to Palestine" and "dirty Jew" and "you're robbing us and our country" and all the different insults that we couldn't understand for what reason and when I came home they used to call us "Christ killer" '. The parents of Kleiner and her friends used to say that these antisemitic Polish youngsters were 'hoodlums' and that intelligent people would not do this. In Kleiner's view, there was an element of class jealousy involved: Poles thought they must be wealthy because Jews 'wore different clothes to go to synagogue on Shabbat' (Sabbath), and also because some Jewish families had Poles to come in to turn the lights on and off for them on Shabbat, who then 'said you are so rich, you got lights, we haven't'. In Kleiner's view, there was not only a class basis but also a religious source for Polish antisemitism, which was actively fostered by the Catholic Church: 'They were teaching them in the churches to hate Jews.'[34]

Class jealousies, whether or nor based in a realistic assessment of comparative wealth, were certainly not the only cause of Polish antisemitism. Morris Danziger lived in the street of Plebańska, not far from the Great Synagogue. He was the second child in his family, and had three sisters. He came from a very poor home, and had to leave school at the age of 12 to help the family income by working; he recalled that he had to work in order to pay for the family's dinners, and that there was never much to eat at home. The family was orthodox Jewish; and after work each day Danziger attended a night school organized by a rabbi. He had to organize his bar mitzvah all by himself. His father was a business salesman selling flour to bakers, but often the bakers could not pay for the flour. Despite poverty, Danziger remembers the pre-war time as one of a 'nice life, nice Jewish community', particularly on the Sabbath: 'came Saturday we enjoy it very much together with other people, friends, life was not bad in that way'. But overall his teenager years were not happy. He could not play football within the city, and if they went out of the city 'we got stoned by non-Jewish people, the gentile people, we got stoned, we got kicked around, it was very hard to go around, there was no place to play ball'. If he and his friends attended a football game between a Jewish and non-Jewish team, if the Jewish team appeared to be winning they had to leave fifteen minutes before the end 'otherwise we could get killed'.[35]

Where the Jewish community was small and the Polish population dominant, experiences could be much worse. Samuel Bradin, for example, grew up in the town of Dąbrowa Górnicza, just to the east of Będzin, where the Jewish community formed a significant but still relatively small minority of the population. As he put it, it was a 'small town, small population of Jews'; his estimate was that out of a population of around 20,000 there were perhaps 4,000–5,000 Jewish people.[36] In his family there were six children, of whom he was the youngest (and eventually the only survivor). He grew up in a 'good family', which was loving and religious, and claims that 'life went on as normal' before the war. His father was in the textile business, working in a retail store selling textiles on the main street of the town; his mother was a housewife. They lived in their own house, several blocks away from the textile store, in an apartment building owned by his father. There were, he recalled, perhaps twenty-five families living there, of whom around half were Jewish and the other half Polish. There were frictions and 'name-callings', but 'we tried to live together'. Polish children were, he believed, brought up to be antisemitic: they would call him and his friends and family 'dirty Jew' and other names, even when they were still very young. In the afternoons after school he attended a Jewish Cheder school, where he learned Hebrew and Jewish prayers. But at his regular daytime school, which was run by Polish teachers, he was often beaten up by Polish boys, as well as being called names; and 'there was not really too much interference' by the teachers: 'a lot of it was ignored', they 'weren't really serious about it, they always looked the other way'. Most incidents happened when the Jewish youngsters had to leave the classes for religious instruction at this Catholic school, and here again the remembered legitimation was couched in religious terms: after classes 'they would attack us, call us "dirty Jews, you were the ones who murdered Jesus Christ and we are going to take care of you"... always after classes, never failed'.

Jacques Ribon (whose original name was Jakub Rybsztajn) had similar experiences. He was born in the small community of Strzemieszyce, close to Dąbrowa. His father was a textile merchant, and owned a dye house. His father was often away, travelling in connection with his textile business, but generally tried to be home for Jewish holidays. Despite the fact that there were three or four synagogues and a religious school in the little town, Ribon attended a public school dominated by Polish children and teachers. Ribon's family was not particularly religious; religion for him was mainly a matter of belonging to a particular group that was perceived as different and treated badly: 'I belonged to a Zionist movement because when I was a little boy, because when I went to school, I was always called a dirty Jew.' In this relatively small community, where Jews were in a minority, he grew up surrounded mostly by non-Jews, and was often called names, which 'as a child...really hurt'. At the age of 6 or 7 he was 'beaten up many times' because of being Jewish. Even some of the teachers in his school were party to the general antisemitism: 'on top of it all, came closer to World War Two we had a German teacher which used to tell us "wait till the Nazis come, he'll take care of you" and he beat us up every so often, the German teacher'. Some of Ribon's fellow pupils were taken out of this public school and sent to a Jewish religious school instead, because of the antisemitism they had had to endure. Outside school, Ribon played mostly with other Jewish children; he and other Jews 'had very little contact or association with non-Jewish' children. He had already become a Zionist as a child, because he felt that he needed to be trained to fight; and he would have gone to Palestine if he had been older when there was still an opportunity. In his free time, like so many other boys in the area, Ribon played football. He concluded, however, about this phase of his life that it had been 'pretty much sheltered other than some of the incidents with the kids in school'.[37]

Sometimes there was simply little contact, with Jewish and non-Jewish communities living alongside each other in symbiotic ways but with little mutual involvement. Mania Richman, for example, came from a family with eight children—four boys and four girls—in the nearby town of Chrzanów. Richman describes this as a small town, with around 3,000 Jews. The family was not rich, but her family life was good. Richman's father had a dry goods business, for which he often had to travel to Czechoslovakia, from where he sent home dry goods that Richman's mother used to sell from their house. Richman attended a Polish school five days a week, and had to make up the schoolwork that she always missed on Saturdays, which was a regular school day for the Polish children. After the Polish school day was over, she always went on to the Jewish school for religious instruction. Her friends were the Jewish girls from school, and she had little association with Polish children apart from picking up the work that she had missed on the Sabbath.[38]

It was quite possible to experience the full range of active antisemitism, social distance, and good, even close emotional relations with individual Poles. Rosa Rechnic, for example, came from a relatively protected and sheltered family home in Będzin. Her father was a committed Zionist, and she recalls that the 'spirit of Judaism' was very important in their lives. So too was education; there was great emphasis on her need to spend time doing her homework, and her free hours outside school were restricted. On the streets she experienced Polish antisemitism even before the Germans invaded. But she feels she was sheltered and shielded by attending an all-Jewish school, and having relatively little contact with non-Jewish people for most of the time. She lived in a building with other Jewish families, did not mix with Polish people much, and avoided contact with Polish people when possible. There was a strong sense of fear and insecurity with respect to the 'outside world'. On the other hand, the family employed a Polish maid: 'We always had Polish girls, they seemed to be close to the family, we treated them as part of the family.'[39] Moreover, Rosa Rechnic's father had, as a youngster, had a Polish nanny, who was allegedly heartbroken when he was later shot dead by the Germans: according to Rechnic, her father's former nanny 'died from heartbreak, that's how much she loved my father'.[40]

The Jewish and the Polish communities thus both intermingled, and kept their distance. Interactions were often for economic purposes only: trading or employment relations between people who were not social equals. Inevitably some of the relations were of economic subordination, with Polish servants being employed in the wealthier Jewish homes. This did not necessarily make for bad relationships, however. One elderly Polish resident of Będzin, Karoline Chajkiewicz (born 1912), remembers very fondly the Jewish family for whom she had worked as a young woman, and in 2008 claimed that she was still plagued by nightmares about members of this family, all of whom, as far as she had been able to find out, had perished in Auschwitz.[41] Another Polish citizen, Henryk Smogór, a veteran of the Polish resistance from a poor working-class background, recalls that in his youth he used both 'to play and to fight' with the Jewish young people in the area of Będzin where he lived. In his old age he had taken it upon himself to try to help preserve their memory, tending a former prayer house and showing photographs of earlier days.[42] Friendship with Jews of their own age was a significant element of many Poles' memories of the time. It was, for example, Rutka Laskier's non-Jewish friend Stanisława Sapińska who saved her 'notebooks' for decades after the deportation to Auschwitz and murder of this Jewish teenager.[43] Rutka's 'diary', written by a young girl on the brink of adolescence, has now come to represent a whole world of experience to which we have little by way of direct access from the time itself. Her reflections on the violence and misery of the world around her, interspersed with thoughts about a teenage boy in whom she was just becoming interested, and comments on other friends, provide a poignant insight into the conditions of life under Nazi rule, and experiences and knowledge of brutality and murder all around.[44]

There was a characteristically mixed pattern to the experiences of Mindzia Schickman (as an adult, Milla Tenenbaum), whose childhood Polish family maid was eventually to save her life and, following the loss of her parents, more or less adopted her as though she were her own mother. Mindzia Schickman was born in 1932 in the small town of Chorzów near Katowice, and spent some of her childhood in Dąbrowa, before moving the few miles to Będzin in around 1937. In 1938 she started school, although her schooling was very soon interrupted by the war. She had two older sisters and one brother, to whom she was very close. She recalls that in 1939 'the SS took over Będzin', but she had already experienced antisemitism before this time. Her childhood, which was otherwise—within the family environment—relatively secure and happy, was punctuated by fear of antisemitic fights. Gentile boys used to throw stones and beat them up when they played in the courtyard behind their apartment; and her father had said they must always run away, and never fight back. She could recall incidents when her dress was torn, and she was crying and hurt; her brother Idek knew he was not allowed to fight back, 'but when he went down, he was beaten up, he said that's fine, but nobody's gonna touch my sister again'. But this happened again and again. When asked by the interviewer if, as a child, she had understood why she was being beaten up, she replied: 'Yes. Because I was Jewish. And Jewish people have to suffer. Jewish people have to take punishment. For what, I didn't understand. I couldn't understand these things. This is normal when you are told that you are not allowed to fight back.'[45]

It was a matter not only of being beaten up, but also of being isolated: 'Nobody really wanted to play with a Jewish person, knowing that the Jews are not acceptable, because if someone would like to play the parents would not allow them . . . Even school, I couldn't go to school.' After she had left school, Mindzia was educated informally in a little group of Jewish religious children: 'It was so segregated, Jews were not wanted, not accepted, not even in school.'[46] This informal schooling probably took place after the German invasion, but Mindzia could recall no time in her childhood before then when, as a Jew, she felt fully accepted in the wider community.

This was, however, not as yet the full-blown racist antisemitism propagated by Hitler, and it could on occasion be combatted by quick thinking rather than physical force. Wajnblum provides an interesting insight into the somewhat confused antisemitism among young Polish people in the later 1930s, an antisemitism rooted in religion rather than in notions of race:

> About two years before the war I had an encounter with a group of Polish antisemitic youth who attacked me in a park and caught me. One of them held a knife at my throat, accusing me of killing Jesus. I desperately pleaded with them to let me go and told them I could not possibly have killed Jesus as he lived some 2000 years ago and in any case I could not have done this to a fellow Jew. This enraged the youth who held me with the knife: he broke the skin at my throat, screaming that he was going to cut my throat because I had the audacity to say that Jesus was a Jew. I was lucky that another more sensible youth pushed his hand away from my throat and told the enraged youth that it is true that Jesus was a Jew. The youth was startled at this revelation and yelled out 'Oh Jesus, why on earth are we then worshipping a bloody Jew?' They started arguing among themselves and in the process I freed myself and fled.[47]

Other survivors remember the area as far more antisemitic over a long period, with a sharp distinction between the Polish population, pejoratively termed 'Polacks' by those who looked down on them, and the differing groups of ethnic Germans and Polish Jews.

Later experiences and the contexts of remembering obviously affected the way survivors interpreted their past. Memories of the lost pre-war community, of lost families, and of pre-war childhoods are bound to be relatively rosy in the light of their traumatic destruction and the sheer scale of the loss. Wartime experiences were also repeatedly rethought in different post-war circumstances, and in the light of the experiences of others. Some survivors, hardly surprisingly, tended to generalize from their own worst experiences. Leah Melnik, for example, recalled very widespread antisemitism in her childhood in Będzin: 'The non-Jews were very anti-Semitic... They say "Jews to Palestine". "It's your house but our street".'[48] In Melnik's view, Poles 'were always anti-Semitic. Even if you told them you would give them everything, they are born anti-Semites. Till now, I suppose.'[49] Melnik inserted her own childhood experiences into the broader framework of antisemitism in post-war Poland and the stories that circulated when she was living in Israel, where fear of Polish antisemitism was widespread. It would nevertheless be wrong to read 'Auschwitz' backwards into the tensions between Poles and Jews in the 1930s.

We can thus gain, with some difficulty, just some small fragments and momentary impressions of the lives of these people, and through them of a vibrant community—with all the internal tensions, challenges, and controversies as well as communal endeavours characteristic of any constantly changing and developing community—that the Nazis eventually designated not merely as 'inferior' to the 'master race' and hence ready prey for exploitation and suppression, but even, ultimately, as 'life unworthy of life' itself.

3
Border Crossings

The German invasion of Poland was a matter of border crossings in more ways than just the most literal one, the military invasion of September 1939. It also marked, over a longer time span, another stage in the transgression of the borders of civilized behaviour, in both small ways and large. Changes had begun in Germany from the moment of Hitler's appointment as Chancellor, with the escalation of state-instigated antisemitism and a growing willingness among Germans to discriminate against those deemed 'racially inferior'—a process of stigmatization and social enactment of racism in everyday life that rapidly escalated into exploitation, progressive exclusion, and violence. Already well before the outbreak of war, hundreds of thousands of people of Jewish ancestry and those of 'mixed race' in Germany from 1933, and the areas that came under its influence in 1938–9, had known only too well just what Nazi racism could mean in practice. One needs only to mention the horrors of incarceration in concentration camps, the violence of the April boycott of 1933 and the November pogrom of 1938, the state-sanctioned discrimination of the Nuremberg Laws of 1935, the escalating exclusion of Jews from professional and social life, from educational institutions, public and leisure spaces, the destruction of their means of livelihood, and the growing pressures for emigration (which itself became ever more difficult in practice) to realize that racist brutality was intrinsic to the Nazi project from the outset of the Third Reich. Jews in Germany, and Austria after the annexation in 1938, had already suffered a form of 'social death' by virtue of Nazi racial policies and German everyday practices in the peacetime years.[1]

But worse was to come from 1939. On some views, the atrocities committed following the invasion of Poland constituted the beginnings of genocide. Nevertheless, to register the evident brutality from the outset is not adequate to the task of explaining how people who viewed themselves as 'decent Germans' could participate in the unfolding horrors of the wartime years.

To understand how people could later distance themselves from involvement in the Holocaust and yet have in fact played a role, however limited, in the way in which it unfolded, we have to make some distinctions. Not everyone was a perpetrator in the obvious senses of committing direct acts of physical violence, or directly giving the orders that unleashed such violence. Yet the Holocaust was possible only because so many people acted in ways that, over a longer period of time, created the preconditions for the ultimate acts of violence.

Udo Klausa was in many ways an absolutely typical case of the very many public servants who found their loyalty to their fatherland subverted in the service of causes that, had they known the ultimate outcome, they might not have begun to support in the first place. But at the same time he is typical of very many who had already turned a blind eye to multiple transgressions along the way—transgressions of which those at the receiving end of Nazi racism were only too well aware, but that seemed to many Germans, including even some who eventually landed up in the belated resistance to Hitler, to be perfectly acceptable ways of treating an unwanted out-group.[2]

While violence was intrinsic to Nazism from the outset, its application escalated massively with the outbreak of war. Yet, even then, the transgressions of what we now consider to be norms of civilized behaviour appear barely to have been noted by many of those entrusted with sustaining and developing the Nazi project. Moreover, beyond the transgressions and atrocities was to lie a less obvious but no less devastating form of systemic violence, both deadly in itself and a precursor to extermination.

Będzin September 1939

Emanuel Wajnblum, one of the few Jewish survivors of Będzin and a teenager at the time, recalls that the initial conduct of the German soldiers who actually marched into Będzin, at the very start of the war, was 'quite good'. As he puts it: 'the majority of soldiers and officers were ordinary young men from all walks of life'.[3] Wajnblum even speaks of 'pleasantness', remembering that a couple of soldiers gave the Jewish children sweets. These soldiers must, however, have been rare exceptions; it is even possible that the soldiers mistook the Jewish children for 'ethnic Germans' (*Volksdeutsche*), to whom sweets had been handed out all the way from the border, on the basis that they were being 'liberated' from the Polish yoke.[4] Yet this first experience of apparent kindness is worth a moment's contemplation.

Given the background of troubles between Polish insurgents and ethnic German minorities in this area over the previous two decades, and the additional whipping-up of unrest between Poles and Germans in the months immediately preceding the outbreak of war, it is quite likely that, in crossing the borders from the reduced German state into what had only since 1919–21 been Polish territory, the soldiers encountered not only massive Polish resistance, but also at least some Silesian Germans who had formerly been Prussian subjects and who now may have genuinely welcomed the apparently 'liberating' arrival of the German Army.[5] Moreover, there was also the question of expectations among this early cohort of army conscripts. The soldiers themselves were predominantly young men: virtually all males born from 1913 to 1918—during the years of low birth rates during the First World War—were called up for active service in September 1939.[6] The principal previous experiences and images of military invasion on which they could themselves directly draw consisted of the *Anschluss* of Austria in March 1938, the occupation of the Sudetenland following the Munich Agreement of September 1938, and the relatively easy invasion of the relatively defenceless remains of the Czechoslovakian state in March 1939. They were probably expecting a relatively easy victory, and at least some degree of welcome on the part of self-defining ethnic Germans in troubled borderland regions. Beyond this, many recent recruits had received relatively little by way of military training, and there was also a considerable shortage of qualified leadership, factors that affected the 'unwarranted' exercise of violence in rather different ways over the first few weeks of the war, from perhaps an initial unwillingness to exercise force to a sudden overreaction.[7]

By the time the soldiers reached Będzin, they were already outside those territories that had ceased being part of the German Reich only after the First World War, and into an area that was predominantly Polish—and Jewish. Whatever the reasons for early and unexpected momentary acts of kindness towards Jewish children, the first days after the invasion were very rapidly characterized by experiences of a quite different character.

Among the Germans' first actions in Będzin was a round-up and arrest of 'notables'—prominent people in the town, whose names were on a list that had been prepared in detail, with full and apparently accurate home addresses, in advance of the invasion.[8] People not on the list of notables were also interrogated and in some cases shot on the spot, in other cases terrorized, under the flimsiest of pretexts. As the official German report put it:

> The protection police [*Schutzpolizei*] embarked on house searches in a number of places and in the process caught several insurgents. In Bedzin three people had to be shot dead.
>
> The security police [*Sicherheitspolizei*] on 7.9.1939 deployed most of their forces. In Bedzin in particular they acted against Jews who were holding back essential goods, putting up prices and keeping back silver coins.[9]

There were also acts of wilful humiliation and public degradation, such as grabbing orthodox male Jews on the street and cutting off their beards.

Although reliable numbers are hard to ascertain, this early violence was clearly on a significant scale. Udel Stopnitsky, a survivor who was interviewed while still in a Displaced Persons camp in September 1946, recalled that, even 'right away, on the first day when they marched in, they took one hundred and seventy Jews and shot them'. The Jews were shot openly in the street, and Stopnitsky personally saw them sitting as though it were 'Saturday night, they were sitting in their silk coats, with their heads... leaning against the wall, and in such a pose they were shot'. He continues: 'They were shot with so much suffering that one could not call it normal suffering. Entire pieces of flesh were torn away.'[10] These Jews were given a burial by the official Jewish undertakers in four graves—two for the men, two for the women—in the local cemetery, with a degree of ceremony that would not be accorded to later victims. It is not clear who was responsible for these very early atrocities.

Rosa Rechnic, resident in one of the more affluent streets of Będzin, remembers that in the very first few days after the German invasion they heard shots outside the windows, and Germans yelling 'Alle Juden raus' (all Jews out), when the men and boys were separated from the women and small children. While the latter were allowed to return to their homes, Rechnic recalls that boys as young as 14 or 15 were grouped with the men, who were then taken away. There were rumours that they were shot in government buildings, and all put into one mass grave in a Polish gentile cemetery. She and others in the community did not want to believe these rumours, and continued hoping for their return, but neighbours from the next building later reported that they had witnessed twenty-nine men and a few women, from two apartment buildings, all of them Jewish, being shot and buried. This was, she remembers, the pattern in every town, where

Germans burned the synagogue, shot some civilians in the street, and emptied some homes, 'to make some impression that they just arrived'.[11] But, she recalls, the grieving period for this incident could not last long because things moved so fast.

The first major act of terror, the horrendous arson attack on the Będzin Great Synagogue and the streets around it on 8 September 1939, was etched indelibly in survivors' memories. This incident was of such significance and severity that those who witnessed it provided vivid accounts, both immediately after the war and even some seventy years later.

Mordecai Lichtenstein, whose testimony was given to the Jewish Central Information Office in May 1945, shortly after his arrival in London, gave a brief factual account (the bulk of his testimony was devoted to an attempt to depict the subsequent horrors of Auschwitz):

> One of the first measures of the occupation force, which consisted of Gestapo and police only, was to burn the big synagogue, the Beth Hamidrash (House of Learning) and the houses adjoining the synagogue. This was done by a special commando, the so-called 'Brand-Commando', which used incendiary grenades. People who tried to escape from the adjoining houses were shot at.[12]

According to another report, around 200 Jews had been driven into the synagogue before it was set on fire.[13]

This incident remained etched in the memories of those who witnessed it for many decades after the event. Wajnblum recalls that the Nazis set 'Jewish homes on fire with incendiary bombs in a densely populated Jewish area in the vicinity of the synagogue, burning down some fifty houses. Hundreds of people had been incinerated or shot while trying to escape the flames of their homes.'[14] Wajnblum's uncle, aunt, and two cousins lived in this area. Their home was burnt down, and they were pursued as they fled to escape the flames. One of them was severely hampered by bad gunshot wounds, but they managed to reach the river and immersed themselves in the water overnight until the attack was over.[15]

Morris Danziger, who lived with his parents and three sisters in Plebańska Street, close to the Great Synagogue, recalled the incident very clearly. At about 6 p.m. on 8 September 1939 they were indoors, but heard shooting all around; they saw the synagogue was on fire, then half an hour later they realized the houses all around them too were on fire: 'there was shooting in the alley and crying', Danziger recalls, 'the shooting went on and on then they [men with guns] went to the next house'. There were, he remembers, soldiers all along the street with guns. Danziger himself jumped out of the ground-floor window of the apartment house in which he and his family lived and helped some women and children out of the house; then everyone ran, while soldiers kept shooting; those who escaped survived the night as best they could in other parts of the town. In the morning Danziger returned to his neighbourhood 'and I saw too many killed people, my friends and my neighbours stretched out like dogs'. There was also, as he put it, no house any more: 'we had no place where to go'; their house had burned down. The Jewish Community (*Gemeinde*) was eventually able to find one and a half rooms for their family to live in elsewhere in the town.[16] Sam Goldofsky was marginally luckier. The synagogue, in which he used to sing regularly, was not far from his house, but just far enough away for his own home to be saved from the flames. He watched the synagogue burning, and claims that the Germans 'put the fire out not with water but with gasoline'; he watched as they shot Jews in the head.[17] In Josef Baumgarten's memory, the outbreak of war was epitomized by the burning of the synagogue, 'like the whole city was on fire'.[18] For Abraham Froch too the memory of this event was deeply traumatic: 'they were chucking these firebombs in the windows, it was the whole Jewish community living right around there, near the temple, it was all connected, this whole quarter, several blocks around, it was Jewish.' He continued: 'it was a pretty tragic story for several weeks, how to eat, where to sleep, where to find people perished in the fires... the fires and the burnt people.'[19] Jews, picked up in the street by the Germans, were then also forced to clear the ruins.

Local Poles also still remember the incident vividly. Irene Gdesz was at the time a girl of about 14, living just across the river from the synagogue. When I talked to her in the summer of 2008, she recalled with evidently continuing horror the sound of screaming and the sight of the synagogue and houses in flames—as well as the sight of people jumping into the river, crying and screaming, and the sight of blood all around. As she put it: 'there, in that river, they shot them... The river was filled with the corpses of human beings... It was a massacre, it was a massacre.'[20] For several days afterwards, according to Irene Gdesz, there were bodies lying in the streets of the area; nightmares about this and other experiences during Nazi occupation still plagued her more than sixty years later. Similarly, Henryk Smogór, at that time a working-class teenager, later a member of the Polish resistance, talked to me in graphic terms about his memories of this event. He had at that time lived in a rather run-down slum district of Będzin, well away from the town centre—an area later taken over by the Germans for the Jewish ghetto, at which stage his own rather poor Polish family had been forcibly moved out—so he was not close to the synagogue when it was set on fire. But curiosity brought him and other local residents to examine the remains once it was safe to do so:

After a couple of days, literally after a couple of days, we looked into these skeletons of the houses and there was burning heat in there . . . There was burning heat in the cellars after all of this, in the ashes. It was incredibly hot.[21]

Smogór then rode on his bike to the Jewish cemetery in Czeladź, where someone had laid out those corpses they had been able to rescue from the carnage:

In that building they were spread on the floor. What I am describing here: old, young, men, women . . . You know, it made such an impression on me, I was 14 years old then . . . Their lips were parted, some gunk was glued to their eyes, something like, they were yellow. These people were yellow. From that smoke or from something . . . And I stared and stared at these people and somehow it had become dark. So I rode downhill on my bike, I have to confess I rode my bike with my hair standing on end for fear, as if I was being hunted by something. Well . . . It was such an experience . . .[22]

The local Polish population were not merely curious: some of them also offered assistance to their fellow citizens, and several Jews owed their lives at this point to the actions of some courageous Poles.

The stories of rescue vary in their details. Rosa Rechnic, who lived a little way from the poorer streets surrounding the synagogue, had seen the flames but did not go near the area at the time. Later, she heard about a priest 'who saved hundreds of Jews', so the story went, by dragging them out of the 'packed' synagogue.[23] This seems less likely than the weaker version of the story, which had a priest coming to open the gates of the nearby Catholic church to give fleeing Jews sanctuary within the church. Precisely who played this role remained a matter of local dispute even into the early twenty-first century. The Reverend Mieczysław Zawadzki is generally credited with having taken the initiative in inviting terrified Jews to shelter within the safety of his church, where they were for the time being safe from any further German attacks—and, given his own elevated position, he too was safe from any reprisals on the part of the Nazis. Surviving the war, Mieczysław Zawadzki was later honoured by Yad Vashem as one of the Righteous among Nations, and there is now not merely a memorial plaque in his honour, bearing his name and recounting his deeds at the side of the church, but also an inscription on his well-kempt tombstone in the nearby graveyard. But some locals think the story was rather different. Elderly residents of Będzin recall that it was in fact a junior priest who first unlocked the gates of the churchyard and let the escaping Jews in.[24] This priest was, however, gunned down by Germans on the spot, and did not live to give any account of his attempt at a rescue. Zawadzki, who in this version had not actually taken the initiative, but subsequently authorized it, later took the credit for the courageous and in the event fatal rescue attempt on the part of his subordinate. Another local Pole who played a significant role in saving lives on this occasion was a surgeon from the local hospital, who managed to smuggle in and secretly give medical treatment to some of the Jews who had been severely but not fatally wounded in the course of the attack.[25]

Who was responsible for the attack on the synagogue? At this very early stage of the war, there were differences between the military and the mobile killing squads or 'special task force units' (*Einsatzgruppen*) in Poland. The 'task force for special purposes' (*Einsatzgruppe zur besonderen Verwendung*), under the leadership of SS Obergruppenführer Udo von Woyrsch, was, of all the special units sent into Poland on the heels of the army, by some measure the most extreme in its actions. Von Woyrsch had on 3 September 1939 received from Himmler the special task of 'radical suppression of the potential Polish uprising... using all available means'—a task he certainly more than took to heart.[26] Just before the commission of atrocities in the Kattowitz area—including the burning of the synagogues in Kattowitz and Sosnowiec as well as that of Będzin—Heydrich apparently personally impressed on von Woyrsch the importance of terrorizing the local Jewish population in the hope that they would then flee the area of their own accord.[27] Direct orders had come from above to instigate acts of terror against the civilian Jewish population—in much the same way as took place following the invasion of the Soviet Union some two years later, although to date this has received less attention from historians.[28]

The *Einsatzgruppen* reports themselves are remarkably laconic on the point of the Będzin events, and, far from taking responsibility for the violence following the invasion of the town, distance themselves from it. The relevant entry in their daily reports merely reads:

> The situation in the area of Einsatzgruppe z.b.V. is for the most part quiet. In the whole area the security and defence police forces are engaged in brisk patrol duties.

There are periodic arrests of rebels. In Bedzin the synagogue has been set on fire. It was possible to arrest the perpetrators.

In Sosnowiec vehicles of the security police and the defence police were shot at. In the ensuing search, a number of rebels were shot dead.

After the burning of the synagogue in Bedzin there was general unrest, in the course of which the police were shot at. A number of summary executions were then carried out. On our side, there were no losses to be complained of.[29]

This report appears to suggest that the responsibilities of the *Einsatzgruppe* were largely limited to dealing with the backwash of the burning of the synagogue. There was merely the pretence of engaging in 'summary executions' of those who had been responsible for the arson attack, or who had actively participated in the ensuing 'general unrest' by shooting at members of the (German) police. According to the local priest's report, on the following day a German in uniform came to the Catholic church requesting 'a grave for 42 Christians... who were shot dead because they set fire to Będzin'. The priest, who had personally witnessed and been to some extent involved in the events, commented in some outrage: 'What perfidy, what a lie, for they themselves, the Germans, set fire to Będzin and murdered innocent Poles.'[30] But clearly the intention on the part of the German occupying forces was to lay the blame for the burning of the synagogue and the murder of so many Jews on local Polish people and thus incite hostility between the Polish Christian and Jewish populations of Będzin.

Other daily reports by the *Einsatzgruppen* of atrocities in the area at this time are similarly laconic and distanced in tone, with no hint of the numbers of real casualties. Even the burning-down of the synagogues in neighbouring Sosnowiec and Kattowitz was barely noted; the relevant official report, for example, merely states that:

The situation is for the most part calm. Only at night are occasional shots to be heard, the source of which could not be ascertained. Industrial works are partly working again, partly they are restarting.

... In the evening hours of 8.9.1939 the synagogue in Kattowitz was set on fire by unknown perpetrators...

And a little later:

The situation is for the most part calm. The defence police had carried out pacification measures in the areas for which it is responsible, in the course of which rebels were shot dead. In Kattowitz there was an attack on an army group. While the security and defence police forces were suppressing this, a synagogue was set on fire and burned down to the foundations.[31]

It is highly unlikely that these and other similar incidents in surrounding localities were purely 'accidental', or carried out by entirely unknown persons. Yet, despite direct orders from Himmler and perhaps an additional impulse from Heydrich, the *Einsatzgruppe* led by von Woyrsch was wary of admitting responsibility in writing for having initiated major acts of violence, reporting only on how the alleged 'perpetrators' and those involved in any ensuing unrest among identifiable 'insurgents' were dealt with—the task with which it had originally been officially entrusted.

As in previous incidents, 'spontaneous' violence, even when initiated 'from above', was also in part carried out by non-uniformed willing assistants on the ground—in this case, probably civilian Germans co-opted to the Nazi cause. In Będzin, unlike other border areas, the Germans involved do not seem to have been part of a pre-existing border protection troop unit, but rather were shipped in especially for the purpose of creating trouble in an area with which they were not previously familiar. Germans who were not part of the *Einsatzgruppe* shock troops, at least visibly, may have arrived in Będzin specifically to assist in this action. Two civilian Germans were actively involved in the attack: Fritz Immhof, an architect from Berlin, and Walter Jensen, an official, were both later accused of having come to Będzin 'in civilian clothes' but 'armed'; together they allegedly 'instigated a mob of Bendzin residents to set on fire the local synagogue and a nearby bloc of 15 houses of Jewish inhabitants'; and they and their 'accomplices' personally shot 'those trying to escape'.[32] 'As reward' Immhof was subsequently 'appointed chief engineer of the Bendzin town administration', while Jensen 'was appointed deputy of the town commander. In 1940 [he] went into business by confiscating Jewish shops.'[33] One interpretation suggests that these two were in fact members of the *Einsatzgruppe*, but wearing civilian clothes in order to make it look as if local agitators had initiated the violence.[34] Whatever their original roles, their later rewards were not in doubt. Right from the outset, brutality and exploitation went hand in hand with a role in civilian 'administration'.

Terror soon achieved the desired effect of rapidly making the newly occupied territory somewhat 'free of Jews', at least in the short term.[35] Many Jews were—as intended—terrified even before the burning of the synagogue, and sought to flee in the very first few days of the war, even before 8 September, thus unwittingly assisting the German plan of making the area 'Jew-free'. But this effect was short-lived. Fleeing Jews were soon overtaken by the rapidly advancing German troops and, realizing that there

Figure 3. An SS officer surveys the ruins of an apartment house on Zamkowa Street, destroyed by the arson attack of September 1939
Yehiel Hershokowitz lived in this building. While he survived a total of fifteen different labour and concentration camps, eventually being liberated from Buchenwald, almost all of his family were murdered, including his parents Israel Josef and Nissel Hershkowitz and his siblings Mordechai Pinchas, Frimet, and Rochma Beila.
United States Holocaust Memorial Museum, courtesy of Benny Hershkowitz.

was no longer any safe place to which to flee, most Jews returned to their homes.[36]

Rosa Rechnic's family, for example, fled Będzin with horse and wagon, and managed to reach the town of Olkusz. Once the Germans arrived there, they returned home. But their stay was short-lived: they were soon moved out of their apartment, because it was 'too nice for Jews to live in'. Her father's employer, Mr Gutman, managed to escape because he had money, but her family had no independent means. Rechnic recalls of this period: 'All the very wealthy people . . . disappeared, that's not to say they survived the war, they went some place else, but they did not survive the war.'[37] Arno Lustiger, aged 15 at the time, managed to get as far as Kielce with his mother, his younger brother, and three sisters before the petrol in their car ran out and they discovered that there was no fuel available anywhere; it had all been requisitioned for military purposes.[38] When they eventually managed to return to Będzin, they discovered that Lustiger's father, a former member of the Będzin Town Council, had been among those arrested. At this time, Arno Lustiger's father was fortunate to be freed after a month or so, which contributed to a false sense of security in the Lustiger family. Later Lustiger's father was no longer so lucky, eventually being taken from Blechhammer slave labour camp, when he was deemed no longer capable of useful work, to be gassed in Auschwitz.[39]

If these early incidents of terror were etched into the memories of survivors for so long after the events themselves, they seem to have had far less by way of effect on the German version of the story. Udo Klausa was not yet present; he arrived to take up his new post as *Landrat* of Będzin only a few months later, in February 1940. On his arrival, his predecessor Dr Grotjan briefed him on the situation, as Klausa recounts in his memoirs: 'He told me of excesses [*Ausschreitungen*] against Jews that had happened before and perhaps also during his period in office. Houses out of which allegedly there had been shooting had been set on fire, it must have been frightful.'[40]

The essentially Nazi notion of dangerous partisans supposedly shooting out of the windows of houses—echoing the *Freischarler* or *Franctireur* (partisan) notions that were already prevalent at the beginning of the First World War—is interesting here.[41] Klausa distances himself from this 'justification' by terming these incidents 'excesses', and by the use of the word 'allegedly' with respect to the accusation of shooting out of house windows; he also hastens to add an explicit note of sympathy, presumably with the Jewish victims of these 'excesses', in the phrase 'it must have been frightful'. Even so, there is a hint of continuing respect for the Nazi version: if it were indeed true that civilians had been shooting at the invading German troops out of the windows of their houses (a point that does not feature in any of the survivors' memories), then—so the Nazi interpretation runs—presumably the Germans would have had good reason to burn the houses and all their inhabitants, whether or not self-defence against invading German troops could be seen as justified, and whether or not all the people living in these houses, including the very young and old, had actually been involved in any shooting. This reported speech gives a good indication of the kinds of 'justifications' prevalent among Nazis at the time.

A potentially more significant aspect of Klausa's account of 'excesses' here, however, is the total omission of any mention of the burning of the synagogue, or of the more than one hundred defenceless civilians held inside it. The ruins of the burnt-out synagogue and the houses all around were still very evident when Klausa arrived in the area, and indeed the devastated area had not still been reconstructed or built over even seventy years later, although grass had covered over the ruins. While echoes of classic Nazi 'legitimations' in terms of reprisal shootings mingle with the later sentiments of sympathy for the victims of direct physical Nazi terror, the central violence not only against individual Jews but against all they stood for in terms of religion and tradition, by burning the Holy Temple and all the innocent civilians within and around it, is not mentioned at all. This is, in view of the scale, the significance, and the sheer visibility of this incident of mass murder, a simply staggering omission in Klausa's memoirs. It might be seen as both symbolizing his previous apparent blindness to the fate of Jews in the Third Reich, and presaging his subsequent failure to engage with the consequences of his own actions over the coming years. Or it might be seen as simply a rather typical selective blindness among many ordinary Nazis with respect to the fates of those who were not part of their own social and political circles: another blank spot among very many. Perhaps Dr Grotjan did not mention it in his briefing, and this was all that Klausa wished to record here. But even so, given that many other incidents that Klausa did not witness personally are included in his memoirs, such as the forcible removal of Poles from their homes to make way for incoming Germans being 'resettled' into the Reich, one would have thought it might have warranted at least a passing mention when describing the situation in the area for which he was taking responsibility. Whichever way we choose to interpret the omission, it can only be registered as a highly curious absence from Klausa's memoirs.

The establishment of civilian administration

The incidents occurring in Będzin—and many other localities in the newly invaded Poland—during the first days and weeks after the outbreak of war do not seem to fit very well with a pattern that has been fairly widely portrayed, in which the initial brutalization of 'perpetrators' in warfare was seen as a precondition for the later escalation of German violence against civilians, particularly following the invasion of Russia in the summer of 1941. In Poland in 1939 it was clearly the case that violence against civilians, indeed mass murder of civilians, was planned, premeditated, and carried out right from the very start, but perhaps with some passing pretence at quasi-militaristic 'legitimation' through notions of 'partisan warfare', 'provocation', or 'reprisal'.[42]

At this very early stage, however, there still seems to have been some distinction between those trained, instructed, and prepared to use violence—namely, the members of the *Einsatzgruppen*—and the reactions of the relatively young cohorts of inexperienced 'ordinary soldiers'. In reaction to further violence perpetrated by the von Woyrsch group further to the east, beyond Kraków, the army at this stage also registered a degree of unrest about the terror, including criticism among the ranks: according to a telegram received by Admiral Wilhelm Canaris of the Abwehr in Berlin from a subordinate in Rzeszów, the 'partially illegal measures' carried out by the *Einsatzgruppen* in rounding up, humiliating, and murdering Jews were being criticized by ordinary soldiers, not least because, 'instead of fighting at the front, young [SS] men were proving their courage against defenceless civilians'; tensions apparently also led to scuffles between soldiers and members of the SS troops.[43]

There is also evidence that attempts were still being made to give a spurious air of 'due legal process', of trying to suggest that shooting of civilians did in fact stand in some evidential relationship with an offence, given the still existing ban on shooting purely as a 'reprisal' measure; thus, for example, a report on 14 September 1939 describes a 'murder commission' that found twenty people 'guilty' by circumstantial evidence, who could then be shot as though they had been formally convicted following proper investigations.[44] Even so, disquiet continued. By 22 September, the rampaging units under the command of von Woyrsch had been called back to base in Eastern Upper Silesia. Yet the partially distancing, partially condoning responses of even the more critical members of the military leadership were at this point at best ambivalent.[45]

The German military campaign against Poland was even at this early stage widely accompanied by atrocities against civilians—atrocities that have been seen by some as in a direct line of continuity with the genocidal suppression of rebellions in the German colonies of Africa in the early twentieth century, and with atrocities in the First World War; although now on a far greater scale, and culminating eventually in a programme of total extermination.[46] Military notions of 'partisans' and 'reprisals' clearly form a major part of any investigation of the military road to genocide. But, in the case of Będzin, mass atrocities against civilians took place even before there could be any question of military 'reprisals', let alone the supposed 'legitimation' in terms of 'combating partisans', 'commissary orders', or absolution from penalties for infringing the normal rules of warfare. Moreover, the army was not only associated with and informed about, but even actively facilitated, the mass murders carried out by the SS from the earliest days after the invasion. Poland was the first place in which Hitler carried out 'the extermination of enemy groups defined in terms of racial ideology', and this, even according to German General Blaskowitz at the time, 'in full public view'; the first steps in the policies of slavery and extermination took place in full view of ordinary German soldiers following the military defeat of Poland in 1939, and not some two years later in the Soviet Union.[47] And the reward for at least one or two of the 'civilians' who had assisted in committing a pre-emptive atrocity was a secure position in the subsequent civilian administration.

Violence initially established German domination; but it was secured only through the rapid routinization of civilian administration. Within weeks of the Nazi invasion and occupation of Poland, the key institutions of Nazi administrative power had been established. The administrative structures had been put in place almost before the military conquest of Poland was secure, and even before the boundaries between the territory to be incorporated into the Greater German Reich and the area that was to become the General Government had been finalized.

By 27 September 1939 the Chief of the Civilian Administration (*Chef der Zivilverwaltung*) in Kattowitz had issued an order, backdated to take effect from 6 September, to establish a 'special Police Authority for the Eastern Upper Silesian industrial area'.[48] This already included the areas of 'Bendzin' and 'Dombrowa-Gornicza' beyond the old Prussian boundaries. On 26 October 1939 a special Border Commission of the Reich Interior Ministry determined the borders of Eastern Upper Silesia to include the new 'Eastern Strip', lying relatively far from Western Upper Silesia with its long-standing predominantly German population, and also beyond the borders of the ethnically more mixed areas of Eastern Upper Silesia that Germany had lost to Poland in 1919–22. The significance of the mining and industrial strength of the area east of Kattowitz meant that, despite the fact that the population was almost entirely Polish, with a very substantial proportion of Jews, from the Nazi point of view the potential economic productivity was worth the effort.[49] On 6 March 1940, by which time civilian administration was on a more stable footing, an order signed by Reich Interior Minister Frick replaced the 'special Police Authority' (*besondere Polizeiverwaltung*) with a regular police authority based in Kattowitz and Sosnowiec.[50] Although the area was incorporated within the expanded 'Greater German Reich', conditions for civilian administration in the 'Eastern Strip' were very different from anywhere else in the Reich. This was hybrid territory indeed.

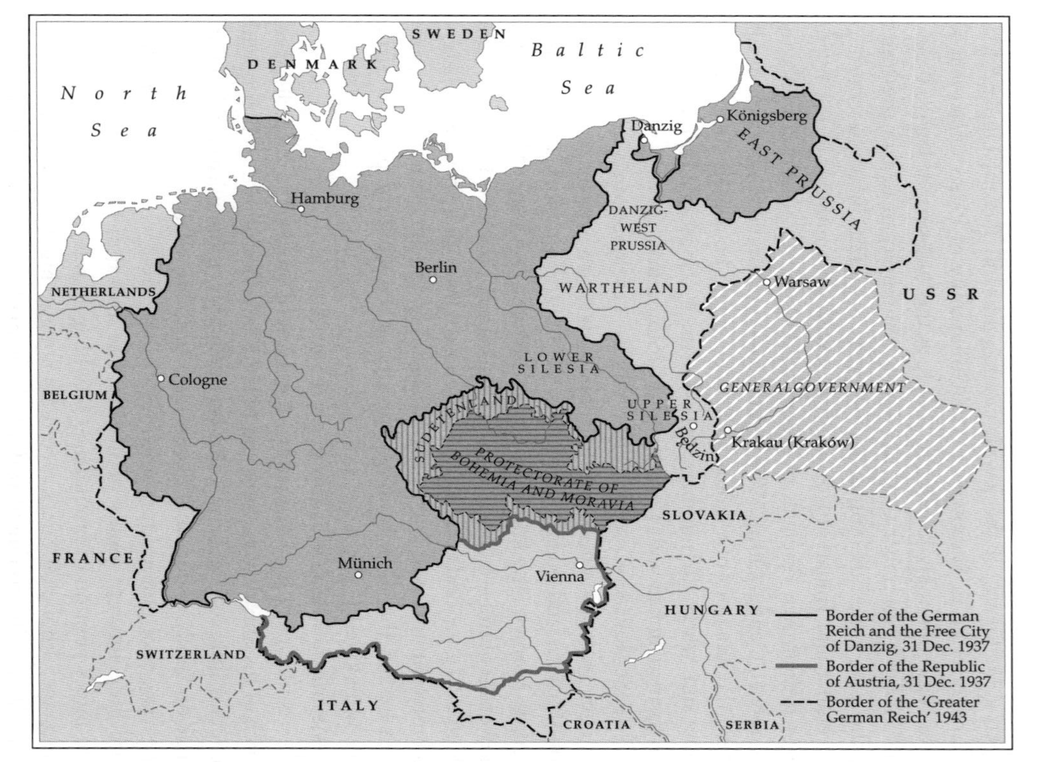

Map 2. The Greater German Reich, showing the *Gau* organization and expansion beyond the borders of 1937

Those who were to be the prime targets of Nazi racial and hence police policies were also being organized, indeed forcibly co-opted into collaboration with their own oppression, right from the very start. Already on 2 September 1939 a Central Office (*Zentrale*) representing the Councils of Elders (*Ältestenräte*) of the Jewish Communities in Eastern Upper Silesia had been set up in Sosnowiec.[51] The Community of Elders (*Ältestenrat der Juden*) was commonly referred to simply as the 'Judenrat' or Jewish Council.[52] In early November 1939, the Jewish community of Będzin, the largest in the area, joined the Sosnowiec umbrella organization; in the course of December and January 1939–40 other Jewish communities in the region formed their own Councils of Elders, which similarly joined in under the Sosnowiec Central Office. Within different communities, organizations fulfilling the functions of a Council of Elders might be named slightly differently; and, where the numbers were too small, a local branch (*Nebenstelle*) was formed, linked with a nearby larger community.

The Sosnowiec Central Office rapidly developed an organizational structure with different departments to deal with law, welfare, health, education, finances and budgetary matters, administration, work, and statistical records. Moniek (also known as Moszek, Moses, or Moshe) Merin was put in overall control—a man who over the course of the next four years came to attract a great deal of criticism from those whose interests he was charged to protect, in the most cruel and unimaginably difficult circumstances, until both he and the overwhelming majority of the Jewish population of the area were killed.

Merin was a highly controversial figure. A man of slight build, he had gone bankrupt in his activities as a commercial broker, and allegedly spent much of his time playing cards and billiards in coffee houses, gambling with generally little success; he was also, unusually in a community placing a high value on family responsibilities, separated from his wife; and he had dabbled in a variety of political movements, switching from one cause to another with little apparent loyalty or success. The arrival of the Germans thrust him into a position of prominence of which he was only too keen to take advantage, although his track record did not give him much by way of credibility within the community. But he soon made up for this in terms of his at times megalomaniac aspirations, as he had responsibility for some 37 Jewish communities encompassing more than 100,000 Jews across Silesia.[53]

Merin appears to have voluntarily offered his services to the Germans, not having previously held any position of responsibility in the local Jewish

Figure 4. Civilians watch forced labour, 1939–43
German civilians and military personnel oversee Jews at forced labour draining the Przemsza River between Będzin and Sosnowiec.
United States Holocaust Memorial Museum, courtesy of Beit Lohamei Haghetaot.

community. Merin's brother Chaim Merin was given particular responsibility for Będzin itself. To assist them in their efforts, they had at their command a Jewish auxiliary police force or militia, recognizable by a broad wristband (worn at cuff level on the same arm as the Jewish Star band) and by a characteristic leather cap. In Będzin as elsewhere, the Jewish Council pursued a highly contentious policy of 'pre-emptive obedience' or cooperation with Nazi policies, producing the lists for labour duties or deportation, requesting the deposit of valuables and goods and the confiscation of furs and other possessions, ensuring people turned up in the right numbers to report for work, seeking people out of their houses (often in the middle of the night), and accompanying them to the German authorities for arrest, interrogation, or deportation.

Merin's power clearly derived not only from the Jewish auxiliary police at his side, but also, to some extent, from his own oratorical abilities and arguments. In Emanual Wajnblum's description, Merin 'was a fiery and persuasive orator', and used his powers of persuasion on behalf of the Germans:

He called numerous meetings and delivered speeches to prominent members and Rabbis of our town as well as to young people, telling everyone to voluntarily meet the demands imposed by the Nazis with deadlines to deliver periodical given quotas of gold, silver, fur coats as well as man-power for 'Arbeitseinsatz' to the labour camps in Germany. As time went on he made persuasive speeches to prominent Jews of our town to meet quotas for deportations to concentration camps.[54]

But for the first two years after the German invasion, no one suspected quite what would eventually develop in this area.

In the meantime, the Jews of Eastern Upper Silesia appeared to be most useful for their labour power. Within a matter of days after the German invasion, with the assistance of the Jewish Council, Jews were being rounded up for forced labour duties. Over the following months, they had their property and livelihoods taken away into the hands of German 'trustees' (*Treuhänder*); some found themselves still in their old places of work but now under German management, others were redirected to work on behalf of new entrepreneurs; some were eventually set to work on municipal or national projects such as the construction of roads, autobahns, and railroad tracks, or in so-called shops (workshops) associated with the production of uniforms, boots, and munitions for the army. Jews and Poles were also periodically subjected to 'raids' and transported to work as forced labourers in labour camps elsewhere, and in other areas of the Reich. At the same time, Jews were moved out of their houses and increasingly concentrated into segregated areas, as part of the Nazis' general project of 'Germanization'.

The Germans may have crossed physical, geographical, and behavioural borders in their invasion of Poland. But those areas that were incorporated into the expanded Greater German Reich were now to be transformed, made to look as 'German' as possible. 'Germanization' was to be achieved by the removal or the subordination and exploitation of non-Germans, with all that this entailed by way of cultural, social, political, and economic transformation. This was a form of 'civilizing mission', certainly a grandiose ambition, and one that would entail massive disruption of people's lives in the area. Quite how disruptive, to the point of mass destruction, was not clear at the start; but it was already an extraordinarily violent beginning.

4

The Making of a Nazi *Landrat*

Once I knew of the involvement of my godmother's husband as *Landrat* of Będzin, I puzzled over what precisely the role involved. It was clearly essential in the implementation of Nazi rule, but had also existed under previous regimes; it might, in principle, turn out to be anodyne. Or it might not.

Historical research has increasingly pointed to a considerable degree of leeway at the grass roots, as functionaries and perpetrators pre-empted Hitler's wishes, in the by-now classic phrase 'working towards the Führer' even before explicit orders had come down from on high.[1] Yet the role of *Landrat* has to date received relatively little explicit public attention.[2] It is well below the level of the classic 'desk perpetrators', of whom Adolf Eichmann is probably the most notorious; it was also below the level of serious decision-making in the Nazi regional administrative and political apparatus, where, for example, *Gauleiters* have featured far more prominently in the public imagination and the scholarly literature.[3] The role of civilian administration also remains outside the circles of the more obvious—and indeed notorious—physical perpetrators, including members of the SS, the Gestapo, the mobile killing squads (*Einsatzgruppen*), and the ordinary police forces or 'order police' units now so readily associated with atrocities.[4]

Moreover, the very word 'administration' tends to strike a dull chord, suggesting neither real power nor much capacity to inflict horror, combined with largely honourable notions of disinterested public service. The widespread connotations of admirable fulfilment of civic duties accompanied by a degree of tedium arguably helped many former lower-ranking civil servants to avoid having to say very much about what they actually did during these years—a relative silence more than outweighed by massive and continuing public interest in the exercise of physical violence against so many millions of victims of Nazism.

Yet civilian administration in the Third Reich was no ordinary form of public service; sustaining and developing the racial state were vital not only to the implementation of early 'Germanization' policies entailing mass population movements, or 'ethnic cleansing' of the newly annexed territories, but also, whether intentionally or otherwise, in paving the way for the genocide that was soon to follow. It is for this reason that the role of *Landrat* is one of considerable relevance to the understanding of recent history; and it is for this reason that Udo Klausa was so concerned that he was, in some way, 'innocently' becoming entangled in inescapable guilt.

Klausa's dilemma was a dilemma shared very widely; it was one in large measure of being constrained by the system to act in ways that had particular consequences, irrespective of personal motives or feelings. The role of *Landrat* was not a role that was apolitical, free of ideology. There was from the outset no way of remaining completely untainted by the Nazi project; the question was rather one of where the limits of 'innocence' might be drawn by any particular incumbent of the role, in terms of their own sense of guilt or moral discomfort. Wherever the Reich Ministry of the Interior might choose to deploy a civil servant, the character of racial policies was by now more than clear; it thus took a degree of basic agreement with Nazi aims to take on the role of *Landrat* in the first place. In this region, and in this role, the translation of colonizing aims into racist practice was to prove more challenging than areas further west in the 'old Reich'. This did not mean that, in 1939–40, everything that was to develop thereafter was already predetermined; but to sustain the Third Reich by active participation in its state structures did require commitment to certain assumptions about 'racial superiority' and the inevitable practical consequences.

Personal ambition and inherited career aspirations, combined with an apparent blindness to the effects of Nazi polices on subjugated peoples that would after 1945 be deemed deeply inhumane, could unintentionally help to lay the groundwork for later implementation of policies of genocide.

The career of a Nazi functionary

Udo Klausa's experiences may help us to understand better some of the typical patterns among those who sought to build a career as young men in the service of Hitler's state, and who later distanced themselves from ever having 'really' been a Nazi. Many civilian functionaries were, for a variety of reasons including career considerations, not only highly trained civil servants and lawyers, but also members of the *NSDAP*. Many later sought to distance themselves from ever having been 'real' Nazis.

What does it mean to be a 'Nazi'? There are many different reasons why a large number of Germans went along, at least outwardly, with the Hitler regime. Some were indeed fanatically committed; some supported particular aspects—foreign policy triumphs, the return to full employment—and disliked others; many were carried by enthusiasm for the 'Hitler cult', the carefully tended adulation for the supposedly charismatic Führer; many others retained a sense of inner distance, and merely acted 'as though' committed while retaining inner doubts and hesitations; some felt constrained, cowed into obedience, but began to mouth the slogans and over time internalized aspects of the world view. Mouthing the official scripts was less easy, however, for those with strong left-wing political commitments or religious and moral frameworks at odds with Nazism, and impossible for those who were cast out by virtue of 'race' or other discriminatory criteria. But younger people who had grown up in a right-wing or conservative nationalist milieu often saw Hitler as the 'solution' to the chaos of the later Weimar years; having little else by way of prior belief systems, they often found it easy to conform to the requirements of the new regime.

The spectrum is extraordinarily complex and broad, and people's attitudes towards different aspects of the Nazi state and changing policies over time could be self-contradictory, mutually conflicting. This complexity, and the prevalence of role-playing, later allowed many people to say, with some belief in their own stories, that, despite appearances to the contrary, they had 'always been against it' (*immer dagegen*). Yet that phrase too is in part a symptom of a later discourse about the Nazi past that was more prevalent in post-war West Germany than in East Germany, where stories about late 'conversion' experiences—for example, while a prisoner of war in Soviet captivity—were encouraged by the communist regime.[5] The distinction between having had strong personal beliefs and 'base motives', or having merely obeyed orders, even became a juridical consideration during sentencing of perpetrators who were brought to trial in West Germany.[6]

This disassociation between inner belief and outer behaviour allowed many people to enjoy a sense of retaining their inner decency while at the same time not risking any loss of livelihood, any compromise over career ambitions, let alone any potentially more serious sanctions; hence never revealing any signs of disagreement or openly showing anything less than apparently full commitment to the regime and its policies. So, even those who to all outward appearances would seem to be highly committed pillars of the regime could have an inner sense of distance from one aspect or another of the Nazi project. For Udo Klausa, a commitment to the Catholic faith caused some difficulty, although not sufficient to affect his relations with his Nazi superiors in any way.

In several respects, Klausa's self-representation is rather typical. A striking feature of Klausa's memoirs of his role and development during the Third Reich is his designation of others as 'Nazis', against whom he had to be protected, in front of whom he had to be on his guard, around whom he had to be very wary. Much of his work as a civilian administrator in Będzin is portrayed as a matter of his doing his best despite the 'excesses' and against the interference of the party. The *NSDAP*, in short, is generally portrayed as something exterior and opposed to him, and very different from the army—which is painted as a potential base for opposition to Nazism—and the civilian administration. Klausa even uses the colours of the respective uniforms to underline his point when describing particular occasions: he turns up in what he terms a 'field grey' suit—presumably his grey *Landrat*'s uniform, perhaps on occasion a civilian grey suit—visibly signalling his distance from the 'brown-shirted' Nazis, at a particular event.

Yet Klausa was himself, throughout the Third Reich, a member of the *NSDAP*, and had been since 22 February 1933. He was one of those who somewhat opportunistically joined the Nazi Party within a bare three weeks of Hitler's appointment as Chancellor (sometimes caustically labelled the *Märzgefallenen* or 'fallen in March', a historical allusion to those killed in the tumult of the March 1848 revolutionary uprisings of Vienna and Berlin). As Klausa put it in his memoirs, explaining why he joined the *NSDAP*: 'One thing was clear to me: They are not going to give up power now . . . So what to do? State service, my declared goal, would probably become unattainable'—unless of course he joined the Nazi Party.[7] Klausa's decision was speeded up by a helpful tip-off telephone call from a friend in Munich: 'Certainly they would soon close membership applications, certainly a totalitarian state would only tolerate a single party, certainly many openings in public service and indeed of any profession would otherwise be closed to me.'[8] The conclusion, for Klausa, was now obvious: 'So on 22 February I dutifully marched into the nearest local party headquarters and declared that I was joining up.'[9] Among the first 25 per cent of *NSDAP* members, Klausa received the *NSDAP* membership number 1,941,466.[10]

This might to some extent be written off in retrospect as pure careerism and ambition. But there was more to this than mere opportunism, and in this aspect too Klausa's experience and self-justifications illuminate those of innumerable others. As he explains:

> this change of regime represented for us the only remaining alternative to an escalating civil war, to a hopeless confusion of our political life with no way out. We actually felt as if we had been saved, in that these endless street battles, demonstrations, police interventions just disappeared, from one day to the next. At any rate one no longer noticed anything of that sort. But one did notice that the new government began, with unparalleled energy, to address the greatest economic evil of the time: unemployment. That was at first expressed in policy orders, but very soon also in practice, in measures visible to everyone. In short: I was waiting to see what would happen, but was not negatively inclined towards this whole development.[11]

Klausa devotes several pages of his memoirs to depicting the sense of excitement and rapid change, particularly with respect to the ways in which the *NSDAP* dealt with the problem of unemployment—'an achievement that one did after all have to recognize'—and the ways in which he was allegedly unaware of the dark sides of the Third Reich.[12] Among the latter, he includes the violence of the SA. It is somewhat odd to suggest he was largely unaware of its activities at this time, since he was himself a keen member of the SA, formally joining on 22 February 1933. He had apparently already applied to join the SA in December 1932, before Hitler had come to power, counting paramilitary training activities in the preceding years towards an accelerated membership application; and he became a group leader of an SA troop within a matter of months.[13]

Klausa's in parts remarkably frank self-portrait of his beliefs and perceptions at the time, accompanied by claims of a degree of blindness, increasingly becomes a portrayal of himself as never having 'really' been a Nazi: within a relatively short space of time in his memoirs, 'the Nazis' are someone else, and he claims that by late 1933 he also 'wanted to disappear from the SA as soon as possible'—something he did not in fact put into practice, which makes it difficult to know whether to give this post-war claim much credence.[14] This is perhaps a key to the ways in which Klausa, like so many others who had joined the *NSDAP* bandwagon in a first flush of enthusiasm, continued to go along with the Third Reich, perhaps with a growing sense of discomfort, but outwardly serving it loyally to the very end; or to the ways in which, after the war, he was able to map back his post-1945 views onto pre-1945 facts, making sense of a biography that could be acceptable in both worlds.

At least in some respects this sort of self-distancing was not merely a convenient post-war ploy in the battle for innocence, but also reflected a sense of differentiation at the time. Many bourgeois members of the *NSDAP* did not feel they had much in common with what they perceived as lower-class rabble, for example. Many former *NSDAP* members later claimed that they had 'only' joined for reasons that were pragmatic, rather than out of ideological conviction or 'fanaticism'. The *NSDAP* was a mass party, which necessarily encompassed many of those who had jumped on the bandwagon when it seemed a good idea, or who had been constrained to join by their employers or other authorities with perceived power over their lives and careers. It may well be that the typical post-war claim of having 'been forced to join' for reasons such as 'to feed the family' or to save one's job, often adduced in denazification proceedings, was more widespread in hindsight than had actually been the case at the time; but it was certainly true for many even at the time of application.

Many former party members, including Klausa, later claimed they had voluntarily joined the *NSDAP* precisely in order to fight against the 'riff-raff' (*Lumpen*) from within, and that being a member of the Nazi Party was the only way in which they could now seek to affect the future. In an apparently private think-piece written shortly after the war, in July 1945, and framed as a debate between the 'victor and the vanquished', Klausa suggested that joining the *NSDAP* had been a way of ensuring that the party 'riff-raff' did not gain the upper hand. Those, like himself, who joined because 'it was no longer possible to fight against the party from outside' were allegedly motivated by a 'sense of duty', and 'each tried with all his might to alter the course' of developments, generally serving in state administration or the economy rather than in party organizations.[15] Klausa also, however, claimed in this piece that the economic recovery over which the Nazi state had presided had earned it respect and loyalty 'for as long as it was not seen through as a criminal regime'; and that 'we [the vanquished] only learned gradually what was really going on in the concentration camps, and this was only fully made known to us by you [the victors]'.[16] In what was effectively a debate with himself—for he was at this point in hiding, fearing internment by the Allies—Klausa clearly could concede neither that he had done anything wrong, nor that he had any reasons for shame; and he still sought to portray *NSDAP* membership in an honourable light. The 'real

Nazis' were others, but those who had been members for more 'honourable' reasons, like himself, had nothing to be ashamed of and did not deserve to be punished.

Whatever Klausa's self-confessed motives may have been, it is also certain that many people did indeed just go along with Nazism out of a diffuse sense of not wanting to stand out against the herd, not wanting to miss career opportunities, not wanting to draw adverse attention to themselves. Particularly for a budding lawyer and civil servant of Udo Klausa's background and generation, it would have taken a considerable degree of courage to stand up and hold out against the pressures of the day—which would in Klausa's case have meant abandoning all his career aspirations and personal ambitions. It took much reflection and considerable courage for one of his better-known contemporaries, the journalist Sebastian Haffner, first to complete his studies and then to leave for a new life in Britain; but Haffner had already been prepared to stand out against some of the prevailing tides of the time among young enthusiasts for right-wing causes in the 1920s, and was possessed of considerable inner resilience; Klausa was a far more typical product of his times, his background, and his generation.[17]

A trained lawyer committed both to a career in civilian administration and to military service—and earlier paramilitary activities, prior to the Nazi acquisition of a state monopoly of violence in 1933—Klausa can be seen as a classic member of what is often referred to as the 'war youth generation'.[18] Born in 1910, Klausa had grown up in the Silesian borderlands and was much influenced by the legacies of the Free Corps spirit in this area. As a schoolboy in the early 1920s he was strongly influenced by the paramilitary activities and skirmishes going on in these violent border regions. In 1925, at the age of 15, Udo Klausa became involved in a group known as the *Gefolgschaft*, or 'The Following', the activities of which he describes as being a camouflaged form of military training. Learning the use of weapons, engaging in field exercises, and indulging in a sense of adventure, with personal commitment and collective camaraderie on a national mission, were common among many youngsters who had observed the First World War from afar, had never really experienced violence at first hand, and who found it hard to accept the German defeat of 1918. 'Nationalism', to many of them, involved a determination to avenge the multiple humiliations of Versailles, and this inevitably included revision of Germany's contested border with Poland.

In addition, Udo Klausa was the son of a *Landrat*—the very profession he too wanted to pursue as an adult. Becoming a *Landrat* had long been his goal: to follow in the footsteps of his father, Dr Walter Klausa, who had been *Landrat* of Leobschütz (now Głubczyce) until 1933 and then—apparently following some machinations by local Nazis who allegedly did not like a Catholic in post—held the post of *Landrat* of Groß Strehlitz until his retirement in 1940, making the appropriate compromises and commitments to the Nazi cause.[19] As a child and young person, Udo Klausa had been much influenced by the family environment, the imposing residence in the stately building that was the *Landrat*'s administrative base, the social circles in which the family moved, and the charitable activities of his mother in her role as the *Landrat*'s wife. This represented for Udo Klausa not only a career but a whole lifestyle and milieu in which he felt at home, and that he wished to replicate in his own professional and domestic life as an adult.

No doubt under virtually any historical circumstances Udo Klausa would have made a very good civil servant—as indeed he proved in his post-war career as Director of the Rhineland Regional Council in the Federal Republic of Germany. The tragedy, for Klausa, as for so many rising civil servants of this generation, was that he came to maturity at precisely the moment Hitler came to power. And, while his father was old enough to enter retirement in 1940, Udo Klausa himself was of an age where, in order to make a career, he had to put into effect the regime's ever more radical policies at this time. The career that he had so longed to pursue, the career to which his father had been so committed, had turned into something rather different. The civil service was now entrusted with putting the policies of Hitler, Himmler, and Heydrich into effect—with particularly virulent implications in the eastern territories of the Reich. To pursue such a career in these circumstances was inevitably to have to make compromises.

But for a fully integrated member of the 'people's community' or *Volksgemeinschaft* of Nazi Germany, the compromises Klausa felt he had to make appear to have been remarkably few. Following a successful period of qualification for state service, including passing the relevant examinations with flying colours, Klausa successfully undertook practical stints in local administration, in which career he made rapid progress up the ranks and garnered glowing letters of recommendation. He managed to combine this with continued military training, no longer with the illegal borderland paramilitary units of the pre-1933 days, nor with the SA as he had done from 1933, but now with the renowned elite Potsdam Infantry Regiment Number 9.

Here, rubbing shoulders with the sons of distinguished aristocratic families, Klausa became close friends with one of the brothers of my mother's schoolfriend Alexandra. Through these personal connections, Klausa not only first met the woman who was to become his wife (and later my godmother); he also made other valuable contacts in high places, including Fritz-Dietlof Graf von der Schulenburg. The Potsdam I.R.9 later gained fame as providing a significant number of participants in the July 1944 plot against Hitler; but even those eventually put to death for their courageous (if belated) resistance were for a long period of time high-ranking *NSDAP* members and active pillars of the regime, coming to the view that the fatherland must be saved from its Führer only when the war was clearly being irredeemably lost. One of the eventual members of this plot, von der Schulenburg, was in the meantime a senior figure in Hitler's regime, in 1939–40 holding the role of Vice President of the Upper Presidium of the expanded state of Lower and Upper Silesia in which the county of Będzin was located.[20] Although others associated with von der Schulenburg later tried to claim a degree of 'innocence by association', Klausa quite frankly admitted in his memoirs that, despite his acquaintanceship with von der Schulenburg, he had known nothing of and had not been actively associated with this plot.[21]

In the mid-1930s, Klausa certainly paid more than lip-service to the racist principles of the Third Reich in his tract entitled 'Race and Military Law' ('Rasse und Wehrrecht').[22] This publication was interpreted—although not excused—by his son Ekkehard as a 'youthful sin' (*Jugendsünde*) motivated by a felt need to reingratiate himself with those in power. Klausa had apparently been under observation by the Gestapo for political reasons, and during a house search a Catholic tract against the writings of Alfred Rosenberg, the virulently anti-Christian racial theorist and editor of the *Völkischer Beobachter*, was discovered on the premises; Klausa thus felt himself to be to some extent 'on probation'.[23] It was also rooted in a desire, developed in the pamphlet, to ensure that the historically elite army officer corps would retain control over who was admitted to the regiment, by retention of the officers' voting rights. This could be interpreted as ensuring that the regiment could not readily be infiltrated by 'officers close to the *NS*[*DAP*]'; despite the fact that Klausa and many others were already members of the *NSDAP*, they appear to have sustained a distinction between themselves and the 'real' or at least the less desirable Nazis.[24] This case is illustrative of the pressures the system seems to have exerted to ensure conformity in expression and action, whatever private differences there may have been, including in this case over religion. The fear of being in trouble appears to have been sufficient to have produced an explicit demonstration of support, contributing in turn to the growing overall climate of state-sanctioned and actively encouraged racism in both practice and theory. It did not matter very much to the victims of this racist climate whether writers of such pamphlets were motivated by genuine belief or by a desire to evade trouble and demonstrate conformity, even while preserving a degree of distance. And on this kind of negotiated compromise the Third Reich was able to expand the ranks of the functionaries who supported its practices while simultaneously believing that—whatever they said and did in public—they were not 'really' part of the aspects of the system of which they disapproved.

Whatever his supposedly elevated motives in seeking to curry favour with Nazis in high places, what Klausa actually wrote in this little book included thoroughly racist assertions such as the following:

> Today there is barely any nation that is made up of a pure race any more . . . The law must contribute to the process by which the more valuable hereditary elements are constantly secured. This takes place through positive furtherance of the racially most valuable people, and through negative selection of the degenerate.[25]

The tract went on to argue that any quite understandable tendency in peacetime to see 'foreigners' as objects of tourist interest must be combated in wartime, when they were enemies of the state. This meant that persons who were 'either not of German or closely related blood' or 'admittedly of the same blood, but degenerate' must be refused entry to army service.[26] Far from being a sole island of decency unrelated to Nazism, in Klausa's analysis here the army was inherently defined in explicitly racist terms: made up of 'racially pure' elements, and fighting to further the alleged interests of the ethnically defined people against others with whom there should be no empathy. This stands in some contrast to his later attempts to portray the army as the last bastion of decency quite distinct from and even supposedly in some sense opposed to the Nazis and their racist project.

It is also notable that at this time, although Klausa seriously contemplated a military career, his health was apparently not up to the rigorous physical demands this would have entailed. He therefore chose, following a demanding stint of military training, to return to civilian administration as his primary career path. After the war it was suggested by Count Baudissin, in an affidavit written on Klausa's behalf for denazification purposes, that Klausa had already had doubts in the later 1930s about pursuing a career in civilian administration, since he apparently felt there was little future for him as a Catholic in the service of the Nazi state; a family story also circulated to the effect that, on the occasion of his engagement to Alexandra, one of her brothers had remarked that this meant 'yet another disenchanted Nazi in the family'.[27] The ambivalence—the strong urge to engage in military pursuits, over which he had already had heated debates with his father while still a student, and an underlying sense of tension as a Catholic in the service of Hitler's state—never entirely left Klausa. Throughout the war years, he was torn back and forth between the two paths.

There are many points in the peacetime years of the Third Reich where even a right-wing nationalist of Klausa's generation might have come to the view that enough was enough. These possible turning points in perception of Nazi politics hardly need enumerating: the boycott and subsequent legislation against Jews in April 1933; the 'night of the long knives' and retroactive 'legalization' of the murder of political rivals in June–July 1934; the Nuremberg Laws of 1935; the annexation or *Anschluss* of Austria, the acquis-

Figure 5. Udo Klausa in military uniform, July 1939
Ekkehard Klausa.

ition of the Sudetenland, and the November pogrom of 1938; the invasion of Bohemia and Moravia in 1939—these are merely a few of the well-known moments when many others (and particularly the victims) realized only too fully the murderous character of Hitler's rule. But at all these points Klausa continued to go along with the regime, pursuing what promised to be a brilliant career in the service of the state. And, like so many other Nazis—Klausa was not at all alone in this respect—he seems neither to have registered fully the intrinsic inhumanity of what was going on all along, nor to have feared the direction in which the regime was heading and the practical consequences of such a path. For whatever reasons, and irrespective of any inner doubts he may or may not have been harbouring at each of these stages, Klausa went on giving Hitler's state full support in his behaviour and professional roles.

By the late 1930s, as the Third Reich expanded its power in Europe, Klausa was ready to take on roles of greater responsibility—roles that, given his demonstrated intelligence and efficiency, were thrust his way in a system that could deploy its state servants with often little regard to their own preferences. During the winter of 1938–9 Klausa assisted in the administration of the annexed Sudetenland, where, despite active involvement at the time in Aussig (Ústí nad Labem), he later professed to have no memory of the burning of the synagogue in November 1938. He then took on a role in the administration of Bohemia and Moravia, following the German military invasion of the spring of 1939. Within a month of the German invasion of Poland, Klausa was 'made available to the Military Command in Posen for deployment in civilian administration'.[28] A handwritten letter by Klausa dated 25 October 1939, ending 'Heil Hitler!', confirms his arrival in Posen.[29]

Klausa's role at this point was that of Personal Assistant to a senior figure in the civilian administration of the newly incorporated Reichsgau Wartheland (commonly referred to as the Warthegau), August Jäger. Jäger was Deputy to Arthur Greiser, dubbed by one scholar as a 'model Nazi' who held the dual party and state roles of *Gauleiter* and *Reichsstatthalter* and was at the forefront of implementing Nazi ghettoization and extermination policies.[30] Jäger was second-in-command in Greiser's civilian rather than party role, but there was precious little to distinguish the inhumane effects of their well-coordinated activities in practice. After the war, Greiser was tried by the Polish Supreme National Court, received a death sentence, and was hanged in Poznań (Posen) in July 1946; Jäger was tried in 1948 and hanged in June 1949. In the Warthegau, if not before, Udo Klausa was certainly exposed to the full meaning of Nazi racial policies in action.

The *Landrat*'s role in the racial state

The position of *Landrat* might at first glance appear anodyne, but the regime that it served was not. This was clear even in the highly politicized way in which it was officially described at the time. The *Landrat* was the modern, bureaucratic equivalent of a former aristocratic paternalism, a head of a district with command over people and resources. Historically, the *Landrat* enjoyed a reputation as both 'uncrowned king' and 'father' of his domain—a reputation in which the incumbents basked, and which, given strong state backing and powers of coercion in policy implementation, the population appears to have recognized.[31] This was the notion of benign paternalism that had informed the atmosphere in which Udo Klausa had grown up, hoping to follow in his father's footsteps. But its mission was—quite explicitly—rather different in the Third Reich.

As a higher-level local government officer, the *Landrat* was charged with carrying out policies passed down from above according to the priorities of the government of the day. And these, in the Third Reich, were intrinsically 'racial'. The practical implementation of racial policy was the central duty of local government at this time. According to the official guide, the *Reichskunde für junge Deutsche* of 1943, the priorities of local government in the Third Reich should consist in the 'preservation and development of the race', and raising 'the racially most valuable people to leading positions'.[32] The *Landrat* may not have been directly involved in executing acts of physical brutality; but *Landräte* in the newly annexed territories were directly involved in the translation of racial policies designed elsewhere into practical consequences for everyday life.[33]

Like so much else in the dynamic, constantly changing structures of the Third Reich, what the role involved in practice changed over time. It seems only to have been at a relatively late stage that Klausa's own perceptions changed, with growing realization in 1942—as deportations to Auschwitz gathered pace—of what precisely he was getting increasingly tangled up in. But the tensions evident later in Będzin were already apparent in the autumn of 1939: the repeated and frequently frustrated desire to serve at the front, knowledge of the brutal character of racial policies on the home front, awareness of the potential difficulties posed by a family commitment to Christianity. Klausa's combination of commitment and ambivalence led him now as later to seek to resolve his inner conflicts by a combination of keeping silent about any differences with the regime, throwing himself into his work—whatever the consequences for the victims of racial policies—and seeking means of leaving for active military service. The latter was something he appears to have been hankering after for other reasons, including attainment of military honours and not wishing to look like a shirker in comparison with his regimental peers, well before any doubts set in about the character of civilian administration.

The political nature of the job following the outbreak of war was already quite clear. *Landräte* in the annexed territories had to oversee crucial issues related to population planning, the mapping, expropriation, and acquisition of confiscated estates and properties, strategies for the 'Germanization' of previously Polish territories, and implementation of a whole gamut of racial policies. It has previously been argued that in some areas, such as the Warthegau, administrative competence might take precedence over party commitment; but this was certainly not the case in Upper Silesia, and apparently not in the Warthegau either.[34] The *Landrat* was a politically sensitive position, in the front line of 'Germanization' policies, and the overlap between party and state was intended from the outset to be extremely close. As Alexandra herself put it, in a letter to the family friend Frau von H., shortly after she and Udo had settled into Posen: 'Here in the *Gau*, there should in principle be a personal union between the *Landrat* and the [*NSDAP*] District Leader, which will hopefully work out very favourably.'[35]

Klausa was well aware of the character of the political role of the *Landrat* and the relevant racial policies even before he took on the post in Będzin. In the Warthegau, he rapidly settled into his new job, despite early qualms as a committed Catholic about the well-known antipathy towards the church harboured by his immediate boss, August Jäger. Jäger was known informally as *Kirchenjäger*—'church-hunter' (as in 'fox-hunter'), a pun on his name—for his earlier prominent role in Nazi anti-Church policies. But, again as Alexandra described it at the time, in practice Klausa found that 'Jäger is a very logical... approachable man, with whom it is very pleasant to work'. The only area of potential conflict was that of religion. Udo Klausa's commitment to Catholicism was possibly exacerbated by the fact that Alexandra had been brought up as a Protestant, and had been a member of a Berlin parish presided over by a pastor in the 'Confessing Church' (*Bekennende Kirche*); this was the wing of Protestantism least susceptible to Nazi takeover in the early days, in contrast to the so-called German Christians, and which was later associated with prominent individuals opposed to Nazism. With respect to differences with Jäger over questions of religion—an early example of the long-term strategy for avoiding points of friction and tension—it very soon became apparent to the Klausas that the obvious solution was to remain silent, as Alexandra explained to a close family friend:

> After this sort of discussion, questions relating to Christianity are carefully avoided. If something is after all touched on in the course of conversation, Udo and I shroud ourselves in ostentatious silence [*hüllen Udo und ich uns in ostentatives Schweigen*]. In this way we are able to get along very well.[36]

Later, in a reference written on Klausa's behalf, Jäger himself emphasized that, despite the fact that Klausa internally 'felt himself bound to his Catholic religion', he had 'in no way' let this get in the way of his 'practical commitment to the National Socialist cause' and his preparedness 'to give his utmost for the Führer's work'.[37]

Right from the start, and even before he was transferred to Posen, Klausa was also ambivalent about choosing between military service and civilian administration, wanting both to play an active part at the front—at a time when early victory seemed assured—while at the same time deploying his organizational, legal, and administrative talents and energies in building up the annexed territories. Shortly after the outbreak of war in September 1939, when the tactic of lightning strikes in the *Blitzkrieg* seemed to promise a rapid end to a successful war, Alexandra wrote to Frau von H.:

> I was terribly sorry for poor Udo, when his regiment had to set off without him... But I think Udo will be able to console himself that, if the war really is over soon, there will be endless people in the same position as him, and if it goes on longer, then they will all eventually get their turn![38]

This first attempt to enter the military fray having been unsuccessful, Klausa threw his energies into administration of the Warthegau. As Alexandra explained in a letter of October 1939—now staying with one of her relatives, Countess von Arnim—Udo had been promoted to *Regierungsrat*, a more senior position in the civil service, gaining 'a very considerable area of responsibility in Posen, which is somewhat making up for the misery of not being at the front'.[39] The tasks Udo faced in his new role seem to have been quite demanding, but also fulfilling, as Alexandra's letter a month later made clear. Following some thoughtful and quite pessimistic comments on the nature and likely outcome of the war, which she predicted as likely to have far more destructive consequences for all combatants than was the case in 1918, Alexandra continued:

Conquering the eastern territories and a farsighted colonization would be one of the few glimmers of light, and could be something great—a parallel to Otto the Great or the Teutonic Knights.—But optimism sinks without a trace if in the light of day you look at what is actually going on in practice.

Udo has a lot to do, a great task, but unfortunately one always has the feeling that, despite putting all possible effort into it, and even given the relatively favourable conditions, everything one does is just like a drop of water falling onto a hot stone.

So Udo is quite happily playing with the idea of going to the front. When this will be we do not as yet know, but that it will be is now definite.[40]

Klausa's desire to go to the military at this early stage of the war is more than evident; but it seems at this point to have been less in protest against the tasks he was set, than in frustration at not being able fully or rapidly to realize the Germans' colonizing mission in the east. The new challenges and responsibilities seemed nevertheless to be compensating somewhat for disappointment about not serving with his regiment. And, apart from the matter of religion, the cooperation—indeed personal unity—between party and state appeared to be working admirably in the Wartheland.

Klausa also appears to have relatively willingly assisted with the racial policies for which his immediate superior August Jäger held responsibility.[41] It was impossible to have been a civil servant in the Reichsgau Wartheland without being cognisant of the brutal policies of mass population expulsions. In his memoirs Klausa distances himself and Jäger from direct involvement in the practical implementation of racial policies. But he never suggests that he was at this stage unaware of what was going on; he even describes a visit with Jäger and SS Gruppenführer Wilhelm Koppe to a barracks where Poles were collected together prior to 'resettlement' in the General Government. Wilhelm Koppe was the Higher SS and Police Leader (*Höhere SS- und Polizeiführer* (*HSSPF*)) in the Warthegau, directly responsible to Himmler for 'ethnic cleansing' and ultimately genocide.[42] It is inconceivable that this trip with Greiser and Koppe was not undertaken as part of Klausa's official duties. Klausa also elsewhere comments, discussing the expulsion of Poles from the Będzin area, that he had had 'quite enough' of this sort of thing during his period in Posen.[43] Thus he was certainly neither ignorant of nor entirely blind to the inherent racism of the new occupation regime.

When talking about later expulsions, Klausa suggests that it was all a matter for the SS, and that he was 'never there'.[44] Yet he also could not have been unaware of the duties of the civilian administrators, including the *Landrat*, in this connection; such duties had already been made known to the relevant authorities during his time in the Warthegau. On 12 November 1939 there was a directive from Koppe in Posen, the administrative centre of the Reichsgau Wartheland, to the effect that all Jews should be deported, as well as all Poles 'who either belong to the intelligentsia or who, by virtue of their Polish national views, might represent a danger for the instigation and establishment of Germanness'. The circular added that 'criminal elements' were to be treated in the same way.[45] This circular, headed 'secret' (*Geheim*), explicitly prescribed the roles of the *Landräte* in rural areas and the City Mayors in urban areas, with unambiguous clarity.

The *HSSPF* Posen ordered that these civilian authorities were to determine precisely what numbers of people were to be forcibly removed from the area, with figures under each of these categories to be submitted by 18 November 1939.[46] Furthermore, the City Mayors and the *Landräte* were to be responsible for establishing the transit camps in which to round up and hold those to be evicted, such that they could then more easily and 'punctually' be put onto the 'trains to be transported away'.[47] Further tasks of the *Landräte* and City Mayors were outlined in some considerable detail, in order to ensure the smooth operation of forcible removal of people from their own homes. More generally, the front line responsibility of the local civilian authorities in the 'evacuation measures', along with all party and state institutions, was again underlined:

> City Mayors and *Landräte* are the persons responsible for the evacuation measures in their areas. All officials of the party and the state are required to give every possible support and cooperation in carrying through the historical task set by the Führer.[48]

There can be little doubt that Klausa was, if only in a subordinate role, involved in these measures in the Wartheland in the winter of 1939–40; and that he was fully aware both of what was going on and who held what areas of responsibility in relation to these expulsion measures. Orders came from the SS to the civilian administration, who were fully involved in the implementation of Hitler's 'historical task'.

Similar lines of command and responsibility were simultaneously being introduced in Upper Silesia. In the winter of 1939–40 SS Chief Heinrich Himmler, Reich Minister of the Interior Wilhelm Frick, and Reich Minister of Food and Agriculture Richard Walther Darré were in intensive discussions about the practical organization and lines of responsibility for the population census and consequent movement of populations. Those charged with 'building up the east' were to work closely with Himmler and the SS, and with the civilian administration at all levels. A circular of 7 December 1939 from the Silesian State President (*Oberpräsident*) in Breslau to the Regional Presidents of Upper and Lower Silesia in Kattowitz and Oppeln explained that the 'resettlement' of 'Poles and Czechs who are enemies of the state' should be done 'in conjunction with the *Landrat*, the Gestapo, the SD [Security Service], the [*NSDAP*] District Leader' and others. Furthermore, 'the *Landrat* makes the final decision, with the Secret State Police [Gestapo], that those designated as "enemies of the state" are to be deported at a given time'.[49] On 8 December 1939 Frick provided detailed additional clarification, running to four pages in total, of the generic lines of reporting and responsibility.[50] If any disagreements were to arise, 'then the Reichsstatthalter shall decide' who in turn reported to the Reichsführer SS, Heinrich Himmler.[51] As far as the local authorities were concerned, Frick made it quite clear the 'the measures for securing German Volk interests' were the responsibility of the *Landrat* in county districts (*Landkreise*) and the City Mayor in urban areas with their own municipal government.[52] Decisions over who was to be forcibly expelled, and who allowed to stay, were thus, in the county or *Landkreis*, the official responsibility of the *Landrat* himself. And this was something that Klausa, a legally trained career civil servant, must have been fully aware of from the outset.

Klausa's appointment as *Landrat* of Będzin

With his long-standing *NSDAP* membership, his strong academic record, and his previous experience in civilian administration not only in the 'old' Reich but also, since 1938, in the occupied territories of the Sudetenland, the Protectorate of Bohemia and Moravia, and the Warthegau, as well as his personal combination of intelligence, ambition, and commitment to the tasks at hand, Udo Klausa represented an apparently ideal choice for this important role. It did not take long—with a little pulling of strings along the way—for him to receive rapid promotion to the long-coveted position of *Landrat*.

Despite a promising start in the Warthegau, Klausa had almost instantly requested a transfer within the administration. In requesting a move, he explicitly mentioned personal reasons: he could barely have settled in when on 25 October 1939 he wrote to the Reich Interior Ministry asking if he could be transferred to Berlin because his wife, Alexandra, was expecting their first child in February 1940 and he wanted her to be somewhere with relatives and a proper home.[53] By November, it appeared that a suitable position had been found with the Prussian Directorate for Building and Finance (*Bau- und Finanzdirektion*) in Berlin—but then, with a little last-minute moving around and juggling of newly nominated personnel, an apparently even better opportunity was pursued: the role of the *Landrat* of Będzin.[54]

In his memoirs, Klausa claims that this opportunity more or less dropped unexpectedly into his lap through a phone call out of the blue, at the beginning of February 1940, from his 'protector'—as Klausa repeatedly portrays him—in Berlin, Dr Hans Dellbrügge. Dellbrügge (born 1902) was a member of the SS and became Government President in Vienna, a senior role in the Nazi hierarchy; in the 1950s, Klausa was able to return the favour, helping to ensure Dellbrügge a post in Düsseldorf. On this day, according to Klausa, Dellbrügge simply telephoned Jäger, with Klausa at his side, to offer Klausa the post; Jäger was prepared to agree on condition that they find him an 'equally diligent successor!', a compliment from Jäger that Klausa greatly appreciated.[55]

Klausa's portrayal of his appointment to the Będzin post is, like much else in his memoirs, a little economical with the details. In fact it had required considerable effort and very likely the active deployment of personal connections to acquire this prize position, since there was, at the time of Klausa's nomination for the appointment, actually no vacancy.

By the spring of 1940, when movements of personnel at the middling and lower levels of the regional offices were still substantial, a list of *Landräte* to head the new administrations had in fact already been fixed. But there was still just room for personal intervention, and a last minute change of locations.

In December 1939, a letter had been sent out requesting experienced officials to take up the new *Landrat* roles in the Kattowitz district, positions that were soon filled.[56] But there remained a serious dearth of qualified personnel to take up posts at lower levels of the administration, compounded by constant haemorrhaging of manpower to the army. As a letter from the Regional President in Kattowitz to the Reich Ministry of the Interior (RMI) in early January 1940 put it, the innumerable tasks relating to the population census, determination of citizenship questions, and 'resettling' people, among other matters, were more than overburdening the limited personnel resources available.[57] Other letters make it clear that there were problems because of people being called away to military service. A letter from a functionary in Liegnitz to the RMI on 19 January 1940, for example, pleaded that no further people should be taken, since it would no longer be possible to guarantee proper running of the *Landrat*'s affairs.[58] There followed numerous urgent pleas, such as that expressed in a letter from Kattowitz on 29 January 1940, to send 'other mid-level officials' or 'state employees'. On 17 April 1940 a letter from the Liegnitz functionary similarly complained that 'on average between 1/3 and ½ of the officials or employees are not available because of call-ups to military service, being transferred to other duties, etc.' and that temporary replacements were generally not up to the tasks demanded of them. Any further loss of personnel would 'endanger' the orderly business of the administration.[59] But by this stage there were no vacancies for the post of *Landrat* itself.

Klausa's appointment to the acting *Landrat* position in Będzin entailed the support of Graf von der Schulunberg, the colleague from the Potsdam Infantry Regiment Number 9 who was the Vice President of the Upper Presidium in Breslau. Graf von der Schulunberg now intervened and 'expressly point[ed] out that this is a matter of the personal wishes of the Gauleiter Wagner'.[60] To put into practice the 'personal wish' that Klausa should be appointed *Landrat* was, however, not a simple matter, given that the position had already been filled. The official dealing with this in the Reich Interior Ministry in Berlin, Theodor Fründt, rather acidly pointed out that one Behrend had already been proposed and approved for 'Bendschin' [*sic*]; Behrend could not readily be sent on to Groß-Strehlitz as suggested, since someone else had already been appointed there, one Studtnitz, who it was now proposed should instead be considered for the office at Goldberg; besides all of which, 'Klausa is also still extremely young' (*Klausa sei zudem noch reichlich jung*).[61] All this has something of the appearance of a slightly nepotistic game of musical chairs, with the person already approved for Będzin being swapped over instead to the Groß-Strehlitz *Landrat*'s office formerly held by Udo Klausa's father Dr Walter Klausa, and the appointee there being sent on to a vacancy elsewhere. Indeed, in a letter from Berlin of 20 February 1940 Gauleiter Wagner in Breslau was told off by Hans Pfundtner, the senior civil servant in charge of appointments to higher levels of the civil service, for trying to change decisions that had been made very recently, indeed decisions that had been made on the basis of his own suggestions.[62]

Nevertheless, the shuffling-around of designated incumbents was set in motion, and in mid-February 1940 Klausa received a letter from the RMI to take up the post in 'Bentschin' [*sic*] after all.[63] This was, however, in view of Klausa's youth, relative inexperience, and what was perceived to be a somewhat 'premature appointment', to be first of all on a period of extended probation, with milestones at one year and again at one and a half years, with final confirmation in post only after demonstrating satisfactory service over the course of a full two-year period.[64] A note from the Regional President of Kattowitz of 1 April 1940 confirmed that Klausa 'took over the administration of the *Landrat*'s office of Bendzin [*sic*] on 21st March'.[65]

Others who were 'sent to the east' to take up administrative posts often saw this as a form of penalty for what had been seen as misdeeds, undue outspokenness, or inadequate service elsewhere.[66] Alexander Hohenstein, for example, received a letter on 14 December 1940 telling him he was to be relieved of his duties as Mayor in a western territory of Germany and sent to take up a post in the Warthegau. On reading this letter, he commented in his diary:

> So this is the way the [*NSDAP*] District Leader wants to get rid of me? This smells strongly of a disciplinary demotion... I've been expecting something along these lines for a long time, after all the constant friction with the party.[67]

This was not the case with Udo Klausa, who appears to have eagerly sought a position in which he could, as he thought, develop his not inconsiderable organizational skills and administrative talents. And Alexandra was equally delighted, for more domestic reasons. She wrote from Berlin to Frau von H. in mid-March 1940, shortly after the birth of her first child, reporting on Udo's move to start the new job in Będzin: 'We are naturally delighted about this turn of things, and I hope above all that connected with this will soon be our own home and the beginning of a [proper] family life.'[68] To suggest that her husband would have preferred a job in a 'colonial wares store', as referenced in almost joking fashion in one of Alexandra's later letters, and interpreted to suggest he did not really want this position of *Landrat*, does not entirely square with the trouble that seems to have been expended in pursuing this post on his behalf to begin with, and the high hopes the Klausas had for their future together in the setting of the *Landrat*'s role—at least when he first took it on.[69]

At this stage, Klausa does not appear to have fully registered the difference in conditions in the newly incorporated borderlands and what he had experienced as a child in the long-established Prussian *Landrat*'s Office in Leobschütz, which was, after all, located in the Oppeln district of Upper Silesia not so very far to the west of Będzin. Moreover, the Klausa family had long-standing family connections in the area. Udo Klausa's great-grandfather, Anton Klausa, had been a substantial administrator of mines and industrial production across a wide area around Będzin, from Tarnowitz down as far as Myslowitz. He had also played a significant role in local politics and community life: in 1842 he had been Mayor of Tarnowitz, to which town he bequeathed an old people's home, while to Myslowitz he bequeathed the cemetery, in which the Klausa family grave was established. This substantial red-brick mausoleum still exists in the well-tended cemetery on the aptly named Ulice Oświęcim, or Auschwitz Road, some 10 miles south of Będzin and 15 miles north of Auschwitz. Anton Klausa had also, incidentally, turned down an attractive offer of working for the Henckel von Donnersmarck business.[70] Udo Klausa's grandfather, Theodor Klausa, had been a member of the Tarnowitz Town Council, as well as managing several mines in the Myslowitz area.[71] Additionally, the area was relatively rich in the country estates of families who were either relatives of or closely befriended with the aristocratic family of Udo's wife Alexandra, including again the Henckel von Donnersmarck family. Other nearby families, such as that of Walrab Freiherr von Wangenheim, were not only friends but also colleagues in local government; von Wangenheim was a neighbouring *Landrat*. So this was essentially a form of home territory for both sides of the Klausa family, even if one where living conditions were effectively those of colonial rule among 'natives' who were considered vastly inferior to the ruling Germans.

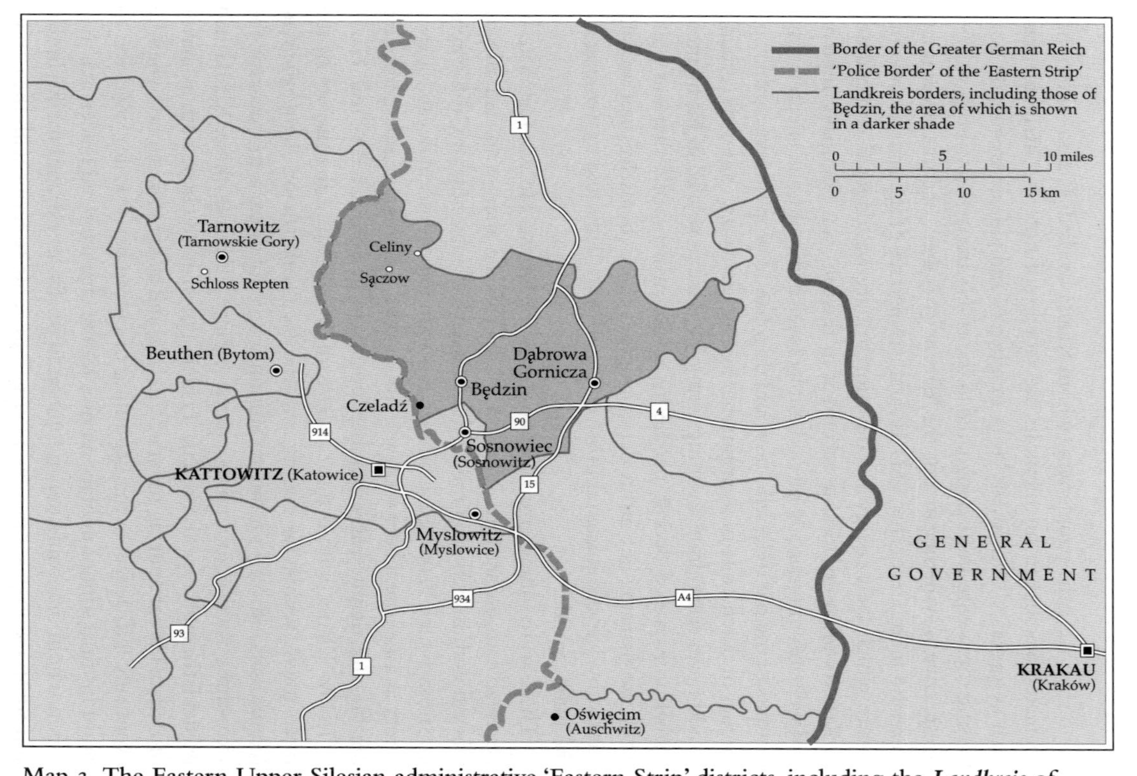

Map 3. The Eastern Upper Silesian administrative 'Eastern Strip' districts, including the ***Landkreis*** of Będzin

The Będzin administration

Who then were the people with whom Klausa worked? Klausa's thumbnail character sketches in his memoirs are worthy of note: he attributes traits such as 'decency' and 'loyalty' to a number of individuals, frequently contrasting them with those designated as the real Nazis or 'brown big-wigs'—irrespective of whether or not the 'decent' members of local government were also members of the *NSDAP*, and irrespective of the actions and policies to which their energy and devotion to duty was directed. As portrayed in Klausa's memoirs, local government in this area was essentially anodyne and well-meaning, largely carried out by loyal, dedicated, and energetic civil servants of the old style, who now and then had to prop up less capable colleagues or defend one of their number against 'the Nazis', but who certainly would never have 'done anything wrong'. We see portrayed in his memoirs a small universe of 'decent' people living in a wider world that was politically problematic; but in his depiction, they were themselves not actually tainted by actively engaging in any evil, and were dedicated to working for the public good.

There were some personal continuities for Klausa. He was fortunate in being able to attract into his service experienced men who had already worked with his father in the *Landrat* offices of Leobschütz or Groß-Strehlitz, from which Walter Klausa retired in 1940 just as his son began his own career as a *Landrat*. There were also others whom Klausa considered honest, reliable, and, despite party membership, not to be considered as 'real' Nazis.

Below Klausa, within the *Landkreis* of Będzin, were the mayors of the three towns within his county, and the local officials or *Amtskommissare* (commissary officers) for the ten administrative subdistricts that oversaw the sixty-three rural communities in the county.[72] Among these, Klausa had particularly high regard for Hans Felden, the man he chose both as mayor of Będzin's neighbouring town of Czeladź, and as his own deputy when he eventually left Będzin at the beginning of December 1942 for what was to prove his final stint of military service. Klausa characterized Felden as a man 'upon whom one could depend unconditionally, an extraordinarily shrewd and adroit man who somehow managed to come to terms with the conditions of the time'. Deploying some of his characteristic turns of phrase, Klausa defended Felden's loyal service despite the fact that Felden's head was sought by the Russians after the war:

Apparently after the Russians occupied the area, a 'wanted poster' for him was put up in Bendsburg. Quite certainly he had done nothing wrong. But one just innocently became—guilty! That was of course the reason for my own departure. After the war Felden became a senior civil servant in the Ministry of the Interior in Lower Saxony... A faithful, decent, loyal man, with whom I remained in contact after the war.[73]

With some other colleagues who had not been of his own choosing, Klausa experienced rather more difficulty. He comments particularly on one Kowohl, describing him as 'an anxious, quite incapable man who was not at all at home in administration', whose work had to be shored up by someone with greater expertise in these matters. Again, however, Klausa was able to draw on his father's contacts: the relevant bureaucrat called in to support Kowohl was 'the former mayor of Leobschütz, Dr Sartory'.[74] In his personal service, Klausa was also fortunate to be able to attract people whom he already knew and trusted, including 'an old colleague of my father's, Ignatz Margosch', who was 'loyal, reliable, [and] had a wife and four sons who were at that time still very small'.[75] Margosch's family even inhabited the bottom floor of Klausa's own official residence as *Landrat*.[76]

In Klausa's summary of his administrative team, he concludes that virtually all of his subordinate colleagues were

decent, not aggressive Nazis, incorruptible... Among them there was even a bearer of the Golden Party Badge, who however never made any difficulties for me. They all had a healthy sense of reserve in relation to party functionaries and restricted themselves to administration. At that time this was far from self-evident.[77]

'Restricting themselves to administration' was not, as we shall see, a guarantee of being able to retain any distance from Nazism. In any case, even the local *NSDAP* functionaries were in Klausa's view people one could deal with, if handled appropriately. Rademacher, the leader of the local Będzin *NSDAP* branch, was, for example, supposedly not too difficult to deal with:

I had a half-way bearable relationship with him, although I was careful not to embark on a collision course. Since of course I was only sporadically in Bendsburg, since I mostly disappeared quickly to the army, I was also more or less successful in getting away without any clashes.[78]

When Klausa was actually present in Będzin, he explains, it would have been unwise to show his true opinions: 'At that time one had to be terribly wary.'[79]

Above Klausa in the administrative hierarchy was his immediate superior, Ministerial Councillor (*Ministerialrat*) Walter Springorum, who was President of the Regional Government (*Regierungspräsident*) based in Kattowitz. Springorum is also portrayed as among the 'decent' Nazis: in Klausa's view, Springorum was 'a decidedly diligent, energetic man with backbone, who would provide real support and cover if one was having difficulties with the "brown big-wigs"'.[80] Curiously, as we shall see, this supposed protector of Klausa against Nazi 'big-wigs' was himself apparently only too happy to sup with the devil—even literally, visiting Auschwitz with Himmler on a couple of occasions, and attending a dinner with him hosted by Gauleiter Bracht—and to participate without any apparent qualms in the implementation of racial policies, up to and even including extermination by gassing. To suggest that Springorum in some way helped to 'cover' and protect those who were at odds with Nazism is a striking misrepresentation of his commitment to the Nazi state and its racist policies.

Springorum was in turn subordinate to the *Gauleiter* and *Oberpräsident* of Upper Silesia, a dual position as head of the state province and the party district or *Gau*. The role was held first by Josef Wagner until 1941, when he fell into Hitler's disfavour, and then by Fritz Bracht until his suicide at the end of the war in May 1945. Furthermore, the *Gauleiter* and *Oberpräsident* held an additional role that was central to racial policies. When in October 1939 Himmler became Reich Commissar for the Strengthening of German Nationhood (*Reichskommissar für die Festigung deutschen Volkstums*), he named the regional leaders of the newly incorporated territories as his deputies entrusted with carrying out the tasks on the ground (*RKF-Beauftragten*); thus Josef Wagner and his successor Fritz Bracht held the triple role of civilian *Oberpräsident*, party-political *Gauleiter*, and immediate representative of Heinrich Himmler as Reich Commissar for the Strengthening of German Nationhood.[81]

The Deputy of the *Oberpräsident* from August 1939 was Fritz-Dietlof Graf von der Schulenburg, who had been instrumental in Klausa's appointment in early 1940. Despite his later role in the July Plot of 1944, von der Schulenburg was at this stage still a supporter of Nazi policies, if already critical of some aspects of practice; he had not as yet evolved into an active member of the resistance, despite some of the post-war self-serving testimonies of former Nazis who had worked with him at this time and later hoped to gain a degree of 'innocence by association'.[82] Von der Schulenburg in fact came into contact with the oppositional circles of the Kreisauer Kreis only in late 1942 at the earliest, possibly only in early 1943. In the meantime, he was concerned to ensure that the new province should be staffed by young, highly qualified, intelligent officials who were also committed Nazis, including Walter Springorum, the President of the Regional Government, and his team of young and ambitious *Landräte*.

Klausa repeatedly professed that he had himself had nothing to do with any acts of physical violence beyond the perfectly 'legitimate' duties of a soldier in Hitler's *Wehrmacht*. The army was held up, throughout Klausa's memoirs, as a model place to have been: he was constantly 'disappearing' to service in the army, portraying it as a last bastion of decency in Hitler's evil world; it is represented as his escape from the complicity that threatened to taint him as a civil servant implementing Hitler's policies on the home front. As he put it—with rather elastic and inaccurate dating, as we shall see—he soon began to realize that even just staying in Będzin would compromise him, and that military service would be preferable:

> [It] was clear to me that I could in no way stay in Bendzin. So I used every opportunity to flee again to the army. That was from the end of June to mid-October 1940, mid-January 1941 until the beginning of January 1942, and then finally from August 1942 onwards.[83]

The army is even characterized as somehow separate from the *NSDAP*, from which, in his memoirs, Klausa also distanced himself (despite remaining a member right through to 1945). The complicity of the army in facilitating and furthering the extermination of European Jews had, at the time Klausa wrote his memoirs in 1980, not as yet been revealed in the full glare of the public spotlight: widespread and very heated public debate on the army's involvement in the Holocaust only took off in the mid- and later 1990s, with the public reception of the controversial 'Crimes of the Wehrmacht' exhibition (shown in numerous locations, with a radically revised second version as a result of critiques).[84]

Klausa repeatedly asserts that even while in Będzin he had nothing to do with any acts of physical brutality and terror, and explicitly distances himself from even having witnessed such acts. When, for example, he was charged with implementation of 'resettlement' measures by Dr Arlt, the Nazi racial expert who had been put in charge of the 'Germanization' programme by Heinrich Himmler, Klausa reiterated his disapproval of such measures following his experiences in Posen.[85] He also explicitly distances himself from having had any involvement with, or even having personally witnessed, acts of terror that were the responsibility of the SS or the police forces.[86] The claim of never having physically been present when something unpleasant or violent occurred is quite typical of Klausa's memoirs. Moreover, despite the fact that members of his own family and close friends had been members of the SS (including brothers-in-law), Klausa repeatedly distances himself from this organization, and claims he advised friends against having anything to do with it. Klausa draws an absolute distinction between his own duties—'only administration'—and the areas that were the responsibility of the SS or police.

As far as his own responsibility for the exercise of physical force in the county was concerned, Klausa recalls with considerable relief that his own remit was limited: the gendarmerie or local constabulary in the predominantly rural areas reported to Klausa in his role as *Landrat*, but the regular police forces in the urban areas reported to the Police President in Sosnowiec, Alexander von Woedtke. Von Woedtke seems to have been a particularly proactive and opinionated person, who was quick to enter into personalized criticism and sharp disagreements; he constantly sparred, for example, with the powerful head of the SS economic empire, SS Brigadeführer Albrecht Schmelt. A member of the SS himself, von Woedtke seems to have tried to make up in his behaviour—throwing his weight around quite vehemently in letters to colleagues and rivals in power—for a lack of any authority rooted in physical bearing: he is described by contemporaries as wearing 'gold-rimmed' spectacles, being relatively short in height and 'broad, fat' in build. He had an 'erect' carriage, a round head, hair that was 'chestnut, sparse, straight, combed back, bald on top', a 'round, full' and clean-shaven face with a high forehead, a small mouth, thin lips, and broad chin.[87] Such detailed descriptions make it relatively easy to identify von Woedtke—and others for whom similarly detailed descriptions are available—in photographs, which provide visual confirmation of the archival evidence of just how closely, for all their jostling for mutual advantage and imposition of their own ideas, different parts of the administration and police forces actually cooperated.

This cooperation was downplayed by Klausa. Klausa makes sharp distinctions between the role and actions of the gendarmerie, on the one hand, and the remaining police forces, the Gestapo and the SS, on the other. Klausa felt he could rely absolutely on the personal integrity of Heinrich Mentgen, the officer in charge of the gendarmerie for which the *Landrat* was responsible. Mentgen was, in Klausa's view, 'an absolutely decent, responsible and dutiful police official, for whom every transgression of police powers was anathema'.

At that time, there was admittedly 'a certain danger' of excesses, 'since Poles and Jews had no rights'. But Klausa is quick to add that they were not really at risk in the area for which his own gendarmerie forces were responsible, since, omitting now any mention of Poles, 'there were no Jews in this area of the county, they had all been concentrated in the three towns, if indeed there had even been any Jews in any other places'. Klausa goes on to comment that 'during my time here there had in this respect been no resettlement'.[88] The significance of these claims—erroneous and misleading in the extreme—will be examined more closely in due course; but the supposed 'absence' of Jews in Klausa's memoirs and remembered areas of responsibility, here as elsewhere, is a consistent theme, and is intrinsically related to the alleged 'decency' of those with whom he worked.

The administration of the *Landkreis* and the county town of Będzin was very closely linked to that of the closely neighbouring town of Sosnowiec. The Police President in Sosnowiec, who from autumn 1940 was Alexander von Woedtke, held police powers over a wide area, including the southern parts of the *Landkreis* of Będzin. Klausa consistently places responsibility for any acts of violence in his area onto the police forces led by von Woedtke. But the records show that in the design and implementation of 'racial' policies the two administrations worked hand in hand. Given the close proximity of the two towns, Klausa also worked very closely with the City Mayor of Sosnowiec, Franz-Josef Schönwälder. There was a division of labour and a division of responsibilities here; but a close and smooth cooperation in pursuit of the same overall goals in the 'Germanization' of the area was never challenged.

This picture of predominantly harmonious cooperation was rather different from that in the 'old' Reich. There, *Landräte* had in the pre-war years often come into conflict with the new Nazi hierarchy, in the familiar maelstrom of clashes and conflicts of authority between old state structures and offices and the new elements of party administration and control.[89] Such conflicts were far less likely in the newly annexed territories, where local administration was set up from scratch, and staffed predominantly by young, keen civil servants determined to make a career and not put a foot wrong. The *Landräte* of the area were, in short, striving up-and-coming young civil servants who had taken on jobs in the administration of this newly occupied territory while still in their thirties.[90] They had received their professional training and served their apprenticeships in the peacetime years of the Third Reich, and were anxious to prove their credentials and make their careers with loyal service at the front line of its expanding empire in the east.

There remains, then, a widely prevalent assumption that it was possible to have been a Nazi with, somehow, acceptable motives and intentions: perhaps mistakenly having supported Hitler as an apparent 'saviour' in times of economic and political troubles in the early 1930s, grateful for the return to full employment and the restoration of Germany's international status in the mid-1930s, perhaps upset at the outbreak of war in 1939 and relieved by easy military victories, motivated by legitimate patriotism—but entirely innocent when it came to any acts of terror committed by a few extremists, Nazi fanatics or members of the SS, and indeed ignorant of any such acts until after the war was over. Variants to this story exist, including twists such as having been under pressure to join the *NSDAP* or an affiliated organization for fear of losing one's job; or having joined in order to fight from within against the 'real' Nazis, who would otherwise have made matters so much worse—and so on. These standard narratives could only be punctured, in the case of particular individuals, by demonstrating that they had actually known more about the Nazi terror at the time, and had been actively engaged in facilitating it, or at least had failed to act against it. This widespread post-war view of Nazism—distinguishing between the 'real' Nazis in the SS and the *NSDAP*, and those who were purely nominal, not actually responsible for acts of terror—is roughly where Udo Klausa took his own starting point in his self-representation.

Klausa claimed, in retrospect, that he was increasingly uncomfortable with the political context in which he had sought to pursue his long-held dream of following in his father's footsteps as *Landrat*. But his representation of his stance at the time, and his dates of absence, are strongly slanted in the direction of what later looked more acceptable. It is also clear, when explored in more detail, that what was meant by 'administration' was far from politically neutral. And it is, to say the least, highly unlikely that someone who had initially been appointed as an 'acting' *Landrat* in February 1940, and was finally confirmed in this position, with a string of strongly supportive references from his superiors in regional government, only in the early summer of 1942—by which time deportations to Auschwitz were well under way—could really have stood out in any way as oppositional in either attitude or behaviour. Klausa could not, on his own admission, risk getting into trouble by exposing his 'real' views too openly.

The disjuncture between the sympathies later intimated in Klausa's memoirs and the record of his activity at the time raises difficult questions about the extent to which the system constrained Klausa to act in certain ways, with the ultimate, if unforeseeable, consequence of facilitating the round-up for deportations to mass murder; or whether his service in a racist cause arose from a combination of career ambitions and underlying agreement with the direction of Nazi policy at least up until the summer of 1942—an agreement that was later denied and the signs reversed under the new conditions of post-war West Germany, reflected in the sympathies explicitly recorded in the memoirs.

Klausa often seems in his memoirs to be struggling to understand the ways in which members of his generation were caught in the crossfire of history, having, as he saw it, very little room for manœuvre, and having been brought up with certain ideals, including nationalist convictions that in other circumstances might have been seen as legitimate patriotism. The underlying assumption that the world was made up of different 'races', with some people genetically superior and others inferior—seen as a matter of scientific fact, rather than political belief—was also very widespread in the circles in which Klausa moved.

These background assumptions were shared by his wife, Alexandra. The relationship between Alexandra and my mother, who left Germany in the spring of 1935, was periodically put in jeopardy when Alexandra voiced her political and 'racial' views too explicitly. In September 1935, for example, Alexandra wrote in glowing terms of the 'feeling of security and protection' occasioned by Hitler's speech at the Nuremberg Party Rally, in which he had discussed the Abyssinian question—to which she explicitly referred—and had announced the infamous Nuremberg Laws that 'legalized' the status of Jews as second-class citizens and pariahs. Two months later, Alexandra explicitly promised not to make any such political remarks in the future: this letter had clearly not been well received by my mother, who, following a period of presumably outraged silence, had apparently responded rather emphatically.[91] What seems to have been seen among some Germans as self-evident was viewed very differently by those who had been discriminated against and ousted from the now 'racially' defined 'national community' (*Volksgemeinschaft*) that dominated their former homeland. Even so, and even at that time, a degree of personal emotional closeness could be maintained by keeping such subjects off the agenda—a pattern that could readily be picked up again after the war, but only by repressing any recognition that support for Hitler's political aims, and failure to empathize with (or even be fully aware of the implications for) those who were excluded from the 'racial community', had played a significant role in making possible all that had happened in between.

Nazism came in many hues, some apparently less respectable than others; inhabiting a human universe of differing personalities, Klausa seemed quite keen to distinguish between the 'decent' and the rest, with little regard for the nature of the system that they were all, in different ways, acting to serve. But racism and rule by terror, whether or not the *Landrat* was personally present or actively involved in any specific act of violence, was part of the professional brief and integral to the political context from the outset.

Udo Klausa was very much a product of his times. His nationalist enthusiasm and desire for military service were evident throughout his youth and young adulthood. His commitment to the SA was superseded by involvement in the army, while his membership of the *NSDAP* was rooted not only in pragmatic opportunism but also in shared commitments with no perception of the human tragedies unleashed by Hitler's state from the very start. The widely shared 'racial' world view, seen as based in scientific fact rather than political choice, enabled Klausa to pursue a career and fulfil his duties with an energy and efficiency that were rewarded with rapid promotion. This was not the fanatical, 'exterminatory antisemitism' seen by some as key to explaining the Holocaust, but a far more widespread set of assumptions about the existence of a hierarchy of 'races', accompanied by a capacity simply not to register the human consequences of policies carried out in service of a deeply racist state.[92] It was perfectly compatible with a commitment to the Catholic milieu that was his family heritage, and that occasioned him some passing discomfort when, sitting among senior Nazi colleagues in the Warthegau, Christianity came up as a subject at the dinner table.

This, then, was Klausa's background and preparation for the administration of the *Landkreis* of Będzin. Therafter, there is a continuing disjuncture between Klausa's portrayal of his time in Będzin and the accounts of the victims of Nazi policies. It is as if there were parallel universes, the one barely noticing the other; yet the actions of the occupiers had a massive impact upon the occupied, as part of a wider system of German rule. While Klausa attributed traits of decency to his colleagues, he appears largely to have ignored the character of the system they were serving so loyally. And those on the receiving end of the blows noticed only the immediate oppressors, the messengers of Nazi rule, with little awareness of the wider system of which they were a part.

5

An Early Question of Violence

When anyone is found out to have been in some sense a Nazi, a widespread response is to ask what, if anything, this person had actually done that was 'really' awful. In post-war Germany it was widely assumed that it was perfectly possible to have been, in some way, an unimportant participant in the machinery of Nazism; and that, even if one had held some rank or office, one did not necessarily have to bear any guilt for having done anything particularly bad. Playing a role in the system and simply obeying orders without being personally motivated to act in the ways that one did—even if acting in these ways actually assisted in causing many deaths—was indeed often wheeled out as a defence strategy in post-war trials in West Germany, bringing a reduction of sentence or no sentence at all. Of the more than 106,496 legal cases that were initiated between 8 May 1945 and 1 January 1996, only 6,494 actually came to judgment; just over 100,000 cases of potential perpetrators never got this far.[1] The attempt at exoneration of some of those who had gone along with the regime, for whatever reason, may or may not be morally acceptable; the rules of criminal culpability overlap with, but by no means fully encompass, other prevalent conceptions of guilt.[2] Moreover, political and pragmatic considerations radically affect the ways in which particular behaviours and intentions are evaluated.

A focus on acts of physical violence, motivated by personal intentions including racial hatred, has somehow permeated both historical and popular perceptions of Nazism. The widespread tendency both to focus on brutal or 'base' motives, and then to see 'obeying orders' as a legitimate form of defence, reducing the notion of 'real' perpetrators to the relatively small circles around Hitler at the top of the political hierarchy and the greatest sadists of the extermination machinery, has helped obscure the way violence permeated the entire Nazi system.

When I first learned of Udo Klausa's role in this eastern territory of annexed Poland, I too—as I now think mistakenly—went down this track of wondering about whether Klausa had personally committed or held responsibility for acts of violence. It was only as I began to explore in greater depth that I realized the sheer extent to which the system in its entirety was based on different forms of terror, and that a search for any one particular act—or relief at finding no apparent area of culpability—was simply to misunderstand the way the system worked. There is, moreover, a yawning gap between the verdicts of post-war legal conceptions and the experiences of those on the receiving end of violence: vast areas miss the restricted legal net entirely.

Distinctions

Views of the system vary dramatically between victims of Nazi racism, and those who were complicit but were later unwilling to acknowledge any guilt, however small. It was and is not a crime, after all, to choose to drop some friends, and to restrict one's personal friendship circles to those seen as socially compatible; but, from the perspective of people condemned to progressive social isolation, the experience appears in a very different light.[3] Views differ too depending on what kinds of standards of guilt are being applied: even to have continued to benefit from the consequences of the actions of the 'truly guilty', or to have failed to oust them from the 'community of solidarity', is in some views to participate in a degree of guilt, whether or not one was even alive, let alone active, at the time the offences were committed.[4]

Legal views also vary and change. Under modern Western systems of law, acts of physical brutality—grievous bodily harm, manslaughter, or murder—are considered reprehensible, though there are variations regarding the conditions under which such acts might be categorized as defensible (as in self-defence) or penalties reduced (by virtue, for example, of diminished responsibility). But there are wide differences of view concerning how to deal with acts committed in the past, when they were state-sanctioned and indeed actively sponsored by the regime in power; changing pragmatic considerations also affect both the definition and the treatment of such acts. While the enforced sale of Jewish property at ludicrously low prices in the 'aryanization' measures of 1938 was soon recognized as grounds for post-war legal claims, it took decades longer for the coercion of people into forced labour to be widely recognized as a crime in and of itself (and not merely associated offences such as incidents of brutality or maltreatment inflicted on forced labourers), and hence to constitute a basis for legal claims for compensation; and victims of Nazi homophobia were unable to gain the status of victims or openly to seek compensation until homosexuality itself was very belatedly decriminalized in both East and West Germany at the end of the 1960s, nearly a quarter of a century after the end of the Reich.

Any attempt now to evaluate the acts of a former Nazi—in whatever sense—is complicated by the need to draw lines with respect to degrees of both reprehensibility and responsibility. To err in one direction may mean to concede legitimacy to essentially Nazi arguments, while to lean unduly in the other, expressing moral outrage about any kind of complicity in the system, may be to gloss over real distinctions in degrees of relative responsibility and the historically uneven distribution of the undoubted overall burden of guilt. It is crucial, then, to be able to combine overall political rejection and moral revulsion with some degree of differentiation in analysis. Understanding how it was possible does not entail exoneration; but then historians are not in the business of judicial determination and passing sentence.

Distinctions between the truly awful and the less culpable Nazis had already begun with early post-war Allied 'denazification' policies. In the western zones of occupied Germany there were five different gradations of assumed culpability, from 'major' and 'lesser' offenders through to 'fellow travellers' (*Mitläufer*) and those who were 'exonerated'. In the Soviet Zone of occupation, a distinction was eventually made between those who were held to have been 'active' and those who were merely 'nominal' Nazis. People facing denazification proceedings naturally shaped their own stories to fit the new categories, hoping to be assigned as low a role in the Nazi hierarchy of responsibility as possible. And, in the subsequent legal pursuit of former Nazis, the focus was very obviously on those who had committed the most heinous crimes, with questions about the baseness and intensity of personal motives as well as the scale of the criminal actions.

In the early years of the western Federal Republic of Germany, there was something of a slowing-down of legal proceedings against former Nazis, once the trials instigated by the Allies in the later 1940s had come to an end. But in 1958 the Central Office of the State Justice Administrations for the Investigation of National Socialist Crimes (*Zentrale Stelle der Landesjustizverwaltungen zur Aufklärung nationalsozialistischer Verbrechen*), based in a delightful eighteenth-century ducal building in the small town of Ludwigsburg just north of Stuttgart, was opened to coordinate the criminal investigations of the German federal states (*Länder*). It began its work with what retrospectively seems a ridiculously small number of staff, given the enormity of the criminal activities of the Nazi regime.

The crimes committed in the Będzin area, the district under Udo Klausa's responsibility, were actively investigated from around 1960, just before the Frankfurt Auschwitz trial began, through to the late 1980s. By virtue of Klausa's position of responsibility for civilian government in the area, his name was used in the very title of some of the files. At first, I thought this archive might hold all the answers for which I was looking.

But perusing the files collated over some three decades of intensive investigation by the Ludwigsburg Central Office eventually made me realize how different, in fact, legal and historical investigations really are. What the legal system conceives to be evidence of criminal responsibility is often not what is of most significance for the historian interested in how a system works, and how people viewed and carried out their roles within it. Historical notions of causation and interpretation do not always overlap neatly or comprehensively with legal notions of individual culpability.

We are now all too well aware of the appalling acts of sadism and brutality carried out by the SS and Gestapo across German-occupied Europe. In the area of Będzin, there are innumerable examples in the files of individual acts of extreme cruelty and violence. Across testimony after testimony, we hear of men such as Rudolf Mildner, head of the Kattowitz Gestapo headquarters and overseer of a 'court' at Auschwitz where death sentences were meted out on the smallest of pretexts after the most minimal of 'hearings'; Hans Dreier, head of the Jewish section of the Kattowitz Gestapo offices, who, along with SS officer Kuczynski, carried out selections over life and death during the mass deportations of tens of thousands of Jews, and perpetrated acts of utmost cruelty in repeated smaller incidents; and numerous others who terrorized and shot people 'while trying to escape'. The criminality of perpetrators such as these is—or should be—beyond doubt. Yet even such a senior Nazi as Mildner, who was captured and brought to testify at the Nuremberg trials after the war, was held to be too 'useful' to the Americans in their post-war fight against communism to be put on trial for his own role in mass murder. Despite all the masses of evidence collected against the perpetrators of criminal violence in this area, some survivors were unwilling to give testimony, pointing out that the initiators were not punished and doubting that any of those who carried out violent acts on the ground would be brought to trial. Given this view, as one survivor put it, 'he wanted to have his peace and hear nothing further of those times'.[5]

If one is interested in the role of civilian administration, however, the records of criminal investigations are somewhat less revealing. Survivors do not remember the men in grey suits hidden away in offices drawing up guidelines for ghettoization, poring over street plans to decide which areas should be made 'Jew-free', or issuing directives about permission to use public transport or restrictions on foodstuffs for those deemed inferior and barely worth keeping alive—even if they were not yet actively put to death. And exploration of the indirect causation of death through malnutrition and maltreatment does not figure high on the legal agenda of those pursuing acts of murder on the scale of millions.

The evidence collated in legal investigations can nevertheless be extremely useful in trying to piece together a wider historical picture. It is, of course, particularly helpful when looking at a system based on repeated acts of violence: a system that is, by its very nature, brutal in the extreme, and prepared to use terror as a political tool on an everyday basis.

But violence comes in a variety of forms, and not only the narrow categories recognized by the German legal system after the war. Both types of terror—the acts of violence that occasioned criminal investigations into individual incidents, and the wider systemic terror that seems to have been beyond the scope of the law—are significant in trying to understand the involvement of ordinary Nazis in this period. This only slowly dawned on me after I had considered not merely individual acts of violence, but also the wider violence that was inherent in the system itself.

Rule by force

By the time Klausa had taken up his post in the spring of 1940, some five months after the burning of the Great Synagogue, violence was routinized and engrained in the system in more diffuse—but ultimately no less murderous—ways. Klausa was selectively briefed by his predecessor Dr Grotjan not only on the early atrocities, but also on the key issues with which he now had to deal.

The implication of Klausa's account in his memoirs is that terror was integral to the initial invasion and early period of the occupation of Poland, but that, by the time he himself arrived in the area, things had settled down—which in one sense was indeed the case. Jews had been forced to come to terms with the fact that now, as Klausa put it, they 'were crammed together in a particular quarter, and lived under the most miserable nutritional conditions'.[6] Typically, we have the hint of empathy in Klausa's later representation—an empathy couched, however, in the passive tense, failing entirely to register any subsequent responsibility for the increasingly constrained and degrading circumstances in which Jews were forced to live.[7] There were no longer incidents of terror on the massive scale of September 1939.

At the same time, however, German rule remained a form of rule by terror, a subject that barely surfaces in Klausa's memoirs. The monthly *Landrat* reports, as well as regular police reports from the wider area, prove instructive in filling some of the gaps in the memoirs about everyday levels of violence, and the need for greater police activity and repression in the area, as well as underlining the ways in which the various police forces and civilian authorities cooperated with one another.

It was clearly not always easy for the Germans to impose their authority. This was evident even at the level of relatively trivial everyday life encounters, when local Polish people often behaved in ways indicating a continuing sense of ownership of their own territory, and hopes for an early end to the occupation. In June 1940, for example, a police report from Sosnowiec commented on the ways in which the local Poles were challenging the Germans in ways large and small. These included walking on the pavements in large groups, then barging headlong into the way of uniformed Germans 'in order to force them to give way'. The German, caught unawares, 'would in that instant not know what to do—and unfortunately gives way. Barely has the Polish group passed the German than they laugh out loud for joy that they have once again forced their will on a German.'[8] While conceding that this was a relatively 'harmless case', the report went on to complain that Poles nearby who witnessed such incidents would also laugh at the Germans. Moreover, 'even in administrative offices' the Poles would 'jabber away in Polish [*polinisieren*], swagger around, impose their Polishness onto German officials and show no interest in German customs and the German language'. It was clear that 'a people with such a low level of culture as the Polish are not worthy of gentle treatment, and they interpret this as weakness'.[9] Moreover, Poles were—at least according to the German police reports—allegedly often armed and willing to put up physical resistance, as well as engaging in robberies carried out by armed bands: 'From this it is to be seen that the Polish subhuman species [*Untermenschentum*] still has at its disposal innumerable weapons, and uses these ruthlessly at any given moment.' There was supposedly incontrovertible evidence: 'It suffices merely to mention briefly the many break-ins and the black market dealings of the Jews.'[10] How black market dealings with Jews were supposed to be connected with Polish armed resistance is not made clear.

But, whether at the level of gesture politics on the pavements, attempts to survive through illegal dealing in foodstuffs, or incidents with real political intent, Polish unwillingness to accept their own subjugation under the German invaders posed a problem for the German administration. And here the actions of the civilian administrators and the gendarmerie in the localities were crucial to trying to instil a sense of massively superior German might.

Klausa's first monthly report as *Landrat*, personally signed by him on 31 March 1940, complained of the lack of adequate police protection for the German authorities and the 'Reich Germans' living in the area.[11] The *Landrat*'s report two months later, on 31 May 1940, summarizes the arrests of members of the Polish intelligentsia, which were carried out 'as generally ordered'. It then goes on to describe a particular 'raid' (*Razzia*) carried out as a joint operation between the criminal police, the gendarmerie, and the local constabulary in the village of Golonog on 16 May. In the course of this 'raid' a 'long sought-after gang robber' and another unknown person, apparently not connected with the thief but who simply happened to be in the room at the time, were shot dead. Klausa applauded this incident:

> It would be desirable if such raids by the criminal police could be carried through more often. They would be useful in reassuring decent members of the population and in demonstrating German strength.—The fact that now as before incidents of robbery are a daily occurrence in the Bendzin district needs little special mention. It will only be worth reporting on this if there is any change in this respect.—Since however the bands cannot always be arrested immediately, raids are the most effective method to combat them.[12]

The significance of establishing 'German strength' in order to reassure the 'decent' sections of the population, even if this entailed killing an innocent bystander, is by this stage not open to question.

Klausa was also proud of the way the gendarmerie—which reported directly to him—was being built up: 'The gendarmerie has been further strengthened through auxiliary gendarmes [*Hilfsgendarmen*]. They are proving themselves in the best possible way.'[13] Force and retribution measures, even when entirely innocent people were involved and murdered, were part of the general policy of demonstrating superior German might.

Even despite the level of terror involved on a day-to-day basis, Klausa does not appear at this stage to have been shocked by the violent character of German rule in the area. Later, he made much of his 'disappearances' to the army, portraying absences on military service as a kind of flight to the last bastion of decency in an otherwise unbearable regime: the front was portrayed as still a place of decency, unlike the home front. But contemporary sources suggest that Klausa's first departure to the army in the summer of 1940 was a realization of the hopes he had been harbouring since the previous autumn, motivated by a desire to be part of the military action and able to participate in the expected glory of victory before it was too late.

Klausa had clearly made a good and energetic start at the prize new job of *Landrat*; and he hoped for a long-term future in civilian administration. But in the early summer of 1940 most Germans had little idea that the war, so successful up to this point, would drag on for so long and end in such total defeat. Like many nationalists of his generation, Klausa was and had throughout the 1930s been torn between the respective lures of civilian administration and military service. His ambitions had long alternated between military and civilian 'service to the state' in a way that not only was characteristic of so many of the males of his generation, but was also integral to the conservative nationalist value system in which his wife, Alexandra, had also been socialized. Again, this outlook was typical of a far wider traditional conservative nationalist as well as Nazi milieu.[14]

From Alexandra's letters in the early summer of 1940, it would seem that the rapid successes of the German Army in the campaign against France made Klausa restive; he seems to have worried that he might miss all the military action and associated honours, such as those already being acquired by one of his brothers-in-law. He seems to have been motivated by a desire to get to his comrades at the front before it was too late to share in the fight and the glory. As Alexandra put it in a letter to her mother:

> It is quite incredible, what our troops have achieved!... Now [Udo] has finally managed to get permission to leave for I.R. [Infantry Regiment] 178 on 1 July, and now in his mind's eye he can see the scornful laughter of his regimental comrades when he catches up with them after all the military action has ended...[15]

On 19 June 1940 Klausa was finally granted official permission by the Reich Interior Ministry to leave for military service, and his date of departure was scheduled for 1 July; it took a few more days, until 6 July 1940, before the regional government in Kattowitz was able to name one Gerhard Rahn as his deputy while he was absent on military service.[16]

Klausa did in fact manage a very brief stint at the end of the campaign in France, which seems to have consisted more in sightseeing than in military action, but his group was then sent towards the eastern borders of Poland with Russia, as Alexandra's letter of 11 July revealed.[17] His absence on military duties at this stage does not seem—as Klausa later presented his stints at the front—to have been any kind of principled 'disappearance' in mute protest against being involved in intolerable practices in Będzin. Military duties do not seem to have been overwhelming at this point. Klausa was able to be present at his sister's wedding in Breslau in late July, from where he went on to Berlin to discuss various matters; and he was present again at the funeral of this very same sister's husband, following a tragic motor accident, later that summer.[18] He managed also to spend some time in August looking for a house that would be suitable as the *Landrat*'s family residence in Będzin. Although Klausa's period of military service in 1940 did not officially end until mid-October 1940, he does not seem to have spent an extended unbroken period of time at the front during the course of the summer.[19]

Before he left for the front, Klausa, his young wife Alexandra, and their baby son were able to spend the first three weeks of June together staying with the Henckel von Donnersmarck family in the nearby Schloss Repten, Tarnowitz, a *Landkreis* adjacent to that of Będzin. Here, accommodated in a castle set in spacious wooded surroundings, they were able to relax together, make social visits to neighbouring families, and play with their small child—whose developments that summer were captured on a small film camera that Alexandra's family friend Kraft Henckel von Donnersmarck managed, after much searching in Breslau, Berlin, and Gleiwitz, to 'find and acquire' in Kattowitz as a present for her 23rd birthday.[20] It was during this period, a time of rest and recuperation prior to Klausa's first stint at the front, that one of the many violent incidents investigated by the Ludwigsburg Central Office took place; an incident that, although in itself relatively small, illustrates wider features of the system of civilian rule and the patchy nature of memory.

Celiny, 6 June 1940

Some 10 miles along the road running eastwards from Tarnowitz lies the tiny hamlet of Celiny, just within the borders of the *Landkreis* of Będzin. Here, on 6 June 1940, thirty-two innocent people were lined up against the wall of a local house and shot dead by German soldiers and gendarmes. The Ludwigsburg Central Office investigated this incident quite intensively.

On 8 January 1972 a local Polish resident, Ignacy Widera (born 1901), gave testimony about this episode to the Ludwigsburg investigators. By the early 1970s, when he gave this testimony, Ignacy Widera was a pensioner, and also secretary and chair of the local community association, something of the village scribe and keeper of local records. From October 1939 to 18 January 1945 he had worked 'for the community of Sączów of which the village of Celiny was a part' and acted as a secretary even for the Germans.[21] In this capacity he had been closely involved in the events of that day, although not personally present at the final meeting when the decision to kill thirty-two innocent people was taken.

Ignacy Widera recalled that 'at around ten o'clock on 6 June 1940 various cars began to drive up', including:

> two Gestapo officers from Sosnowiec, two criminal police officials from Sosnowiec, the deputy of the *Landrat* of Będzin, the Kommandant of the Gendarmerie in Sączów—who came from Bavaria—, the Kommandant of the Gendarmerie in Tapkowice by the name of Auer Ernst and the mayor of the community in Sączów Ernst Heinrich.[22]

This gathering talked for about three hours in the community hall of this little hamlet. Then the participants—notably including both members of the various police forces and district and local civilian officials—repaired to the gendarmerie offices in the nearby village of Tapkowice, where 'the final verdict was reached'. At about three o'clock in the afternoon two trucks drove up in Celiny, 'out of which the condemned were unloaded at the side of the house belonging to Stanislaw D.'.[23] The area was then surrounded by military forces and members of the gendarmerie.[24] The prisoners were made to stand in two rows against the wall of Stanislaw D.'s house, as Ignacy Widera reported:

> One row was commanded to lie down on the ground while at the same time the first row was shot dead with machine guns, and then the second row... Where the corpses of the murdered people were taken is not known. Bloodstains led in the direction of Będzin. I myself investigated as far as Siemonia.[25]

The events were still very much alive in the memories of elderly individuals decades later. In the 1970s there was a local campaign to raise the money to erect a small memorial, well off any tourist tracks.

Local residents are still only too keen to talk about the event. Józef G., an old man by the time I talked to him in 2008, still vividly recalled this day when, as a teenager, he was tending cattle in the field across the road from the house, and witnessed this brutal execution.[26] There were, he too recalled, militia all around, and a great commotion as the shooting took place; finally the bodies were thrown back onto the lorry, leaving trails of blood, and he watched it drive off. Once we had stopped in the street and talked to Józef G., neighbours joined in and took us to see the site of the killing. The wall against which the thirty-two people were shot remains pockmarked by the bullet holes, daubed now with dashes of red paint to intimate their bloody origins; there is a memorial stone, for which money had arduously to be raised among the local community; and fresh flowers are often laid there, to keep the memory of former compatriots and relatives alive. We were also invited into a local house to see the files that had been kept of the campaign to raise money for the little memorial, and several residents were only too keen to explain what had happened there.

According to the current version of the story, the shooting of thirty-two innocent people was in reprisal for the shooting of a German gendarme the day before.[27] Two Poles had apparently become involved in a dispute with

Figure 6. Celiny memorial
The memorial in the village of Celiny, erected in the mid-1970s on the wall of the house against which thirty-two innocent people were shot in 'reprisal' for the death of a German gendarme on 6 June 1940. The list of names includes only the Christians whose names were known to the local priest, and not the names of the three Jews, who remain unidentified.
Conrad Fulbrook.

the gendarme, provoked by a disagreement over the legality of ordering a certain dish in a local hostelry: that particular cut of meat was not supposed to be available to Poles under the rationing system introduced by the German administration. The Poles had initially succeeded in escaping from the fracas by bicycle, but were caught up by the gendarme, on a motorbike, in Celiny; here, a further scuffle had ensued, in the course of which the gendarme was fatally wounded. In a slightly different version of the story, the German gendarme had not even been killed by the Poles but had died as a result of crashing when, somewhat inebriated as well as angry, he took a corner too fast in pursuit of the two Poles.[28] Whatever the truth of the matter, the latter knew they were in for trouble and rapidly escaped; they were later nowhere to be tracked down.

The local notables whose names had some months previously been registered by the Germans as potential 'hostages' in the event of any trouble had been rapidly warned by friends and relatives of the potential danger of their situation, and they too managed to disappear to safe hiding places overnight. The next morning, therefore, when the designated 'hostages' could not be found, there were long discussions among the German authorities over how best to proceed. Finally, after several hours of inconclusive debate in Sączów, as described by Ignacy Widera, the group relocated to the nearby gendarmerie offices in the village of Tapkowice. This gendarmerie post was in fact situated in a house that had been requisitioned by the Germans and previously owned by Ignacy Widera's family.[29] There, following what must have been a relatively brief discussion, the order was eventually given to produce further, quite unconnected, 'hostages' from the prison in Sosnowiec. The group of thirty-two men (twenty-nine Catholic Poles and three Jews) who were brought in the back of a lorry from their prison that day had initially been incarcerated for all manner of reasons, including minor infringements of the most trivial of the new rules imposed by the German occupation, political resistance, and sheer bad luck. They were now brought out to the scene of the scuffles of the night before; and every single one of them was made to stand in a row against the wall of the house, where they were shot dead, at point-blank range, in 'reprisal' for an offence with which they had absolutely no connection whatsoever.

Was the *Landrat*, Udo Klausa, involved at all in the cold-blooded murder of thirty-two innocent civilians at Celiny in June 1940, and, if so, in what capacity? On the one hand, he was technically on leave at the time; on the other hand, he was staying barely 10 miles away, easily reachable by telephone for advice (or even in person) if necessary. Circumstantial evidence suggests that at least some higher authority was involved in the final decision to shoot.

According to Ignacy Widera's quite precise testimony in response to the Ludwigsburg war crimes investigations in 1972, it had taken a long time on the morning of 6 June 1940 for the German authorities to reach a decision about what to do in response to the killing of the German gendarme the night before. The highest authority who was present in person at the main deliberations, which took up the whole morning, was the *Landrat*'s deputy—who perhaps had some qualms about reaching such a major decision on his own. According to local belief in the summer of 2008, the final decision was ultimately taken by the civilian administration 'at the highest level'.[30] The word on the street nearly seventy years after the event is, of course, merely a reflection of persisting local legend. It is nevertheless curious that, following a full three hours of apparently indecisive deliberations in the community hall in Sączów, from ten o'clock in the morning until one o'clock in the afternoon, the entire party decamped to the gendarmerie headquarters in the nearby village of Tapkowice, where the final decision appears to have been reached with some considerable speed. And less than two hours later, the truckload of prisoners had been brought from Sosnowiec, some 15 miles away across mainly small country roads, to be shot on the spot.

Why was such a decision so speedily reached in Tapkowice—or was a previous, rather tentative decision merely ratified by a higher authority at this point? The only district authority immediately superior to the *Landrat*'s deputy was, of course, the *Landrat* himself. This is perhaps why it was the *Landrat* who was being investigated by the Ludwigsburg authorities in relation to this incident.

To the legal investigators for the Ludwigsburg authorities, Klausa professed that he was already in France at this time. In one statement he claimed that he was present in the Będzin area only from February to May 1940; in another, that he was present only from February to April 1940.[31] In his memoirs, by contrast, Klausa recalls that he went to the front 'at the end of June'; but, as far as the Ludwigsburg investigations were concerned, he claimed to have already been well out of the area.[32] Yet Klausa was in fact still in the area, seeking to rest and acquire a level of physical fitness pending his hoped-for departure for military service.[33] Although on leave, he was still formally in charge, and indeed, on the date the Celiny incident occurred, did not yet know whether or not his request to join the troops in France would be successful. On 12 June 1940 Klausa unofficially heard that his call-up for military service might be quite soon.[34] His immediate superiors in the regional government in Kattowitz, as well as the Reich Ministry of the Interior in Berlin, record on 19 June 1940 that he had now formally received permission to be freed for military service; and he was actually called up to join his regiment only on 1 July 1940.[35] He had also not as yet been officially replaced in his capacity as *Landrat*. His deputy, Assessor Rahn, was formally put in place only with effect from 6 July, a full month after the Celiny killings.[36] Yet the Ludwigsburg investigators appear to have accepted Klausa's claims that he was away on the 'French military campaign and then East Prussia', which got him off the hook from any further investigation of the matter.[37]

Although formally on leave, then, Klausa was still physically present in Schloss Repten on this day. It would have taken very little time for the *Landrat* to come in person to contribute a more decisive voice to the discussions; or he could readily have been contacted by a telephone call from the gendarmerie post at Tapkowice—which was distinguished by having a telephone line at that time—to ratify a decision about this 'reprisal' killing.[38] Whether either of these surmises is correct, we shall never know; obtaining approval for the proposed course of action by making a quick telephone call to the *Landrat* is certainly a plausible scenario.[39]

There are, of course, other possibilities. Klausa might have ensured that, being on leave, he should not be disturbed even for a brief telephone discussion of a serious incident of this sort. The indecisive group headed by the *Landrat*'s deputy might perhaps have sought confirmation from some other authority, such as the Police President in Sosnowiec; but this was a matter concerning the local gendarmerie who reported to the *Landrat*, and Celiny was geographically outside the area of responsibility of the Sosnowiec police forces. It is also unlikely that authorization would have been sought from the regional government in Kattowitz by going above the head of the *Landrat* without his prior knowledge. It was the *Landrat* who in terms of his official role would bear formal responsibility in principle, whether or not he explicitly authorized the Celiny 'reprisal' murders in practice. Moreover, Klausa was not, as he later claimed for the Ludwigsburg investigations, as yet absent in France on military service; but he was certainly keen to establish that he was 'not there' at the time of the killings, a claim that would have provided a defence against possible legal charges.

Although we cannot establish whether or not Klausa himself was directly involved in the decision to shoot, he must at some point soon afterwards have known about the event. There seems even to have been an official *Landrat*'s report—probably written by Klausa's deputy—provided the very next day. The *Landrat*'s general situation report at the end of June—when Klausa was back in charge before departing for the front—includes the following lapidary summary, which seems to have reduced the number of casualties by two: 'As a retribution measure for the murder [of a gendarme] in the Sontschow area 30 Poles were shot dead by court martial. I refer to my report of 7 June 1940.'[40] Klausa could also have refreshed his memory when looking back over the *Landrat*'s files on his return from military service in the autumn. He does not, however, recall the episode in his memoirs, despite the fact that the mass killing featured quite prominently in the Ludwigsburg investigations; and despite the fact that he not only (falsely) claimed that he was away in France at the time, but also (equally falsely) that the gendarmerie, for which he was responsible, was never involved in any unwarranted acts of violence.

It is, however, possible that such an incident might at the time have seemed more or less routine, barely notable, easily forgotten by those in charge of German administration and not personally exposed to the direct horror of the killing. Given the *Landrat*'s use of words such as 'retribution measure' (*Vergeltungsmaßnahme*) and 'shot dead by court martial' (*standrechtlich erschossen*) it must by this time have seemed, for the German occupation authorities who believed they had a right to rule by force, merely to have been all in a day's normal business. Under the later Nuremberg Principles, however, this cold-blooded murder of innocent civilians as 'hostages' would have fallen under the heading of a war crime, as would any complicity in the act.

In the light of the enormity of the other crimes that were soon to engulf the area, the Celiny incident eventually paled into insignificance in the memories of the Germans involved. Moreover, for most people after the war this incident would scarcely bear mention in comparison with the crimes committed on an infinitely larger scale at Auschwitz. For the little Polish community that was so closely affected, the murder of innocent civilians in their midst was far less easy to forget. But this was only one of many bad memories they had of the German occupation.

The context of terror

The Celiny episode, appalling though it was, was far from an isolated occurrence in this area of German-occupied Poland. Terror as a measure to frighten off the rest of the population was consciously deployed as a tool of the occupation. There were widespread memories of a whole range of incidents of terror under German rule.

Polish residents of Celiny not only recalled this reprisal killing, but also very soon began to tell us of their own troubles with the local gendarmerie. One man recalled a night when he had been caught by gendarmes after curfew, sharing in meat that had been slaughtered illegally by a local farmer. The gendarmes not merely confiscated the meat, but held the young people overnight, making them lie flat on the floor all night, and repeatedly walking or treading on them, including across their hands. As this man, who at that time was a teenager learning his father's trade as a carpenter, recalled:

> And I remember as if it was today—they went into this building, collecting all persons standing in the street. We lay down on the floor and they walked on top of us like this... When they carried these meats out of the house I remember someone stepping on my hand and I thought he had broken my fingers.[41]

The youngsters were all terrified that they would be sent to Auschwitz for having broken both the curfew and the regulations concerning meat. Two girls who had been in the group started to run away, and shots were fired after them; but the girls succeeded in escaping, knowing the hilly terrain better than did the German gendarmes who were in hot pursuit. The rest of this little group were eventually released after a frightening night being physically assaulted; the carpenter's son feared he might never be able to practise his trade again after the damage done to his hands, but fortunately in the end they healed.

They were not the only local Poles to be punished for what they had considered to be minor infringements of the newly imposed German laws; and for some the consequences were far more severe. In the company of an interpreter, I visited the hamlet some seventy years after the mass murder of 1940. Still living inside Stanislaw D.'s house, the outside wall of which had been used for the 'reprisal' shootings, was one of his family, Sylwina D., along with her daughter, Zofia N.[42] At the time of our visit Sylwina D. was elderly, and unwell; her daughter Zofia therefore recounted her story to us. Sylwina D. had been a schoolgirl when the Nazis invaded, and had, along with five friends from her class, refused to report for forced labour for the Germans, defiantly announcing that she would prefer to continue to go to school. For this, all six teenage girls had been sent to Auschwitz; she was one of only two girls to survive the experience. Zofia N., her daughter, told us that her own life had been massively affected by the way her mother had been treated in Auschwitz, with ill-health and lingering psychological consequences for decades thereafter.

These were everyday incidents in which the gendarmes were involved, and not even always ones that entered the official records or needed much by way of approval from above. The Będzin area was not unique; it simply provided variations on a far wider pattern in areas incorporated by the Germans or under German occupation.

A glance at the police daily 'morning reports' (*Morgenmeldungen*) for the period 19 May to 8 July 1940 for the area of nearby Jaworzno (a few miles to the south-east of the *Landkreis* of Będzin), for example, reveals that an almost identical incident took place just one day before the Celiny incident. The shooting of a German gendarme in Jaworzno also resulted in a mass 'retribution' killing, an incident in which members of the local gendarmerie again played a central role. The Police Battalion 83 had searched in the woods some 4 miles east of Jaworzno 'without result' for the 'criminals who had fled'; as a result of their fruitless search for the culprits, some twenty others, entirely uninvolved in this incident, were arrested and executed:

> In the afternoon hours of 5.6.40 twenty violent criminals were arrested by the Pol[ice]-Bat[talion] 83 together with forces of the responsible gendarmerie in Cienskowitz as a retribution measure and handed over to Pol[ice]-Bat[talion] 82 for execution.[43]

It is not made clear why these twenty people, murdered in retribution for the killing of a German gendarme, an act in which they had not been involved, were designated as 'violent criminals', since they do not seem to have been in custody for any other offences before their arrests.

Just a few weeks after the Celiny incident, a similar but far more visible, public ritual of humiliation and brutality took place in the neighbouring district of Olkusz (Ilkenau). On what became known in the little town of Olkusz as 'bloody Wednesday', 31 July 1940, in 'reprisal' for the death of one or two German gendarmes (accounts vary), all the men who could be found were gathered together in public places, and made to lie face-down on the ground for seven or eight hours. During this time, they were insulted, hit with weapons, humiliated, and ridiculed. Jacob Schwarzfitter, interviewed while in a Displaced Persons camp in 1946 by David Boder, an American psychology professor, recalled the incident with continuing horror:

The punitive expedition took place because sixty kilometres [around 38 miles] from the city were murdered by bandits two gendarmes. But they felt it useful to make of it a political incident. And it was ordered to make responsible for it the peaceful [civilian] population. We were led out at daybreak, with our hands up, they jabbed us with bayonets and we were compelled to run. When we arrived at the square, we had to pass a cordon. On both sides stood SS men, with [metal] rods, belts, rubber truncheons, clubs, and they beat us. Every one had to go through. People went through the cordon, and emerged covered with blood.[44]

Poles and Jews alike were subjected to the maltreatment, but Jews appear to have been singled out for particularly brutal treatment. Forced to lie as though making up the paving stones of a path, they were walked over by German soldiers and police wearing heavy boots. 'Out of the Jews who had been brought there a living pathway was created, over which the Germans walked.'[45] Jacob Schwarzfitter commented: 'After lying for eight hours we were ordered to get up. Everyone was pale and black. We all looked like dead men.'[46] There could be appalling outcomes, for both Jews and Poles, as one eyewitness recalled:

One Jew by the name of Glajtman [Gleitmann] was maltreated by a German to the point where he lost consciousness, with the German standing on the face of the Jew, who was lying down, and seeking to keep his balance, and continuing until the face of this Jew was squashed to pieces. After this water was poured over the Jew. Another Jew was forced to beat his colleagues, etc. After this all the Jews were transported off somewhere in a truck.

After the Jews had been taken away, the Germans began, in a gruesome and sadistic manner, to step on, beat, and maltreat the Poles who had been brought there.[47]

There were several deaths as a result. Two people were taken off in lorries, one 'who sought to escape was shot dead, Priest Marian Luczyk was beaten unconscious, and Priest Piotr Maczka died on 10.8.40 as a result of the consequences of what he had suffered on the square at that time'.[48] The few survivors remained horrified by this incident many years later; Benjamin Weizmann (born 1910), for example, as well as many others, remembered the 'bloody Wednesday', when, following the death of a German, all Jewish men between 16 and 30 had to lie flat on the ground all day.[49] Israel Zukermann (born 1913) recalled not only the incident itself, but the further consequences:

On 31 July 1940 there was the so-called Bloody Wedesday in Olkusz. Because a gendarme had been killed, on this day all Jewish men aged 13 and above had to gather in several squares and lie on the ground until midday. Some days after this eighteen Poles were also supposedly arrested.[50]

Further 'reprisal' measures were carried out in this little town some two weeks later, on 16 August, when a further twenty men were executed.[51]

'Bloody Wednesday' in Olkusz was perhaps a particularly extended and brutal series of incidents, seared in local memories for decades in part because it affected all the families of the town: Poles and Jews alike, the elite and the ordinary citizens, the priests and the peasants. But in its details and individual elements, this horrendous composite incident simply illustrated what was, over the years of Nazi occupation, a common pattern: the total disregard for human life and well-being in the interests of terrorizing the population into submission and establishing German domination.

It would seem, then, that a threshold of violence—in terms of the killing of entirely innocent people as a 'retribution measure' for acts with which they were not connected—was being widely crossed at this time. To the Nazi functionaries responsible, even if they were not the ones directly pulling the trigger, such killings apparently were considered not to be murder, but rather a means of demonstrating German strength and imposing effective 'administration'. In this respect, then, perhaps an incident on the scale of Celiny could be forgotten relatively easily: memory tends to work best in relation to incidents that are unusual and stand out, or have high personal relevance and associated emotional charge, not those that are routine, everyday events—as anyone recalling the menu for a special dinner, as opposed to what they ate on a random Tuesday a few weeks previously, will readily be able to test for themselves.[52] For this reason, perhaps, a member of the German administration who was not himself personally involved in (let alone on the receiving end of) the event might later not have remembered specific incidents in a context where terror had become so prevalent.

But terror was not merely a matter of incidents such as these, however horrific they were for those involved. There was a far wider form of violence involved in the imposition of German colonial rule. This included the 'confiscation' not only of Jewish possessions—gold and silver, radios and cameras, jewellery and furs—but also of their homes and properties, workshops and factories, all the means by which Jews had made a living. German 'trustees' took over Jewish shops and businesses, leaving them with few independent means of survival and exploiting their labour.

Samuel Kucharski, who was deported to a slave labour camp at the age of 16, and whose family were murdered in Auschwitz, managed to survive the war although severely and permanently disabled as a result of his experiences. Kucharski's parents had owned a small shoe factory and shoe shop, which were taken over by a German businessman by the name of Rudolf Braune. When interviewed in 1960 in a Bavarian sanatorium for people with chronic lung diseases, Kucharski recounted:

In Bendsburg there were many Jewish businesses whose owners all shared the same fate that my parents and I had to suffer. The chairman of these trustees was Rudolf Braune, who is now apparently living in Hamburg... This Braune took away most of our family property and that of other Jewish citizens, who at that time still possessed Polish citizenship. I personally consider this manner of behaving to be theft.[53]

Carrying out or benefitting from such theft did not, however, entail any legal consequences or criminal proceedings in post-war West Germany.

The very character of everyday life under German rule was predicated on acts of violence at one remove from the immediate sight of the Germans who benefited. And the latter did not always even consciously register quite the character of the system in which they were integrally involved. To call them mere 'bystanders' is to ignore the way in which they were actually beneficiaries of the systematic oppression of others.

The 'Villa of the Jew Schein'

No doubt at the start the Klausas held out very high hopes for their new life, and in particular setting up their family on a long-term basis here, with Alexandra playing the 'first lady' role of *Landrat*'s wife, as her mother-in-law had done for so many years for Udo's father in Leobschütz.[54] But the Second World War meant that now the conditions, demands, and tasks of the post were very different. And for the *Landrat*, even domestic arrangements entailed a form of border crossing.

In late August 1940, Udo took Alexandra to visit Będzin. As she put it in a letter to her mother, Udo 'had a lot to discuss there, and I wanted to take a look at the house'. Alexandra's first impressions in August 1940 were not favourable:

The town is incredibly hideous, wretched, dilapidated, dirty, I've never seen anything like it. The streets are teeming with grimy, ragged, disgusting Jews. There is hardly anyone not wearing white armbands, but even they are filthy. Some of the Jews talk German, everything [*sic*] else Polish.[55]

Nor did Alexandra think much of what she saw as the ugly housing stock available. After some consideration of apparently unpalatable alternatives, a decision was reached: it was the 'Villa of the Jew Schein that we have now finally nominated as the *Landrat*'s residence'.[56] In one of her regular letters to Frau von H., an older woman who was a family friend and close neighbour in Berlin, Alexandra described the house in detail:

The only habitable house in Bendzin is the villa of the Jew Schein, a big industrialist who fled in time. Externally the house is ghastly, but internally very civilized [*manierlich*]: six large rooms, a hallway, rooms for the maids, kitchen, bathroom, etc, All very comfortable. So we can be contented about the house, it can be made very pretty and agreeable, and that is after all the main thing. In such a dreadful nest [as Bendzin], life is after all necessarily concentrated primarily on one's own home.[57]

Alexandra appears to have given no thought whatsoever to the question of where 'the Jew Schein' who had 'fled in time' might now be living, why he might have had to flee in the first place, or the ethics of simply taking over someone else's house in this way. In the years that followed, she did in fact concentrate her life primarily around the house and her growing family.

The villa was clearly quite sizeable, since not only the Klausa family and their own domestic staff but also Udo Klausa's trusted work colleague and house manager, Ignatz Margosch, could be comfortably accommodated. In his memoirs, Klausa states:

I myself moved into an empty villa (Schajn) as my work-related home in Post Street, across the road from the post office and perhaps a kilometre from my office. It was a hideous modern building, but with its garage and sanitary facilities was quite habitable. Margosch took up his domicile on the bottom floor, I took over the two top floors.

...Now we had also had enough of the frequent and long separations in our marriage, and we furnished the house as best we could.[58]

He too gives barely a second thought to the previous inhabitants, not even reflecting on the reasons why the villa was 'empty'.

Given that Germans took over only the better villas, and that the only well-to-do Jewish family by the name of Schein (in whatever spelling) in Będzin was that of the well-known philanthropists and benefactors of the orphanage, it would seem certain that this villa had been the home of the family of Cyrele (also known as Cyrla or Cesia) Szajn (or Schein).[59] Cyrele Schein (née Przepiórka, born 1882) 'came from one of the finest Chassidic families in Warsaw', and married Icchok Szajn (Izak Schein, born 1882), an industrialist and one of the pillars of the Będzin Jewish community. She became a substantial philanthropist and social activist: she was central to the fund-raising and foundation of the Jewish orphanage, which was located not far from this villa. She was widely respected for her activities in the inter-war period, prior to the Nazi invasion, not only as a major benefactress of the orphanage but also for her work as a Town Councillor.[60] The villa belonging to the Schein family was located in a side street just off the main road that ran alongside the railways tracks, perhaps 100 yards or so from the road running under the railway to the other side, just before the main railway station. Close to the railway station on the other side of the tracks was the very substantial building endowed by Cyrele Schein, the Jewish Orphanage—now dilapidated, and bearing no sign either as to its former function or in memory of the scenes that were to be played out in it during the years of Nazi occupation. Despite Alexandra's comment that they had 'fled in time', the Scheins did not make it through the 'final solution': Cyrele Schein was last heard of and very probably murdered in the Kołomyja ghetto in 1942; her husband Izak was murdered in Auschwitz in 1944.[61]

In the autumn and winter of 1940–1, Alexandra did her best to settle into the 'villa of the Jew Schein', organizing the acquisition of appropriate furniture, including a removal van (somewhat unusual in wartime) with desired objects sent from Berlin and from the family estates. At the age of 23, and with her first baby, Alexandra clearly wanted to set up her marital home in the style to which she had been accustomed throughout her life to date. Seemingly unaware of the inherent paradox of the situation, Alexandra was particularly stressed at having to keep an eye out all day in case anything among the newly delivered possessions went missing:

> At the moment I'm sitting in chaos in the house. The Berlin furniture van was unloaded today, and everything is standing or lying around... [The painters] will supposedly be finished on Thursday, and then I can at least unpack the Berlin things. Until then, my sole occupation is to walk around and stand around in the house the whole time, in order to prevent any of our things 'sticking to the fingers' of the Jews. That is a very annoying business, since they steal like ravens.[62]

In a letter written a few months later, with apparently no self-consciousness or sense of irony, Alexandra rejoiced at some length about the knock-down prices at which she was able to acquire furniture that had been confiscated from Jews:

The trustee who sets the prices for the Jewish furniture was just here. It all went very quickly, and I think I will take everything without thinking it over for long.

Alexandra listed prices for each of the items: a living room carpet was the most expensive, at 350 Marks, followed by a clearly sizeable dining table at 75 Marks, accompanied by twelve dining chairs at a further 75 Marks, and a coffee table at 5 Marks, as well as apparently rather more ordinary furniture for a maid's room (a bed, a mattress, a wardrobe, four chairs, and a bedside table), which together came to a grand total of just 30 Marks. She concludes:

For a total of 535 Marks one can probably buy the whole caboodle; I've saved this much, actually rather more than this, since January. With the surplus I can buy a bed etc. for the little brother, as long as I can find one. Beuthen and Kattowitz are really terrible Nigger villages [*Negerdörfe*], one can't get anything there.[63]

Udo Klausa too recalls that they were able to buy 'very nice pieces of furniture' in Prague—but without any intimation of who might have been the previous owners.[64]

Alexandra's subsequent letters are full of details of domestic matters, as befitted a young mother with a new baby, accompanied by complaints about the quality of her domestic servants, discovering, for example, 'yet again a lack of cleanliness with respect to the baby's cooking equipment'.[65] There are occasional intimations of the quality of social life, and the lack of breeding of the local army officers, for one of whom she had provided lodgings, who then even turned up in *slippers* (underlined in her letter) to let her know that he was leaving. As social company, the local military was less than helpful:

And the fact that the Commander has not rendered a visit to me is certainly agreeable, but not a sign of the best breeding. I would otherwise have invited him now and then to a good meal; I also have tolerably good wines, and could have invited along *Landräte* from the vicinity too.[66]

It was clearly not entirely easy for Alexandra to emulate the style either of her aristocratic mother in Berlin, or of her mother-in-law, who had played the role of wife of the *Landrat* so well for Udo Klausa's father in Leobschütz and Groß-Strehlitz. Alexandra's letters convey her characteristic sense of humour—but they betray also the prejudices and blindness characteristic of the upper stratum in a colonial situation. While 'stealing' was what the natives did, the 'confiscation' by the new ruling class of the homes and furniture of the inhabitants of the occupied territory was on this world view an entirely different matter, one to which it was not worth giving a second thought. For all her efforts to set up house and home, however, Alexandra never did come to feel at home in Będzin.

It might have been expected that Udo Klausa, given his local links and family background, including the nearby Klausa family mausoleum, would have felt somewhat more at home in both the role and the region, even if it was just beyond the old Prussian borders; and that he would have had more than the usual sense of proprietorship in the still patriarchal value system of Prussian civilian administrators.[67] But the tasks with which he was faced in this new historical context were arguably very different from anything for which even his upbringing and ideological socialization had prepared him.

At this early stage there is, however, no evidence to suggest that Klausa was shocked or concerned about the intrinsic violence of the German occupation regime, which he continued to support in his public role.[68] And if he were privately already stressed about the visible widespread violence of the situation, there is no record of this in his post-war writings: he records no memories of these violent incidents in his later memoirs or self-defence statements referring to his own time in Będzin, referring only to the 'excesses' that had occurred before he arrived, or those taking place when he was absent or after he had left. And, while Alexandra was trying to establish a lifestyle along the lines to which she had previously been accustomed, life was very different for those who were deemed 'racially' inferior. Alexandra—like so many other 'Aryan' Germans—was able to benefit more or less unthinkingly from the misfortunes of others, even while she registered a degree of discomfort in her new surroundings. The conditions under which the Jews of Będzin were being forced to live, by contrast, were continually and massively deteriorating, and this as a direct result of the policies imposed as a matter of 'mere administration' by the functionaries of the Nazi regime.

6

'Only Administration'

Why did Będzin appear so disagreeable to Alexandra on her arrival in the summer of 1940? Why were the streets 'teeming with grimy, ragged, disgusting Jews', who were easily to be distinguished because they were 'wearing white armbands'? How had the town so rapidly declined from being the flourishing centre of trade, industry, learning, and culture described by Jewish survivors to the state in which Alexandra found it—a place in which she was never able to feel at home, accustomed as she was to living in the German capital of Berlin, and moving among cultured and well-to-do Germans?

The transformation was a direct result of Nazi policies of 'Germanization'. This word no longer meant bringing German laws, language, and culture to those peoples whom the Germans had conquered, as it had done in previous periods of German expansion; rather, it now meant moving and exploiting 'inferior' groups, defined in 'racial' terms, to make way for Germans and to service their needs.

Alexandra's reaction was not atypical for people of her generation coming for the first time to the eastern provinces and being exposed for the first time to the realities of Jewish life under Nazi rule. There was a widespread reaction of revulsion when German soldiers first witnessed the state of Jews in the towns and villages, the segregated living areas and the provisional, makeshift or more carefully constructed ghettos established by the Nazis, as they made their way in conquest across Eastern Europe. Very few Germans made the connection between Nazi policies and the all too visible evidence of Jewish and Polish degradation. Many simply saw this as confirmation of the racial stereotypes they had been served in Nazi ideology. And, given the horrendous conditions elsewhere—as in the enclosed ghettos with rations reduced to starvation levels—and the enormity of what was to follow, the state of Jews in the more 'open' ghettos that preceded the final enclosures and deportations to extermination generally eluded adequate attention in its own terms. Even many survivors demote the early years of Nazi occupation to a relatively hazy phase, prior to the more sharply etched memories of the horrors that came following deportation to the slave labour and death camps. This too is perfectly understandable.

It only dawned on me slowly that there was an insidious form of violence exercised through the imposition of the Nazi policies of 'Germanization': policies that prioritized the needs and aspirations of the Germans, subordinating all others to the overall goals of the Nazis, in different ways according to 'racial' category. This might be called systemic violence—a form of violence inherent to the system of Nazi occupation rule.

Klausa held direct responsibility for the implementation of these policies. As he put it in his memoirs: 'My service in the district of Bendsburg [*sic*] was limited in practice to current administration. After all, one couldn't develop any larger initiatives.'[1] It is, therefore, in 'current administration' that the impact of Klausa's contribution as *Landrat* must be sought. And it is here that we have to try to understand the historical significance of a distinctive mentality, with particular priorities and areas of apparent blindness, as well as the sometimes startling gaps in memory and later representation.

The controversial question of whether such goals and associated policies can, from a later perspective, be seen as the 'forerunners of genocide' should not distract us from registering their horrendous effects on people at the time.[2] As one survivor put it, the 'conditions already at that time made life into hell'; and, in the words of another survivor, 'for us Jews every day at that time was ghastly [*grausam*]'.[3] Nor should the apparent tedium of the word 'administration', or the post-war connotations of administration as something entirely a-political, lead us to accept with little further investigation the conventional defence strategies of those who had formerly served the Nazi state. Ordinary antisemitism appears to have allowed Klausa at this time to ignore the consequences on the victims of the policies he was charged with implementing.

Although things changed rapidly and radically during the first two years of Nazi occupation and administration of the area, this period was clearly distinguishable in a number of ways from the 'exterminatory racism' of 1942 and beyond. The facts of what came later should not, retrospectively, cloud our perception of the earlier years. Death was a frequent by-product, rather than a primary goal, of Nazi policies towards the Jews in this area in 1939–41.

But at the same time, these policies were far from innocent. Nazi policies of 'Germanization' entailed the ousting of Jews from their homes, the expropriation of their property and means of livelihood, the rounding-up and deportation of able-bodied adults to forced labour, the break-up of families, restrictions on freedom of movement, reduction of rations, maltreatment of those transgressing newly imposed regulations, and the spreading of a general atmosphere of terror in the face of unpredictable brutality. All this caused immense suffering among the victims of Nazi racism. Colonial racism was accompanied by policies of utmost inhumanity.

Moreover, Nazi policies during these years were not innocent in their longer-term consequences, however little individual functionaries, Klausa included, might have intended the later outcomes. Racial policies meant that living conditions for Jews rapidly deteriorated, creating mounting 'problems' with respect to public health and leading some Nazis to see mass murder as the only possible 'final solution' to their self-created 'Jewish problem'. The progressive degradation in the conditions of life for Jews, with progressive restrictions on freedom and ultimately effective incarceration, also helped to lower their capacity for resistance, and played a significant role in making the Nazi task in the final round-ups and deportations that much easier.

'Only administration' on the part of civilian administrators—who might not have been motivated by any form of 'exterminatory antisemitism', nor intended to play a role on the path to the gas chambers—cannot be considered from outside this historical context.

Absent spaces

Looking for traces of the ghetto in Będzin some seventy years later is not easy. There is a memorial to the ghetto—but it is a memorial only to the very last phases of ghettoization: a memorial to the enclosed and linked ghettos of Kamionka and Środula, which were inaugurated in the autumn of 1942 and to which the Jews of Będzin were sent prior to their final deportation in the summer of 1943. It is placed in the open space where Jews were collected before their final deportations, to make Będzin 'Jew free' (*judenrein*). There is, even in this area across the railway tracks and some distance from the centre of Będzin, no demarcation or guide to precisely which streets and houses constituted the former ghetto.

But there is no memorial at all to the streets in the centre of Będzin where, for most of the three years prior to the final 'cleansing' of Będzin (to use the Nazi terminology), growing numbers of Jews were cramped into a restricted area, thrown into ever more crowded housing in the narrow streets of an impoverished district near the former marketplace. There is not even any sign that a remaining open space in this district was once the Rynek or market square—but which is now half obliterated by a dual carriageway road slicing through past the castle, running eastwards towards Dąbrowa. It is hard to imagine that somewhere over 20,000 people managed to live within a few streets in this area, making way for the Germans to take over the better houses and the better parts of town for their own use.

Nor are there any memorials to the former ghettos that were created in other places in the *Landkreis* of Będzin, with the concentration of Jews into just a few streets in the neighbouring towns of Czeladź, Strzemieszyce, and Dąbrowa. As one drives westwards from Będzin up the hill towards Czeladź, the road passes the former Jewish cemetery—which still remains relatively well preserved, including a very well-tended memorial to one particular family as well as the wider community, erected by a survivor. But, arriving in Czeladź itself, I had to use an old sketch map dug up in the Katowice archive, plotted against the road layout on a modern map, to identify the particular streets—just a couple of blocks—that had become the ghetto into which all the Jewish residents of Czeladź had been forced. There is no memorial here to their former presence or the significance of what now look like the perfectly ordinary, rather run-down streets of a Polish satellite town of the Katowice industrial conurbation. Similarly, around the streets of Strzemieszyce, now just a small suburb of Dąbrowa, there is nowhere any visible sign marking the streets where hundreds of Jews were concentrated, in order both to remove them from the sight of the conquering Germans and to free up their former homes in better areas for the new ruling class.

There is no memorial in these streets to their former Jewish occupants.[4] Nor are the actions that forced Jews into ever worse conditions present in the private memoirs or the legal testimonies of the former German occupiers. The parallel universes of Germans and Jews, and the ease of failure of memory on the part of the former about the fate of the latter, were in part created and sustained by the imposition of physical separation.

What of Klausa's views on implementing policies of 'Germanization'? Given the speed with which things developed in the years from 1939 to 1942, it is perhaps plausible to take the view that a young up-and-coming civil servant—even one who had gained some experience in the horrendous early days in the Warthegau—might have thought that, after a while, policies would settle down and a new *modus vivendi* be achieved (although one that would clearly be more acceptable to the German beneficiaries than to those on the receiving end of such policies). Moreover, the *Landrat* was not directly responsible for making policy. Orders came down from people higher up the Nazi hierarchy, including Klausa's immediate superiors in regional government, and ultimately, of course, the Reich Ministry of the Interior in Berlin, the SS and Police Chief Heinrich Himmler, and the Führer, Adolf Hitler. The directives on racial policy that came down from these quarters were, as we shall see, faithfully carried out by Klausa, and had continuing consequences for the local population even after he had left the area. It is possible that Klausa continually suffered from 'nerves' as a result of sensing the inhumanity of these policies. Yet a curious feature of Klausa's memoirs is his failure to register the significance of his responsibility with respect to the Jewish population of his area—or indeed, more generally and throughout the Third Reich, to register much explicit awareness of the impact of Nazi policies on Jews.

The challenges of 'Germanization'

In the Reichsgau Wartheland, a previously Prussian region with a higher percentage of resident Germans, the solutions spearheaded by the *Gauleiter* were relatively simple: at first, dumping members of 'unwanted' categories (including large numbers of Poles) over the border into the General Government; and, from the spring of 1940, starting to concentrate the remaining Jews into ghettos, the largest of which was Łódź (in German, Litzmannstadt).[5] These 'solutions' were, for a variety of reasons, less feasible in the areas of Eastern Upper Silesia, including Będzin, that had never previously been under German control.

The ethnic mix in the Upper Silesian borderlands was complex. This area was very different from the 'old Reich' (*Altreich*), where relatively small numbers of assimilated German Jews lived among their fellow German citizens. A so-called police border separated the predominantly German areas around and to the west of Kattowitz from the newly conquered, formerly Russian Congress Polish territories to its east. This served to protect the relative 'civilization' of the readily 'Germanized' Kattowitz from the neighbouring Polish territory. Beyond this strip lay a further border: the new border between the expanded Greater German Reich and the General Government under Hans Frank.

The area in which Będzin was located, between the police border to the west and the new Reich frontier to the east, was known as the 'Eastern Strip' (*Oststreifen*). It was initially designed as a transitional dumping ground for those deemed to be ethnically unwanted, who could be expelled from 'Germanized' areas to the west, pending—as was initially thought—further deportation eastwards into the General Government. Thus a population that already had a high percentage of Jewish inhabitants found the numbers swollen further by those exiled to this area against their will, from their homelands further west.

A state in which policies are organized on 'racial' lines has to know precisely who belongs to which category. One of the first and primary tasks of civilian administration in Eastern Upper Silesia had been to clarify the 'racial' distinctions between Jews, Poles, and those who by virtue of their claimed descent and outlook were compatible with and potentially able to become part of the 'Germanized' society run by the new settlers.[6] An official survey of inhabitants in the province of Kattowitz carried out in the week of 17–23 December 1939 asked residents to put themselves in 'racial' categories. Despite the fact that these categories were strongly disputed, people had to cooperate in order to obtain an identity card, an essential document for survival in this period. West of the police border, the danger of being deported in the interests of 'Germanization' meant that many Polish people claimed some measure of German descent in order to be categorized as 'ethnic Germans' (*Volksdeutsche*), also then being entitled to privileges such as higher food rations and better employment prospects. Many realized only too late that, for males, it might also mean being called up into the German armed forces. In the 'Eastern Strip', there was at this early stage no apparent danger for Poles of deportation or other evident disadvantages—although these were soon to materialize—and so the survey produced somewhat more accurate figures; only a tiny minority claimed ethnic German descent.

Some figures are in order here. At the time of Klausa's arrival in Będzin in the spring of 1940, just under half the inhabitants of the town itself were Jewish. The numbers soon began to rise as a result of German policies. While the 'Eastern Strip' became a dumping ground for Jews from areas further west, Hans Frank, the Governor-General of the rump Polish state to the east, refused any further movement of Jews into the General Government that he controlled. Numbers also began to swell as a result of Jewish decisions about relative survival chances. Jews who had fled eastwards after the German invasion frequently returned to their homes, having found conditions no better elsewhere; and Jews from the General Government often moved westwards, assuming that conditions could not be worse than they were under Hans Frank's rule. Subsequent movements—deportation to forced labour camps, movements 'concentrating' Jews who had originally lived elsewhere, rising mortality rates, and fluctuating birth rates—meant that this was a highly unstable population; but the percentages initially remained high. On 15 September 1940 Moses Merin, in his capacity as head of the Central Office of the Jewish Councils of Elders in Eastern Upper Silesia, provided figures for different communities. Będzin's population was still around 50 per cent Jewish, with some 25,000 Jews. Sosnowiec, with marginally fewer Jews—around 23,500—was nevertheless a considerably larger town: Jews made up only around one in five of its total population of 115,000. Elsewhere in the region for whose Jews Merin was responsible, the next largest concentration was at that time to be found in the town of Oświęcim (Auschwitz), with some 5,600 Jews making up nearly 47 per cent of its overall population of 12,000; within a few months, in the spring of 1941, the Jews of Oświęcim would be resettled in the nearby towns of Będzin and Sosnowiec, as the Auschwitz concentration camp and associated slave labour facilities were expanded. The other significant areas of Jewish population were to be found in the towns of Chrzanów, with 8,000 Jews or nearly 45 per cent of a population of 18,000; and somewhat more than 5,000 Jews in each of Zawierce and Dąbrowa, which had total populations of 33,000 and 37,000 respectively.[7] There were also smaller communities and families living scattered across the villages and hamlets of the rural areas.

But, whichever way the figures are calculated, and at whichever date a census is taken, Będzin had the biggest 'problem' in terms of Nazi racial policies: it had both the highest absolute number of Jews and the highest overall percentage of Jews in any population anywhere in the Kattowitz region. In the light of these figures, and particularly the Będzin total population of somewhat over 50,000, roughly half of whom were Jewish, an extraordinary comment is later made by Klausa. He recalls, when introducing the area in his memoirs, that in 1943, the year his family left for good, the town of Będzin had around 27,000 residents.[8] He makes no connection between this and the figure he cites on the following page, of the fact that in his area of responsibility had lived 'perhaps 40,000 Jews, who at the time of my arrival were already recognizable by virtue of the fact that they had to wear white armbands with the star of Zion'.[9]

Clearly in Klausa's own account virtually half the town's residents had been deported or murdered; it was by now, to use the horrendous Nazi expression, effectively 'Jew free'. Yet he does not explicitly register or reflect on this massive loss of population, or his own role in population movements and control, in the state-ordained attempt to 'Germanize' the areas incorporated into the Greater German Reich.

The nature of the project of 'Germanization' varied massively. West of the border, 'Germanization' was effected by enforced expulsions of Jews and targeted Poles, and containment of remaining unwanted elements. By 1 October 1940 the City Mayor (*Oberbürgermeister*) of Kattowitz was able to report that there were now only German kindergartens and schools in the city, and that all church services were now held only in German. 'Non-German' property (*nichtdeutsche Grundbesitz*) was being expropriated, and Polish and other organizations had been repressed.[10] Kattowitz was well on track to becoming a truly 'German' city. East of the border, the situation was, as indicated, far more complex. Yet there was a determination to develop radical 'solutions' to this self-imposed problem.

Plans for the 'Germanization' of the area were given a major boost when Himmler himself made a personal visit in October 1940. The *Kattowitzer Zeitung* carried a description of Himmler's tour of the area, accompanied by Governor and Gauleiter Fritz Bracht, as headline news, 'Reichsführer SS Himmler in Eastern Upper Silesia'.[11] The new plans included a horrifying calculation: the town of Będzin was ultimately to have its population reduced from 55,000 to around 15,000.[12] No details were given at this time as to precisely how this dramatic reduction was to be achieved; but it was quite clear that the 30,000 or so Jewish inhabitants of Będzin were to have no place in the future 'Germanized' conception of their home town. Dr Fritz Arlt, in charge of the resettlement programme as the Kattowitz representative of Heinrich Himmler, also personally visited the *Landrat* of Będzin, Udo Klausa, to ensure the smooth settling in of 'Volksdeutsche'—people considered to be 'racially' German—into new homes and new lives in the Będzin *Landkreis*.[13] Moreover, designated by Himmler as responsible for the 'population list' (*Volksliste*), which involved categorizing people by 'race' or ethnic group, the *Landräte* of the area had to attend periodic training courses in 'racial' matters at a *Gauschule* or *Gau* training school.

None of these developments were in any sense secret. The 'struggle between peoples' and the ultimate aim of rendering the area essentially 'German' was a major theme in the area, a central point of propaganda, and widely trumpeted across the local newspapers. Under the headline 'Who can be considered German in the East?', readers of the *Kattowitzer Zeitung*, for example, were informed on 4 October 1940 that 'SS Oberführer Rudolf Wiesner, MP, spoke about "The tasks of the resident Germans in the settlement of the German Eastern territories"'.[14] Announcing that there had to be considerable movement of people in the area, and that in particular the Polish had to be moved out, in classic Nazi declamatory tone the speaker 'gave a terse overview of the fight of the Pole against the German, which for the latter only meant suffering, repression and terror'.[15] It was made absolutely clear: 'One thing is clear to all those who have lived and had to fight in Poland: Those who once brought misfortune to our homeland must leave the land.'[16] A little over a week later, the paper had a major half page spread under the headline 'Sosnowitz—a town with a future!' Fearful that readers in Kattowitz might be relatively unaware of this neighbouring township (virtually a suburb in the Kattowitz conurbation, connected by an easy tram-ride), the newspaper posed on their behalf the following questions: 'Sosnowitz—where is it? Is it a place in which there are *only* Jews, or are other people also to be found there?' There then followed the story of how German officials were going there to build it up, including Pg. (*Parteigenosse*, Nazi Party Member) Franz-Josef Schönwälder, the City Mayor who was Klausa's civilian counterpart in this neighbouring town, the borders of which directly adjoined the borders of the town and *Landkreis* of Będzin.[17] On 17 October 1940, the *Kattowitzer Zeitung* described the taking-over of Jewish concerns into German hands—that is, the robbery of Jewish possessions and livelihoods—as being 'freed from the Jewish spirit'.[18] And, in order to get the antisemitic message across, on 20 October the deeply prejudiced and stereotypical portrayal of an avaricious eighteenth-century 'court Jew' in the film *Jud Süß* was given a whole page review under the banner 'A film by the great actors'.[19] The antisemitic agenda continued on 4 December with a pernicious piece entitled 'The face of the eternal Jew'.[20] Altogether the newspaper was at this time lively, full of optimism and advertisements, and clearly committed to the project of 'building up' a 'racially pure' community in what seems to have been experienced by the invading Germans as some sort of 'wild east'.

'Germanization' of the area for which he was responsible was a task with which, on Klausa's own admission, he was relatively happy to cooperate—at least in part. This part related to treatment of the incoming Germans, those who were coming 'home to the Reich' (*Heim ins Reich*). As Klausa puts it in his memoirs, although he was unhappy about the forcible expulsions of Poles deemed necessary to make way for the resettlement of Germans, 'I pursued with more commitment the task of caring for the German population that was streaming into the area'.[21] Here, he seeks to gain the moral high ground by emphasizing that he insisted on the incoming Germans having the right to attend churches. His efforts to ensure the possibility of religious observance were also emphasized in positive testimonials on his behalf after the war.[22]

There can be little doubt from contemporary sources that Klausa was indeed concerned to make the 'resettlement' of Germans into the *Landkreis* as smooth as possible for the newcomers. He gave instructions, for example, that the administration should 'ensure all possible ways of easing' the situation for the incoming Germans, including the 'preparation of new areas for living in', and giving them preferential treatment in 'acquiring furniture from the Polish property which has been seized'.[23] There is no hint of recognition in this contemporary document that the 'seized' goods and furniture should not have been taken from their rightful original owners and handed on to incoming Germans in this way. It is a simple expression of the mentality of conquest, seeing forcible robbery as in some sense legitimate acquisition.

In his memoirs, Klausa also suggests that the reverse side of the 'resettlement' coin—that of moving people out, in order to make way for those being moved in—was something with which he would have nothing to do, having, he claimed, had 'quite enough of this' during his stint in Posen.[24] He emphatically distances himself from the actual practices of removing Polish people from their homes and sending them into the General Government, in order to make way for incoming German 'resettlers', and typically shifts full responsibility onto the SS. With some self-contradiction, Klausa claims that he both witnessed terrible scenes that were carried out by the SS, and yet was never actually present: 'There was no need or opportunity for any participation. It was all done by the SS, and at best one could stand by with tied hands and see what heart-rending scenes were being played out. I was never there.'[25] Only a few pages later in his memoirs, however, Klausa concedes that the gendarmerie, for whom he held responsibility, did in fact assist in the 'resettlements'.

Klausa may not have been physically present at the forced expulsions of Poles with their 'heart-rending scenes'. Yet he officially held responsibility for rehousing and forced population movements, with the civilian administration working closely hand in hand with the police authorities to ensure that Nazi resettlement polices were imposed as 'smoothly' as possible.[26] The records of the time indicate that the *Landrat* was responsible for and deeply involved in the expulsion of people from their own homes and their forcible 'resettlement'. But, leaving aside his later appeals to sympathy on behalf of those affected in these 'heart-rending scenes', Klausa's memoirs betray not the slightest hint of any sense of guilt, nor even recognition of his own role in causing this suffering. Indeed, he seeks actively to disassociate himself from having borne any responsibility at all in relation to the victims of the policy, as opposed to the German beneficiaries, for whose ease of settling in he takes some credit.

Several of Klausa's former acquaintances testified after the war to the difficulties he had supposedly experienced as a result of his Catholic family background, and his undoubted personal concern to ensure the possibility of religious practice for incoming Germans—for whom the alleged difficulties of church worship in Upper Silesia may have been retrospectively rather overstated.[27] Without wishing to enter into any theological discussion here, it does nevertheless seem notable that Klausa's sense of 'Christian' commitment seems to have been severely restricted to those he saw as members of his own 'racial' community. He does not seem to have followed the injunction in practice that 'thou shalt love thy neighbour as thyself'. Rather, he behaved in conformity with the very widespread Nazi separation between the 'racially' defined in-group and others, seen as inferior, subordinate, and not to be treated with similar respect and concern. On the evidence, Klausa seems to have been capable at the time of not fully registering the consequences of German racial rule on those who were subordinated, and at a later date did not seem to remember these less than morally elevated aspects of his role.

Ghettoization as removal and segregation

It is not only the impact of resettlement policies on the Poles that Klausa managed to overlook or forget in his memoirs. There is also barely a hint of what actually went on with respect to the tens of thousands of Jews he recalls living in the *Landkreis* of Będzin. In a brief comment, Klausa seeks to imply that, if there had been any relocation, this had already taken place before his time. Referring to the northern areas of his district, Klausa comments: 'There were no Jews in this part of the district, they were all concentrated in the three towns, if there ever had been any Jews in other areas. During my time no resettlement in this respect took place.'[28] This, like much else in Klausa's representation of the experiences of Jews in his *Landkreis*, would appear to be a revealing, and indeed in this case a massive, failure of memory. It is also yet another failure to register the effects of German policies on those who were their objects and victims.

The images of the large enclosed ghettos of Warsaw and Łódź have impressed themselves on post-war conceptions of what a 'ghetto' looked like under Nazi rule. Yet ghettos came in many different forms and sizes; they were constructed for different purposes in different contexts, changing over time; and they lasted for varying periods, with some persisting for a period of years while others were only transitory. The term 'ghetto' itself was also used in different ways, with changing meanings over time.[29]

In Będzin and the surrounding areas, three major phases of ghettoization may be distinguished, with different underlying purposes. In each of these stages—which were overlapping, and unfolded with variations in different locations in the region—German control over space, people, and movement was central, and this was, of course, intrinsically political. The first stage, from the autumn of 1939 and continuing throughout the occupation period, involved ousting Jews in order to make way for incoming Germans, stigmatizing and segregating Jews, and making 'Jew-free' areas for the Germans to enjoy in whichever way they wanted. The second stage, effected progressively over the course of 1940–2, involved further concentrating and confining Jews to particular quarters, and increasingly controlling and limiting their movements, as well as restricting interactions between Jews and non-Jews. The final and mostly clearly demarcated stage in this area, in 1942–3, was that of ghettoization as effective incarceration, explicitly designed as preparation for final deportation to extermination.[30] The stages were not predetermined, nor part of a preconceived or well-designed plan; they arose from a combination of local initiatives and negotiation of practical difficulties, with different interests competing in the planning, design, and execution of changing policies. But retrospectively a certain logic can be discerned in this progression; each stage brought with it new 'problems'; the resolution of these 'problems' in turn exacerbated conditions and demanded more radical 'solutions'.

At each stage, the local administration, under the overall responsibility of the *Landrat*, was directly in charge of the processes of ghettoization, stigmatization, restriction on freedoms, and degradation of the living conditions of the Jews. It might be plausible to call this 'only administration', but it was administration of deeply racist policies, with utterly inhumane consequences for the victims of these policies.

The underlying thrust of Nazi polices at this time was to remove Jews from areas designated for the sole use of Germans, while exploiting them as labour. Segregation was further supported through increasing restrictions on freedom of movement, in a variety of ways, with potentially severe penalties for those caught transgressing the new rules. Jews were rendered visibly different, initially through the wearing of armbands, later stars sewn onto clothing; and they were issued with identity cards that were always to be carried and produced on demand. Associated with ease of identification at any time and in any place were measures placing ever more demanding physical restrictions on when and where Jews were even to be seen, radically curtailing their freedom of movement.

Klausa obviously took over when much of this was already under way. He did not initiate these policies, but rather picked them up and sought to ensure effective implementation, even at the most detailed everyday level. The wearing of armbands, for example, had already been introduced during the winter of 1939–40 (as Klausa rightly recalled in his memoirs), but in the summer hours it was not being comprehensively observed; nor were the curfew times. At this stage, Jews appear to have been still making an attempt to assert their rights to exist and walk the streets of their home town. Klausa played what for him was no doubt a routine role in trying to ensure that these German-imposed regulations and restrictions on the behaviour of Jews should be observed. The police forces under von Woedtke and the gendarmerie under Klausa clearly worked together to try to ensure both effective monitoring and implementation of policies and penalties.

On 25 May 1940, Klausa issued a directive to the officials in charge of those rural communities, villages, and hamlets that were under the control of his own gendarmerie forces rather than the Sosnowiec police. This circular referred both to curfew hours for Jews in the summer, when they were permitted to spend an additional hour out of doors, and to the problem of wearing light summer clothing without sleeves. On Klausa's orders, if Jews were wearing clothing without sleeves during the summer, then they must 'wear the blue star of Zion on a white background in the same size as before on the left breast of their clothing'. Anyone found failing to follow this order 'should be arrested immediately and taken straight to the nearest

Gestapo office'. If there were no such office nearby, then they should be held for three to five days, and the police headquarters in Kattowitz was to be informed. Finally, 'the Jews themselves must bear the costs of their arrest and must pay immediately. If they are unable to pay, the Jewish community is responsible.'[31]

But there seems to have been little by way of developments in terms of Jewish compliance. A confidential police report on the situation in Będzin on 8 June 1940 reported:

The behaviour of the Jews on the streets is as cheeky as ever. They only give way when an official in uniform is visible. The curfew for Jews is not being observed. It is almost impossible for the police patrols to catch these Jews, since when the police turn up they immediately disappear into houses. It would be very helpful to have patrols in civilian dress.[32]

A further police situation report of 11 June 1940 complained:

The behaviour of Jews demands greater attention. Despite the order recently given to the leadership of the Jewish Community that Jews should give way on the streets not only to people in uniform but also to all other Germans, there has been no noticeable change in the behaviour of the Jews on the streets. The native cheek of the Jews is strengthened by the fact that the [Jewish] Communities constitute a sort of authoritarian organization that ... is already now coming forward with complaints against police officials, if they are on occasion rather sharply handled by these.

The police report suggested that, despite the lengthening of the curfew in summer to 21:00, it should rather be the case that

the Jews should only be allowed to use certain streets after 19:00 and these in the Jewish quarter, and should not be allowed to move around in the main streets any more, unless a more radical prohibition is passed that would prohibit Jews from entering certain streets altogether.[33]

The latter suggestion—restricting the streets that could be used by Jews—was very quickly put into effect. By 24 June 1940, the situation report included, with some satisfaction, the comment: 'The introduction of the Jewish ban on certain streets or sides of streets in the towns of Sosnowitz, Bendzin, and Czeladz has been received with satisfaction by the Reich and ethnic Germans, and partly also by the Poles.'[34] But the question of ready identification through the wearing of armbands had still not been adequately solved:

There is no decline in the attempts of Jews, in particular young females, to go around in the streets without wearing the armband. It therefore seems necessary that the Stapo [police] should make greater use of the practice of holding them for a lengthy period of time in an ersatz police prison.[35]

On 25 June 1940, having just returned from his three-week break in Schloss Repten and picking up routine administration again in the few days before he left for the front, Klausa issued an additional qualification to his earlier order with respect to enforcing the wearing of armbands and the penalties for those Jews found without identification: 'If there are no adequate arrest cells in the individual gendarmerie headquarters, the arrest will be carried out by the external service of the state police.'[36] Clearly the civilian administration and the police authorities were working very closely together on this issue. In September, the curfew times were again restricted to the shorter daylight hours.

If Jews were restricted in when they could go out, they were also restricted in where and how far they could travel. Much attention was devoted to the question of Jews using public transport, in an attempt to separate Jews from 'Aryans'. As one police situation report put it, using the classic language of the supposed dangers of pollution by contact with Jews:

The separation within compartments of Jews and Aryans, carried out by the Dombrowan streetcar authority, is to be seen as an inadequate regulation, since the purpose of the separation, the prevention of infection through contact with Jews, can only be achieved if the Jews are directed towards separate trams cars.[37]

A circular banning Jews from the use of public transport entirely was issued from Kattowitz in December 1940, although the translation of this prohibition into practice appears to have caused considerable problems.[38] A circular of 30 January 1941 attempted to reinforce the point that any 'Jews who use the above-mentioned means of transport without a certificate from the police authorities demonstrating permission to travel are to be arrested immediately, reported and held for five days'.[39] In ways small and large, Jews were being systematically restricted in where, how, and when they could move and travel, and the parameters of their lives were being progressively reduced.

These restrictions were not anodyne; the consequences of transgression could be and often were fatal. In the autumn of 1940 David Apfelbaum's father was caught after curfew and beaten up by the German authorities.

He was so severely injured by this beating that he could not move, and he died of his injuries three months later. The funeral was held in the nearby town of Olkusz on 3 December 1940; Apfelbaum, then aged 20, had to obtain a special permit to go to Olkusz for the funeral. There he learned the contents of his father's will; his 'legacy' was to take on responsibility for looking after the whole family. At this point in the interview—like so many survivors at moments of traumatic memory—Apfelbaum broke down, and simply said: 'what can I tell you . . .'.[40] Other Jews were deported to Auschwitz for offences such as 'not wearing the armband, staying on the street a few minutes after the curfew hour, riding a tram in an area in which persons of Aryan descent lived, also being present in such an area without special permission, and even crossing the street in a manner contrary to regulations'.[41] Once in Auschwitz, they were likely to die of illness and brutal maltreatment even before the programme of mass extermination got under way. Their deaths were reported back through the Jewish Council: it was common knowledge that people sent to Auschwitz would not survive this punishment for 'having been guilty, in the opinion of the Germans, of some offence' against these increasingly restrictive regulations.[42] Klausa may have seen the imposition of such regulations as a matter of mere administration, relatively trivial in itself; but the consequences for the victims were not.

There were continuing discussions of how to develop further the segregation, physical separation, and progressive isolation of Jews. The early and somewhat haphazard ousting of Jews from their homes and forcing them into increasingly overcrowded areas specifically designated for Jews was followed, in the autumn and winter of 1940–1, by discussion of creating a clearly demarcated ghetto. Clearly the examples of the ghettos in the Warthegau city of Łódź (created in the spring of 1940) and, in the General Government, Warsaw (created in October 1940) provided examples inspiring the local Nazi leadership.

The question of ghettoization was complex, in part because it involved not only the civilian administration and the police authorities, but also the Principal Trusteeship Office for the East (*Hauptreuhandstelle Ost* (*HTO*)) and other interested parties at national and regional levels. There were continued disputes over the precise means and stages of the segregation of the Jews, often accompanied by strong personal animosities. The Police Chief of Sosnowiec, Alexander von Woedtke, clearly took considerable initiative in driving ghettoization forward, despite practical considerations raised by others who had to deal with a range of economic and labour consideration issues. But nowhere in the twisting tale of the segregation of the Jewish population of this area is there a whiff of human empathy for the plight of the Jews themselves to be found: policies are always weighed in terms of what would be most opportune and beneficial for the Germans at any given point in time. Since circumstances changed quite rapidly—not least as a result of the Germans' own policies, the consequences of which were often not adequately, if at all, thought through in advance—so too did views on the question of ghettoization, 'resettlement', or 'evacuation'.

In Sosnowiec, Jewish property was forcibly taken over with effect from 1 August and Polish property from 1 September 1940.[43] On 1 October 1940, the *HTO*'s announcement that Jewish and Polish property was going to be taken under its administration occasioned considerable popular unrest. There was particular uproar among members of the local Polish population in Sosnowiec, who were aware of the earlier enforced population transfer of around 30,000 Germans from the Lublin area in exchange for Poles 'resettled' from the Warthegau and feared that they too would be sent off to the General Government. Moreover, the city authorities were worried about the resettlement of some of the more prosperous and professional members of the Polish community, including medical practitioners who provided valuable services to the community; the latter could not necessarily be expected to live 'cramped up in the quarters deemed less suitable for Germans' (*in den für Deutsche weniger geeigneten Wohnvierteln zusammengedrängt*); class considerations here seemed at least partially to weigh in the balance against 'race'. Worst, from the point of view of the City Mayor, Franz-Josef Schönwälder, was the loss of tax income from property-owners, since the *HTO* did not pay in the way previous private owners had done; and the fact that former Polish property-owners were now having to rely on municipal benefits in order to pay rents for which they had not previously been liable, and had no means of paying. Meanwhile, because of the lack of any private German market or customer base, there was a serious problem about attracting German entrepreneurs into the area who might make up the difference in municipal income. By the end of November, the situation with respect to Polish bad temper and underground political activities had worsened, to such an extent that Schönwälder was suggesting there should be at least a temporary halt to measures against the Polish population.

No such arguments would be relevant to the situation of the Jewish populations of Będzin and Sosnowiec, however. But, even here, there were difficult practical considerations. The Police President von Woedtke was strongly in favour of establishing a ghetto, but the City Mayor, Schönwälder, pointed out that the proposed area was also the location of many of the enterprises that had been taken over by the Trusteeship Office and were being administered by Germans. Establishing an exclusively Jewish ghetto in this area would massively disrupt economic productivity.

As far as the *Landkreis* of Będzin was concerned, in response to von Woedtke's proposal for an open ghetto Klausa pointed out there were varying considerations in different areas of his relatively extensive territory. Purely pragmatic considerations about what was feasible in the circumstances—no questions were raised about the intrinsic inhumanity of the enterprise—appeared to be all that mattered to Klausa at this stage:

> A solution to this question is not in my view very urgent, but can be carried out without much difficulty in Czeladz und Strzemieszyc. In Dombrowa it will be considerably more difficult, and in Bendzin I fear it may cause serious disruption to economic life. The procedure of the property company, of freeing up main roads one by one, seems both a more organic process and one that promises to be more successful.[44]

In Klausa's view, it would in this way be possible to exclude Jews from desirable streets while not as yet excluding Poles or Germans from what would otherwise have been designated purely Jewish areas; economic enterprises in the predominantly Jewish zones would not as yet be affected, while for Germans better areas could be rendered 'Jew free'.

Developments along the lines supported by Klausa appeared to be in sight: a letter from von Woedtke to Regional Governor Springorum of 14 December 1940 indicated a strong desire to proceed with 'in the first place cleansing the main and shopping streets as well as the main residential quarters from the Jewish population'.[45] Jews were thus to be excluded from areas where they had historically lived, worked, and socialized, and were to be forced into ever more restricted and overcrowded quarters in poorer areas of town.

Following a discussion on 8 January 1941 between Klausa as *Landrat* of Będzin, von Woedtke as Police President of Sosnowiec, Schönwälder as City Mayor of Sosnowiec, and the Regional President Springorum, it was decided to begin to concentrate the Jews within certain confined districts, and to make other areas 'Jew free', without at this stage constructing an enclosed ghetto along the lines of Łódź or Warsaw, in the sense of an 'area of town that is demarcated from other urban areas and secured accordingly'.[46] This meeting illustrated the ultimate responsibility of the *Landrat*, and the close cooperation between civilian administration and police authorities, in implementing anti-Jewish measures and in particular segregation and ghettoization.

Regional President Springorum summarized the decisions as a 'plan, designed according to ethnic–political considerations and entailing the separation of those areas to be reserved exclusively for Germans and the designation of living quarters solely for Jews'. The plan entailed 'freeing up certain streets that, because of their significance for transport or because of the fact that they contain housing of above average value, are to be cleared of Jews, and designating particular residential quarters for the exclusive habitation of Jews'. The corollary was 'the designation of certain streets, due to their significance for transport or their better residential quarters, for the exclusive habitation of the German population'. The lines of responsibility and duty of cooperation were made absolutely clear: ghettoization was 'the responsibility respectively of the towns and under the oversight of the *Landrat* in Bendzin'. While the civilian authorities were responsible for the planning and development of rehousing policies, the police authorities were also responsible for their implementation in practice.[47] Given that Klausa personally signed a letter on the same day that Springorum sent out the summary of the decisions they had jointly come to some ten days earlier, there can be no doubt that he was at this time still present and actively in charge of the affairs of his *Landkreis*.[48]

At this stage, then, Udo Klausa was personally involved in the development of policy and the continuing process of ghettoization of the Jews. There are some intimations in Alexandra's letters that Klausa was suffering from 'nerves' at this time, although the causes are not made explicit. On 6 November 1940 Alexandra wrote from Schloss Repten, where she was at that time staying, to a family friend, Frau von H., that 'our Bendzin residence is still not in a fit state to move into, and I am leading a very uncomfortable life between Repten and Bendzin'. She continued:

> Udo has an incredible amount to do, which would be easy to bear and even enjoyable, if only he did not always suffer, to a greater or lesser degree, from pressure of nerves on top of it all, which just makes him completely knackered [*kaputt*]. Quite

apart from everything else, he has inherited the totally labile nerves of his mother, so that he is in a simply terrible state, and only getting worse. I hope that in this respect there will at least be a small improvement when he has a habitable home and comfortable conditions in his private life, and I can care for him a bit. But it won't help very much as long as the other matter doesn't improve![49]

Klausa's nervous state may well have been in large part related to an as yet unsettled home life, combined with a highly demanding workload. Even a relatively junior member of his workforce, a telephonist, was expected to work a regular fifty-six-hour week at this time.[50] He possibly felt a need to exert his authority: he was still very young for this post—having just turned 30—and had responsibility over subordinates in the district who were mostly older even if not always as intelligent or effective as he was. He undoubtedly felt the need to prove himself to his regional superiors, given his still precarious probationary status. Furthermore, Klausa seems to have had an inherently rather delicate physical constitution, evident already in the later 1930s when he did his first major stint of military training with the Potsdam I.R.9 and decided to return to a career in civilian administration for health reasons.

What the 'other matter' might consist in is not made clear here. We can speculate that it related to an inner sense of discomfort on Klausa's part with his civilian role and a desire to leave the job he had so much coveted; but it might also relate to the impending one-year milestone in his probationary period, with his desire for confirmation in that role and need to prove himself, despite his wish to return to military service as soon as possible. He clearly was experiencing some sort of inner conflict, and one that his wife could not articulate clearly, or did not wish to write about explicitly in a letter under the political conditions of this time.

By early February 1941, shortly after he had consigned the Jews to their fate in ghettoization, Klausa appears to have been hoping to get back into military service. Again Alexandra's veiled references are unclear: she tells her friend that Udo 'is not well, the work here is too demanding'. She was by now 'almost hoping that he can realize his desire to go back to his regiment at the end of February. He would certainly recover well there.'[51] Although the comments made are again opaque, members of Klausa's family later sought to interpret them as veiled references to growing doubts about the course of policy in the area. Yet, whatever nervous strain he may have been suffering from, Klausa's professional actions were entirely in conformity with what was required of him in his role at this time.

Policy continuities and developments

The policies inaugurated by the German administration continued to have a major and devastating impact on those whose lives were affected, whether or not the *Landrat* was physically present in the area at any given time. There was a clear continuity in the direction of policy, whatever the discontinuities in Klausa's own periods of physical presence in the area. And these were the conditions under which Jews now had to live, whether or not Klausa himself was present in the area he had helped to shape.

'Resettlement' of the Jews of Będzin and Sosnowiec proceeded systematically, according to the plans laid down in January 1941. By early March 1941, an administrative assistant for the *Landrat* of Będzin, Assessor Pilz, reported that the plans for moving people around 'according to ethnic–political considerations' were in train. But unforeseen difficulties had arisen, because the Trusteeship organization could not winkle people out of their homes because of a legal technicality—extraordinary, given the other far less than legal measures being taken in the area with apparently few or no scruples—relating to the Silesian law regulating tenants' rights. The *Landrat* was, accordingly, going to make an application to have this dealt with as quickly as possible. On hearing of this little technical hitch in the smooth and 'legal' expropriation of Jews and ousting them from their homes, Regional President Springorum sent a note to the relevant authorities in charge of these matters, instructing them to the effect that, when the *Landrat*'s application arrived, they were to give it fast-track treatment in the light of the earlier decisions taken on segregation.[52]

The *Landrat*'s intervention to speed matters up with respect to ousting Jews from their homes clearly had some effect. The enforced movement of Jews into poorer quarters now proceeded rapidly. Already a week later, 467 Jewish residents of Będzin had been forced out of their homes, although this paled in comparison with the 1,339 people in Sosnowiec who had at this time been ousted.[53] Overcrowding of the Jewish families, forced in ever greater numbers into ever more cramped quarters, was further exacerbated by continued movements of Jews in from areas designated as 'Jew free' west of the police border, or communities moved from elsewhere in the 'Eastern Strip' to clear territories that the Germans had designated for other purposes.

In March 1941, for example, the German settlement of the Auschwitz area was massively expanded, with several villages being entirely cleared of their Polish populations to make way for incoming German camp staff and their families.[54] Plans for the expansion of the Auschwitz concentration camp as well as the 'Germanization' of the town of Oświęcim (Auschwitz) entailed the removal of some 8,000 local people from the villages around the site of Birkenau, while, in the week of Pesach (Passover) in early April 1941, the entire Jewish community of the town of Oświęcim was expelled. It seems that the originally intended resettlement of around 6,000 Jews from this area into the General Government was blocked, ostensibly because the *Reichsbahn* was unable to provide trains. The Jews were then to be sent, instead, on foot to the nearby towns of Będzin and Sosnowiec. In the event, at very short notice transport was arranged: 5 trains each with 20 goods wagons and 12 passenger coaches took some 2,000 Jews to Sosnowiec, and a further 3,000 to Będzin.[55]

One of those forcibly ousted from his home in Oświęcim was Jakob Rosenbaum, a teenager of 15 at the time.[56] He recalls that, within weeks of the German invasion, everything had been confiscated, including his family's

Figure 7. Resesttling Jews into Będzin, spring 1941
Relocation of Jews from the surrounding communities, including Oświęcim (Auschwitz), to Będzin.
United States Holocaust Memorial Museum, courtesy of YIVO Institute for Jewish Research.

business and home. They initially moved into one room in his grandfather's house in Oświęcim, and were somewhat fortunate in being able to work in a bakery in this building from which they could obtain extra bread. His sister was, however, taken away after four or five months to forced labour in a woman's camp in Germany, along with his cousin, from whom they subsequently received a few postcards before losing contact. When Jakob Rosenbaum and his family, along with the rest of the Jewish community of Oświęcim, were deported to Będzin, a lot of the older people were simply shot dead on the spot rather than 'resettled'. Those killed included his own grandfather, who was shot in front of everybody in the middle of a public square. Rosenbaum further recalls that the Będzin ghetto was run for the Germans by Jewish administrators, who 'did all the dirty work for them', crowding ever more families into one room. He, like others, was forced to go and watch the public hanging of Jews: 'There were no trials, no jury, there was one German said hang and you hung, that's it, and you could not appeal, nothing.'

Despite the worsening overcrowding in the Będzin ghetto, those who survived the repeated 'resettlements' were at this time still lucky. Gauleiter Fritz Bracht, who had paid a visit to Auschwitz with Himmler in March 1941, made a curiously grim remark to the Governor of the General Government, Hans Frank, on 2 May 1941: 'It would be simplest to eliminate, by the quickest and perhaps rather painful way, everything that is not German in the *Gau* of Upper Silesia.'[57] While at this time Bracht's remark was arguably just one of those characteristically brutal Nazi utterances with little immediate implication for practical policy, the Jews who in 1941 were 'resettled' from Oświęcim to Będzin would over the following two years be retransported back to their home town to be murdered in the gas chambers of Auschwitz-Birkenau.

Inevitably, overcrowding brought growing health hazards as well as psychological distress. By 4 June 1941 the Leader of the Jewish Council of Elders, signing himself 'Moszek Israel Merin', reported to Regional President Springorum that 'as a result of the resettlement housing density is already at five people per room'.[58] But in his view resettlement was proceeding too fast, and the Jews could no longer cope with the housing conditions, particularly given the health dangers in the heat of the summer. Jews had now been asked to clear by July the house numbers 21–25 and 22–56 on the two sides of what the Germans had renamed as the Old High Street (*Alte Hauptstrasse*), a task that Merin held to be impossible in the current circumstances, given that they were already horrendously overcrowded: 'The 34 houses that come into question are inhabited by 858 families, 3,150 [!] souls. A resettlement of such a large number of people requires a corresponding period of time and a corresponding area in which to live.' Moreover, already some seventy families were still homeless as a result of the most recent 'resettlement' measure, and there was no adequate accommodation into which they could move. As Merin pointed out, there were also serious health considerations to be taken into account:

> The part of the town in which the Jewish inhabitants have been resettled contains houses of the oldest type, the most elementary comforts are not present in these houses, they have no water supplies, the privies and rubbish bins are often in a condition beyond words.
>
> The Committee of the Jewish Representative Community that is responsible for overseeing the sanitary conditions—particularly with this degree of overcrowding and in view of the coming summer—will not be in a position, given the lack of the most elementary hygienic facilities, to prevent the threatened danger of epidemics and furthermore will not be able to control the situation in the case of an outbreak of infectious illnesses. Any further overcrowding of the Jewish inhabitants under these conditions is of great danger, quite apart from the fact that it poses significant difficulties.[59]

Merin ended, on behalf of the Jewish community, that 'we politely request' that any further moves should be delayed in the light of these problems.

How this must have felt and smelled at the time is hard to imagine. Alexander Hohenstein, a Nazi functionary and small town mayor in the Warthegau, one day took an unannounced walk in the ghetto area of his town. In his contemporary diary entry there is a graphic description of the unbelievable squash of people walking up and down huddled together in large groups on the streets, the overcrowding inside the miserable hovels with an average of seven people living in one room, having to take turns to sleep in the one or two available beds that had to be used for everyone, the unbearable, nauseating stench of the buckets that had to function as toilets, and that were also kept in the same room, in close proximity to the receptacles used for cooking.[60] Conditions were very probably not dissimilar in the old and decrepit housing quarter of Będzin into which Jews were now being forced. A German propaganda film of the time includes scenes from the ghetto with throngs of people in the streets, appearing to a viewer today somewhat like a demonstration or march, but in all probability just an everyday scene of massive overcrowding.[61]

The German responses to Merin's pleas on behalf of the Jewish community were less than sympathetic. The Mayor of Będzin put in writing to the *Landrat* on 24 June 1941: 'The German population really could not be expected to live together with the Jewish parasites any longer, or to have to make their way through the respective streets. Therefore action must be taken immediately.'[62] Springorum considered the views both of the German administration and of the Jewish community representatives, and on 30 June 1941 pronounced:

> I consider the complaint of the leader of the Council of Elders of the Jewish Community to be unfounded. Since the further internal resettlement of the Jews in the town of Bendsburg is urgently desired and there is sufficient habitable space available for this, I have as of now permitted the resettlement to continue.[63]

On 8 July 1941 Springorum wrote to the *Landrat* complaining about the (German) Property Company, who had apparently taken undue note of the Jews' views, which he thought should be no concern of theirs, and had failed to consider the broader political implications of the situation. In Springorum's view, the medical policy considerations in particular were issued not 'on behalf of the Jews, but precisely for the protection of the German population'.[64] Clearly, as long as the comfort and health of the latter were assured, conditions for the Jews could continue to deteriorate, whatever the consequences for them.

Jewish experiences of the early phase of ghettoization

To understand the *Landrat*'s role, and the continuing consequences of German policies even when the *Landrat* was himself not physically present, requires both an effort of the imagination and a trawling of wider sources than those policy documents produced by the officials involved. In part because the process was long drawn out and piecemeal, in part because the developing ghetto areas in Będzin, as well as neighbouring Sosnowiec, were neither as large nor as clearly well defined as the big ghettos of Łódź and Warsaw, alongside a multitude of other smaller or more transient ghettos they are only now beginning to gain a place in the historians' corpus.[65]

We cannot do justice to those who lived—and died—in this period of occupation and exploitation, prior to the major deportations that began in 1942 and the final stage of ghettoization that followed, without trying to gain a sense of lived experience. The subjective material available is patchy, but potentially rich. There are few surviving letters or other personal materials from this time—the diary of the teenager Rutka Laskier dates only from the spring of 1943—but there are large numbers of testimonies, memoirs, and oral history interviews with survivors. From these and other sources, it is possible to gain at least some sense of the major issues and the ways in which different individuals responded to the circumstances and challenges of this time.

In the memories of survivors, the different phases of Nazi policy formation are not always clearly distinguished. There are memories of frequent moves, discomfort, hunger, fear, loss, overcrowding, individual traumatic moments, acts of violence against family, friends, neighbours—but which particular period or policy was the precipitant of the particular event or the general deterioration in conditions is not always clear, and dating is often extremely hazy. This is in part because many of those who were interviewed only in the 1990s were still children at the time of the Nazi invasion; it is also in part because the moves themselves were piecemeal, and, while some families were repeatedly moved, others found themselves subject to sudden 'resettlement' only once or perhaps twice. Even in surviving documents of the time (such as letters to and from the labour camps) feelings and emotions may be expressed with immediacy, but details are often omitted for fear either of censorship or of causing concern among loved ones. Yet certain themes stand out, and a composite picture, made up of a mosaic of different individual stories, can emerge. And they emerge in the context of policies introduced and sustained by the German regime, including the civilian administration.

Yetta Kleiner, who was 11 when the Nazis invaded, recalls that they had to move out of their home very early on and move into another house with another family. Her sense was that there had been nowhere to run; that everything was 'already too late'. Her family had previously lived in an apartment consisting of just two rooms and a kitchen, 'but it was ours'. The move hit them very badly, psychologically as well as physically: 'Everyone was distressed, my mother was crying, my father was just going around, he was powerless, as a man.' Then there came the announcements about handing in jewellery, gold, furs; and that, if a Jew was caught with any of these items, it would mean the death penalty. Kleiner remembers these announcement being conveyed on placards in both German and Polish, as well as announcements through loudspeaker horns, with members of the Gestapo driving around in jeeps barking out orders from cars; people had to run and obey, thinking this might save their lives. Her memory of these events was that it was chaos, 'grabbing whatever we could', 'possessions we could carry with us', at very short notice, with the whole household disrupted. They had been given the order, they knew they had to fulfil it, the family was 'so frightened', the Germans were 'standing with rifles, any movement you made that was wrong you had the rifle into your body hitting you'. Kleiner commented: 'It really hit us very badly, my father was ready for a nut house, when they took his business away'; 'and our home, just a year before the war our parents had just furnished our home, and it was all gone, in a minute'. They were moved into a single room with another family, and remained there until the Kamionka ghetto was formed some three years later. Before then there was constant fear of the repeated raids, during one of which her brother was taken away to a labour camp. In another, her father, who was at the time praying in his prayer shawl, was taken away; she never saw him again. She was now left with just her mother and sister.[66]

Rosa Rechnic similarly commented that: 'As far as I'm concerned, the ghetto started almost immediately, because people had to move out of certain quarters, of certain areas, which necessitated looking for another apartment, uprooting yourself, being in smaller quarters', moving constantly. 'As the ghetto area kept getting smaller and smaller we had to keep moving from apartment to apartment.' Meanwhile, the German occupiers 'took over the beautiful apartments, possessions and everything'. Her family first of all tried to take in additional members of their own extended family, but then also had to accommodate strangers resettled from other areas, finally living in a shared small room with a curtain between themselves and the others living in the same room. These eventually included two elderly people who had, Rechnic remembers, just arrived from a transport: they were German Jews, 'so quiet, timid, pathetic'.[67]

Marion Landau's family had before the war lived in the relatively affluent street of Sączewskiego. When the so-called trustee, or *Treuhänder*, took over his father's textile business, it was quite clear that this man did not know very much about the business; Marion Landau, by now a young adult of 21, continued to deal with day-to-day matters: 'I was the one to run the business under the Germans until they deported me.' The family had already, before the invasion, tried to hide some of the fabrics, which had been sent for safekeeping to another town, where one of his mother's relatives had a store. At that point: 'We were alarmed, not about our lives, we never imagined what can happen, but about our merchandise we tried to save, to send to that small town, about 100 miles away from Będzin.' They were forced to leave their home soon after the German invasion. Now 'it was one room that we were allowed to live in, thanks to a distant relative of my father's that allowed us to move in with them . . . I didn't know of their existence because that was a completely different part of the city, because we happened to have lived in a more fashionable part of the town and that was in the old city of Będzin that we moved to.'[68] Life changed dramatically in a myriad of respects:

Every few days there were different announcements, not allowed to have radios, not allowed to read the papers, not allowed to go to school, every few days something different, so little by little, little by little, in Będzin they told us that we have to get out of our place and move to the Jews' section, and in between we were being harassed day and night, you could hear . . . that they were harassing different sections of the town, we could hear the screams, and . . . every few days they were making arrests, caught people walking the streets, onto buses, and that sort of thing.[69]

As a young adult with particular skills and resources, as well as considerable luck, Landau was able to develop techniques and strategies that ultimately helped him to survive. For those who were less well placed or younger at the time, the situation was more difficult.

Helen Balsam was 12 years old at the time of the German invasion. Her father was in the Polish Army; following its rapid defeat at the hands of the Germans, he was rounded up in Zamość, where he stayed till 1941; hence he had no identity papers on his eventual return to Będzin. Helen's family therefore had no man in the house in the early months of the German occupation, and were very soon moved into an area she already called the ghetto: 'it was in a very old area of town, near where the cemeteries were, very narrow streets . . . a very poor neglected area.'[70] Excluded from school, she was put to work in a factory, which she remembers only as 'something with leather', located on the outskirts or just beyond the ghetto area. She could not remember where or how her mother obtained any food, but 'there were no stores that you could go in and buy' except bread: 'bread you could buy'. Her mother brought home food, 'but it was very little, very little food'. 'Everyone had to work, everyone.' Her family was quite Zionist in orientation, and she went to a Zionist youth group a few times, which was, she remembers, preparing them to go to Israel after the war.

Mindzia Schickman (named Milla Tenenbaum as an adult) was only 7 years old when the war started.[71] Her memory of the loss of the family home and possessions was traumatic. The SS came initially, she thought, just to take all the furniture: 'There was no power and there was no saying no, we were really helpless.' One SS man started playing with her mother's hair, then physically grasped her mother, at which point Mindzia's father became very angry. The SS officer took his pistol out, and continued to take Mindzia's mother towards the bedroom, but Mindzia's father grabbed and lifted the SS officer and threw him down the steps, while her mother started shaking. She was not the only one:

> We all were shaking, we didn't know from where [my father had] the courage . . . but this policeman stood up and took his gun and walked away. The next day they came and took all the furnitures [*sic*], and a few days later they came and took my mother away.[72]

Mindzia was not at home when her mother was taken away, 'but when I came home I was told that it's okay, that she was taken to work'. This was a common experience: 'From every family they took one or two people out and they sent them away to work . . . it was something that we accept, we had to accept that, you cry, you wipe your tears, and you have to accept, those are the facts, but nobody knew where they are taking them.' She never heard from her mother again. 'No. Never. Never never.' When asked what impact this had on the family, and how her father had reacted, Mindzia replied: 'I think we were taught to hide our feelings. One thing, that my father never showed emotions. I was very young . . . I felt my brother is there . . .'. Mindzia's brother Idek was at this stage, and for some time afterwards, extremely important for her survival. Even so, 'I was all confused at the time'. Shortly after this incident, they were moved from their home at Kościuszki 2, 'and they were segregating streets, the Jews were not allowed to walk on any street, only one street'; the place they moved to 'was like one room, a garage room'.

The designated Jewish residential areas were not as yet enclosed physically, but there were severe restrictions on where Jews were permitted to go. When asked 'Was this ghetto enclosed?', Helen Balsam replied, 'No, no, but you couldn't move freely.'[73] David Apfelbaum similarly recalled that the ghetto was a closely designated area.[74] Marion Landau described this early period of the Będzin ghetto as highly restrictive, despite its lack of physical means of enclosure. The designated part of 'old Będzin' was 'a very congested area with small streets and very old homes':

> There was no wall, it was not a walled ghetto, but we were not allowed to move around all the rest of the town, the parks, or there was a castle that I always used to go for myself on a Saturday with a book, Saturday was closed to business…and none of these places were allowed for Jews to visit or to walk through, except for these particular few streets which we called the ghetto.

Landau emphasizes that 'we were kind of walled in by all kinds of commands and edicts from the Nazis'. Even so,

> it was a vibrant community as much as it could be under the terrible circumstances that we lived in, with every day people being deported, caught in the streets and they put them on trucks, and raids at night, knocks at night at all different places, people running around, moving from place to place, trying to hide, still we managed to somehow, as a matter of fact we had…Jewish plays…that people were performing and we did the best we could under the circumstances to survive until of course there was nothing left for us but run around and hide, hide as much as we could until they caught up with us anyway.[75]

With variations according to the circumstances of the interviewees and their families, these sorts of descriptions and recollections come up again and again.

Whatever his private doubts may or may not have been, there is no evidence that Klausa in any way explicitly registered any reservations in principle about the continued infringement of the human rights of Jews and the enforced deterioration in their conditions of life. Conditions for the Jews, and the further constraints and overcrowding caused by the implementation of the ghettoization plans sealed in January 1941, continued radically to affect the lives of the Jewish inhabitants—for they were no longer citizens, as they had previously been—of Będzin, whether or not Klausa was physically present in the district or away at the front. The same was true of other aspects of their working and living conditions at this time.

7
Means of Survival

Alexandra's letters to her mother during the three years she lived in Będzin are full of requests and thanks for additional foodstuffs; mentioning delicacies brought by one of her brothers from the western front, attempts at rustling up additional fruit from the orchards and gardens of nearby friends and relatives, or the glass jars necessary for making the preserves that would be essential for seeing her growing young family through the winter. She registered dismay when the market of Będzin eventually closed down, in her letter suggesting this might have had to do with Jews being sent to labour duties elsewhere. There is also much talk in her letters of making and mending; of having a tailor come to stay to measure her for new clothes, then wondering whether, in view of a suspected pregnancy, this would really be worthwhile at that particular time; whether particular colours of clothes could go together; what to do about having the soles of a pair of her mother's shoes mended, once the previous—Jewish—cobbler 'had gone', with no question about why he was no longer in his accustomed place. She records disapproval of the behaviour of domestic servants, including a maid, and of local officials who did not accept the kind of hospitality she would have liked to offer. She clearly did not like the environment in which she was now living, but did her best to compensate by periodic visits to friends and relatives west of the 'police line', in the areas surrounding and north of Kattowitz, such as Beuthen and Tarnowitz.[1]

There is little doubt that German women of Alexandra's social background found conditions in the new colonial situation of the 'wild east' not at all what they had been accustomed to at home in the 'Old Reich', nor what they would have aspired to in the relatively elevated social situation of *Landrat*'s wife. Yet registering the petty discomforts of wartime circumstances in this annexed territory seems to have precluded any sense of how those subjugated by the Germans were living, literally, on the other side of the garden fence. As a young mother, Alexandra seems to have been primarily wrapped up in family matters; or perhaps she sustained a characteristically humorous style in her letters and concentrated on domestic concerns, since this was what she felt most appropriate to communicate to her mother. But so many Germans, and not only Alexandra, seem to have been able to live in their own social worlds, relatively unaffected by the miseries of those who were increasingly being removed from their sight and herded into ever more cramped and segregated conditions.

It was in some respects easy for the civilian administrators and beneficiaries of Nazi rule to disassociate themselves from the victims of Nazi rule, the more they were removed from their sight. Moreover, lack of physical contact could lead to having no sense of their own involvement in the system. Paradoxically, this was a blindness shared by Jews, who also had only a partial view of the world, but for rather different reasons.

Most survivor testimonies reveal just how little interaction they had with any Germans beyond the immediately brutal thugs dealing out orders and blows, and the occasional more benign German employer. Most interaction between the Jewish inhabitants and the German authorities was conducted through the intermediaries, the local representatives of the Jewish Councils of Elders. There were still, but increasingly limited, interactions between Jews and Poles: many local Poles remember that after a while they had little to do with their former Jewish neighbours, and knew little about the conditions under which they were living; but some individuals were vital in helping Jews, while others played a role in denouncing them.

Unfree work

From the very beginning of the German occupation, Jews had been coerced into forced labour. Jewish properties were expropriated, and Jews set to work by private employers, the German 'trusteeship' office, or municipal labour organizations. Labour camps were also established early on, with periodic 'raids' of the young and able; as David Apfelbaum remembers, 'by October [1939] already they get at some youths, men and women, and then send them away to *Arbeitslager* [labour camps]'.[2] From the autumn of 1940, others were forced by the newly established Organisation Schmelt to work for the SS, or were 'rented out' by the SS to private employers, who shared the profits of exploitation of 'cheap labour' between them. Conditions varied, but underlying all accounts by Jews of experiences of work under Nazi occupation was the radical loss of control over their own freedom and material resources.

Abraham Kimmelmann described how the early forced labour schemes operated. There was very little contact with the German authorities organizing the work schemes, since the Jewish Council acted as intermediary: 'the Jewish Community Council would get this kind of an order, they would take the lists, the card index of every Jewish inhabitant and would send him a note that on such and such a day, such and such an hour, and at such and such a place he should appear' for work duties. Jews had to do 'the hardest and the worst work... In the worst frost, in the worst snow... People had to sweat, people had to shed their blood, and with all effort one had to finish the work.' Moreover, work was often accompanied by physical violence: 'One word was enough to make one grab the shovel and to do his utmost. But there were also among them such sadists who wouldn't talk at all, they were just beating.'[3] Mordecai Lichtenstein corroborates this picture: 'Jews were forced to do road work, debris clearing, and similar kinds of hard work. Slackers were shot on the spot.' Some of those in charge gained a particularly bad reputation: 'The worst brutes of the Schutzpolizei were Zybis and Miczko, who used to beat up and shoot Jews, and who also employed Jewish informers.' The system itself bred corruption: 'The informers blackmailed Jews and then shared the spoils with their police superiors.'[4] Violence against Jews was now exercised indiscriminately by Poles, by newly registered 'ethnic Germans' who felt themselves to be a cut above their Polish neighbours, as well as by the German occupiers.[5]

As long as the ultimate numbers added up, it was possible for richer and more privileged Jews to buy, bribe, or barter their way out of disagreeable situations, and to ensure more favourable treatment for members of their families, as Kimmelmann noted: 'Those with plenty of money, these would hire a poor Jew, pay him for the day according to agreement, and that fellow would work for him.'[6] Many people without the means to buy their way out nevertheless still sought to evade forced labour duties; but it rapidly became clear that severe consequences would follow. As a police report in June 1940 put it:

> Recently there have been a rising number of cases in which Jews, who have been ordered by the Jewish community to report for forced labour, have refused to take up work. The Stapo is asked to deliver such work-shy Jews for a while to the ersatz police prison.[7]

David Apfelbaum recalled that very early on he had to get an identity card, marking him as Jewish. Some Polish people he knew became *Volksdeutsche*, ethnic Germans, in order to gain privileges; and Germans from the Reich or local 'ethnic Germans' became managers or 'trustees', forcibly imposed on formerly Jewish businesses that had been confiscated from their owners.

The German authorities kept a close eye on the way in which the seizure of property and means of livelihood was affecting the Jewish population under their control. In his final report of 1 March 1940, Klausa's predecessor Grotjan had noted that the 'numbers of Jews with no means of existence is growing ever bigger', and pointed to the risk of 'outbreak of epidemics' owing to the lack of food.[8] Nor, it would seem, was the Jewish Community any longer in a financial position to support increasingly impoverished members of the community. Grotjan considered various measures, including 'giving up the activities of the Jewish people's kitchen, in which already nearly 40 per cent of the Jewish population receive their midday meal for free'.[9] A more permanent measure appeared to him simply to be 'resettling' the Jews outside this area entirely:

> In view of the difficulties mentioned above, which are daily growing ever greater, and also because the housing situation of the daily growing numbers of Reich officials, employees and workers is becoming ever more urgent, the solution of the Jewish question in this area has become extraordinarily urgent. I therefore request most emphatically that implementation of the evacuation measures against the Jews should be carried out as soon as possible.[10]

At this stage, moving the Jews out was not yet a euphemism for murder, as it was later to become. But the underlying issues were already visible: enforced hunger and overcrowding inevitably led to the threat of infectious diseases, which could potentially pose a problem for the growing German community; and the ever-increasing size of the latter meant further enforced overcrowding of the Jews. And meanwhile, 'resettlement' of the dispossessed and hungry Jews into the General Government was not an option, so that, as conditions deteriorated further, the search for a 'solution' would eventually become ever more radical.

In late May 1940, the *Landrat*'s report, with Klausa now in full charge, noted that 'the Jewish workforce is still for the most part lying idle'.[11] But within a matter of months, this situation changed radically: work became apparently central to the survival of the Jews of Eastern Upper Silesia—

until genocidal racial ideology took precedence over economic rationality and pragmatic priorities.

By the autumn of 1940—just at the time the *Landrat* and his wife were settling into the house formerly owned by the Schein family and setting it up with furniture that had been seized from Jews—a report from the Police President in Sosnowiec commented that 'the behaviour of Jews has not changed. Their economic situation has become more fraught due to the ever-increasing seizure of furniture etc.'[12] On the same day, the police forces in Czeladź registered a sense of satisfaction in a job now virtually completed:

> Insofar as properties in the built-up area were in Jewish or Polish possession, they have been taken over by the Trusteeship Office... In Czeladz there are only poor Jews, they behave for the most part peacefully. At most they give cause for intervention because of illicit trading.[13]

A draft report from the Sosnowiec police sections covering both Będzin and Czeladź made remarkably similar comments, presumably drawing directly on the Czeladź report:

> The urban properties of the Poles and Jews are being increasingly taken over by the Trusteeship Office... The Jews are remaining calm. Their economic situation is getting worse because of their progressive exclusion from economic life. They seek to improve this through increased illicit trading.[14]

The report coming from the principal seat of local government, Będzin, additionally noted some of the less desirable consequences, from the Germans' point of view, of the German expropriation of Jewish property:

> The Property Company Ltd has already taken over the properties of the Poles and Jews... Now as previously the Jews are engaging in illicit trading, in part they are still active in their [former] shops under commissary administration. But they are being progressively more and more excluded from work and economic processes. This is the only explanation for the fact that so many Jews are always lounging around on the streets. Naturally therefore much of the workforce is lying idle. So it is proposed that they be pulled into communal works. Poor Jews will be supported by the Jewish community.[15]

But 'solutions' were soon at hand for the 'problem' the Nazis had created, that of Jews hanging around and engaging in illicit trade in order to try to survive, once their own businesses had been forcibly taken away from them. Many Jews continued to work in enterprises that they had formerly owned themselves, but were now under the control either of the Trusteeship Office or of private entrepreneurs. Others were simply uprooted and had to make a new start.

Poles too were affected. Even though some Poles had at first manœuvred themselves into relatively privileged positions, many others were not so lucky and got caught up on the receiving end of forced labour for the Germans. And local Polish people too soon became only too well aware of the penalties for seeking to evade forced labour. As one Sosnowiec police report put it, following an incident in which Poles who had failed to report for work duties had been deported to Auschwitz:

> The numbers of work-shy Poles at the employment office had declined rapidly in the last two weeks. It would thus appear that the arrest and deportation to the concentration camp of 19 Poles . . . did after all have the desired effect.[16]

But there was effective segregation with rather different working conditions for Poles and Jews.

Within Będzin and the surrounding area, a great network of 'shops' developed, employing the now dispossessed Jews, including youngsters who had been forcibly prevented from continuing their education: workshops and factories producing army uniforms, boots, and munitions and continuing trade that had already been carried out prior to the invasion, but now under German 'trustees'. This work brought together and altered the interrelations between different social classes.

Henrietta Altmann recalled that, when she had to go to work in one of the 'shops' (workshops) run by Alfred Rossner, she met members of the Jewish proletariat for the first time in her life, and was highly conscious of class differences. She was an educated young woman, speaking Polish and German; but her fellow workers from less privileged backgrounds spoke Yiddish. They were easily able to do the work, whereas she, a child of the intelligentsia, did not even know how to sew on a button. She was teased and ridiculed by her fellow workers and felt very hurt. Roles changed from her having been in a 'position of advantage in childhood and early youth to a position of disadvantage when it came to survival'. She had been taught Hebrew, and now tried to learn Yiddish in order to understand her co-workers.[17]

There were notable differences between individual employers in the ways they treated members of their labour force. Like Altmann, Apfelbaum too worked as a tailor in a 'shop' run by Alfred Rossner, making uniforms

Figure 8. Rossner workers' group, March 1941
Jewish workers employed as forced labourers making German uniforms at the Rossner factory, Będzin.
United States Holocaust Memorial Museum, courtesy of Yad Vashem Photo Archives.

for the German Army. They and many other survivors praised Rossner, on whom Yad Vashem posthumously awarded the honour of being named one of the Righteous among the Nations. Alfred Rossner was born in 1906, had pre-war connections with socialists, and had previously been employed in Berlin in the factory of a Polish Jew with whom he remained close friends. In Będzin he employed large numbers of Jews in his 'shop' making army uniforms and other clothing. The Rossner workshop was technically under the aegis of the Organisation Schmelt, but Rossner appears to have run it with a high degree of personal authority. Once deportations to Auschwitz were under way from May 1942, the special blue identity card, or *Sonderpass*, which was granted to Rossner workers provided protection not only for them but also for two other members of their families. Rossner also made frequent visits to Berlin to obtain confirmation that the production of uniforms in his factory was essential warwork, hence succeeding for over a year in protecting 'his' Jews in much the same way that the much better-known Oskar Schindler did. As Altmann recalled, Germans were 'the most bribable people' and 'on our behalf Rossner was doing the bribing'.[18] Moreover, Rossner had taken the trouble to learn Yiddish, and was able to communicate with his workers; contemporary documentary film footage shows him smiling benignly among a group of workers.[19]

Although Rossner undoubtedly profited from both cheap labour and substantial bribes, there is much evidence in the testimony of those affected that he was well-disposed and humane, with genuine concern for the fate of those Jews whose lives depended on his continued capacity to employ them. At the time of the final ghetto clearance in August 1943, Rossner underwent personal risks to rescue as many Jews as he could from the deportation trains and hide them in his premises; but in December 1943 Rossner too was arrested by the Gestapo and in 1944 died by hanging while in imprisonment—either as a result of suicide, as the official story had it, or killed by the Gestapo, as many Jews believed.

The unique system of forced labour under the control of the SS, known as the Organisation Schmelt, was of major significance in the area. It was named after SS Brigade-Führer Albrecht Schmelt, Police President of Breslau from 1934 to 1942, who in October 1940 took on the additional role of 'Special Commissary of the Reichsführer-SS for the Deployment of Foreign Labour' (*Sonderbeauftragter des Reichsführers-SS für den fremdvölkischen Arbeitseinsatz*) in Upper Silesia, with his headquarters in Sosnowiec. The Organisation Schmelt employed what one survivor, Arno Lustiger, described as 'tens of thousands of Jewish work-slaves'.[20] At one point, Schmelt controlled some 158 camps in Silesia and a further 19 in the Sudeten territories; by the time he left the area and removed his headquarters to Annaberg in September 1943, he had enriched not only the SS and the employers who profited from such cheap labour, but also his own coffers to the tune of some 100,000 Reichsmarks.[21] Some Jews were employed building autobahns and improving the infrastructure for military movements; some were employed making army uniforms and boots; others making ammunition; others making huge wooden crates or cases for transporting large bombs in freight trains across Europe. This level of production was key to the war effort in terms of both infrastructure and materiel; it came to an end only with the virtually complete annihilation of the Jewish community of Upper Silesia in the course of 1942–3.

The civilian administrators, including the *Landrat*, were closely involved in ensuring that the seizure of Jews as labourers for the SS should proceed smoothly; it was also made very clear to them what the penalties would be for any Jew seeking to evade a round-up. A letter from the Regional Government President, Springorum, on 21 November 1940 informed all the *Landräte* in his region of the new arrangements with respect to Schmelt and the Jews in their own districts. The Council of Elders of the Jewish Community was to provide lists of names of all Jews, male and female, capable of work and not already usefully employed; and the implementation of the new system would 'require the constant and energetic cooperation of all the local police forces'.[22] Springorum further warned that any Jews caught 'because of a breach of the duty to report' for work would be sent to a newly set up 'Jewish collection camp' (*Judensammellager*), located 'in the new Jewish school on Gleiwitz Road'.[23] Moreover, he was well aware of the potential conflicts this would cause for the Jewish Councils of Elders in the area, who were likely to be the target of considerable criticism within the Jewish community for cooperating with the Nazi administration in this way. Thus 'appropriate police measures' were necessary to ensure that the Jewish Councils were able to fulfil their task on behalf of the Germans.[24]

The Jewish Council was thus put in an extremely awkward situation—not helped by the personality of the man leading it, Moses Merin. As Henrietta Altmann put it, describing the Jewish Council, 'very soon it developed into an arm of the Gestapo'. When asked in what respect, she replied: 'Well, by giving them an order, tomorrow you have to provide me with 5,000 Jews.' Moreover, there was a 'disease of corruption—you could bribe people to exempt you'.[25]

The civilian administration of Będzin was not only party to cooperation with the Schmelt organization; it was also itself a direct employer of Jewish forced labour and well aware of the conditions under which such workers were deployed.[26] There was initially the worry that the Schmelt organization might drain away all available labour, but an arrangement was reached. As Klausa put it in his *Landrat*'s report of 29 November 1940:

> The danger exists that in the coming summer there will be neither Jewish nor Polish workers for communal work projects. Cooperation with the Special Representative for Jewish labour [Schmelt] is very good. After a first intensive discussion, all my requests for the reclamation of particular Jews who are indispensable for certain work purposes were granted.[27]

At this time, camps were constantly changing in character, with mixed inputs from local business, the regional and local administrations, and, later, Auschwitz. The camp at Lagischa, for example, situated around a mile and a half north of Będzin, was founded in 1941 for construction of the Upper Silesian Electricity Works. The firms 'Klotz' and 'Haga' from Będzin oversaw the construction works in Lagischa, under the guidance of the Kattowitz-based EVO (*Energieversorgung Oberschlesien*). The first part of the construction project was dedicated to building the slave labour camp, with double electric fences with barbed wire to contain the workers; Jewish slave labour from Będzin and surroundings was deployed for this purpose. Udo Klausa reports in his memoirs that one of his least onerous duties was to serve on the Supervisory Board (*Aufsichtsrat*) of the Upper Silesian Electricity Works, but he seems neither to have made a site visit nor noticed the deployment of Jewish slave labour in this area.[28] In 1943 the Lagischa camp became an official satellite camp (*Aussenlager*) of Auschwitz, with appalling conditions and virtually no food supplies (what food there was for the prisoners was driven over daily from Auschwitz), alongside much sadism on the part of the SS and brutal maltreatment and shooting of slave labourers.[29] By this time, of course, Udo Klausa had already left the area for the front.

Conditions in these camps varied, but at least for most people in the early period of German occupation there was some degree of communication possible between the workers in the camps and their families at home; many families knew roughly where their relatives had been taken, even if they could gain only veiled glimpses of the lives they were leading. Some families were able to maintain relatively frequent contacts between those members of the family who were in camps and those who remained at home. Hundreds of letters exchanged between Sala Garncarz, who survived seven labour camps, and her loved ones at home in Sosnowiec remarkably also survived, and provide compelling insights into the experiences and perceptions of this time. Sala's 18-year-old sister Raizel was in fact the one whom the Jewish Council had named to report, on 28 October 1940, for 'six weeks' of a labour camp, since the family was too poor to pay the 'head tax' that would have given them exemption.[30] But, at the age of 16, Sala offered herself in place of her frail and scholarly elder sister. Already on the train to camp, Sala began writing her diary, noting:

> My dearests! If you could have looked deep in my heart, you would have seen how desperate I was; still I tried to keep a smile on my face as best I could, though my eyes were filled with tears. One must go on bravely and courageously, even if the heart is breaking.[31]

But Sala was fortunate in one respect; already on the platform was an older woman, who, seeing her misery in last-minute separation from her mother, promised that she would take care of her. This older woman, who characteristically wore a smart hat at a jaunty angle, was called Ala Gertner. On 29 October 1940, the first day after their arrival at camp, Sala describes Ala Gertner thus:

Miss Ala also cheers us up, she is such a terrific and courageous girl. Even though she came from a wealthy home, she is able to adjust to present circumstances without fighting them; what's more, she is able to give us hope. Our dinner consisted of barley soup, which was less than tasty. Well, that too shall pass.[32]

Within one week at camp, when it came to the Sabbath and she could not mark it with her family, Sala was particularly devastated: 'I walked around like a lunatic for I had nobody to share my sorrow, nobody to console me as I cried my eyes out, finding it hard to breathe; it was stifling.' She was relieved when Ala returned to the barracks, although she could barely talk to her: 'I prefer to write such things down, since I don't know how to talk about such matters.'[33] Sala was fortunate enough at this time to share a bunk in the barracks with Ala, who comforted her frequently, as evidenced again and again in diary entries and letters home. Despite the support of her older friend and protector, and growing friendships with other workers, who included people she had known from home, Sala was unable to surmount the miseries of separation from her family and friends. She wrote on one occasion that:

The world is moaning, life is terrible, and there is much to lament. Is it any surprise that I am seeing people's misfortune, their sufferings and the injustices done to them? . . . there is a void around us.[34]

Separation on Fridays, missing the family as they marked the Sabbath, was always particularly hard for Sala.

The family at home also worried about Sala, and were explicitly delighted about the way in which Ala Gertner seemed to have taken a special interest in protecting and comforting her as best she could in the circumstances. But the family did not always receive the messages Sala sent through the official channels of the Jewish Council. As Sala's elder sister Raizel noted in one letter:

Now, dear Sala, we received the greetings you sent through friends. But Mr Merin and Mrs Fanny Czarna did not give us your regards. We were very upset at how they behaved, since you wrote that we should receive greetings through them.[35]

But the exchanges of letters more often give us glimpses of mutual concern than full descriptions of conditions: even apart from the possibility of censorship and unduly critical letters not getting through, neither side wanted to worry the other side unduly.

Survivors often paint a more general, frequently brutal, picture of conditions over lengthier periods of time. Morris Danziger, for example, was first sent to a camp at Ottmuth, where he was put to work on constructing autobahn highways or railroad tracks. Despite having too little to eat, and feeling unwell, he remembers that he never complained about ill-health, but pushed himself to work without stopping. After about six months he was sent to another camp in Upper Silesia, which he describes simply as 'a very bad place'. Here, he was engaged in road construction. Every day, he had to walk 10 miles each way to work on the job, which consisted of hard labour pushing trucks through the mud. He often arrived drenched, having to work in wet clothes, wearing the same rags every day, and working from six in the morning until four in the afternoon, when he walked back to the camp. Here, there was not much to eat, 'then sleep, that's it'. He was with around twenty workers for about four or five months in this place, then was sent to Blechhammer. Here, he not only received brutal treatment himself, but was also forced to witness 'doctors' injecting air into prisoners' veins so that they would die; his job was to hold the candles while the doctors did this. He feared the same would eventually happen to him. Other brutalities included a prisoner being buried up to his neck because he had 'stolen' some potato peelings. The following morning this prisoner was taken to the washroom, where he was hosed down with water and then killed.[36]

Once labour groups such as those for the Reich Autobahn construction were taken over by the Schmelt organization, many Jews became effectively slave labour with neither wages nor adequate provisions, living under unsanitary and brutal conditions. Moreover, from the autumn of 1941 onwards periodic 'selections' took place in these camps, so that anyone found unfit for work would be sent to Auschwitz to be murdered. The most important of the Schmelt camps became, in 1943, part of the extensive network of satellite camps under the overall administration of Auschwitz and Groß-Rosen. But the use of forced labour, where workers were held under appalling conditions, seems to have been acceptable well beyond the ranks of the SS. And, despite the fact that workers were technically within the borders of the Third Reich, it has been suggested that conditions in these camps, which ranged in size from between 100 to over 1,000 workers, were more comparable to conditions in the General Government than to other labour camps in the Reich. Those who were employed in their home towns (although often no longer living in their own homes) at least had the benefit of being close to family, friends, and relatives. But they were no longer in control of their own businesses, means of livelihood, or conditions of work; and there was an immediate and radical reduction in their quality of life, in just about every respect.[37]

Klausa must have been well aware of the conditions of forced labour, given that the municipal authorities were a major employer of Jewish workers living in the locality. He may barely have registered the character of forced labour for the Electricity Works, but he was himself directly responsible for one forced labour camp and could not have avoided registering conditions at this camp. The civilian administration, on a very small scale by comparison with the SS, was involved in the running of a labour camp for railway line construction in the Golonog area of the *Landkreis* of Będzin. Here, some 300 Jewish workers were held against their will, guarded by a combination of police officers, members of the SA, and the local gendarmerie, under the overall control of the latter, who reported directly to the *Landrat*. Conditions in the camp were made clear in a report from Heinrich Mentgen, head of the Będzin gendarmerie, to Udo Klausa as *Landrat*:

> The camp is still without drinking water. The wash barracks is still being built. Sanitary and toilet facilities are available . . . The Jews deployed here remain under constant guard. The camp is surrounded by a high wire fence to prevent anyone from escaping.[38]

We are talking here about 'only' 300 people being held in conditions that even Mentgen conceded were not as yet in a fit state for human habitation: 300 human beings enclosed and constantly guarded, forced to remain and to work against their will. One of the survivors of this camp reported, shortly after the war, on the appalling conditions in which he had lived and worked, describing how Jews had been held together in primitive barracks, for a long time with no cooking equipment or facilities and very little to eat—small portions of bread, margarine and bitter black coffee, supplemented by a watery soup—and forced to do hard labour on railroad construction for eleven hours a day, from six in the morning until five in the evening.[39]

Mentgen's report came in at a time when Klausa was perhaps feeling ever less comfortable in the role of *Landrat*.[40] But the existence of this labour camp and the role of the gendarmerie in guarding the inmates and overseeing the operations do not find a place in his memoirs. Nor does this appear to have affected his view of Mentgen as an inherently 'decent' police official who would not tolerate any excess or transgression.[41] Again, overseeing a small camp of forced labourers was clearly just a routine part of what, in the Third Reich, was deemed to be 'only administration'.

Arrests and deportations

Będzin Jews tried very hard to gain employment in one of the Rossner shops, and to avoid being arrested and deported to forced labour camps elsewhere. Later, it would turn out that at least a few of those who had gone to labour camps far away from the area had, in the end, higher chances of survival than those who stayed and were eventually sent straight to Auschwitz, as Rosa Rechnic pointed out:

> The poorest and least affluent people went first to the *Arbeitslager* [work camps], which turned out to be a blessing in disguise, and those that had connections and position remained till the very end. As a result of that they went to Auschwitz.[42]

But for the first couple of years of Nazi occupation, fear of 'raids' and being taken away from home plagued and overshadowed every day and night.

Wherever they were working—whether for private entrepreneurs, the army, the Schmelt organization, or the civilian administration—Jews were essentially viewed as movable pawns to be seized and deployed in whichever way it suited the Germans to exploit their labour. Jews of working age were never safe from the possibility of sudden arrest and deportation. The precise numbers and moments of likely arrest were somewhat unpredictable.

There were many small 'actions', in which groups were rounded up and sent first to the 'transit camps' (*Durchgangslager*) or 'Dulags' in Sosnowiec and Będzin. From there, they might either be destined for forced labour service or, if they had been arrested for some offence, sent to the nearby concentration camp of Auschwitz. Survivors recall almost weekly deportations to Auschwitz of groups who had been held first in the orphanage near the railway station.[43] For two years or so, Auschwitz was 'merely' a traditional concentration camp: a place for the concentration of forced labour, with high death rates from starvation, disease, torture, or being put to death for some alleged 'offence'. 'Auschwitz' functioned not even as an 'open secret', but rather as an explicit threat, alongside hangings and other public forms of severe punishment.

On 1 March 1941 the SS leader Heinrich Himmler carried out his first inspection of Auschwitz. He was accompanied not only by the Higher SS and Police Leader (*Höhere SS- und Polizeiführer* (*HSSPF*)) Erich von dem Bach-Zelewski, but also by the *Gauleiter* and Governor of Upper Silesia, Fritz Bracht, the Kattowitz Regional Governor—and Klausa's immediate superior—Walter Springorum, as well as representatives of the major chemicals production concern, I. G. Farben.[44] The regional civilian administration, including the 'decent' Springorum, was thus as fully informed of ongoing developments as were the industrialists who so massively developed the site for exploitation of slave labour in this area.

The fear of being arrested and taken away was ever present. Elias Burstyn felt that he and other Jews were never safe on the streets, even if they observed the regulations about areas that were out of bounds, and curfew times, because people were always being picked up and taken away; so 'we had to hide'.[45] Abraham Froch too remembered constantly having to hide to avoid round-ups: people would be picked up from their apartments at night, or rounded up in the street and simply taken away to labour camps.[46] Rosa Rechnic commented that, 'from the very beginning, they were catching people in the street'. These people were sent to work camps, which at that time were much feared.[47] Meanwhile, those with more resources managed to hide, evade round-ups and selections, or bribe their way out.

The official figures bear out these memories of repeated round-ups. On 19 March 1941, for example, 775 Jews were arrested and taken to the 'Dulag' in Sosnowiec; on 24 March 931 Jews in the town of Będzin were arrested and taken to the Dulag; on 25 March a further 35 were caught; on 28 March the figure was 183 Jews; but on 1 April 1941, by contrast, the search for Jews 'fit for work' had failed and 'there were no successful arrests of Jews'.[48] On 21 April, 378 Jews were arrested and taken to the Dulag; the report comments laconically that, 'apart from shooting the Jew Holländer, there were no incidents'.[49]

Poles too were subject to sudden arrest and deportation as forced labourers, generally to the 'Old Reich', including the industrial heartland of the Ruhr area. In the course of May 1941, for example, round-ups varied with figures of 600, 578, 1,000, 802, 900, and 252 Polish labourers being arrested and sent off as forced labourers to Germany.[50] Conditions in the Dulag in

Sosnowiec were dreadful, but for those arrested for forced labour only temporary; they were relatively quickly moved on to one of the numerous labour camps in the vicinity, dotted all around the extended sphere of interest of the SS in Eastern Upper Silesia.

Details of instructions and arrests varied slightly. On 4 November 1941 Alexander von Woedtke, the Police President of Sosnowiec, issued a very precise order to members of his police force, requesting the arrests of 'only the named Jews and no substitutes'.[51] These 'named Jews' were presumably being specifically arrested for alleged offences. The following day, there was to be a far larger round-up of Jewish women to be sent to work as slave labourers in the Old Reich: on this occasion, the instructions were still very precise, but the remit slightly broader. Only those women were to be rounded up who did not hold one of the special coloured work ID cards, were not visibly old or too ill to work, and did not have children. Von Woedtke's order of 4 November 1941 to his police forces instructed them to exclude 'Jewesses who hold a blue, green, pink or yellow identity card' from the Schmelt organization; 'married or single Jewesses with children' and 'Jewesses who are visibly ill or physically disabled'.[52] Ironically, because of the relative 'protection' given to women with dependent children at this time, some women thought it would help to save them if they could become pregnant. The following year, it was precisely such women with babies who were among the first, along with the elderly and the ill, to be selected for instant death, while those deemed sufficiently able-bodied to be exploitable as slave labour were still among the 'saved'.

On 7 November 1941, there was a fairly damning police report on the lack of success of this 'action'. Only 349 women of the 1,600 on the list had actually been arrested. The police forces had not been able to locate the other 1,251 women, who had successfully managed to hide during the course of the 'action'. In the words of the report, this was because they had got wind of the planned arrests and had hidden in all manner of places, including with Polish families: 'the Jewesses sought out every conceivable nook and cranny in which to hide' and also 'found hideouts with Poles'. The attempt at arresting Jews in Będzin the previous day had had exactly the same outcome. The Police President in Sosnowiec drew the relevant lessons from these experiences:

> An obviously limited success, as yesterday, can be very detrimental to the authority of the state and the German police.

Therefore measures are required that will from the outset ensure the full success of special actions.[53]

Future round-ups were to be carried out with less advance warning, and more ruthlessly.

Rations and food supplies

Work was essential to survival; but it was also insufficient for survival. The problems of hunger and difficulties with obtaining adequate amounts of food were compounded by the risks and penalties associated with attempts to obtain enough to eat by means that had become, as a result of Nazi policies, now not only illicit but extremely dangerous.

Klausa as *Landrat* was responsible for overseeing and reporting on the situation with respect to food supplies in the area. In his memoirs, and indeed in the archival evidence too, there is evidence of pride at his achievement in finding strategies of increasing agricultural production and delivery of, for example, eggs; there are also suggestions about the ways in which reorganization and new strategies might work to improve the food supply. All this, however, was in a context where there were several classes of citizens: not merely Germans, Poles, Jews, but those who had enough to eat in order to survive and those who did not, unless they resorted to more desperate and now illegal measures.

Jews were severely restricted in what they could buy. Ration cards were distributed according to 'racial' categories. Poles received more than Jews; but even so the allotted rations for Poles were well below standards required for health and maintenance of weight and labour productivity—the latter being of most concern to the Germans.[54] Those Jews who did heavy labour or important work received a better ration card allowance than those who did light work or no work. Potatoes and vegetables predominated on Jewish ration cards.[55] Germans received the best rations—a reason why some local people were tempted to claim German ancestry, as a report from Czeladź noted:

The ethnic Germans here are all very happy that, compared to the Poles and Jews, they receive privileged treatment with respect to the distribution of rations, because in contrast to these they receive the Reich ration cards. The conjecture that this is the only reason why many of the ethnic Germans professed themselves to be German cannot be dismissed out of hand.[56]

The rations allotted to working Jews in this area were better than those in the ghettos of Łódź and Warsaw, where death by starvation was a daily occurrence, in massive numbers. Photographs and film footage of the Warsaw ghetto show corpses lying in the streets or being carried away on carts to be tipped into mass graves, people shivering and huddling against walls, children of uncertain age with apparently enormous heads and stick thin, bony legs and bodies staring apathetically into space; the death tolls were horrendous, and the smuggling in of potato peelings or a piece of bread could make all the difference between living or dying between one day and the next. This was not the appearance or experience of the Jews of Będzin: the workforce of Upper Silesia was for the most part being fed just enough to sustain at least partially productive labour in the vast network of labour camps and 'shops'. But the fact that they were not dying daily in large numbers of starvation and diseases exacerbated by malnutrition should not blind us to their suffering from hunger.

Abraham Kimmelmann, interviewed while in a Displaced Persons camp in 1946 by the American scholar Dr David Boder, recalled the difficulties in great detail:

> It was forced labour. It was without pay. They did not pay. Later they paid 1 mark 70 per day for the work of eight or even ten hours. But you can imagine, what could one buy for 1 mark 70. Or what could one purchase for it?... That would be all right, 250 grams of bread would be enough, but if one gets only bread, if one can't get potatoes or corn flour, and no fat; can one live on 250 grams daily? People had to support each other and help out each other. It is just impossible to be starving. When a person is hungry he is ready to do anything. So what could he do? One looked for somebody who would bring in bread on the black [market] or flour and one paid more, and in order to pay more one needs money and so 1 mark 75 wasn't enough.[57]

Other survivors, interviewed at a much later stage in their lives, often clearly remember suffering from hunger but cannot recall how they obtained food or even, in some cases, what it was they had to eat.

Helen Balsam, a child of 12 at the time of the Nazi invasion, remembered the difficulties. Even though her mother brought home food, it was insufficient. Their family had no real contacts with Polish people, and were unable to obtain additional foodstuffs through personal acquaintances.[58] Henrietta Altmann recalls having needed 'vouchers', obtained from the *Judenrat*, for food.[59] Samuel Bradin remembers that the main issue was food:

'everyone was fighting for survival'; a loaf of bread or a potato was one of the most valuable things in life.[60]

Gunter Faerber could not actually remember what food they had eaten in the ghetto: 'I remember what we had in the concentration camp but not what we had in the ghetto.' Clearly his memories of later starvation rations outweighed his memories of what he had obtained to eat while in Będzin, although he could recall particular strategies of survival at that time. His family originally came from Lipiny, Świętochłowice, to the north-west of Kattowitz, in the ethnically mixed border territories that had been the subject of Polish–German disputes after the First World War. Faerber's wider family included ethnic Germans, some partially Jewish cousins, and Jewish relatives who were protected from Nazi persecution because they lived in mixed marriages.[61] Having been deported from their home in Chorzów to Będzin with the ethnic 'cleansing' of the areas west of the police border, Gunter Faerber's family was moved around and lodged in different houses, ending up in the ghetto area across the railway tracks; Faerber was set to

Figure 9. A food store in the Będzin ghetto, 1939–43
Vendors selling food at an outside market in the ghetto.
United States Holocaust Memorial Museum, courtesy of Beit Lohamei Haghetaot.

work in a factory making utensils, formerly under Jewish ownership but confiscated by the Germans. Although not being local had not helped with the housing situation, this and the mixed family background now came in useful as far as food was concerned. First of all, Faerber managed to obtain Polish food coupons on the black market via his Jewish grandmother, who was still living on the western side of the police border; and, secondly, he ran only a limited risk of being recognized when he took off his Jewish star and tried to buy food in Polish shops. On one occasion when he was in a Polish shop, as he recalled, the man behind him in the shop either knew him, or pretended to recognize him, and shouted out to the shopkeeper:

> 'You mustn't serve him, he's a Jew!' But I poo-pooed it of course and I didn't look Jewish and I spoke German fluently, better than the shopkeepers did, better than the Poles, so they accepted it and they sold me the bread and let me go.[62]

He was lucky, too, that he had always spoken German with his parents and with their friends, but Polish with his own friends.

Locals had a far greater potential problem with being recognized. On one occasion Helen Balsam tried to obtain additional food by going into a Polish shop to buy groceries that were forbidden to Jews, and very nearly succeeded, being blonde and blue-eyed and not obviously of stereotypical Jewish appearance. However, a Polish woman in the shop recognized her 'and said this is a Jewish girl, she shouldn't be here'. As Balsam commented: 'That was the only time I went and I had that experience and I didn't go again.'[63] The difficulties with being recognized in shops by their former Polish friends and neighbours were ever present, although some were more successful than others in passing off as non-Jewish.

Other means of obtaining additional food included purchasing food at extortionate process from local farmers. In the summary of a survivor, Mordecai Lichtenstein: 'The weekly rations allotted to Jews were very small... People who had not the means to buy extra food from farmers could not exist on these rations.'[64] Those formerly well-to-do Jews who had followed German orders to hand over all their wealth—gold, silver, money reserves—found themselves unable to make the extra purchases necessary to sustain life through black market purchases. So the formerly well-to-do Jews faced a choice between two evils, as Abraham Kimmelmann, aged 12 at the time of the Nazi invasion, remembers:

> If one was very much afraid, and he could not hide the things, so he surrendered them. But if one was more adventurous and wanted to take chances, then he hid it.

And on that depended the life of people. Because if one had no money one could die from starvation.[65]

Others had not had additional means in the first place, or what they had by way of spare wealth was soon used up in the battle to survive. Those who sought to survive by dealing on the black market, or by altering their ration cards in the attempt to get a scrap more to eat, faced appalling consequences if they were caught.

Retributions

Radically reduced rations on which alone it was impossible to survive, brutal treatment for seeking to find sufficient food to stay alive, and shooting on the spot for 'slacking' or any apparent infringements of rules, were everyday experiences in Będzin under Nazi occupation. Even infringements of minor rules, or simply being somehow in the way, or out of place, could potentially bring deadly consequences.

Many smaller arrests, of groups ranging from a handful to a few dozen people, were for minor 'offences'. These included Jews being out at night after curfew, being found in areas or on roads where Jews were not permitted, being found without identity papers or with the wrong ID cards. Jews from the General Government and the Warthegau, who had witnessed the increasingly horrendous conditions of enforced starvation in the ghettos of Warsaw and Łódź, often sought to escape or return to Eastern Upper Silesia, having heard that working conditions and rationing levels were somewhat better in this area. But this was risky: they too were subject to automatic arrest, imprisonment, and deportation if caught. On 26 February 1942 Rudolf Mildner, at that time Head of the Gestapo in Kattowitz and head of the Political Department (Camp-Gestapo) in Auschwitz, sent a circular concerning such 'illegal' Jews, entitled 'The illegal immigration or return of Jews from the General Government and the occupied part of Russia'. Mildner had noticed 'that in recent times a large number of Jews have illegally entered or returned to this area of responsibility from the General Government and the occupied parts of Russia'.[66] But they could not get ration cards without getting illegal papers; so a crackdown on forgeries and card swindling would ensure either starvation or capture.

Often those rounded up for deportation were held briefly in the former Jewish orphanage—of which Cyrele Schein had been a benefactress—since it was situated conveniently close to the main railway station of Będzin, directly on the railway tracks to Auschwitz. This was referred to at the time as a transit camp, or 'Dulag'.[67] Miriam Liwer (née Kaminer), who had been born in Będzin in 1905, described these smaller 'actions':

> I knew of these actions because I worked in the kitchen of the orphanage. Particularly those Jews were collected up in the orphanage who had illegally come to Bendsburg from the General Government. These people were then loaded onto trucks, weekly, and taken to Auschwitz. These actions were always led by the Gestapo man Kat.[68]

These 'smaller actions' often served to punish by death those who had thought they had escaped precisely that fate by illegally crossing the border to get out of the General Government, as well as many others arrested for minor transgressions of the highly restrictive rules—traffic regulations, curfew times, area boundaries, rationing rules—imposed on them by the German occupation authorities. Just after the war ended, Mordecai Lichtenstein summed up his experiences in this period:

> Anyone breaking the regulations was ruthlessly dealt with, e.g. anyone crossing the road not at the prescribed angle, or having even the smallest quantity of provisions not allotted by the ration scheme, had to report to the police. That meant 'Aussiedlung' (deportation)...[69]

Szalom Herzberg remembered that Jews would be arrested for 'minor offences, such as not wearing armbands, entering the areas reserved for people of Aryan descent without permission' and even for illegally 'buying or selling bread'. They would be held in the orphanage, 'from which transports of Jews were continually going to Auschwitz'.[70]

Klausa, living in the house formerly owned by the Schein family, had a daily walk to his office along the road on the other side of the railway line from the orphanage. The railway line, and the end of the station platform, could not have been more than around 100 yards from the *Landrat*'s house. These incidents, even the very existence of the orphanage, found no place in his memoirs.

Violence could be exercised entirely unexpectedly, randomly, and from totally unknown quarters; potential victims were never safe, even when engaged on entirely harmless and permitted pursuits. The testimonies of survivors, who gave evidence in the early 1960s, are full of examples of brutality: again and again and again they report on individual incidents of violence. Miriam Liwer, for example, gives a graphic description of a baby being ripped away from its mother's breast, held up by the legs and bashed against the wall, at which point she saw how 'the skull of the tiny baby shattered and its brains flowed out onto the floor', in full view of its mother.[71] Arno Lustiger recalls that his uncle, who was employed on road-building, was sitting at the road side eating lunch one day, during the allotted lunch break, next to his good friend Max; for no apparent reason, Max was suddenly shot dead on the spot.[72]

Everyday humiliation accompanied the system of repression; failure to play one's allotted part in repeated incidents of degradation could bring about horrendous acts of reprisal. As Arno Lustiger recalls:

> I remember a scene on the main street of Będzin, Malachowska Street. The District Leader of the *NSDAP* had taken up his quarters in the villa of a rich Jewish industrialist. I saw how his son, a little Hitler Youth in uniform, pulled at the beards and hit passers-by, particularly elderly Jews. No one dared to intervene against him. In this sort of a situation one could only clench one's fist in a trouser pocket. Had a single hair of the boy been ruffled, the Nazis would probably have had the whole family transported to Auschwitz.[73]

These incidents of petty terrorization on the part of an 11-year-old boy on Będzin's high street were so frequent that they were even captured in the drawings of an artist, Ella Liebermann-Shiber.[74] Born in Berlin, like other Jews of even only half Polish descent, she and her parents had been expelled from Germany in November 1938 and settled in her mother's home town of Będzin. A teenager at the time, she subsequently survived Auschwitz and settled in Israel, and shortly after liberation began through the medium of art to try to work through her traumatic experiences and express the emotional enormity of what she had witnessed.

From very early on both Jews and Poles in the local population were well aware of the meaning of arrests and deportations. Not only were they terrified of being arrested for fear of what might happen; the German authorities generally made little or no attempt to disguise the consequences of arrest, and used the threat of Auschwitz as a means of terrorizing the people, Polish as well as Jewish. Moreover, when local Polish people provided assistance in Jews' attempts to hide, they knew not only that they were at risk of arrest and of the death penalty, but that their whole family would be subjected to similar penalties if any one of them were caught helping a Jew.

This acted as a massive deterrent; many survivors report only short periods during which a member of a Polish family would help or hide them, for fear of the potential consequences if caught.

Poles who had been involved in black market dealing, or illegal slaughtering of animals for meat, or refusing to be sent to forced labour, were liable to arrest. Here, the gendarmerie were often involved, particularly when the individuals in question lived in the small villages and hamlets of the *Landkreis* that were not under the overall control of the Police President in Sosnowiec. The experiences could be appalling for those concerned. Many suicides among Poles were related to fear of the consequences of arrest. On 24 January 1941, for example, the butcher Stanislaw S. was found hanged in the gendarmerie prison cell of Wojkowitz-Koscilene, having been arrested for illegal slaughtering; a similar fate soon befell Stefan W., who was found hanging in the prison cell of Gendarmerie-Posten Wojkowice Komorne, having been arrested for selling meat on the black market.[75] Ignać D. had been sent by the Będzin Labour Office (*Arbeitsamt*) to forced labour in Salzgitter on 8 May 1940. Following a brief holiday at his home in the village of Grodziec, he refused to return to Salzgitter, and by late November 1940 was terrified of the potential consequences. His daughter Danuta, in her testimony following his suicide on 27 November 1940, explained what had happened that morning, when her mother had gone out to do the washing:

> My father said to me, I should go out with him because he was frightened of the gendarmerie, since they would certainly be searching for him because of his refusal to work. At home he was very worked up and this settled a bit once I was outside with him.[76]

Later that day he was found hanged. Peter K. committed suicide on 6 September 1943 'in part because of fear of punishment'. He had been interrogated on 2 August 1943 because he had 'allegedly in secret given an English prisoner of war in the mine foodstuffs (eggs, bread, cherries etc.) and was therefore interrogated. Since this time he has been depressed.'[77]

There were also public hangings of Poles by the Germans. On 12 June 1942, for example, more than ten Poles who worked in the Bankowa-Hütte were hanged for alleged sabotage and political activity. The execution took place at four o'clock in the afternoon, and the victims were left hanging until nine in the evening; their relatives were forced to watch. Andrzej Krol, the son of one of the men who was hanged, recalled that a 'German wearing

Figure 10. A public hanging of Poles in Sosnowiec, 1939–41
Civilian spectators and German police look on during the hanging of ten Poles in Sosnowiec.
United States Holocaust Memorial Museum, courtesy of YIVO Institute for Jewish Research.

civilian clothes' read out the verdict, to the effect that the victims were being sentenced for politics and sabotage. The men had been arrested at different times, but were brought together for the collective hanging. Marianne Krol, the wife of one victim, recalls that he was arrested on 28 April 1942; Leon Maro, the son of another, remembered his father being arrested around one month earlier than this; Aniele Gruchala, wife of another victim, says he was arrested on 16 May for having allegedly 'printed brochures and leaflets, inciting people to sabotage and reading illegal newspapers'.[78] In another hanging, eleven Poles were hanged in 'reprisal' for the killing of a German gendarme. Udo Klausa's name, in his capacity as *Landrat* of Będzin, appeared as the official signatory on the public announcements of these hangings. But in the Ludwigsburg interrogations he was able to claim that he was absent from the area at the respective times: he 'had not given instructions for the killings and therefore knew nothing about these incidents'.[79] It is quite likely that the name of the *Landrat* would appear automatically on the posters that went up announcing such public spectacles, with little or no personal intervention required by the *Landrat* himself. It is also possible that his association in his official capacity with these acts was yet another aspect of the situation that Klausa, in the spring and early summer of 1942, appears to have been finding increasingly distasteful; but, incapacitated by vague symptoms of ill-health and 'nerves', he had as yet little idea of how to get away from it without jeopardizing both his own career and his family's situation.

For Jews, taking measures to evade a slow death by starvation—dealing illegally in foodstuffs or ration cards—often meant a far more rapid death by summary execution. There appear to have been relatively frequent public hangings as punishment, which large numbers of people were forced to attend and watch as a warning. These hangings were sometimes held in the marketplace, frequently also in the Jewish cemetery of Będzin. Often the bodies were left up hanging for hours after the event in order to achieve maximum impact on members of the community, including their own family and friends.

Memories of hangings in the Będzin area are reported again and again in the testimonies taken in conjunction with war crimes investigations in the early and mid-1970s. Witnesses generally agree that the reason given for the hanging of Jews had to do with illicit use of ration cards or dealing in foodstuffs on the black market; but they differ considerably with respect both to the remembered date of the hanging, and the numbers of people who were executed, ranging from just two to as many as five or six. Aharon Feldberg (born 1920), for example, recalled that he was 'once a witness to the hanging of three Jewish men in the old Jewish cemetery in Bendzin. They had supposedly traded in ration cards.'[80] Jakob Muszynski (born 1921), following a discussion of the major selections of 1942 and 1943, added:

> Between these actions I have described there were many smaller actions... For example, I remember that once at the old Jewish cemetery several people were hanged, because they had allegedly forged or sold ration cards. This hanging I watched myself. It was carried out by the police in Bendsburg.[81]

Wolf Zawader (born 1901) mentioned the hanging of Jews 'at the cemetery on the Sarwalle [*sic*] Street because they had been involved in black market dealings'; although he could not recall the exact date, he thought it was 'around 1942'.[82] Dow Isachar Zalmanowicz (born 1925) also recalled 'a hanging of four Jews, who, on the orders of the Germans, were hanged in the old Jewish cemetery, supposedly because they had been involved in the black market'.[83] Ischak Muszinski (born 1899) remembered that he 'witnessed the hanging of two Jews . . . because they had been dealing in ration cards'.[84] Sonia Strochlitz (née Pfeffer, born 1928) similarly remembered witnessing a hanging, which she thought perhaps took place in 1941; she could not recall having had any idea, as a child of around 13 at the time, why the hanging was taking place.[85] Szmuel Krystal (born 1922) also mentioned a hanging, thinking it was in 1941.[86] David Auerbach (born 1925) saw in 1941 'how in the neighbourhood of the first Jewish cemetery in Bendzin 5 or 6 Jews were hanged'.[87] Chaim Michal Silberberg (born 1900) also remembered a hanging, which he vaguely dated to 1941.[88] Abram Skoczylas (born 1915), remembered the hanging of Jews by the name of Stern and Scheinemann—several witnesses name these individuals—and thought it was 'at the end of 1941 or the start of 1942'.[89] This particular hanging, which in fact took place in April 1942, just one month before the first major deportation, was perhaps significant as a signal; we shall return to it below.[90]

Survivors also gave slightly differing answers when offered a list of names and asked which individuals they could remember. They rarely knew the names of individuals with broader responsibility for developments, whom they did not have occasion to meet in person. David Auerbach commented only that 'who was responsible for these killings is beyond my knowledge'.[91] Aharon Feldberg commented that, while having no idea who was responsible for the hangings: 'I can only remember that before the hanging a German read something out to the effect that the Jews were impudent [*frech*] and were therefore being exterminated.'[92] The people survivors best remembered were those with whom they had personal and often physically violent encounters. Auerbach remembered particularly the 'leader of the gendarmerie of Bendzburg [*sic*] Mentgen' as one of the most violent, alongside Dörfler. In addition:

> The most notorious German was the member of the uniformed police Mitschke. He was about 30 years old, had a round face and blue eyes, was of medium height and dark blond and had a brutal facial expression. Of him it was reported that he had killed many Jews. He beat me so hard that I can still barely hear out of my left ear . . . Further, I know the member of the uniformed police Wolf. He was a dog handler and I myself saw how he set his dog on Jews, and how the dog then tore out pieces of flesh from people. He was the second Mitschke.[93]

Jakob Muszynski testified:

I remember Mitschke and Doerfler, who, so I heard, is supposed to have shot Jewish people. The same is true for Seidel and Wolf. I can also remember the leader of the police forces Abesser... I also remember the name of the Landrat Klausa. I saw him personally at many smaller actions.[94]

Ischak Muszinski remembered 'apart from Baucke [the Gestapo chief] the names: Dörfler, Nowak, Mitschke, Wolf, Ertel, and the Landrat Klausa'.[95] These two are the only ones who specifically mention having seen the *Landrat*, Udo Klausa, present at violent 'actions'. Even during those periods when he had not 'disappeared' to the army, Klausa was clearly not a highly visible or notable physical presence on the streets of Będzin, at least as far as survivor memories and perceptions are concerned.

There were comparable hangings in the neighbouring district of Olkusz (Ilkenau). Israel Zukermann (born 1913) remembered witnessing in 1941 or 1942 the hanging in Olkusz of 'three or four' people. 'It was said that they had, without permission, several sausages with them. Among the hanged were Gleitner, Matzner and Pinkus.'[96] Rubin Apelstein (born 1925), also recalls a hanging in Olkusz:

I remember too that, around 1941, three Jewish men were hanged in the market-place in Olkusz on the orders of the Germans, because they had allegedly been involved in black market dealings. The Jewish population in Olkusz had to come and watch this hanging. Who was responsible for ordering this hanging is beyond my knowledge.[97]

It is possible that these memories of a hanging in Olkusz in fact were part of a well-coordinated series of hangings, alongside the public hangings of April 1942 carried out simultaneously in Sosnowiec and Będzin, and at the same time in a number of other locations in the run-up to major deportations to extermination centres.[98]

The rapid imposition of the death penalty for minor infringements of German rules, without great public fanfare and staging, was, however, a frequent and regular occurrence. It is hardly surprising that there were so many memories of executions and other forms of humiliation and 'punishment'. Public acts of terrorization as a means of demonstrating what was beyond the boundaries of the 'moral' universe of the Nazi 'people's community' were repeated weapons in the Nazi arsenal, and this against anyone—including Poles and even those categorized as ethnic Germans—

who did not fit in with the new norms of the Nazi 'people's community'. They were ritual acts intended to underline the boundaries of acceptable behaviour, and to drive home by public display the penalties for transgression.

Even a cursory survey of local newspapers shows up reports of several death sentences within a week or so of each other. The *Oberschlesische Zeitung* was only too keen to report incidents of capital punishment, with—given its readership—a particular emphasis on 'ethnic comrades' (*Volksgenossen*) who had 'chosen' to put themselves outside the 'moral universe' of the German 'racial community', and on unacceptable behaviour (including resistance) among Poles, rather than on actions against Jews. The *Oberschlesische Zeitung*, for example, reported the following events within the space of two or three weeks in the early autumn of 1942. Just after a large article on 'The Warsaw of Today: A New Heimat for Thousands of Germans', there was a piece on a 'Polish horse thief' who was 'shot while trying to escape'.[99] Several issues had short notices on people who had been 'executed for black market dealings' or for hiding 'bandits', including the case of five women from Janow, aged between 29 and 50, who had hidden two people and their 'booty'. Two were sentenced to death, and two to imprisonment.[100] Two days later, it was reported that a 27-year old man had been sentenced to death for stealing. He was German but 'in the justification for the sentence the judge explained that W. had himself, through his extensive deeds, excluded himself from the people's community [*Volksgemeinschaft*]'.[101] The following Tuesday, seven people were sentenced, some to death, for 'forbidden slaughtering' (*Schwarzschlachtungen*) of animals for meat.[102] On the Friday of the following week, it was reported that a man aged 35 had been put to death as a 'spy'.[103] Death was ubiquitous for those who did not conform to the rules of Nazi occupation.

What was perhaps distinctive about the public hangings of Jews was that members of the Jewish community were forced to come out and witness them in large numbers. They were thus not merely used as a reactive 'punishment' of an individual for a specific offence, but were carefully designed and prepared in advance, irrespective of the alleged deeds of those to be hanged, as a form of collective warning to the entire Jewish community.[104] Ritual humiliation and terrorization were as significant as retribution in the extraordinary measures to which the Jewish population of the area were subjected.

Self-preservation and resistance

Despite the daily experience of misery, hunger, and degradation, attempts were made by the Jewish victims of Nazi policies to deal with the situation as best they could, as they sought both survival strategies for the present and possible ways to escape or oppose these intolerable conditions. But it increasingly became clear that such strategies would be met with massive and public force. Few at first realized where it would ultimately end.

Many Jews appear to have thought this was the worst it could get, and that the war would be short; they sought to try to make the best of the new circumstances. For a while, as Abraham Kimmelmann put it, people 'began to manage in various ways', even if not all were successful:

> One would do business on the black, others would work overtime, people would simply risk their lives somehow to get through, and those who could not do it, who did not have enough courage or were too much afraid, these had to starve. And so many went caput [*sic*], died right before me... Sometimes we played cards. We still laughed. It wasn't yet so noticeable. People had still some money from before the war and so people could manage somehow.[105]

For some two years after the German occupation had begun, no one imagined quite what would develop in terms of Nazi policies of extermination. It was more a matter of trying to get through until there was some improvement.

Josef Baumgarten, who had three brothers and three sisters, recalled that his family initially talked about leaving Będzin, but they did not have enough money to buy tickets: 'because it takes money to get out... we just didn't have the money'. So their philosophy was: 'just see what's going to happen, just try to survive day by day...'. His father had owned a tailor's shop, but the Germans sought 'to liquidate all the Jewish stores, take everything out'. They were then moved out of their home: 'about 1940 they took us, my parents and my sisters and brothers to a ghetto'. A 14-year-old at the time, he was put to work in a factory. He remembered first having to wear a star on his left arm, and later having a star sewn onto his clothes that could not be removed. After that it was 'hard to get along in this city because they noticed it... that you are a Jew'. On one occasion, there was an incident where he was threatened with a 'gun in my head'. He was fortunate on this occasion to have been able to escape; he ran home crying, and the memory of the fear remained with him all his life. Later 'they took my parents away, we didn't know where or what, they went to a camp . . .'. Then 'a year later they came in again they took myself and two brothers . . . my sister was already in Birkenau . . .'.[106]

Wherever they ended up working, the loss of livelihood and the threat not merely to economic status but also to the sense of self and self-respect was a major blow to many adults. Terror, panic, and a fear of abandonment were also common experiences among younger Jews, whose parents or older siblings had been drafted into the local labour force, or deported to forced labour camps elsewhere.

Premature responsibility for care of the household was then often thrust onto even very young children. Mindzia Schickman, whose mother had been deported to a work camp when she was still only 8 years old, within a year found herself almost solely in charge of the family's domestic needs. Not only her father but also her elder brother Idek as well as her much older sister Sala were forced to go to work; now, as the youngest, Mindzia remained at home 'and prepared meals and prepared for next, that they could take to work, there was very little to eat, and whatever I could do in the house at that time, I was nine years old'.[107] The family were extremely lucky in having a very close Polish friend, Cecilia Krzeminska, who far from abandoning them gave ever more help to them. She would wear a

> huge red nice heavy shawl . . . and under the shawl she had always a loaf of bread, candies, a little flour, she brought a few potatoes, and she also was living on cards . . . but she went to work, cleaning houses, and whatever they give her to eat she would save and bring home and she brought it for me.

At this stage Poles could still enter the Jewish area, although Jews could not themselves leave it: 'She was able to come to the street that was only for Jews'—and she was willing not only at that time, but also as conditions further deteriorated, to take ever greater risks in helping Mindzia to survive.

For many Jews, in this period before the programme of mass extermination got under way, resistance entailed an attempt to survive not only physically, but also mentally and spiritually; to keep their traditions, culture, and love of learning alive. Jochanan Ranz recalls the development of an unofficial 'library' of books that were collected and held in Podwale Street.[108] Seeking to continue with an education did not only mean learning Hebrew or Yiddish, or acquiring the necessary practical skills and making preparations to leave for Palestine. Once the schools had been closed and she was no longer able to go to regular lessons, Lea Eisenberg benefited from the fact that a woman living in the same house—there were by now many families living squashed into one house—was able to teach her German. She even managed to read poetry by Goethe and Schiller, and learnt how to write in Gothic script.[109] Lea also went out for an hour to two to walk the streets, to meet and talk with other young people. Such momentary oases were just that—a short-lived respite:

> But in the evening the horror started. They used to come, bang on the door, and take some of the people out, like cattle. The older people who lived with us in the kitchen went immediately with the transport.[110]

Lea's own family did not remain intact for long. Her father had refused to work on the Sabbath day. On subsequently returning to work he was severely beaten and sent home; he died eight days later.

Even and perhaps especially in this atmosphere, the attempt to live for more than just the next meal was immensely valuable. Jochanan Ranz, for example, provides a detailed description of active Jewish social and cultural life, and particularly of the youth organizations. He describes the lively debates and diverse political movements among young people, the unofficial 'libraries' with circulation of reading matter from the large personal collections of one or two well-educated individuals, and theatrical and musical performances despite all the difficulties. Sporting activities were rather more curtailed through the effects on energy and health of the very poor food supplies, and the more general fears of being shot if caught on the street at the wrong time, falling foul of the bad mood of a particular Nazi, or failing to have observed orders of which one was unaware. The Zionist youth organization provided a centre of activity, community, and debate for more than 2,000 young people. Unaware at first of the full scale of the impending doom, young people engaged in sometimes ferocious debates over what kind of a future they would build, and whether they should remain in Poland or try to leave for 'Eretz Israel', the promised land.

A particular centre of such discussions was what Jochanan Ranz and others have called a Kibbutz. The establishment of this already pre-dated the Nazi invasion, and its headquarters moved at some point to Kołłątaja Street, the main street running across town just below the castle and the Catholic church; in addition, it gained the abandoned site of an old coal mine in a poor suburb of Będzin, 'Little Środula' or Środula Dolny—an area later to be part of the enclosed ghetto prior to the final deportations. On this derelict land Jewish activists established a centre of agricultural production,

Figure 11. A meeting at the 'Farma', 1941
Jewish youth at the 'Farma' agricultural collective attend a meeting.
United States Holocaust Memorial Museum, courtesy of Benjamin & Hanka Schlesinger.

known as the *farma* or farm.[111] This actually pre-dated the war, and was already in existence in the summer of 1940 when Udo Klausa commented on it in one of his early monthly reports as *Landrat*. He expressed a degree of puzzlement about the prominent role of intellectuals in an agricultural enterprise, followed by a slightly snide remark, using a typically stereotyping expression about the 'Jewish trader' in the singular, concerning the way in which Jewish dealers were still in some way making profits:

> Attempts here to shape the *Jewish state* [underlined in original] into a self-contained entity persist, particularly as far as the economic side is concerned. The Jews have leased a large plot of land near Bendzin and are cultivating all manner of vegetables there on their own account. It is notable that this work is being carried out almost exclusively by the Jewish intelligentsia. School-age youth and students in particular cannot find any other means of livelihood here. The resident Jewish trader is obviously still carrying out enough by way of deals.[112]

If the *Landrat* thought growing vegetables was the key purpose of the farm, Jewish survivors placed far greater emphasis on intellectual, cultural, social, and political activities, as Arno Lustiger recalls:

> The centre of activities in Bedzin was the *Farma*, an agricultural estate. Under the pretext of vocational retraining, numerous young people could come together here in order to hold meetings, sing Zionist songs, and forge plans for an uncertain future.[113]

One of those actively involved was Samuel Rosencwajg, who after the war changed his name to Shmuel Ron. Ron recalled this farm as an oasis in an otherwise awful situation:

> At that time this farm was a glimmer of hope in the darkness... A thoroughly active life predominated at the farm. Heated debates were on the daily agenda, the Sabbath and holy days were celebrated, and one met up with friends. There was a lot of singing—an opportunity for us to give expression to the storm in our souls. Despite the external difficulties many comrades picked up a pen and wrote, others sang, some rehearsed plays, others organized literary evenings—and of course debates. These meetings between the various ideological movements allowed a unique oasis to develop outside the reality of the ghetto. The estate was also a 'breeding ground' for activists in the centre of the underground movement... On the estate three languages were spoken—Polish, Hebrew, and Yiddish—and in this way I came closer to the Yiddish language than had been possible for me in my parents' house.[114]

Although the *Landrat* did not seem to realize it—and would probably have been horrified if he had—the activities of this 'farm' thus went well beyond the economically useful production of vegetables.

Shmuel Ron was himself a member of one of the many youth movements in the area, the Hashomer Hatzair. Right across Poland, this movement was organized by young people who wanted to study, to build up new forms of political and social life, and to continue to teach those children who had been forcibly ousted from schools with the Nazi takeover of power. According to Shmuel Ron, from the ranks of this youth movement also came many of the later leaders of the uprisings in Warsaw, Vilna, Bialystok, and elsewhere.[115] Hashomer Hatzair carried out a range of activities, including providing less fortunate families with additional food, and maintaining links with people on the 'Aryan side', in the hope of forging resistance networks. In these activities they cooperated with other Jewish youth movements that were also highly active in the area, such as Dror, Gordonia, and Hashomer Hadati. They disdained and often came into active conflict with members of the local Jewish Councils, with variations depending on different individuals, and clashed in particular with the Central Office of the Jewish Councils headed by Moses Merin in Sosnowiec.

Another participant in the life of the farm was Siegmund Pluznik, who eventually managed to escape from Będzin to Palestine, with an alarming number of close shaves, arrests, and repeated escapes, over the years 1943–4.[116] Many individuals were involved in attempts to organize human chains of trustworthy helpers along escape routes, using false identities and accompanying false papers, finding addresses of individuals who would be prepared to offer refuge and assistance along the way. These attempts were often sabotaged and the individuals involved betrayed by the Jewish Council, as in the case of attempts to get passports to emigrate to South America.[117] Some courageous individuals, whether or not they were participants in this unique 'farm', sought to acquire weapons and forge links with resistance movements elsewhere in Poland and Eastern Europe.

These endeavours were fraught with dangers, not least because the Polish resistance groups were often highly antisemitic and did not welcome Jewish members into their groups; and because individual Poles found they could make considerable sums being paid by Jews to find weapons or lead them to friendly partisan groups, and then even more financial gains by double-crossing and betraying them to the Gestapo. Ranz gives a vivid description of the way he alone survived from among his group of ten who had been lured into just such a trap:

> It rained with bullets from all sides. Our people fell one after another. I still ran and saw that I am the last. I don't know where the thought came from. My brain told me to fall down and play dead. I did so by lying with my face to the earth without moving. It whistled a few more series from the machine guns and it turned quiet. The Germans came nearer and considered the dead bodies. They laughed sadistically. With them was the Polish guide. He counted the bodies and said, 'That's all of them. There were ten.' They looked around and left. I didn't move for half an hour and listened fearing a trap. Then I got up and went back in the direction we came. I went the rest of the night until I came to a road. From there I played a Polish boy and reached the Ghetto.[118]

A Pole by the name of Socha had led two groups out to meet partisans who then betrayed them to Gestapo. Socha was, after the war, put to death.[119]

Samuel Bradin, like many other survivors, recalled that any kind of resistance faced numerous difficulties: not only were the Jewish Councils 'collaborating' with the Germans, but there were also huge problems with respect to the Polish population of the area: 'We talked about resistance but it wasn't possible, because if we made contact with outside the ghetto we were double crossed by the Poles.'[120] They would take the money supplied by the Jews in return for weapons, without supplying the latter, and then the Jews would be caught by the Gestapo, 'so we had the impossibility to resist'. As Bradin summarized the situation: 'The Germans were the common enemy of the Poles and of the Jews, but against the Jews the Poles were totally united with the Germans.' He concluded: 'So they too worked with the Germans to eliminate the Jews.' Ultimately, 'we were pushed into a corner where we had no way out, we had no place to run'.[121]

For most Jews in Będzin, fear of massive reprisals, and the basic and indeed overwhelming need to conserve sufficient energy to work, in order to be able to feed oneself and one's family, took up all the time and physical resources available. In Arno Lustiger's summary:

> The solution propagated by the [Jewish] Council of Elders of 'salvation through work' made a lot of sense to many people—also because of lack of alternatives, since armed resistance appeared to be a romantic, dangerous undertaking that threatened the whole community.[122]

At this point, no one could have predicted that even work would no longer ensure their continued existence: that a dead Jew would eventually be more highly valued by Hitler and Himmler than a Jewish slave labourer.

The debates went on, sometimes to the point of exhaustion, as to whether the best strategy was to try to survive and sit it out, to mount an armed rising and engage in active resistance against Nazi rule, or to escape and flee to a place of safety elsewhere. These debates were carried out against a backdrop of uncertainty as to what was going on in the wider world—Jews had no legitimate access to newspapers, their radios had been confiscated, and they were almost entirely reliant on word of mouth, illicit sources of news, and rumours from the 'Aryan side'—and also a widespread unwillingness to believe that an already appalling situation could, within a relatively short space of time, become even worse. 'Resistance' became quite another phenomenon once they realized with certainty that the alternative was inevitable death.

Meanwhile, the local leadership of the Jewish Councils of the area, coordinated in its Sosnowiec headquarters by Merin, was still under the illusion that full cooperation with the Germans was the only way forward.[123] Merin had by now developed what has been termed a 'messianic complex', believing that his 'Central Office' or *Zentrale* would be able to coordinate the activities of Jews not only within the Dombrowan region for which he was held responsible by the Germans, but also right across Germany, Poland, and Czechoslovakia. At this time, unlike the Jews whom he was supposed to represent, Merin was able to travel quite widely, and sought to coordinate activities and exert his authority against other prominent Jewish leaders. The latter, however, were sceptical of his ambitions, and refused to submit to him as in any way a superior authority.

In the short term, Merin carved out a position of some power—within severe limitations—and privilege for himself. He also coordinated many offices and activities that genuinely provided some degree of assistance in terms of shelter, clothing, food, medical help, and supplies to those whose livelihoods and homes had been snatched from them; in a sense, he assisted the Germans in a coordinated effort to reduce massively the standard of living of expropriated Jews without a catastrophic collapse of any infrastructure for sheer survival. Hundreds of local Jews with good intentions of assisting members of their community worked within the network of offices run by the

Figure 12. Jewish militia give orders to Jews, 1939–43
Jewish police officer Zeidman informs a group of young men about the order to vacate the Zederman house on Zawodzie Street.
United States Holocaust Memorial Museum, courtesy of Beit Lohamei Haghetaot.

Jewish Central Office, including, for a while, Ala Gertner, after she had returned from the labour camp where she had been with Sala Garncarz.[124] The activities of the Jewish Councils thus provided something of a buffer and safety net for those in desperate need, even if at the same time corruption was rife, and individual acts of bribery could often ensure that in the short term wealthier Jews were able to purchase a degree of relative privilege and protection from some of the harshest effects of German policies, while those without means were more readily delivered up to their fates. At the same time Merin coordinated the activities of the Jewish militia, who carried out many tasks that might otherwise have been the domain of the Gestapo; who knew and moved among fellow Jews and so were more easily able to target and deliver up 'appropriate' victims; who were open to bribery and corruption from both sides, Jewish and German, and thus able both to protect or denounce at whim; and who could develop small messianic complexes of their own, pursuing personal vendettas and feuds in their ever so slightly elevated status in this oppressed underworld. Merin also, at this time, actively dissuaded people from strategies of non-cooperation, and succeeded in more underhand ways in preventing Jews who would have liked to escape or resist from pursuing their aims, even directly betraying some of them to the Gestapo.

In the eyes of many of its critics, the Jewish Central Office did little other than assist the Nazis in their task, until the Jewish leadership too was no longer needed and followed the rest down the railroad tracks to Auschwitz, as Wajnblum recalled:

> I remember [Merin] explained the situation of the Jews in the Zaglembie district as different from the Jews in the protectorate areas of Poland, as our district was annexed to the German 3rd [*sic*] Reich... In desperation most Jewish people had pinned their hopes on this self-proclaimed false Messiah. As it turned out he was not a man to be trusted. Mr Meryn's energies were primarily directed to satisfying the demands of the Gestapo and in doing so he efficiently helped the Nazis with the liquidation of the Jewish community in the whole of the Zaglembie district.[125]

In the longer term, no amount of collaboration with the Nazis would ever buy the freedom of even the few remaining collaborators who, once they had outlived their usefulness in delivering up the prey, would themselves finally also be cast away.

8

Escalation, 1941–1942

Murder, violence, and brutality took place in less obvious forms than the later West German system of justice was prepared to recognize. Slow death by starvation, or as a result of illnesses that proved fatal because of malnutrition, low immunity, and being forced to live in conditions of overcrowding and poor hygiene, were perhaps less visible, more indirect forms of homicide than were beatings, torture, shooting, or gassing; but these were nevertheless deaths directly caused by Nazi policies of persecution—deaths that under 'normal' circumstances would warrant charges of criminal neglect or manslaughter, if not actually murder.

We do not know what inner doubts Udo Klausa may have been having at this time. The systems of forced and slave labour, the policies of rationing entailing deliberate malnutrition, the hangings and other forms of retribution, were simply the system of colonial racism, a form of business as usual; certainly nothing worthy of particular mention in Klausa's memoirs. He does not distinguish between any 'before' and 'after' as far as his absence in the army in 1941 was concerned, nor does he pick up some of the points that were remembered so acutely by survivors of Nazi exploitation and terror—not even those where we know from the archival sources that he was not merely physically present, but holding a degree of official responsibility. There is no mention of the labour camp at Golonog, run by his loyal and 'decent' colleague, the head of the gendarmerie, Heinrich Mentgen, who reported to him personally on the 'sanitary' and security arrangements; there is no mention of any public hangings, of which he must have been aware and in all likelihood witnessed; there is no mention of the agonies of separation when friends and family members were deported to labour camps, nor the daily miseries of those subjected to enforced starvation through the system of rationing imposed by the Nazi regime with the full knowledge and imprimatur of the *Landrat*.

Military absence

In both his memoirs and his defence statements, Klausa repeatedly bases his claim to innocence on his frequent and lengthy 'disappearances' to the army, implying that he consciously chose, as something of an act of inner resistance, to offer himself for military service at the front despite officially being registered as 'indispensable' on the home front. There seems to be some inner, psychological truth to this story as far as Klausa's third absence, from December 1942, was concerned, despite major factual inaccuracies in the details of his account; and there may also be an element of truth in relation to his second period of military service in 1941. But here, as for the third absence, Klausa does not give an entirely accurate representation of the nature of his departure, when strenuous attempts by the civilian government to gain indispensable status for Klausa were unsuccessful. Given the significance for Klausa's overall story, the character of his absence in 1941 is worth some consideration.

Klausa's second 'disappearance' to the army in the spring of 1941 may or may not have been accompanied by a desire, as he later claimed, to get away from unbearable circumstances in Będzin. Certainly letters from his wife to her friend, Frau von H., suggest continuing concerns about his 'nerves', although it is far from clear that contemporary concerns were the sole cause of his nervous state (as we have seen, Alexandra suggests that this 'labile' state was a long-term disposition, perhaps inherited from his mother).[1] If there were any inner concerns, they were certainly well hidden. The records show that Klausa's civilian superiors were more than satisfied with his work in the area. On this occasion, the return to military service came about, against the will of Klausa's superiors in Kattowitz, as a direct result of the army's need for further manpower in the run-up to the invasion of the Soviet Union.

It is quite clear from the files that the regional administrative hierarchy did its utmost to keep Klausa. The importance attached to Klausa's personal presence and responsibility as *Landrat* of Będzin at this time is emphasized repeatedly by Regional President Springorum. It is also clear from this correspondence that Klausa was seen as not merely going through the motions of doing the job of *Landrat*, but rather as energetic, proactive, and indeed central to the success of the 'Germanization' policies that were now about to enter a more radical stage.

On 18 December 1940 Springorum first stated that Klausa's services were urgently required in the district; on 21 December 1940, he reiterated his arguments when writing to the local military recruitment offices in Kattowitz requesting 'indispensable' (*uk*) status for Klausa.[2] On 21 January 1941 Springorum pleaded with the Reich Ministry of the Interior (RMI) that, despite Klausa's recent return from the front in mid-October 1940, he could in principle still be called up at any time; and that it was untenable that the 'district leader best acquainted with the numerous important tasks [and]...the difficult ethnic situation in the district should be away for any longer period of time, or could any day be called up again for military service'.[3] This request was initially granted on 28 January 1941, allowing Klausa *uk* status until 31 July 1941, but then the decision was suddenly reversed by a telegram from the Military Recruitment Office in Berlin, presumably in the light of further preparations for 'Operation Barbarossa' in the coming summer.[4] Further requests were turned down by the Army High Command (*Oberkommando der Wehrmacht*).

But, if military preparations were hotting up at this time, so too were developments in racial policy in the annexed territories—where Klausa's presence seemed equally urgently required. The tone of subsequent letters from Springorum, including one on 18 February 1941 to the RMI, became even more strenuous: 'I allow myself to emphasize yet again that there are special tasks immediately facing the district of Bendzin that make the presence of the *Landrat* himself essential.'[5] Springorum also wrote to the Military Recruitment Office in Berlin on the same day, urging them to reconsider in view of 'the important political measures that are to be carried through in the district of Bendzin that is administered by Dr Klausa'.[6]

The battle continued, the situation apparently somewhat exacerbated by Klausa's membership of the elite Potsdam Infantry Regiment 9 (I.R.9). As the Berlin army authorities explained on 25 February 1941, Klausa could not apply for indispensable status 'since he is in a military unit that, by order of the Military High Command, is exempted from all granting of "indispensable" positions'.[7]

Yet the administration did not give up easily, now even bringing Hitler into the fray on their side. By 26 February 1941, the RMI had itself taken up the fight for Klausa's 'indispensable' status, now also writing to the military recruitment offices in Berlin, and even adducing the 'Führer's orders' as a clinching argument, adorned with a large red 'Confidential!' at the top of the page:

The presence is urgently required of the *Landrat* Dr Klausa in the district of Bendzin. In the next few weeks there are tasks facing the *Landrat* that are of special importance and that demand the presence of the *Landrat* himself. In general the work is particularly difficult in the eastern territories incorporated since the Polish campaign. But the greatest difficulties exist in the district of Bendzin and in its neighbouring district of Chrzanow. The district of Bendzin with 250,000 inhabitants, among which there are some 60,000 Jews, must, according to an order of the Führer, be resettled [*ausgesiedelt*] over the next few weeks.

The use of the word *ausgesiedelt* is interestingly different from a previously used term, *umgesiedelt*, although both are readily translated as 'resettled' in English; rather than 'resettling' people *within* an area (as with *umgesiedelt*, 'moved around'), the implication of *ausgesiedelt* is that of moving people *out*. Later, the term 'evacuated' was often used as a euphemism for deportation to murder. The usage here suggests that the earlier attempts in the Sosnowiec and Będzin area to render the better areas 'Jew free', designating certain areas for the use of Germans only while resettling Jews within restricted and poorer areas, was soon, on the Führer's orders, to be displaced by something altogether more radical. Although not spelled out explicitly, this may have referred to plans for possible expulsions into the General Government or to other larger ghettos; or it may have been a relatively vague reference to something more extreme, perhaps based on a rant by Hitler; we have little means of knowing what was implied here, although the actual course of developments thereafter can be traced in some detail.

It certainly suggested that Springorum was well aware of population planning and racial policy with respect to the Jews, and that the *Landräte* were viewed as essential to implementing plans developed at the highest levels. Moreover, Klausa was seen as personally vital to a successful outcome of this enterprise. The letter continues (with a characteristically cruel and untrue sideswipe at the allegedly continuing economic strength of the Jews):

It is, therefore, necessary to get the Jews out, which in view of the powerful economic position of this population group in the district of Bendzin is bound up with unbelievable difficulties... These measures can only be carried through if the experienced leader of the district is available... This is thus a special and exceptional case, so that I urgently request the release of First Lieutenant [*Oberleutnant*] Klausa. If ever a position of a civilian character in state service is also worthy of particular consideration in view of military requirements, then it is precisely the district of Bendzin that justifies such consideration.[8]

Yet, despite such urgent pleading by the civilian government, the combination of the elite status of the Potsdam Infantry Regiment 9 and the preparations that were under way for the invasion of the Soviet Union meant that Udo Klausa, now at the prime age of 31, could not be released from availability for military service at this point. On 11 March 1941 Fründt, on behalf of the RMI, confirmed that Klausa could not be spared from the army.[9]

The attempts in the winter and spring of 1940–1 at obtaining 'indispensable' status for Klausa were ultimately unsuccessful—but it was certainly not for want of trying. So Klausa's second stint in the army, for most of 1941, can hardly be interpreted as a 'flight' from an unbearable situation in Będzin; and, far from having chosen to 'disappear' in silent protest against what was going on in the area, he had played such a significant role in implementing Nazi policies that his continuing presence and leadership were highly valued by his superiors. He was clearly viewed as a key link in implementing Hitler's radical racial policies. Any inner ambivalence he may have felt—and which may have been expressed in what Alexandra repeatedly referred to as his 'nerves'—was certainly not evident as far as his behaviour and fulfilment of professional duties at the time was concerned.

Klausa thus spent the summer of 1941 fighting on the eastern front, before being invalided out in the early autumn. In his memoirs of his experiences at the front, there is very little mention of real violence; merely an anecdote about entering a home where the family were obviously afraid he would kill them. According to his account, it was only later, after having confirmed his entirely gentle intentions towards them, that he realized they had been afraid of him because they were Jewish. This rather typical story—with its characteristic self-portrayal as both innocent and ignorant—is the only hint we get in his memoirs that Klausa was even aware of the murderous policies against Jewish civilians following the invasion of Russia in June 1941. His army unit went through areas that were in the thick of massacres, yet Klausa appears to have had little or nothing to do with them, and precious little awareness of the atrocities taking place, with the backing and support of the army, all around. The memoirs of other members of his regiment also provide little other than accounts of German heroism, honour, struggle, and suffering.[10]

We know from many other sources that such accounts are notable for what they leave out; there is much historical evidence to suggest that experiences of the mass murder of Jewish civilians on the eastern front had a major impact on ordinary German soldiers.[11] And it is notable that more

Jews and other civilians were killed by bullets and summary executions than in the gas chambers of the dedicated extermination camps.[12] As innocent and heroic an experience of war as Klausa portrays in his memoirs is highly implausible. Nevertheless, he later claimed that he had never personally witnessed anything on the lines of the atrocities shown in the notorious *Wehrmacht Ausstellung* (Army Exhibition) of the mid-1990s.[13]

Whatever his experiences on the eastern front, Klausa did not emerge from his second stint of military service in a good physical or emotional state. In the heat of the battle, Klausa had a complete physical collapse. Following serious illness, medical treatment (including an intestinal operation), and an extended period of convalescence, Klausa finally returned to his role as *Landrat* in late 1941. He nevertheless continued to suffer from physical malaise, including long-standing stomach problems. His symptoms may or may not have been, at least in part, psychosomatic; there is no way of making a medical diagnosis at this historical distance, and no definitive diagnosis was produced at the time.[14] But Alexandra's comments in a letter to Frau von H. in February 1942 are revealing:

> Udo is a real worry; he is still really very unwell, and the burden of work is taking its toll on him, so that there is really no prospect of recovery. There is also a lot of aggravation [*Ärger*], which of course affects the health of nervous people. For Udo has still not been confirmed as *Landrat*. The reasons are obvious. But that one of the main reasons is the fact that he went off to war is quite incredible. Yet this is the case.[15]

So clearly factors other than, or in addition to, his physical ailments were affecting his 'nervous' state at this time.

One of the major concerns preying on Klausa's 'nerves' was that of ensuring that he was finally promoted from his probationary status to the permanent role of *Landrat*, repeatedly termed his 'dream career'. The delay in confirming his permanent position because he had gone to the front could charitably, after the event, be interpreted to mean an allusion to possible doubts on the part of superiors about Klausa's supposedly quasi-oppositional stance in 'disappearing' to the army. On the other hand, given the glowing references from his superiors, it is far more likely that the Berlin authorities were simply mindful of the fact that Klausa, having been physically absent from his duties as *Landrat* during a significant part of the probationary period, had perhaps not as yet had sufficient time to demonstrate his abilities in that role. After all, on his initial appointment critical comments had been made about his extreme youth and relative inexperience, thus requiring the extended probationary period of two years.[16] He had to make up for this by demonstrating commitment and efficiency in a relatively short time. There is no conclusive contemporary evidence to support his post-war claim that his religious commitment had caused further delays in what was already to be an extended probationary timescale, although the family heard rumours and grumbles around their announcement of their son's birth using religious phraseology ('by God's grace').[17] It is certainly the case that Klausa's commitment to Catholicism had been occasion for comment in one of his references, but only in order to dispel any doubts that might have arisen about his simultaneous commitment to the Nationalist Socialist cause. As August Jäger (the 'Church-Hunter'), for whom Klausa had acted as personal assistant in the Warthegau, had earlier summarized the situation: 'In his practical work [Klausa] always demonstrated energy, capability, stamina and reliability'; in the difficult questions around the Nazi project of 'building up' the new 'Germanized' society (*Aufbau*), Klausa's attitude was also always characterized by a mindset of 'initiative and stimulation', so that Jäger 'learned to treasure him as a colleague in the truest sense of the word' in his own areas of responsibility. Despite his Catholic faith, Klausa's ideological and practical commitment to the Nazi cause was, in Jäger's view, absolute.[18]

In the event, the long-awaited promotion did not come on 20 April (the Führer's birthday), as had initially been rumoured, but only some three weeks later. This delay is relatively insignificant, and there is nothing at all in the official records to indicate any doubts whatsoever about Klausa's capacity for and commitment to the job—quite the opposite, in fact.

Nevertheless, letters from Alexandra both to her mother and to the close family friend, Frau von H., throughout the following months testify to Klausa's continued poor health.[19] Throughout the spring and summer of 1942 Alexandra repeatedly comments on the state of Udo's 'nerves' and his hopes that a 'rest cure' will render him fit for further military service. She also reiterates his continuing desire to return to the army, although commenting that in his current condition he is simply not fit enough. Medically, however, he showed no definitive or easily diagnosable symptoms, and as time passed and he continued to suffer from lassitude he increasingly feared that to try to describe his listlessness to a doctor would be seen merely as attempting to shirk his military duties. He was clearly not in a fit state to return to the army, yet equally unable to provide any simple medical evidence to this effect.

Whatever the character of this syndrome of malaise, the records from the archival sources suggest that Klausa continued to fulfil his role as *Landrat* impeccably. He picked up Nazi policies where they were at the time of his return, and continued to carry out orders from on high with his customary efficiency and intelligence. Clearly there could at this point be no hint of any inner doubts Klausa may have been having about the direction in which Nazi policy was heading. And it was just as he returned from the front and picked up the reins of the *Landrat*'s position again that policies were shifting gear in an ever more ominous direction. Here again, whatever Klausa's inner feelings may have been, in public he carried out his duties as *Landrat* in exemplary fashion. And—just as in the case of those 'ordinary men', members of police battalions who had qualms about pulling a trigger, but nevertheless shot and hit the target—it was the actual behaviour of Klausa and others in a similar position, not their possible inner doubts and well-hidden thoughts, that had historical consequences for the victims of Nazi racism.

Ghettoization as concentration and containment

From the summer of 1941, mass killings by shooting Jews into graves were gathering pace in the east, and in September the use of Zyklon B gas was tried out in Auschwitz. When in September 1941 Jews in the 'old Reich' of Germany (*Altreich*) were required to wear the yellow star, the same measure was introduced for the Jews in the newly incorporated territories, along with increasing restrictions on movement. On 20 September 1941 Springorum sent out a general directive to all the *Landräte* and Police Presidents in the districts of Kattowitz, Gleiwitz, and Sosnowiec to the effect that, from 22 September 1941, all Jews must wear the yellow star on their clothing at the height of the heart and that 'from this day it is forbidden for Jews to leave the area where they live without written permission from the local police authority; it is also forbidden for them to wear orders of merit, badges of honour and similar symbols'.[20]

From the autumn of 1941 Jews were also to carry new identity cards with photographs (*Lichtbildausweise*), to reduce the possibility of getting by on false papers. These measures were of sufficient importance to have the personal intervention of Reinhard Heydrich, Himmler's Deputy in the Reich Security Main Office (RSHA), confirming the details.[21] The SS organization labour leader, Schmelt, wrote in a letter of 12 November 1941 to Merin,

Leader of the Jewish Council of Elders, about calling in the old identity cards. Jews needed to turn up in person to hand in their former pink and green identity cards, which would lose validity, at which time a decision would be taken as to whether they would be issued with new cards. Schmelt threatened that, if they did not turn up, their factories or places of work would be closed and they would not get valid new cards.[22] For some Jews these cards could, over the coming months, make the difference between a temporary reprieve and prolongation of life, or selection for instant death.

The restrictions on movement that had been introduced in early September precipitated further developments with respect to the identification and physical concentration of Jews. In the *Landkreis* of Będzin, despite substantial recent resettlement measures and designation of areas forbidden to Jews under the *Judenbann*, there was still no totally enclosed and entirely self-contained ghetto. It therefore now became imperative to clarify where exactly and what constituted a 'Jewish residential area'. This effectively inaugurated a second stage of ghettoization.

The 'residential area' was now defined as being 'that political community... within whose municipal area the particular Jew is resident'.[23] This somewhat circular definition proved of little help in practice. Particularly in the outlying more rural areas and small communities of the *Landkreis* of Będzin, the local functionaries (*Amtskommissare*) found some difficulty in implementing the order that Jews could no longer leave their own 'residential areas'. For example, in the community of Sączow, where the small villages of Celiny and Tapkowice were located, the responsible functionary complained that 'bringing together the Jews in a particular community within this part of the district would be hard to carry out, since the inhabitants here mostly have their own houses, which are only sufficient to meet their own housing needs'.[24] A characteristically pre-emptive suggestion, couched in a distinctly distasteful tone, was a communication from the local functionary of the parish of Strzemieszyce, who thought that Jews should be banned not only from using public transport, but even from riding in their own horse-drawn carriages: he felt that 'Jews should go on foot', since 'the conduct of Jews, increasingly preserving their flat feet, provokes irritation not only among Germans but also among a large proportion of Poles'.[25]

In October 1941 Klausa was still being represented by his deputy, Jansen, who on 15 October suggested that Jews who were spread about too much in isolated hamlets across the *Landkreis* should be concentrated in three major locations: Zagorze, Niwka, and three places within the Amtsbezirk of Strzemieszyce, leaving the other areas as 'de-Jewed' (*entjudet*), a classic example of the Nazi use of the possibilities of German grammar.[26] The construction of this word is worth reproducing in English—which does not have an equivalent single term—to drive home its full significance.

By November 1941 Udo Klausa was actively back in charge of the *Landkreis*, and picked up this policy with characteristic efficiency. It may be noted that the ordered resettlement and concentration of Jews in the 'thinly settled northern parts' of his county gains no mention in his memoirs—he could not even seem to remember whether or not there had indeed ever been any Jews in those parts—but his actions at the time certainly made a considerable impact on those affected in practice.

Klausa now wrote to the local functionaries in the parts of his district that did not come under the control of the Sosnowiec Police President, and requested further concentration of Jews in each area. Klausa felt that, in the light of the previous orders, it was now 'essential in local districts to bring together Jews into one or two places and create so-called Jewish communities. It would be expedient to de-Jew [*entjuden*] the principal communities.'[27] He further requested that his local officials should report back to him on progress in their respective areas of responsibility after a month.

From late November through December 1941 reports duly started coming in from the local functionaries saying which areas had been 'de-Jewed', and where and how many remaining Jews had been concentrated. In Sączow, despite earlier concerns, some progress had been made: 'The fifteen Jewish families resident in this part of the district have been accommodated in the villages of Niesdara and Tombkowitz. Putting them together in one village is at the moment not possible because of a lack of housing.'[28] Wacław Widera, at that time a young boy, recalled well the Jewish families living in Tąpkowice. One was a baker, whose house was almost opposite his former family home. Later, he was told by his father that he need no longer complain about that particular family, since they had all 'gone up the chimney'.[29]

On 29 December 1941 the local functionary of Strzemieszyce reported back to the *Landrat* in a characteristically long and unpleasant letter, boasting that he had succeeded in concentrating '89 Jewish families with 332 people' into two particular areas, both known for having the worst housing conditions, compounded now by overcrowding: 'While in Kazimierc the necessary space for incoming Jews was won by moving out Poles, in particular moving them out of the worst housing in the Black Sea district, the accommodation in Strzemieszyce was achieved by denser occupancy of the existing Jewish housing.'[30] The local functionary of Grodziec, who had by 4 December 1941 succeeded in concentrating all the 166 Jews of the community into one street, put in a request that they should be further moved out in order to make Grodziec 'completely Jew free... I assume in this connection that the Jew will not be required for the education of youth here, for training them in the [Nazi] world view.'[31] The local functionary of Zombowitz dutifully reported that he had already managed to concentrate the Jews into just two areas, and was now undertaking further measures to get them all into the area of Bielowizna: 'In the course of this resettlement over a period of time we will achieve the de-Jewing of the main community.'[32]

Figure 13. Forcible removal of Jews from their homes, 1942–3
Jews, who have been forced to vacate their homes, load their belongings on to horse-drawn wagons for transfer to the ghetto—where there would not be enough space to accommodate their furniture, much of which subsequently remained piled up on the streets. The man wearing a white cap and brandishing a stick is a member of the Jewish militia, overseeing the removal.
United States Holocaust Memorial Museum, courtesy of Beit Lohamei Haghetaot.

Yet, despite all this increasing restriction on movement, there were still some Jews on the loose, including Jews seeking to escape from the General Government. Dr Mildner, head of the Gestapo in Kattowitz, issued a directive to all *Landräte* to the effect that any Jews who had entered illegally from the General Government must be arrested if found; they were to be distinguished by not being registered with the relevant police authorities.[33] Heydrich again intervened personally to urge further restrictions on the capacity of Jews to travel: this was 'to be reduced to an absolute minimum'.[34] Jews, even when on forced labour duties, were only to be allowed on public transport if they lived further than at least one hour or 7 kilometres (about 5 miles) away from their workplace, and in only very few other exceptional circumstances.[35] Springorum also weighed in on this topic, as late as 22 April 1942.[36]

As was by now usual when any directive came from on high, further tightening control over the Jewish population of the area for which he was responsible, Klausa in his role as *Landrat* ensured that polices were put into effect in every last little corner of the rural communities and parishes of his district. And within a matter of weeks the usual little white notes came back to the *Landrat* from all the functionaries to show the ways in which they were carrying out the policies, and reporting on successes in their areas.

Compared with the problem of 'resettlement' of Jews and their concentration within restricted areas, restrictions on the use of public transport were easier to implement: local commissaries either replied simply that there were no means of public transport in their areas anyway (Sontschow, Golonog); or that, by now, there were no more Jews in their areas (Bobrowniki, Lagischa, Zombkowitz). As usual, the letter from the *Amtskommissar* in Strzemieszyce provided additional emphasis, with the report that restrictions on the use of transport were unnecessary because his area was by now *Jew free*, underlined.[37]

Increasingly, it was held that Jews should not merely be restricted in where they could live, and what forms of transport they could use, but that they should be kept under surveillance at all times, including being escorted in groups to and from work. In early November 1941, Police President von Woedtke, the Gestapo leader Dreier from Kattowitz, and Prof. Dr Köttgen, a legal adviser to the Kattowitz government (and well-respected academic lawyer in West Germany after the war) came together to discuss the issue, which would entail further resettlement and 'concentration' of Jews, with strict regulations about their capacity to move outside the designated areas.

A variety of possible scenarios were mooted, noting that some Jews were already 'collected together as in a camp' so could be taken in groups to work; but appropriate measures still needed to be taken in the case of others, so that they could be 'brought to the workplace in closed formation'.[38] The priority was very clear, namely:

> Such that not only in the workplace itself, but also on the journey to the workplace Jews are kept together under the oversight of a non-Jewish person provided by the employer. Under all circumstances it must be guaranteed that the Jews will be constantly under control and will have no opportunity to leave the group on their own initiative.[39]

Effective imprisonment at all times was thus under way. It had already been substantially achieved for those who could be taken to work in enclosed groups, but there remained the 'problem' of those employed on an individual or geographically scattered basis.

It was difficult for the German authorities to know how best to put all this into practice, with some evidence of disagreement between Schmelt—in charge of such a wide network of forced labour—and Police President von Woedtke. Schmelt was highly critical of von Woedtke's supposedly obstreperous policies with respect to issuing special passes, thus allegedly preventing those of 'his' Jews who worked in army uniform factories from getting to work by 5 a.m. or leaving after the late shift at 10 p.m.—an indication of the sheer extent of exploitation of Jewish labour in this period. Regional President Springorum in Kattowitz even drafted a letter to Himmler requesting advice and guidance on this matter.[40] Meanwhile, further physical concentration and enclosure of Jews were taking place.

In the autumn of 1941, Hans Felden, the mayor of Czeladź and trusted colleague of Klausa (following Felden's long experience in local government under Klausa's father), developed plans for a closed ghetto for his town. He reported on 23 September 1941 that, of the total population of 23,000 in his town, some 1,200 were Jews. These 1,200 people he now managed to 'concentrate' into a small 'Jewish quarter', encompassing a mere couple of blocks on the outskirts of town, situated a short walk from the main road and tram transport route to Będzin. In view of this, he wanted to make other areas 'free of Jews':

> In view of the relatively small number of Jews I consider it appropriate that the Jew ban [*Judenbann*] is extended across the whole area of the town with the exception of the Jewish quarter and the connecting street to the tram stop.

Furthermore, many of the Jews working in the immediate vicinity were in any event employed by the municipal authorities:

> 162 Jews are employed in concerns here, of whom most are employed by the town administration... A certificate about employment should be prepared for individual Jews, so that they can attend their workplaces.[41]

An attached list showed that 114 of the 162 Jews employed locally were in fact employed by the town administration itself, and thus readily kept under close control.[42] The remainder, in Felden's view, could be kept under surveillance as they went in closed work groups to the tram station, located conveniently nearby on the main road to Będzin.

As von Woedtke put it in a report of 23 February 1942 to the Regional President in Kattowitz, 'a self-enclosed Jewish quarter' had now been introduced in Czeladź, with the intention that the 'ban on Jews' (*Judenbann*) would prevent Jews from being seen anywhere else in town. In his reply, the Regional President wondered whether, at this stage, it might still be worth

Figure 14. Tailors in Czeladź, 1939
Tailors in a garment factory that made children's clothing in Czeladź. The factory, which had belonged to the Urman family, was taken over by the Germans in 1940. Among those pictured is the donor, Salomon Urman (on the right at the back of the room), and his sister, Pearl Chaya (second row on the right).
United States Holocaust Memorial Museum, courtesy of Salomon Urman.

considering reserving only certain areas to be free of Jews and for the exclusive enjoyment of Germans.[43] The Jewish quarters where Jews were by now concentrated were not bounded by walls and barbed wire, as were the ghettos of Łódź and Warsaw. But, given the severe and frequently fatal penalties for transgressing the boundaries and entering 'Jew-free areas', the decision had not entirely dissimilar effects in practice. It was merely a question of drawing precise boundaries and borders.

This discussion was in the end overtaken by events. It was easy enough, in May 1942, for the two blocks of streets into which the Czeladź Jews had been squeezed to be rapidly surrounded by police and militia. Felden's work in ghettoization had massively facilitated the task of the police forces. The Jews of Czeladź were easily rounded up, and those selected as unfit for work were taken to Będzin, from where they were deported to be gassed in Auschwitz. It was only a matter of months before the remainder suffered similar fates.

Irrespective of the details of the discussions in the spring of 1942—the 'problems' were by no means simple to solve, and the 'solutions' increasingly radical—there is a more significant underlying point. The nature of ghettoization had by this time clearly shifted, from the earlier one of ousting Jews from the better quarters, which could be taken over by Germans, to that of ensuring not only that Jews were no longer to be seen in areas reserved for Germans but also that they were increasingly constrained in every aspect of their movements and everyday life, whether at home, on the way to and from, or actually at work. This was no longer ghettoization primarily for purposes of ousting Jews from the better areas in order to free up desired spaces for Germans, but rather—or additionally—ghettoization for concentration, containment, and increased control of the Jewish population. They were increasingly confined, encircled, under constant surveillance. And whether the civilian authorities intended this or not—we have no way of knowing, for example, precisely what motives lay behind the initiatives taken by Klausa's trusted deputy, Hans Felden—such policies certainly had the consequence of making the subsequent job of round-ups and deportations very much easier.

The Jews had thus been crowded together, squeezed into cramped accommodation and cleared out of the better areas of town. Even so, this was seen as inadequate to achieving the eventual goal of full 'Germanization'—rendering the entire area 'free of Jews'. Police President von Woedtke retained a strong sense of distaste for conditions for Germans living in the area, who still had on occasion to encounter Jews. On 26 January 1942, following many small incidents, he commented:

If the German population here is in a situation where living space has to be shared with Jewry, then it is understandable that they desire to be able to move around on at least some streets without having to be exposed to the repulsive appearance of Jewish creatures.[44]

Within a matter of months, the situation was again to change dramatically—not only as a result of policies designed elsewhere, but also helped along massively by the antisemitic rhetoric and practices of local officials. The increasing 'concentration' of Jews by the 'de-Jewing' of other areas, and the increasing control over their movements outside tightly designated areas, were to prove extraordinarily helpful to the Nazi police forces when it came to the round-up and deportation of the Jews. And, regardless of whether or not this outcome could have been foreseen by the civilian functionaries implementing the policies, they also never seemed to register the intrinsic inhumanity of these polices at any time, even well before it came to the deportations. Klausa and his colleagues, including his highly regarded subordinate and later deputy, Hans Felden of Czeladź, had taken leading roles in the further degradation and effective imprisonment of the Jews in the *Landkreis* of Będzin, with apparent regard only to policies ordered from on high and German 'racial' interests.

The tightening of the noose

Try as they might in their letters to the teenager Sala Garncarz, who was still away in a labour camp, members of her family living in Będzin's neighbouring town of Sosnowiec could not entirely conceal their own hunger and related illnesses. On 23 March 1942, Raizel confided, not to her sister Sala, but to her brother-in-law, just how bad things were becoming for the family. Since the deportation of her own husband, there had been no breadwinner, and rations were so far below adequate that remaining members of the family were simply wasting away. She commented that: 'I am sick in bed and my dear Father is very weak. I tell you, dear Mother will not survive this... I'm not going to survive this.'[45] Yet when writing to her younger sister Sala just five days later, while indicating just how upset she was that the family had no matzo for Passover—and indeed nothing at all to eat—Raizel adopted a tone of false jollity, not wanting to worry her young sister and neatly managing to evade answering the more difficult of her many questions:

We haven't sent you any matzo. No, I couldn't express it in words if I took half a lifetime. Dear Sala, we beg you a thousand times for forgiveness, but we're not going to have any matzo either. There is no possibility that we will get any...

Remember, don't worry, everything is fine with us. One can't look particularly good either (how can we)? You're asking if our dear Mom still looks as she used to. You're asking that we write often; I can do this to please you. Then I hope that I'll only have good news to report...

Remember, don't cry, don't cry, don't cry![46]

At this point the family was constantly ill and apathetic with incessant hunger. But worse things were in store.

Some two weeks later, while on her way home, Raizel was forced—along with a huge crowd of other unwilling spectators—to witness the hanging of the brother and father of one her friends, Bela Kohn. The two men had been accused of black market dealings—in a desperate effort to stay alive and feed their families. It was not until 23 April that Raizel was able to write to her sister, and then only briefly:

We don't know exactly what's going on. Bela Kohn is in distress because her brother died. What else can I say? Don't worry about us and calm down. I really don't have enough to say to merit a letter and no patience either.[47]

'What was going on' appears to have been a concerted campaign of terror at this time, perhaps to drive home to Jews the superior power of Germans and to indicate that there was little point in putting up any kind of resistance or breaking the rules in any way.

Bela Kohn's brother was Mayer (sometimes spelled Mejer) Kohn, at that time aged 30 and the father of two young children, David and Renia. His wife Bronka, née Broder, came from Będzin, and was one of six children; her parents ran a tobacco and stationery shop at 52 Malachowski Street. She married Mayer Kohn in the early 1930s, and moved with him to Sosnowiec. Meyer was hanged alongside his father Nachun Kohn, after their dealing in ration cards had been reported to the Gestapo by an informer. A close family friend, Avraham Susskind, was among the estimated 5,000 Jews who were forced by the Nazis to stand and watch the hanging, and who remembered it with emotion even many decades later:

He was hanged. Mine God, to take people for nothing and hang them up!... He did not die right away... Mayer saw me, I was very close to him... He was talking to me, quietly, while they were putting the rope around his neck. He spoke to me the last words from his life. He said: 'Please take care of my children.'

The minute it was finished, people went home. Everyone from the Kohn family was waiting at [Mayer's wife] Bronka's house, Bronka with the children with her mother-in-law Dina.[48]

Avraham was not able to keep his promise to his dying friend. Not only was Avraham unable to help look after his friend Mayer's children, who were subsequently transported and murdered in Auschwitz; the ration levels decreed by the Nazis were insufficient to sustain life, and Avraham's own two children, 5-year-old twin daughters, died of starvation in the ghetto even before it was finally 'cleared' and those remaining adults and children deported to be gassed.[49] Bronka Kohn, and her children David and Renia, were later murdered in Auschwitz; only one of Bronka's six siblings survived. The stories of these two families point up, in the saddest possible way, the lethal consequences of Nazi occupation policies even before, or outside of, murder in the death camps.

As with so many other such incidents, the head of the department dealing with Jewish affairs in the Kattowitz Gestapo, Hans Dreier, was closely involved in this incident. In her 1969 testimony, Eugenia Dancygier recalled many 'atrocities and barbarities', including the hanging of Jews for dealing with ration cards or forbidden foods; she remembered Dreier as having been the 'initiator of many executions of Jews and Poles', including that of an acquaintance 'by the name of Kohn, the former owner of a shop in Modrzejowska Street'.[50]

On the same day, 13 April 1942, some 5,000 people were made to watch the hanging of two Jews in the old Jewish cemetery of Będzin, on the corner of Zawale Street. The official police report records that the hanging took place at 5 p.m., when many people would be on their way home from work. Survivor testimonies record that on the previous day they had had their identity cards confiscated from them at work, and were made to leave work early on the day of the execution in order to arrive in good time to take up their positions to see this public execution. Only once they had watched the hanging would their work identity cards be returned to them.[51] The area was closed off, and people had already been made to take their place at four in the afternoon. The corpses were removed only at a quarter past seven in the evening.

These executions appear to have been planned with more care, designed to function as a public spectacle, than were the many individuals hangings carried out as a relatively routine form of punishment.[52] The hangings in Będzin and Sosnowiec had been orchestrated in advance, in meticulous detail, by the Police President in Sosnowiec.[53] The execution in Będzin was to take place one hour later than the one in Sosnowiec. As much thought was given by the police authorities to questions of security and seating arrangements as might be appropriate for a modern open-air musical concert: this was to be not a simple punishment for an individual offence, as had happened innumerable times, but rather a mass spectacle, intended to have a major impact on members of the audience, who were, according to category, to have very different kinds of place from which to view the spectacle. As the draft of a report on the event noted:

There were special viewing areas for members of the German audience, so that they were separated from Jews and Poles... While in Sosnowitz the spectators took up their positions in a relatively narrow space, in Bendsburg the spatially more extended square allowed for a better set-up.[54]

The report on the Będzin hangings noted with apparent satisfaction that there were 'no disturbances, no infringements of the prohibition on photography'.[55] A rather indistinct contemporary photograph, clearly taken illicitly from behind someone's shoulder and from some distance away, suggests that nevertheless the chance of capturing a record of the spectacle was held by at least one member of the audience to be worth taking the risk; the early post-war drawing by the then teenager Ella Liebermann-Shiber also gives us a strong impression of the impact of this event, as do the many memories.[56]

Despite the relatively less favourable topography for a mass audience, effective impact could also be organized in Sosnowiec. It is worth quoting at some length to gain an impression of just how carefully this public event was staged:

It was also felt to be particularly agreeable that Germans and ethnic Germans were allowed to set themselves up on the northern side of the gardens (the place of execution of judgment) and that the western side of the square was kept completely clear. As a result the public consisting of Jews and Poles, who took up their positions on the western pavement side of the Modrow alley at the same level as the gardens, also had a good view of the place of execution of judgment. And because the military procession took up its position on the southern side of the gardens, it was clearly visible from in front, that is by practically all spectators; the desired effect was

Figure 15. An illicit photograph of the April 1942 hanging
It was strictly forbidden to take photographs at this well-orchestrated public event, which some 5,000 Jews were forced to watch for over two hours before they were allowed to return home. This photograph was probably taken by a German civilian.
United States Holocaust Memorial Museum, courtesy of the Żydowski Instytut Historyczny.

therefore not lacking. On the eastern side of this park around 750 Jews took part as enforced spectators.[57]

It required the permission of the civilian authorities to ensure that the regular restrictions on Jews' movements would be lifted in order to ensure the maximum audiences and the 'desired effects'.

Was there a particular significance to these two simultaneous spectacles? Public hangings appear to have taken place over a wide range of different locations at around the same time, about one month before major deportations, and planned with similar care some days in advance. There are many eyewitness testimonies to this effect, as, for example, in the neighbouring district of Chrzanów, where, according to one report: 'Representatives of the German authorities with their wives and friends assembled at the execution site. They were laughing while the persons condemned to death were the object of ridicule.'[58] These coordinated public spectacles of mass hangings do not seem, as in other cases of retributions, to have been in direct response to a particular crime; it seems there was a policy of 'any Jew will do', although infringements of German rules (including not only black market dealings but also very trivial 'offences') were adduced as the ostensible 'reason' for these executions. Members of the Kattowitz Gestapo, including Hans Dreier as the official responsible for Jewish affairs, seem to have been heavily involved in the organization and implementation of the spectacles, examining the sites in advance and making arrangements for setting up the gallows, in the process no doubt liaising closely with local officials.

In the case of a small town in the Reichsgau Wartheland, we have the contemporary evidence of the local mayor and *Amtskommissar*, Alexander Hohenstein.[59] Hohenstein recalls in painful detail the way in which he was visited by two members of the SS several days before the intended hanging, and requested to find a sixth person for the gallows. It was not as if the gallows were already in existence: they were to be specially constructed to accommodate a half dozen Jews, and the SS informed him that they were prepared to supply only five of them, local Jews who had in the meantime been incarcerated in Łódź. He was to find the sixth. On protesting against this, he was told that all Jews were criminals, and anyone could be used for the occasion; whether or not he could identify someone who had actually committed a crime and deserved to be punished for a specific offence, they were all fit to be put to death in any case. Following several days of agonized thought and even discussion with the local Leader of the Jewish Council, Hohenstein refused to find a sixth victim; on the designated day of the hanging, that part of the gallows remained empty. The event itself was highly disturbing; Hohenstein could hardly bear to watch as local Jews were deployed to put the nooses around the necks of their own family members and friends, and the whole community was forced to watch. He stood in the allotted place as local head of the civilian administration, but stared at his shoes rather than enacting the appropriate gestures expected of an official in his position. He was also horrified to find that some thirty Jews were in fact being held in the back of the truck driven in to deliver the five designated victims; on asking who they were, he was told that the hanging was part of a series, and they were simply driving around a variety of places hanging them in batches in each place as they passed.

Hohenstein's refusal to deliver up a sixth victim to the gallows, his bearing of evident discomfiture on the day, his previous kindnesses to both Poles and Jews—he had even once invited the Jewish leader and his wife to a social evening in his own home—all contributed to increasing difficulties with the local party. Ultimately, he was called up on charges of disciplinary offences, forced to resign from his office, stripped of *NSDAP* membership, and banned from any future career in the German civil service (*Beamtentum*). Despite his broader commitment to bringing what he still held to be superior German 'civilization' to the 'primitive' eastern provinces, he was forced to return to the Old Reich, where he worked for a while in industry before being sent to the front. After the war, despite this quite honourable stand against the way Nazi racism was becoming evidently murderous, Hohenstein was held to be in the compromised category 3 of Nazi offenders, and subsequently—ironically, given the similar ban under Nazism—he was unable ever to pick up a civil service career in the Federal Republic of Germany.

The case of Hohenstein offers a very instructive comparison to developments in the Będzin area around the same time. The incident recorded in Hohenstein's diary bears a striking resemblance to the similar orchestration of public spectacles in Sosnowiec and Będzin. The events in Hohenstein's small town took place exactly one month before the round-up of the entire population of the ghetto, their incarceration in the local church where any potential for physical resistance was massively weakened, and their subsequent deportation to gassing in Chełmno. The hangings in Sosnowiec and Będzin took place almost exactly one month before the first major deportations to gassings in Auschwitz. It seems highly likely that these, and the events organized in nearby areas of Silesia at the time (as in the Warthegau), were specifically intended as warning signals to the community of victims—and possibly also tests of loyalty among civilian officials.

There is no direct contemporary evidence of Klausa's presence at the hangings in Będzin, although two survivors do recall his presence at many 'small actions', of which this event may well have been one.[60] Given the clearly compulsory nature not merely of attendance but of public display of support in the case of Hohenstein, it is almost inconceivable that a place of honour in the audience would not have been reserved for someone in the senior capacity of *Landrat*, and that he would not automatically have been expected to attend and contribute to the appropriate official legitimation of the event. Hohenstein was, after all, merely a local functionary, answerable to and significantly below the level of the *Landrat* in his area; Klausa's role was the equivalent of that of Hohenstein's superior, who in fact instituted the disciplinary proceedings against Hohenstein for staring down at his feet and not displaying the appropriate attitude in public at the hangings in his town. Moreover, as we have seen in relation to the hangings of Poles for alleged sabotage, Klausa's signature as *Landrat* appears to have been automatically added to public announcements of hangings, whether or not he was personally involved, implying a degree of official responsibility for such an event.[61]

Klausa was certainly physically present in Będzin and in office with full responsibility in April 1942. Indeed, he was at this time eagerly awaiting full confirmation of his post as *Landrat*, still expected for 20 April, and would therefore have been extremely unlikely to have wanted to put a foot wrong as far as meticulous fulfilment of his duties was concerned. His defence of absence on military duties, to which he appealed when other hangings were investigated by the Ludwigsburg authorities, was certainly not valid on this occasion. We do not have any direct evidence either of his absence, or of his presence and personal participation in this particular event. But the direct comparison with the Hohenstein case is suggestive. For his evident reluctance to enter into the intended spirit of the spectacle, Hohenstein ended up in disciplinary proceedings and was stripped of both party membership and state offices. Klausa, whose appointment as *Landrat* had initially been on a probationary basis, was just a few weeks later rewarded with promotion to the full status of *Landrat*. In the promotion papers and letters of recommendation, there is no evidence whatsoever of any possible hint of departure from the party line in conduct or attitude; quite the opposite, in fact.

Whether or not he was personally present at the hanging, or chose to stay away, at the time Udo Klausa could not have overlooked an event of this significance, which brought the centre of town, the seat of his municipal administration, more or less to a standstill. Yet there is no mention of it in his memoirs. Had he been upset by this incident and wanted to distance himself from it, he might have mentioned it in his memoirs as one of the many possible reasons for wanting to leave the area; the omission or gap in his memory about such a major event is striking. Yet again, in his memories of his time as *Landrat*, we have a past without violence.

Klausa was proposed for final confirmation of tenure in the office of *Landrat* with a series of supportive letters of reference, written in March and April 1942. Regional President Springorum initially proposed him in glowing terms:

> Klausa has, in the particularly difficult conditions of the Bendsburg district, been goal-oriented and successful in his work... Particularly following his participation

Figure 16. Old Jewish cemetery today
The patch of park that is the unmarked site of the old Jewish cemetery in Zawale Street, Będzin, where a public hanging took place in April 1942 (see Figure 15). *Conrad Fulbrook.*

in the war he possesses, alongside a secure basis of knowledge, a calm assurance in his appearance and behaviour. He reaches rapid, clear and independent decisions that he ensures are efficiently carried out. It is precisely his leadership in office since taking up his duties again in Bendsburg that has demonstrated that he has fulfilled the preconditions for final nomination as Landrat.[62]

Springorum's superior, Gauleiter Bracht, could only endorse this praise on behalf of the *NSDAP*, adding simply that Klausa 'has in the course of good cooperation developed a relationship of trust with party offices'.[63] These sentiments were further endorsed by the Reich Minister of the Interior, who in his letter made good use of phrases already supplied by Springorum and Bracht.[64] The official confirmation of Klausa's nomination as tenured *Landrat* was dated 12 May 1942 and given Hitler's seal of approval on 15 May 1942—one month after the hanging, and just as the first major deportations to Auschwitz had begun.[65] Whatever inner conflicts Klausa may have been experiencing, in the light of pressures for public conformity and promotion to a permanent position as *Landrat*, he was arguably able to go through at least the outward motions in a more satisfactory manner than was the lower-ranking functionary and local mayor Alexander Hohenstein. There was no visible evidence of any break on Klausa's part with the official line of the Nazi regime up to this point, and much to suggest that he had more than fulfilled his duties to the satisfaction of his superiors at the highest levels.

Like so much else that went on in his area, Klausa does not mention the hanging in his memoirs. Elderly local Polish people do, however, remember the hangings vividly. Irene G., for example, recalled very clearly walking back from her grandmother's house nearby, and, still a young girl at the time, being stopped and forced to watch.[66] But the hangings were not memorialized in any way in the public culture of Będzin of the early twenty-first century when we visited; indeed, the nearly deserted patch of green alongside a couple of roads, at the intersection of Zawale Street, cannot even be recognized as the 'old Jewish cemetery'. A couple of benches, with old men drinking beer and a dog barking and running around wildly, a few trees and an old wall, form now a small patch of land that can hardly be dignified with the name of park. Without an old map or specialist knowledge, it would be impossible to know what events had taken place here in April 1942: that 5,000 people had been gathered, so many against their will, to watch the hanging of men who were killed merely because they had tried to stay alive.

It was only as policies shifted into an altogether more sinister gear—instant murder rather than slow death by neglect, illness, starvation, or retributions—that Klausa appears to have had growing qualms about the enterprise in which he was so closely involved. In this, too, he was entirely typical of very many Germans. Even some of those who later ended up involved in the 1944 July Plot were still active supporters of the regime at this time. Ordinary racism, everyday exploitation and suppression, were still within a Nazi 'moral universe' prioritizing the 'master race', a mental framework that so many seem to have found acceptable and were prepared to sustain in all aspects of their official roles. More obvious and direct forms of murder of civilians, particularly in large numbers, seemed to some at least to be on a different plane. While for some the escalation of genocide in 1942 began to precipitate a break with Nazism, for others stirrings of conscience simply rendered continued fulfilment of their duties rather more uncomfortable. It is at this point that the tales told by memory and the facts of the historical record begin to drift increasingly apart, as some of those involved later arguably sought to represent how they had felt rather than how things had actually been at the time.

9

Towards Extermination

Auschwitz was always an open threat, used to instil fear and obedience into the population. Even well before the development of techniques for killing Jews by the use of poison gas (Zyklon B) and the emergence of a concerted effort to exterminate every Jew in German-dominated Europe, Auschwitz was widely known as a site of imprisonment, extreme brutality, starvation, illness, and high mortality rates, including killings by various forms of torture, shooting, and hanging.

Yet, however awful life might be, few Jews in the surrounding area could imagine, given their crucial role in production for the German war effort, that the fruits of their labour might eventually be valued less highly than the fact of their deaths; that exterminationist ideology could displace the exploitation of labour for military purposes. The realization that the unthinkable was in fact true spread among those targeted as victims of mass murder over the spring and summer of 1942.

This period, when thousands of Jews were deported from the Będzin area to their deaths in the nearby gas chambers of Auschwitz, also appears to have been something of a turning point for Udo Klausa, although perhaps not always in the ways he described. It seems likely that at this time a crucial threshold in the acceptability of racist policies began to be crossed as far as he was concerned. But the evidence of Klausa's responses is patchy; and his own later story does not entirely match with contemporary sources. It is impossible to reconstruct with any certainty what his inner feelings and considerations at the time really were. Some elements of his story—particularly his alleged ignorance about Auschwitz—are highly implausible. Some details, such as the date he repeatedly gives about his departure from Będzin, as well as the reasons for his return to the army, are simply false: factually incompatible with what the archival evidence reveals. Some parts, including the stories Klausa himself tells, do not add up to a coherent picture, and are open to a number of possible interpretations. Almost certainly what we have in Klausa's later account is an attempt to convey some of his own perceptions of the situation, but they do not fit very well with what other sources suggest.

It is at this point that the significance of my own double role—as both professional historian and a personal friend of the family—becomes particularly relevant. For the mutual contradictions and the ambiguities of the stories and sources can lead to a variety of possible conclusions.

Had I not known the family well, I would have been led instantly to what would appear the most plausible of these interpretations: that, in his post-war self-representations, it was simply a case of a former Nazi lying about his past in order to cover potentially guilty tracks and evade having to take any kind of responsibility for the past—an emotionally potentially unbearable burden, even if never leading to establishment of guilt in the restricted legal sense of the term. It would thus be possible to write this story with a degree of cynicism—and, given the scale of the consequences of such behaviour in terms of 'making Auschwitz possible' (on which more below), it is not only survivors, and the friends and relatives of victims, but indeed anyone with a concern for humanity who might hold such cynicism to be justified. The story could thus quite easily be written as essentially one of indictment.

On the other hand, the evidence of Alexandra's repeated comments in her letters about her husband's nervous state during the summer months of 1942, as well as what I have been told of very open post-war discussions within the Klausa family, suggest far more personal disquiet at the time than the more cynical account of a convenient post-war cover-up would probably allow for. Comments in contemporary letters suggest an inner state to which we cannot have secure evidence-based access, but they do imply that Klausa was intensely ill at ease during the period of the first major deportations, and particularly in the run-up to the major selections and deportations of August 1942. Despite his later protestations of complete ignorance, even he concedes that in general terms he was aware of the massively criminal nature of what was going on at this time, and the clues in his own self-representations provide strong evidence of a wish to be personally disassociated from these events.

The story could thus be one not of indictment but of interpretation: of relatively (un)sympathetic understanding of the dilemma in which Klausa found himself, caught between the demands of an office and a role he had always coveted and that represented the summit of his career ambitions, and a remarkably late but growing realization of the sheer criminality of the Nazi enterprise that he was, through exercise of his official duties, functionally helping to sustain.

Klausa was—like so many other ordinary Nazis in the Third Reich—in this sense caught by the system; and now, the escalation of antisemitism into a comprehensive programme of mass extermination went way beyond the kind of colonial racism that he had supported up to this point. The problem was that by virtue of his official role he was of necessity both knowledgeable and involved in practice in a variety of ways: the pleas in his memoirs of ignorance and innocence cannot actually be sustained in the ways he wanted, without serious gaps and reshaping of the narrative. But the dissonance between what he felt and the truth of the situation would later have been too great to live with in any comfort: the story thus arguably had to be massaged to fit the sense of self and an acceptable post-war identity rather than the actual facts of the situation.

It is in this very ambiguity and complexity that we can see how people who had initially felt they were doing a perfectly honourable job in the civil service, and who were indeed also prepared to go a very long way down the road of intensely racist practices in Hitler's regime, finally baulked when they realized the full horror of where Nazi racism was leading. In several other cases, individuals in similar situations, or coming to similar realizations, refused to go along the road of conformity and facilitation any further, or even, in some few instances, began to think more actively about engaging in opposition. Basic antisemitism of the sort that had made it possible to ignore the painful and inhumane consequences of policies of expropriation, ghettoization, enforced malnutrition, and coerced labour, did not necessarily lead directly into being one of 'Hitler's willing executioners' when it came to the gallows, the bullets, and the gas chambers. Understanding this complexity does not entail condoning the racism that had led so many so far down the path of supporting Hitler's horrendous enterprise; but it does go a long way to explaining how the 'final solution' became possible, as the very last step on a road on which so many had accompanied the Nazi project up to this point. And it does help to explain the post-war stories and professions of both horror and ignorance of so many other Germans.[1]

'Ordinary Nazis' were, in their own self-perceptions, quite different from those whom they saw as the 'real' or 'fanatic' Nazis, in the company of whom they felt they had to mind what they said and how they behaved. On any historical analysis, it is clear that the *NSDAP* was never a monolithic entity, and there were always differences between 'moderates'—if this is not an entirely inappropriate word in the context of what any commitment to Nazism entailed—and radicals or extremists. But, without the mass support in principle and practice of those who felt they were engaging in honourable service of the Nazi state, and who indeed often did not even view themselves as 'real' Nazis, extreme 'solutions' would never have been made possible.

Udo Klausa never claimed to have entered the resistance at this or any subsequent point; he served his country loyally throughout the war, indeed receiving a personally signed award from Hitler for his bravery in one particular battle, an award he saved in his personal files. He claims rather to have expressed a more muted courage, in offering himself up to return to the front rather than remain and be party, in however distant a way, to the crimes in the locality of Auschwitz. If the evidence is examined closely, this story does not quite stand up in the way that he tells it. Yet it was this—effectively a gesture of potential self-sacrifice—that Klausa perhaps internally intended; it was certainly this story with which he personally identified; and for this reason his self-representation departs from the story actually told by the archival evidence. The self-representations thus made psychological sense, and allowed Klausa (and members of his family) to live with his past as an honourable man, whatever the historian may want to say about the actual sequence of events and the functional role played by the *Landrat* in the unfolding horror of the fate of the Jews of Będzin.

It is in this combination of inner ambivalence and outward conformity that some of the answers as to how Auschwitz was possible may be found. And it is here, perhaps, that the author, as both historian and family friend, also has the greatest conflicts to overcome in explicating and interpreting the course of events over the summer and autumn of 1942.

The transition to the 'final solution'

There had, already since 1940, been periodic arrests and deportations of Jews to Auschwitz—generally as a result of some minor infringement of the innumerable regulations to which they were increasingly subjected, but also for failure to follow the orders of the Germans passed on via the Jewish Councils.[2] The levels of torture and brutality exercised in Auschwitz, as well as the prevalence of disease and acute malnutrition, were widely known both among those who were threatened with Auschwitz as punishment as well as those charged with upholding Nazi notions of law and order. Moreover, *Landräte* in the area had been officially informed of the use of deportation to Auschwitz as a penalty for non-compliance with, for example, the demands for labour on the part of the Organisation Schmelt.

Even at a relatively early stage, well before the construction of the extermination centre in Birkenau, it was widely known among the local population that, although Poles might return from periods of incarceration in the main prison camp of Auschwitz, Jews generally did not. Often the only news that came back was a request for money to deal with the ashes of a person who had supposedly died from 'natural causes' within a matter of days or weeks after arrival. In one case, thirty-two men were sent by Lindner from a work camp to Auschwitz for alleged 'sabotage'; soon telegrams were sent to their families requesting 30 Reich Marks each for return of the ashes.[3] In another case, as Michael Lasker testified in 1961, a group known to him were arrested and suffered a similar fate:

> They put the people who had been arrested into the 'orphanage' in Bedzin from where, after about two weeks, they were taken by the Katowice Gestapo to Oswiecim (Auschwitz). A few days later telegrams were sent from Oswiecim with the notification that so-and-so had died as a result of a seizure and that the relatives could receive an urn with his ashes if they would pay 30.-RM for it to be sent. All these telegrams arrived via the Jewish Community in Sosnowiec.[4]

Repeated incidents where those deported were never heard of subsequently could leave little doubt in people's minds about the essentially murderous character of Auschwitz even before they heard of the development of mass extermination through gassing.

Klausa too could hardly have been unaware of the escalation of genocidal policies at this time. Following the military invasion of the Soviet Union in the summer of 1941, mass killings of Jewish civilians took place in which *Einsatzgruppen* were assisted by ordinary police forces and local collaborators, often with the knowledge and logistical backing of the army. Both Klausa and one of his brothers-in-law were serving on the eastern front at this time; despite Klausa's protestations to the contrary, they can hardly have been unaware of what was going on, even if it is true, as he claims, that Klausa himself never personally witnessed any atrocity. One of the major problems with these methods of killing was that they were hard to hide;

they were much talked about among troops as well as civilians in the region (such as road engineers and others working in the area) and many soldiers wrote home about dreadful scenes they had witnessed.

Klausa is unlikely to have known about the experiments, in the course of the autumn of 1941, to find 'better', more 'efficient', means of killing, including the use of Zyklon B gas, first used on Soviet political prisoners in Auschwitz on 3 September 1941. But other developments in the technology and practices of mass killing were beginning to be talked about among local functionaries in the vicinity of the new extermination centres over the course of the coming winter and spring. In early December 1941, Jews from the Łódź ghetto were 'selected' for gassing in Chełmno (Kulmhof in German) by exhaust fumes piped into the back of vans into which they had been herded; once all those in the van were dead, the bodies were tipped out and buried in mass graves dug in a nearby forest. Knowledge of this was already circulating in nearby areas, and spread relatively rapidly among the community of potential victims with the clandestine movement of Jews across a far wider area. Even local functionaries well below the level of *Landrat* became aware of what was going on with the Jewish communities in their areas of responsibility.

The Warthegau *Amtskommissar* Hohenstein, for example, noted in his diary entry of 28 December 1941 that the Jews in the ghetto of the town where he was mayor were aware of mass murder already at the end of December 1941, when killings in Chełmno had been going on for only three weeks; they believed the rumours, while he was at this time unwilling to concede any truth to the stories. Hohenstein recorded the remembered conversation in a diary entry shortly afterwards: although the words are unlikely to have been remembered precisely, even so soon after the event, the gist of the discussion is likely to be authentic. He had invited the leader of the Jewish Council and his wife, Herr and Frau Goldeborn, for a totally illicit social evening, which he knew could cost him his 'head and neck' if news of it spread to his superiors. The key conversation that evening was reportedly opened by Frau Goldeborn, saying that she felt that they were heading towards 'an inevitable, evil fate, a terrible end'; she spoke of the 'gruesome rumours' that were going around among the Jewish community.[5] The Goldeborns' fears proved prescient: within four months they too had been deported to Chełmno for gassing. Hohenstein's last act of kindness to this Jewish couple, treating them as human beings, did in the event cost him, if not his life, then at least his job, despite his having chosen an evening when all the house personnel had been given leave, and the gendarmerie were preoccupied with birthday celebrations in a local hostelry and unlikely to be observing any comings and goings at his house. On tip-offs from an informer, however, this social evening was one among several elements leading up to Hohenstein's eventual dismissal from his post.

Auschwitz, not Chełmno, was the centre to which the Jews of Eastern Upper Silesia were sent to be murdered. In the spring of 1942, the use of Auschwitz was massively transformed and extended: in addition to being a major centre for imprisonment, torture, and slave labour, Auschwitz now evolved into what was to become the largest dedicated extermination centre of the Third Reich, with the development of specially designed gas chambers and crematoria at Auschwitz–Birkenau. And, given the proximity of Będzin to Auschwitz, Jews from this and neighbouring communities in the Dąbrowa industrial region were at the forefront of the unfolding programme and the developing psychological tactics as well as enhanced technology of mass murder at Auschwitz–Birkenau.

Local people widely began to suspect that these deportations were of a rather different nature from the previous deportations to the labour camps, although suspicions were roused only in faltering and partial steps, with 'knowledge' accompanied by a widespread sense of disbelief and continued hope against all the evidence. Potential victims were reliant primarily on rumours spread by word of mouth. They also drew conclusions from the demographic profile of those now being deported. The subsequent total silence of these groups also gave considerable cause for concern.

Gunter Faerber, for example, recalled the moment in February 1942 when the Jews of Beuthen (Bytom in Polish), where his grandmother lived, were brought through Będzin on their way to Auschwitz.[6] The men had some time previously already been taken to labour camps. Two large army trucks of Jewish women from Beuthen were brought 'straight to the station, they were queuing at the station':

> I was still given a chance to say goodbye because we knew already, how we found out I don't know, that the women of Beuthen are arriving, from other little towns as well. I went down to the station, I saw the long queue of women.[7]

Faerber asked permission of a Gestapo guard to go up to his grandmother, who was with her sister, 'and I said goodbye, and that was the last I saw of them and the whole transport was moved out by train and I never saw her again and I never heard anything [about] where they went to'. Faerber knew it would be his final farewell to his grandmother, since he was certain of the deadly nature of the train's destination. Realizing that elderly women were unlikely to be setting off for labour camps, and then hearing nothing more after their departure, were highly significant for concerned family members, and a composite picture soon began to build up. The lack of any further news at all was in stark contrast to the relatively frequent exchanges of letters and parcels that took place between people in labour camps and their families at home, as in the case of Sala Garncarz and her family in Sosnowiec.

This was new, and it was almost unimaginable. For a little over two years after the Nazi invasion of Poland, Jews had been systematically robbed of their possessions, maltreated, humiliated, starved, and on occasion killed. But during this time the Jewish inhabitants of Będzin had been primarily exploited for their labour power and productivity in a highly industrial area, one that appeared crucial to the German military effort. Jews elsewhere, particularly in the large ghettos of Warsaw and Łódź, had suffered far worse conditions, with daily mass deaths from starvation and disease. But in the spring of 1942, even in Silesia where Jewish labour was essential to the German war economy, there was a pronounced and noticeable shift in policies. Repression and exploitation were progressively displaced by the escalating policies of mass murder, now seen as the 'final solution' of the Jewish question. If labour remained for the time being protected, within a year and a half even those who were for the time being deemed fit to work would be murdered.

The first gassings of Jews from Upper Silesia, including very probably Gunter Faerber's grandmother, took place on 15 February in the gas chamber of Crematorium 1, in the main Auschwitz camp.[8] From 20 March, Jews were killed in the newly installed gas chambers of a converted farmhouse in Birkenau, the so-called Bunker Number 1.[9] For the following several months, deaths took place as a result of fatal injections, being shot 'while trying to escape', disease, starvation, and torture. Gassings also continued to take place in Auschwitz I, where 'improvements' in the 'efficiency' of the procedure of mass murder were continually improvised. We know from the rare testimony of a survivor of Auschwitz, the former Kapo (prisoner functionary) Filip Müller, something of what awaited a group of Jews who were deported to Auschwitz in May 1942: they were among the first to be wilfully deceived into thinking that this would merely be a shower, a tactic that assisted their relatively cooperative quietude in entering the gas chambers.[10]

Following earlier outbreaks of panic among the arriving groups of people destined for death, and the difficulties experienced by Kapos in undressing the corpses after they had been gassed, it was on this occasion that the SS improvised techniques for 'calming' the new arrivals by misleadingly telling them they were merely going to have showers before going to work, and persuaded them to undress in the open air prior to entering the gas chambers. Although this had some effect—at least to the satisfaction of the SS men involved—it became increasingly clear that gassings in Auschwitz I were too public, and that the centre of killing operations should be moved to the ever-expanding complex at Birkenau, some 2 miles away on the other side of the main railway lines.[11]

Many of these early transports, instantly gassed on arrival, were from Będzin or Sosnowiec and the surrounding towns and villages. Indeed, the first time the numbers are in the thousands is with the mass deportations from Będzin and Sosnowiec when in early May 1942 some 5,200 Jews from Eastern Upper Silesia were killed in the gas chamber of Bunker Number 1.[12]

The escalation of killings, May 1942

The first mass deportations from Będzin and Sosnowiec were scheduled to take place over a few days starting in early May, and were planned in advance in meticulous detail, with instructions given to the local police forces already on 8 May, several days in advance of the planned 'action' in Będzin of 12 May.[13] It seems that the stepping up of numbers deported to be killed took place following a couple of weeks in which Himmler had repeatedly met Heydrich, in widely separated geographical locations: Friedrichsruh, Berlin, Munich, and Prague.[14]

Perniciously, the Jewish Council was directly involved in 'selecting' this first major transportation of the elderly, disabled, and very young, who were to report for 'resettlement', accompanied and controlled by members of the Jewish militia as well as regular German police forces. In Sosnowiec, a total of 1,200 Jews were supposed to present themselves at a school in readiness for 'resettlement'; but by the third day only some 150 of those on the list had actually shown up. The Leader of the Jewish Councils of Elders, Moses Merin, was then central to the organization of a somewhat violent hunt, which finally produced a significant number of Jews for deportation from Sosnowiec and Będzin.[15] The official sources report that on 12 May 1942, in

Figure 17. Round-up of Jews in Dąbrowa for deportation, April 1942
German soldiers rounding up Jews on Francuska Street in the Dąbrowa ghetto.
United States Holocaust Memorial Museum, courtesy of Sidney Schlesinger.

Bunker Number 1 in Birkenau, 1,500 men, women, and children were gassed with Zyklon B.[16] In total some 4,000 Jews were rounded up over a period of just a few days.[17]

Although some Jews clung to the forlorn hope that deported groups might genuinely be going to 'resettlement', others sensed that this was wholly implausible. Polish railway workers were already telling the Jews of this area that the destination was Auschwitz, and also what this now entailed.[18] The round-ups were thus accompanied by panic, terror, and many people being shot on the spot as they sought to resist capture and deportation.

An early post-war source described the 'action' of 12 May 1942 in Będzin, recording how Jews had been collected up from the poverty-stricken streets of the now massively overcrowded Jewish quarter around Zawale Street, by the old Jewish cemetery where the Jews had been publicly hanged only one month earlier:

There is in Bendzin a street on the other side of the castle hill, not far from the Przemsza [river], called Zawale. It was called 'cold arse' by the Jewish population. Most of the Jewish poor people had lived there previously in small houses, half falling down. This quarter was surrounded in the early morning by police and militia, and everything that was alive was driven onto a large square and taken from there to the orphanage.[19]

On the occasion of this round-up, another 'selection' appears to have taken place in the orphanage across the railway tracks, carried out by Gestapo officials including Hans Dreier and Kuczynski, prior to being taken to Auschwitz via Sosnowice station. There were two further 'actions' in the following days to try to achieve the total numbers desired, including the deportation of orphaned Jewish children and all the inhabitants of the Jewish hospital.[20] The role of the Jewish militia in assisting in these round-ups was highly contentious, both at the time and later. Hirsch Barenblat, commander of the Jewish militia in Będzin, had to take a leading role in these events. He was subsequently tried for his collaboration, both in Poland immediately after the war and again in Israel in the early 1960s, at which time he was assistant conductor of the Israel National Opera. Identified by a Będzin survivor at a concert in June 1960, Barenblat was subjected to investigations, leading to his arrest in 1961. Although in 1963 the Tel Aviv District Court convicted Barenblat of collaboration and sentenced him to five years' imprisonment, the following year the Israeli Supreme Court overturned this decision, and Barenblat was acquitted in February 1964.[21]

The round-ups and deportations in which Barenblat and others were forcibly involved took place in full view in the streets of central Będzin; the orphanage where people were held was the scene of considerable violence and police activity; and, given the logistics and planning involved, as well as the evident disruptions at the time, it is difficult to believe that the *Landrat* did not know about any of this.[22] In a somewhat self-contradictory statement to the Ludwigsburg authorities, Klausa does on one occasion concede that the civilian administration was officially informed about such actions—allegedly 'generally' only *after* they had taken place—and that he assumed that the transports went to Auschwitz, at least at the final clearance of the ghetto. In the words of the Ludwigsburg summary:

[Klausa] claims that the SS with its various establishments had control of the whole Jewish question and that the administration was generally only informed about measures against the Jews when they had been carried out. He assumes that the Jews on the clearance of the ghetto were sent to Auschwitz.[23]

Whether or not he was informed before or only after the deportation on this occasion, Klausa cannot have been unaware of it. But this May 1942 deportation of several thousand Jews to their deaths finds no place at all in Klausa's memoirs. Indeed, even his apparent clarity about the character and destination of deportations fades from his statements over time, as we shall see.

Meanwhile, there seemed little improvement in Klausa's state of health. He was able to go on a 'rest cure' for some weeks from 20 May to late June 1942. Alexandra's letters to her mother at this time initially express concern about how to pay for this period of recuperation, then relief that she had been able to find the money out of current income rather than drawing from her savings; she finally expressed the hope that the regional government would in the end finance or at least greatly subsidize the rest cure.[24] While he was away, Klausa received the very welcome news that his initially provisional, probationary appointment as *Landrat* had finally been confirmed as permanent; he even received a congratulatory telegram from his deputy, Jansen, sent to him on 29 May 1942.[25] This appointment at a relatively early age, despite the delay in receiving it, was a source of some personal pride.

Following Klausa's return from his rest cure at the end of June, Alexandra several times comments in letters to her mother that, while her husband appeared outwardly recovered and in a good physical state, his 'nerves' were terrible. In a letter to her mother of 28 June, following a complaint that since the cobbler, one Goldman, had gone 'away' (presumably deported) the shoe repair service was no longer satisfactory, she writes: 'Udo came home on Friday [26 June]. He looks well and sun-tanned and has rested up. But up to now the rest cure has really achieved no success with respect to his nerves, this is really too dreadful.'[26] A few days later, on 2 July, Alexandra complains that the market stalls were closing down and Jews presumably being 'sent to labour duties elsewhere'. After comments about the state of the garden, her pursuit of fresh fruit and vegetables with the help of Udo's colleague and house manager Ignatz Margosch, her children's activities and other domestic matters, Alexandra comments again on her husband's state:

> He came back with the usual benefits of a vacation, looks well, has rested up and has been well fed. But any success of the rest cure with respect to his nerves is actually not at all evident, this is very bad.[27]

In a letter of 29 July, some four weeks after Udo's return home, Alexandra complains again about Udo's state:

Udo's rest cure was money absolutely chucked away, I find him unchanged, if not in an even worse state with respect to mood and energy levels. Of course even the slightest benefits of his period of recuperation have long hence dissipated. It is too ghastly. And on top of this he wants to go back to the front in the autumn, because he is hoping to be able to endure it better if he has himself transferred to a motorized unit.[28]

From this it is clear that something was deeply troubling Klausa, something that had not been 'cured' by the food and relaxation of the rest cure. Moreover, it is also clear—and this is significant in relation to Klausa's own later story of a turning point with the August deportation and the sudden offer to return to the army—that he was already at this stage aiming to return to military service in the autumn. It is more than likely that at this point Klausa knew about the mass deportations to Auschwitz—something about which he quite probably did not talk to his wife (or if he did, she was not prepared to put any such intimations in a letter to her mother), and which may well have been troubling him immensely, accounting for the worsening of mood and depression.

There was, then, no sudden decision to offer himself back to the front following the witnessing of a deportation in August, as represented in Klausa's memoirs, but rather a view of the future already being discussed in July. It is perfectly possible, indeed very likely, that his terrible 'nerves' were connected with knowledge of what was going on at this time; and that his later attempt to imply ignorance of deportations until August, and then claim he left immediately, were related to the hope that he could thus disassociate himself from the genocide of which he was arguably becoming all too well aware.[29]

Growing realization and 'knowledge'

Deportations on a smaller scale continued over the weeks following the mass round-up of May 1942. Chaim Michal Silberberg (born 1900) recalled that 'between the three large actions virtually every week there were smaller actions in which always some tens of Jews were deported'.[30] Miriam Liwer recalled weekly transports—on Wednesdays—from the orphanage; not only Jews from Będzin but also sometimes from further afield in Silesia, and even from Holland, were held here before being taken on to Auschwitz.[31] Again, Dreier, Mildner, and others from the SS and the Kattowitz Gestapo headquarters were closely involved. And it had already become increasingly clear that Jews were being sent to Auschwitz and murdered.

Klausa's colleagues higher up in the hierarchy of civilian administration were certainly closely acquainted with developments in Auschwitz. Klausa's immediate superior in Kattowitz, Springorum, in fact visited Auschwitz on the evening of 14 May 1942—just after the deportation of some 4,000 Jews in total from Sosnowiec and Będzin—and had discussions with Rudolf Höss about the relations between the SS and municipal authorities. On this visit, he was accompanied by other members of the civilian administration, including a relatively low-level local functionary, and met representatives of industry.[32]

Both Springorum and his immediate superior, the *Gauleiter* and Silesian Provincial Governor Fritz Bracht, accompanied Heinrich Himmler on his visit to Auschwitz on 17 July 1942. This was followed by a social evening in Himmler's honour, hosted by Gauleiter Bracht in his villa in Beuthen, in the company of both Springorum and Auschwitz Commandant Rudolf Höss. We know that the methods and scale of killing were discussed explicitly at this event. On this occasion Himmler apparently drank rather more wine than he was accustomed to, and appeared relieved and relaxed. He seems to have talked rather more openly about his plans for extermination than he might otherwise have done in such a social event with a relatively extended guest list.[33] An ordinary industrialist, Eduard Schulte, whose mining company actually owned this villa, now on loan to Bracht, was among those attending the event. He was sufficiently incensed by what he gleaned from the conversations that evening that he risked his own life to get the news of the extermination policy out to the Allies, via contacts in Switzerland.[34] Schulte's attempts to warn the world and avert the impending mass murder of Europe's Jews did not have the desired effect.

Curiously, Springorum, in Klausa's evaluation, was, as we have seen, a thoroughly decent man who would provide protection against the 'brown big-wigs'.[35] This comment was made by Klausa in the context of seeking, yet again, to draw a sharp contrast between the brown-uniformed 'Nazis' and the grey-suited civilian administrators such as himself. Yet the evidence suggests that this is an entirely inappropriate distinction, given the prevalence of *NSDAP* members in civilian administration (as was Klausa himself), and the demonstrably close cooperation between all involved in the escalating process of 'Germanization'.

The deportations and killings continued to escalate. Indeed, immediately after this visit, on 19 July 1942, Himmler actually ordered a stepping-up of the pace of extermination, aiming to render Poland entirely 'Jew free' by the end of the year. The scale of killing was now such that it became ever more obvious across a wide area.

Shortly after his visit to Auschwitz, Himmler also ordered, via Eichmann's office, that the corpses in the mass graves that had been dug earlier in the year should now be dug up and burned, and the ashes disposed of in such a way that no one would ever be able to count the numbers.[36] By the summer of 1942, the bodies that had been buried in large pits near the gas chambers were apparently beginning to putrefy in the heat. As Pery Broad, a member of the Waffen-SS who worked in the Political Section of Auschwitz, recalled:

> The sun shone hotly that summer upon Birkenau, the only partially decomposed bodies began to fester and a dark red mass poured out from gaps in the ground. The resulting stench was indescribable. Something had to be done about it and quickly.[37]

It was also clear that, as killing measures were being stepped up, some better method would have to be found to dispose of the growing volume of corpses. Even burial could not adequately dispose of the traces.

The decision was then taken to dig up the mass graves and burn the bodies on a great pyre, visible for miles around. In the description of Auschwitz Commandant Rudolf Höss:

> we started to burn [the corpses], at first on wood pyres bearing some 2,000 corpses, and later in pits together with bodies previously buried. In the early days oil refuse was poured on the bodies, but later methanol was used. Bodies were burnt in pits, day and night, continuously.[38]

One eyewitness, himself an SS officer at the camp, later described with horror the effect that witnessing this burning had on him; he claims he felt particular revulsion at the way in which 'the Kapo there . . . made fun of the fact that when the bodies started burning they obviously developed gases from the lungs or elsewhere and these bodies seemed to jump up, and the sex parts of the men suddenly became erect in a kind of way that he found laughable'.[39] His own response was merely to ensure that he worked in administrative tasks, sorting money taken from the victims, and insulating himself from any direct contact with a mass murder to which, at that time, he had no principled opposition. Pery Broad recalled in his 'Reminiscences' that, in the original crematorium of Auschwitz I,

the smoke did not always rise above the chimney in transparent, bluish clouds. It was sometimes pressed down to the ground by the wind. And then one could notice the unmistakeable, penetrating stench of burnt hair and burnt flesh, a stench that spread over many miles. When the ovens, in which four or six bodies were burnt at the same time, were just heated, a dense, pitch-black smoke coiled upwards from the chimney and then there was no doubt as to the purpose of that mound. Or when at night a tall flame issuing from the chimney was visible from afar.[40]

It was no better when bodies were also being burned on the pyres in Birkenau:

In the countryside a little farther from the camp, a countryside, by the way, which was less marshy and very lovely, one could, for long weeks, see dense, whitish smoke clouds rising towards the sky from several spots. Nobody was allowed to come near these places without a special pass, but the stench betrayed the truth about which people around Birkenau had begun to whisper.[41]

The situation was made worse by the growth in numbers being murdered.

Höss recalled: 'During the spring of 1942 the actions were comparatively small, but the transports increased in the summer, and we were compelled to construct a further extermination building', which in turn further added to the growing number of corpses for disposal.[42] He complained that 'during bad weather or when a strong wind was blowing, the stench of burning flesh was carried for many miles and caused the whole neighbourhood to talk about the burning of Jews'.[43] He went on: 'Moreover the air defence services protested against the fires, which could be seen from great distances at night.'[44] In Broad's summary:

the great pyres were spreading such a stench that the whole countryside, many kilometres in width, had been infected. At night, the red sky above Auschwitz was visible for many miles. But it would have been impossible to do away with the immense quantities of corpses, both of those who had died in the camp and of those who had perished in the gas-chambers, without the huge pyres... Gossipy sentries were punished for talking; they were supposed to be guilty of betraying the secrets, but it was by reason of the unmistakeable sweetish smell and the nightly flames that the surrounding neighbourhood learned about the goings-on in the camp of death. Railwaymen used to tell the civilian population how thousands were being brought to Auschwitz every day, and yet the camp was not growing larger at a corresponding rate. The same information was supplied by the police escorts of the transports.[45]

Testimony given at the Nuremberg trials, straight after the war, suggested that the flames above the camp

> could be seen as far away as the Upper Silesian city of Kattowitz, some thirty kilometres distant... Even more disconcerting than the flames was, however, the drifting smell of burning flesh from the area of the camp... If the wind was south-easterly... even the inhabitants of Kattowitz could discern the strangely sweet smell.[46]

A report from a resident of Anhalt, some 6 miles north of Auschwitz, much later gave very similar evidence:

> When the camps were in operation, one would be able to see the factories of Auschwitz and Monowitz from the hill of the neighbouring town. But above all when the wind blew from that direction, one smelled them.
>
> ... it stank everywhere, sometimes almost unbearably, of burnt hair. And if the weather was right and you forgot to close the windows, a kind of fatty-slimy soot settled on the furniture, the dishes, and the floor, and got stuck in your hair... When they were children... they climbed the nearby hill and saw the smoke rising in the distance.[47]

The countryside around Auschwitz is gently undulating, with Auschwitz itself in something of a lower, previously swampy area in the river valley. Considering this question from higher vantage points while driving along the highway today—when we are more than used to seeing the distant glow of city lights when heading towards major urban areas at night—one cannot help but wonder how at that time anyone could have even sought to hide what was going on in Auschwitz, once the burning had started.

And indeed there is much evidence to suggest that rumours spread rapidly, given the all too visible evidence. Many people either lived close to the camp, or interacted with it in the course of their work, further spreading rumours about one of its primary functions. As far as Jews in the region were concerned, such rumours were confirmed by the fact that it was highly unlikely that transports of the elderly, the sick, and the very young were being taken to labour camps; and that those of their friends and families who had been taken to Auschwitz were never heard of again.

Disposal of the bodies, and the visibility of this disposal, was not the only problem for the Nazis. Public health—including the health of their own SS troops and other personnel, as well as the local industrialists employing slave labour—was a major concern. The overflowing of sewers caused health hazards for the local population, quite irrespective of the epidemics among inmates of the world's largest prison and murder site. Again, the local civilian administration was of necessity involved. Klausa's superiors Springorum and Bracht repeatedly visited Auschwitz, and knowledgably discussed the problems of drainage in the area, including a further site visit in September 1942, which included the local *Landrat*, to discuss how to deal with drainage in view of the ever-growing population in the camp.[48] The *Landrat* of the *Landkreis* of Bielitz in which Auschwitz was situated, to the south of Będzin, was particularly well aware of the consequences for his territory of the increased activity over the summer months. He claimed in one of his regular reports to Regional Governor Springorum that he had, 'in closest cooperation with the state health authorities and the Concentration Camp Auschwitz, taken all possible measures to prevent the further spread of epidemic typhus'.[49]

Moreover, the system of policing and 'justice' in the whole Kattowitz area was closely linked with Auschwitz. The 'Summary Court' of the Kattowitz State Police was held once or twice a month in a special 'courtroom' in Block 11 of Auschwitz I, next to the infamous 'black wall' where executions were held. It was presided over by Dr Mildner, often accompanied by others who were notorious in the surrounding area for their cruelty, including the much-feared SS Hauptsturmführer Hans Aumeier and others. Periodic 'commissions' would visit from the local Gestapo. Prisoners from all over the area, including prisoners from the Będzin area interned in the prison in Myslowitz, were brought here to 'stand trial' and face interrogations, accompanied by torture and often followed by execution. SS Hauptscharführer Franz Nowak was commander of the transit camp ('Dulag') in Sosnowiec: Jews from Będzin and Sosnowiec were frequently brought through this transit camp on their way to forced labour camps or to Auschwitz. While Nowak was in the habit of cruelly beating detainees, when paid high bribes he would also on occasion allow Jews to escape from this camp.[50] There were also close personal links between the Auschwitz staff and the Gestapo personnel in Sosnowiec and Kattowitz. SS Hauptsturmführer Peykart (also spelled Peikert), for example, was in 1942 head of the Sosnowiec Gestapo; in 1943 he was transferred to Oświęcim Gestapo, from where he was transferred to duties in Birkenau. The Ludwigsburg investigation suggested that in 1943 he 'commanded the final deportation actions against Jews in Bendzin and Sosnowiec' and 'supervised and attended all the proceedings and murdered personally a great number of Jews'.[51] It is inconceivable that Klausa's close colleague, the Sosnowiec Police Chief von Woedtke, was as ignorant of all this as he later sought to claim.

Even Jews at some considerable distance from the camp soon heard about its operations in some detail, giving an added urgency to preparations for resistance. By the summer of 1942, Jews—particularly those in the various youth movements—were beginning to coordinate resistance movements across Poland. Hadasseh Rosensaft, who was at that time a young mother and dentist in Sosnowiec, recalled, for example, that her brother Jumek was a member of a Jewish underground movement made up of members from diverse groups, including 'Ha-No'ar ha-Tsioni, Ha-Shomer ha-Tsa'ir, and Gordonia'. This grouping had links with resistance fighters in the Warsaw area and elsewhere:

> In June 1942 Mordecai Anielewicz, later the commander of the Warsaw ghetto uprising, illegally visited our underground resistance groups and told them about the situation of the Jews in other parts of Poland, about the deportations and gas chambers and crematoria. After Anielewicz's departure, the groups intensified their work; they had connections with the Jewish Committee in Switzerland, especially with Saly Mayer, the Swiss Jewish leader and representative of the American Joint Distribution Committee (AJDC), which helped get Jews visas for South American countries.[52]

Shmuel Ron too reports on the increasingly urgent activities of youth resistance groups at this time. They managed by various means to smuggle news into the ghetto from the outside world, to forge links with people outside, to obtain weapons and train themselves in their use; they discussed ways of obtaining false papers in order to hide on the 'Aryan side', or to emigrate or escape illegally under false identities; they debated and despaired of what they saw as the unduly depressive, pessimistic responses of those who simply resigned themselves to their fate.[53]

Yet they also realized that such outlooks and attitudes had been ground into people by the effects of more than two years of oppression by the Germans. Living under Nazi rule had reduced them, physically and emotionally. Shmuel Ron even noted the dramatic changes in his own father's approach to life over this relatively short time:

> My father, who in 1940 took the risk of fleeing and got as far as Aachen in western Germany, was in 1942 a broken man, at a loss and virtually helpless. He was still looking for solutions, in particular for my little sister, but reality finally caught up with him. For reasons that he alone can judge, my father returned to a zealous piety such as I had never known in him during my youth.[54]

Other families of Ron's acquaintance found themselves in horrendous emotional dilemmas. When an elderly member of one family, for example, was on a list for deportation, he went 'voluntarily' to his death despite the best efforts of his family to persuade him against presenting himself at the allotted place, for fear that an attempt to evade the round-up would put all the members of his family at risk, ensuring death not just for himself but for all of them. In many other families, when one member was listed for deportation, others 'voluntarily' went with them—adult children with elderly parents, parents with younger children—unable to bear the thought of loved ones going alone to their deaths.[55] A frequent attempt to retain at least some tiny sense of a degree of 'freedom' was to have a strategy for killing oneself before the Germans could do it, thus choosing one's own moment and means of death.

At this time Moses Merin, the regional Leader of the Jewish Councils, was cooperating fully with the German authorities in drawing up such lists for deportation, still actively collaborating with the Nazis under the illusion that by delivering up half of 'his' people he would be 'saving' the other half. Rabbis here as elsewhere spent long hours debating whether such a strategy was ethical and in accordance with Jewish teachings, and whether it could be viewed as a lesser evil. Despite differences of view and the ambiguous outcomes of such discussions of principle, Merin persisted in this approach, apparently believing that he could pursue his 'messianic' goals and build up a basis of supreme power by virtue of proactive assistance to the Germans. He personally oversaw deportation round-ups, waiting until the Jewish militia had surrounded the designated homes and pulled out those whose names had been listed in advance; he would then personally hand them over to the Germans for deportation. The continuing 'raids' and smaller deportations were thus being carried out with full participation from this would-be 'king', as Mordechai Chaim Rumkowski, the Leader of the Jewish Council in Łódź, had dubbed him.[56]

Reports of the extermination centres in Poland and Silesia, and the mass killing of Jews across Eastern Europe, reached the outside world from the early summer of 1942 onwards. There were perfectly credible reports from such a range of sources—not only escaped Jews, the Polish Government in exile, and eyewitnesses, but also German soldiers writing home, and even the public statements of prominent Nazis themselves—that there could be little doubt within the German Reich, in the occupied territories, in the neutral countries, and among the Allies fighting Nazi Germany that the

Jews of Europe were being sent to the east not for 'resettlement' but for death. There was no comprehensive overview of the sheer scale and the precise character of killing; some communities had less access to information than others; some could not help being (or perhaps only partly consciously chose to be) incredulous; and there were any number of political and practical considerations that put barriers in the way of substantially ameliorating the plight of European Jews and other persecuted groups.[57] Within Germany and occupied Europe, the voices raised against such murder were few and for the most part ineffectual. Arguably one of the most significant forms of resistance was at an individual level: to assist in the hiding of individuals who were targeted for persecution; to provide food, medicine to those already imprisoned; and to pass messages between prisoners and their families. But such strategies could by definition save only a tiny minority of those caught in the trap of Nazi rule.

Whether in the great pyres of flames or the tall smoking chimneys, the factory of death at Auschwitz was not hidden away from public visibility in the manner of the 'Operation Reinhard' death camps of the east—Bełżec, Treblinka, and Sobibór. Although Bełżec was conveniently situated close to the railway tracks, in full view of a little town, it was hardly in a great centre of industrial production, and was a long way from the borders of the Greater German Reich. Both Treblinka and Sobibór were genuinely hidden away in the depths of the forests and countryside, barely to be found without knowledge of their precise location. But Auschwitz was different. It was smelled for miles around, visible from miles around, spoken about for miles around; by the summer of 1942, when killings of thousands of Dombrowan Jews were getting under way, it is simply not plausible that a *Landrat* living a mere 25 miles away, responsible for the town with the largest total number of Jews, travelling around the area and regularly conversing with his colleagues in local government in neighbouring counties, could 'not know' about this place of extermination.

Auschwitz was not a killing centre that could easily be ignored by those living in surrounding areas—and arguably least of all by those who were officially charged with removing Jews from their homes and corralling them into enclosed areas for easier control and deportation.

It is, therefore, perfectly understandable that Klausa's rest cure was of little help as far as his 'nerves' in the summer of 1942 were concerned. For this seems to have been the point where Klausa began finally to grasp that he was in danger, as he repeatedly put it, of 'innocently becoming guilty'; of becoming responsible, by virtue of his position and practical involvement, for something that even fanatical Nazis—including Himmler and Höss—explicitly recognized as almost beyond what even their world view could attempt to 'legitimize', something extraordinarily hard to swallow without qualms.[58] Mass murder in the gas chambers, rather than the distress, devastation, and deaths caused by previous policies of humiliation, expropriation, and ghettoization, marked perhaps the parting of the ways between 'fanatical' Nazis and those Nazis who had gone along with 'everyday' forms of racist oppression but were not prepared to countenance explicit policies of extermination.

The question now was really one of what difference such inner distancing might make in practice, given the conflicts between growing, if extraordinarily belated, awareness of the intrinsic criminality of the regime, and the continued behavioural conformity demanded of those committed to the Nazi system. Even now, it was possible to continue outwardly to go along with the system, to fulfil official duties, and to fail to 'see' what such conformity brought by way of consequences.

10

The Deportations of August 1942

By late July1942, local Jews were becoming increasingly aware of their intended fate and making every effort to hide or evade deportation. They could no longer be counted on to cooperate with the demands of Moses Merin and the Jewish Council; nor, arguably, could the Jewish Council any longer be fully depended upon to cooperate with demands to collect up large numbers for deportation. The first phase, in which the Jewish Council assisted in the round-up and selection for deportation was over; Jews now had to be entrapped by other means.

The sports ground selections

The major selection and deportation 'action' that took place in August 1942 was different in several respects both from the deportations that had already taken place and from those that were yet to come.

First, it relied on trickery and deception to get Jews to collect themselves together in a place that would easily be overseen and guarded: they were coerced, effectively, into temporarily imprisoning themselves. This made the preliminary round-up for deportation much easier than it had been in the less well-planned raids of May 1942, when so many had managed initially to escape.

Secondly, 'selections' between those fit to work and those designated for death took place on the sports grounds where the Jews were collected. This selection was carried out in full view of local townspeople; it was not the pre-selection by the Jewish Council for the earlier round-ups, nor the later notorious—and by now iconic—selection on the infamous 'ramp' of Auschwitz by the man who has come to represent the epitome of evil, the Nazi doctor Josef Mengele.

This was a selection carried out, furthermore, not only by representatives of the forces of repression (SS, Gestapo); local employers also participated. Their representations about the ways in which holders of particular employment identity cards were essential for work helped, at this stage, many Jews to be selected to remain rather than to be transported for instant murder. Given the criteria for selection—usefulness in employment, age, and health—it was more than evident to the victims of the procedure what was afoot; the significance can hardly have been lost on the local employers either, and indeed some (like Rossner) did their utmost to save not only their own employees but also additional members of their workers' families.

This major event massively disrupted normal patterns of life and work in the town, as the regular curfews and 'Jew bans' were lifted and the labour force was out of action during the period of selection. It was not something that could be overlooked, nor something that people in the area could plausibly claim they 'knew nothing about'.

Least of all, of course, Udo Klausa and his wife Alexandra—and not only because of Klausa's official role in the area. The Hakoach sports ground was directly opposite the 'villa of the Jew Schein', where the *Landrat*'s family had made their home. Alexandra could not have avoided seeing what was going on within a few yards of her garden.

The official report of events in Będzin, drafted on 20 August 1942, discusses how this 'action' took place in the two different sports grounds, over a period of five full days, from the early morning of 12 August 1942 until the afternoon of 17 August.[1] It explains that a total of some 23,000 Jews were gathered, from among whom some 4,700 were selected for deportation. The latter had to be collected and retained, as was by now standard practice, in the orphanage building on the other side of the railway line, as well as—given the sheer size of this 'action'—in a couple of other locations.

The selections began on Wednesday, 12 August 1942; the first transport to Auschwitz left on Friday, 14 August, and trains continued to run until the last deportation from the railway station took place the following Tuesday, 18 August 1942. A final planned transport on Wednesday, 19 August, 'had to be cancelled, because around 1,000 Jews had escaped the deportation by fleeing in the night of 18.8.42'.[2] This 'action' took place not over one lunch

Figure 18. Bus station today
The main bus station in Będzin, on the unmarked site of the former Hakoach sports ground, where the major selections took place in August 1942. Just behind the bus station is the site of the former *Landrat*'s villa. The main road to the railway station runs off to the right of the photograph, with the train tracks running parallel to this road.
Conrad Fulbrook.

hour, as suggested by Klausa's account in his memoirs discussed further below, but over the course of a full week. It resulted in some 10,000 murders of Jews from Sosnowiec and Będzin on their arrival at the gas chambers of Birkenau, and many individual deaths as a result of being shot 'while trying to escape' before being put onto the trains, or even while clearly not 'trying to escape', as in the case of the babies who were shot or whose brains were bashed out, witnessed by many survivors, and the deaths of others (particularly among the elderly, the sick, and the very young) as a result of thirst, exposure, and infirmity while waiting in the selection fields.

The police report, of which drafts as well as the final version are retained in the files, had some difficulty discussing the numbers of deaths that occurred during these days, and the rather peremptory ways in which these had been dealt with. As one version put it:

> Since at the actions on 12 and 13 August a number of Jews who wanted to flee from the collection places were shot dead by the Gestapo or were so badly injured that they soon died, and furthermore that in the collection camps some suicides

occurred, it would in such cases be appropriate if the Gestapo were to ensure that the necessary formalities for burying the corpses were completed immediately, particularly since it is very often a case of people whose identity can no longer be confirmed.[3]

This report on the cold-blooded killing of people seeking to escape transportation to a later place of murder made it quite clear there would be no attempt to inform relatives, nor indeed any expectation that bereaved relatives would be in a position to do much about funeral arrangements in these circumstances. And there can be no doubt from survivors' accounts that the scenes were very bloody indeed.

The round-up was initially disguised as an identity card procedure, very likely because of the growing knowledge of the murderous character of Auschwitz among the Jews of the area. The Jewish Council issued an order, several days before the allotted day of assembly, that all Jews—even the very young, the very elderly, and those unfit to work—must show up in the designated locations in Sosnowiec and Będzin, dressed in their best clothes, in order to have their identity cards authorized; anyone failing to comply would henceforth be an illegal, at risk of arrest and deportation. As one survivor, Tusia Herzberg, recalled:

Before the 12th of August 1942 the local Jewish Council made known to the Jews an order from the Gestapo, according to which all Jews had to turn up in alphabetical order at the sports grounds. In the case of non-compliance with this order the whole family would be severely punished.[4]

A few days earlier, what in retrospect were revealed as dummy run identity card checks had been carried out in Czeladź and Strzemieszyce, following which all the Jews were released to go home—a further part of the elaborately staged deception, to enhance the likelihood of the deceit being successful, given the difficulty otherwise of gathering Jews peacefully for such a purpose. As Hadasseh Rosensaft, a Sosnowiec dentist who went on to lose all her family, including her 5-year-old son—her 'little sunshine'—to the gas chambers of Auschwitz, later commented: 'It was a cruel trick.'[5]

Jews had to arrive at precisely the same time on the same day at the four separate selection points in Sosnowiec and Będzin. Of the total of 23,000 Będzin Jews called for selection on this day, some 15,000 were told to report to the Hakoach sports ground in the Bahnhofstrasse (Railway Road), with a further 8,000 collected on the Sarmacja sports ground in the Talstrasse (Valley Road), a location substituted at the last minute in place of the Police

Riding School, previously designated as the second selection place.[6] Many of the Jews who were mustered at the sports ground near the river were employed in concerns of particular significance to the German war effort, so were less likely to need transporting through the town to the railway station. The Hakoach sports ground nearer the railway station was particularly useful in view of the higher percentage of these Jews who would need to be held in the nearby orphanage pending deportation to Auschwitz, or to slave labour camps elsewhere. But families were not broken up, so there were also the very young, the sick, and the old in both locations.

The most immediate account we have of this process by one of the victims is a diary entry written just a few months later by Rutka Laskier, who at the time of the selections was still only 13 years old, and who did not in the end even live through another summer. Rutka wrote a 'notebook' during the first few months of 1943 that has, remarkably, survived. On 6 February 1943 she thought back to the events of the previous August, and wrote in her notebook that she would 'try to describe that day so that in a few years, of course if I'm not deported, I'll be able to remember it'.[7] Rutka and her family awoke at four in the morning, and after an unusually good breakfast left for the Hakoach sports ground. It took a while to make their way there: 'There were thousands of people on the road. Every once in a while we had to stop, in order to let the crowd in front of us proceed.' They reached the sports ground at half past six, and 'were in a pretty good mood until nine-o'clock'. At this point it became clear that something much more sinister was afoot than merely an identity card check: Rutka 'saw soldiers with machine guns aimed at the square in case someone tried to escape (how could you possibly escape from here?). People fainted, children cried. In short—Judgment Day.' The weather added to the difficulties: 'People were thirsty and there was not a single drop of water around. It was terribly hot. Then, all of a sudden, it started pouring. The rain didn't stop.'[8]

Given the numbers involved, Jews had to wait several hours until all were corralled and enclosed. Only then could the actual process of selection start, in this way preventing the possibility of knowledge leaking out from one place and adversely affecting the likelihood of Jews being successfully duped in another. As one survivor, David Kane, commented, people were no longer likely to be very cooperative if they had any cause for suspicion, and the way the Jewish Council had led the selections of people from their homes and off the streets earlier in the year was also no longer an option: 'We knew that people were shipped to Auschwitz–Birkenau, we didn't know about many other camps but Auschwitz–Birkenau was well known.' The Jewish Council was no longer able to facilitate round-ups, 'so after a while what happened is that the Germans gathered up the Jewish [people] from the entire town and placed them in a stadium'.[9]

Selections on the Sarmacja sports ground began in the morning, carried out by Messner, who was in the course of the afternoon replaced by Hans Dreier; Mildner, the head of the Kattowitz Gestapo office, was also present for a while, observing the proceeding; on the following day, another person by the name of Kronau took over selection duties.[10] On the Hakoach sports ground, the selections started only at about three o'clock in the afternoon, with the arrival of the SS officer Friedrich Kuczynski and the process of sending people into different, cordoned-off areas of the field reserved for different groups. Rutka Laskier had a clear oversight of what the four groups meant: '"1" meant returning home, "1a" meant going to labour, which was even worse than deportation, "2" meant going for further inspection, and "3" meant deportation, in other words, death.'[11] It is quite clear that even as a 13-year-old Rutka had few illusions: deportation for her meant instant death, forced labour seems to have implied a longer period of suffering before a delayed death.

Those involved in carrying out the selections included not only members of the Gestapo and the SS, but also representatives of the SS Schmelt labour organization, and individual local employers and representatives of the Trusteeship office. Survivors recall 'German civilians' as well as SS and Gestapo officers.[12] The Kattowitz Gestapo official in charge of Jewish affairs, Hans Dreier, was particularly active. Described as 'around 30 years old, tall and thin',[13] Dreier seems to have driven around Sosnowiec and Będzin in order to be present in more than one of the selection grounds. Tusia Herzberg, for example, recalls his presence in the Hakoach sports ground:

> When I arrived with my husband at the sports ground 'Hakoach', this place was surrounded by armed Germans... On the grounds there were around 15,000 Jews... I also saw how Dreier held a stick in his hand and how he bloodily beat several Jews.[14]

Dreier was also involved in the selections taking place in Sosnowiec over the same period. Eugenia Dancygier (née Fajner) recalls that 'Dreier shot right into the crowd of people':

> With a smile on his lips and a revolver in the hand he went very slowly past the prams and shot at the babies. One mother, who was standing near to me—she

was called Najman and lived in the street 'Ulice Sienkewicza 14'—suffered a nervous shock when she saw the innocent victims of Dreier streaming with blood. She screamed 'where is my child?' Dreier came up to the woman and instead of an answer he shot her down. The woman died immediately. Towards evening Dreier sought out a few of us, I was among them, and gave us the task of clearing away the dead bodies and laying them against the fence. He said of this: 'Away with the shit.'

Pen and paper would not suffice to write down all the terrible murders of Dreier.[15]

Dreier, representative of the Gestapo's section for Jewish affairs, was clearly particularly memorable for his violence; but he was far from the only German who was present and active in making selections.

There was a group of individuals representing the various elements in the Nazi system with a particular interest in distinguishing between those Jews who might be useful and hence selected for life, and those destined for immediate death. Kuczynski was active in selections all around the area on behalf of the SS; and Lindner was present at the selections on behalf of the Organisation Schmelt, where he had already gained a fearsome reputation for his violence when inspecting labour camps, unleashing his dog on terrified victims and beating and shooting prisoners.[16] Some of the major employers of Jewish labour in local factories, such as Alfred Rossner and Rudolf Braune, came to intervene on behalf of 'their' workers. Rossner in particular gained a reputation as 'saviour' among Jewish families who felt they were being rescued, even if only temporarily.

Members of the Będzin municipal administration were also participants in the process of selection for deportation. Participation by these civilians in selection processes did not necessarily mean they were helping to 'save' Jews. Officials of the Będzin administration were not merely aware of the selections; at least one of their representatives, involved in trusteeship business, was an active participant in the procedures. This was a man by the name of Walter Schroeder or Schroeter (the spelling varies in different documents). In the summary produced by the Political Department of the Jewish Agency for Palestine dealing with 'Records of War Criminals, Instigators and Perpetrators of Crimes against Jews', Schroeder participated 'voluntarily in the deportation and extermination proceedings against the Jews of the town'. He had a reputation for handing Jews over to the Gestapo, as well as searching 'for Jews hiding in bunkers', whom he 'handed... over for execution'.[17] Schroeder was recognized and remembered by a number of survivors.

Szalom Herzberg, for example, a former factory owner in Będzin, had been moved from his home to the ghetto area in the overcrowded streets of the old town centre.[18] Along with thousands of others, he duly showed up for the sports grounds selections, and recalled quite clearly the participation of civilians, including Schroeder, in the selections and in shooting Jews:

I saw the corpses of the dead Jews lying on the ground. I saw how German civilians with pistols shot Jews. With my own eyes I saw how Schroeder, who was wearing civilian clothing, shot at Jews who fell down dead. I was standing about 10 metres away from him and saw how he held the pistol in his hand and shot several times.[19]

Herzberg knew it was Schroeder because he had previously met him in the course of his work in the factory.[20] In physical appearance he 'was of medium height, perhaps 40 years old, had blue eyes and was strongly built'.[21] But it was Schroeder's clothing that was most distinctive. Another survivor, Alexander Gattmon, recalled that Schroeder 'did not wear uniform but was always dressed in a half-military style in knickerbockers'—again, helping ease of identification in the photographic evidence.[22]

In Gattmon's view, 'Dreier, Lindner and Kutschinski' were primarily responsible for the selections, but 'there were also other Germans present'.[23] These included Schroeder, whom he knew quite well from other incidents: as he put it, 'I know him so well because he often prowled around the ghetto'.[24] Schroeder 'was a sort of Trusteeship Officer or member of the tax or price controls or the municipal administration, who was well known to us all because we had to fear him greatly'. Gattmon and his friend Harry Blumenfrucht had once escaped from the ghetto to the 'Aryan side' but were spotted by Schroeder:

He was acquainted with the Blumenfrucht parents and thus also knew Harry. When he noticed him, he drew others' attention to him by shouting 'stop, Jew', and set his dog on him, whereupon Harry was caught by the Germans and taken to the police. There he was tortured for several days and finally hanged.[25]

It was the German director of a shoe factory, Rudolf Braune, who conveyed the message of Blumenfrucht's hanging.[26] Miriam Liwer (née Kaminer) recalled that Schroeder 'was always accompanied by a dog and was notorious among us; I heard that he had killed many Jews'.[27] Chaim Michal Silberberg too remembered Schroeder's presence at the 1942 selections.[28] It is dubious in the extreme that Schroeder would have played such a prominent and memorable role had he not been participating in an official capacity at this event.

The selections were carried out by holding Jews in one part of the sports ground and then calling them up to the tables in turns, where they were evaluated by Dreier, Kuczynski, and their associates in terms of different criteria: age, health, current employment status, and potential usefulness or otherwise for work. In principle, as Rutka Laskier and others noted, there were four different groups to which a person could be allocated.[29] It rapidly became very obvious to people who were waiting their turn to be called up to the selection table what the criteria were for each group. Those with 'special passes' (generally known as a *Sonder*, short for *Sonderpass*) indicating that they were currently working for Germans in the network of 'shops' (workshops), including those run by Rossner, were released to go home. Young people with different work passes, indicating that they were working for private employers, were kept aside for consideration as to whether they should now be sent to labour camps. Families in which only a few members were in employment were also often kept aside for the time being, their fate to be determined after further consideration. But the old, the young, the evidently ill and infirm, and people without appropriate work identity cards or obvious capacity to work were to be sent straight to Auschwitz.

When Rutka Laskier and her family were called up, they were separated; Rutka was just old enough to be selected to be sent to a labour camp, as were some of her friends of a similar age. She felt 'stunned', yet for her the 'weirdest thing was that we didn't cry at all, at all. We didn't shed a single tear.' Having been allotted to a group for labour camp, Rutka was held overnight pending transportation. But some time after one o'clock in the morning, she managed to escape:

> My heart pounded. I jumped out of a window from the first floor of a small building, and nothing happened to me. Only my lips were bitten so bad that they bled. I was completely torn apart. When I was already on the street, I ran into someone 'in uniform', and I felt that I couldn't take it anymore. My head was spinning. I was pretty sure he was going to beat me... but apparently he was drunk and didn't see the 'yellow star', and he let me go.
>
> Around me it was dark like in a closed cabin. From time to time flashes of lightning lit the sky... and it thundered. The journey that normally takes me half an hour I did in ten minutes.[30]

In retrospect, we know that Rutka might, in the long term, have stood a better chance of survival had she not made her dash for freedom and had instead, as selected for work, been taken to a labour camp. The majority of those Będzin Jews who did actually manage to survive the war were those who had gone to labour camps, or had gone into hiding, before the final ghetto clearance.

Given the sheer numbers involved, it was difficult to get through the selection process on the sports ground very quickly. There was considerable violence, as Rutka Laskier and others recalled: 'I saw many more disasters. I can't put it into words. Little children were lying on the wet grass, the storm raging above our heads. The policemen beat them furiously and also shot them.'[31] Even the sheer length of time over which the process was drawn out took its toll on the victims, as Jochanan Ranz recounted a little over a decade later:

> Three days and three nights people stood sometimes under a strong rain waiting their turns. The SS men after 'working' a few hours took a rest or went to sleep drunk. At night it was cold and women with children suffered hard.[32]

Because Jews had not expected to be held in this way for so long, they had come with insufficient supplies of food and water: 'Many of them fell unconscious especially little babies.'[33] If any of them stirred, however, the penalty could be fatal, as Gattmon recalled: 'We had to sit on the ground and were not allowed to stand up. Very close to me, a woman who had got up was shot dead by the Germans. Her corpse lay next to me the whole night.'[34] The length of time also was helpful, however, for those attempting to engage in resistance and helping to rescue people, as recounted by Ranz:

> Already on the stadium we organized children into 'running groups'... The children were gathered in groups and told to run on a signal through the line of guards. Part of them succeeded in running through but part had to go back under the beating sticks of the Jewish militia and shooting of the SS guards...
>
> Members of the youth organization risked their lives wearing false armbands like special assigned auxiliary militia. They simulated crying and beating people and so drove them to another field.[35]

In this way at least some were, for the time being, rescued from deportation.

Those present at this selection were terrified of what was likely to happen if they were allotted to the wrong group, or if the family was separated in the process. The refusal to believe in what they at the same time knew to be true was widespread, so people were extremely apprehensive but at the same time unwilling to acknowledge that their fears could indeed be true.

As Henrietta Altmann put it, they 'had no illusions' when they saw that it was 'the old and the sick, the infirm, the abandoned children, the children from orphanage, mothers with children' who were being taken for deportation. But, as she recalled, 'the desire to live was such that it obscured all logic'.[36] She and other Jews 'couldn't believe we had to die'. It was simply beyond psychological or logical comprehension: 'All Jews have to die because Jew is not allowed to live and you just can't see yourself in the group that is going to die.' The outlines were clear, but the details remained vague, unimaginable: 'We did not know what form that destruction was taking. There were rumours that were unacceptable to our mind.' The new policies were simply unprecedented:

> Our parents and grandparents remembered Germans... but they were civilized people. I mean the concept that they murder people was impossible. We believed that we might be starved and that we will die from starvation... but to take people to murder them is inconceivable, inconceivable.[37]

However inconceivable, many people knew this would be the outcome if they did not take active steps to gain selection into one of the groups still slated for survival.

Lea Eisenberg vividly recalled her experiences of the selection in the Hakoach sports field. Eisenberg's family was not called up for selection on the first day, but had to wait overnight, through the driving rain, before being called up. Then her mother and sister were sent to the deportation group, and she was pushed into a different group: 'And I started to run off to my mother and they started to beat me and pushed me away and that was that.'[38] She never saw her mother and sister again.

Others were luckier, at least for the time being. Zosia Baigelman had gone to the selections with her uncle and some other members of her family. At the time she was only 14 years old. But her uncle, on reaching the table where the selections were being made, said that she was his wife, so she was allowed to remain; she would otherwise probably have been taken for forced labour. In her interview, she recalled, with tears, how a lot of people were separated from their children: 'Like cattle... we stopped being human.' She also remembered the sense of not knowing what it would be best to do, or what it meant to be sent to one side or the other; she felt she was extremely lucky that her uncle was quick thinking at this point.[39]

Like many others, Gunter Faerber too recounts that they waited all through the unbearably hot first day, and then through the night while it rained; finally at six o'clock the following morning they were called up for selection, facing SS men who had just arrived. Faerber puts his own release down to the fact that his family had a German friend aged around 20, who was, as he put it, 'one of the good times girls' and very friendly with a Gestapo man. She used to visit them in the ghetto, and they gave her valuables such as gold watches and earrings; he thinks she put in a good word for them with the Gestapo, so that when their turn came all four members of his family were released back into the ghetto. 'That was another incident where we survived for, until the next time, and we carried on our normal work, our normal chores, for a few more weeks or months after that.'[40]

The Szpringer family had a highly unusual experience. Apart from one of the brothers, Issa, who had fled to Russia at the outbreak of the war and was by now in a Russian labour camp, there were six remaining members of the family. They were summonsed to arrive together at the Sarmacja sports stadium in the Talstrasse, down near the river in Będzin. Here they recall that people were being divided into three groups by a 'notoriously vicious SS officer named Mesinger'.[41] The youngest Szpringer daughter, Laya, was still just a small child, too young even to wear a yellow star, and hence destined with certainty for the group designated for death; but on the advice of one of her older brothers, she managed to run for Group One (those to be released), by hiding behind a couple who had just been sent in that direction during a period of 'pandemonium' when 'the police had their hands full controlling the panicking crowd'.[42] The other five members of the family—the two older brothers, Moishe and Yossel, their sister Dora, and their mother and father—all managed to get themselves categorized as fit to work, unusually as a complete family unit. They surmised that Mesinger might have been using them purely as an example at a particular point in the proceedings, in order to show others waiting that it was possible for a family to remain intact, thus luring people unsuspectingly towards certain separation: they had boldly walked forward at a point when the militia were 'having increasing difficulty in moving people up to the table', since 'more and more of the families became aware' of the character of the selections.[43] Once in the area fenced in for Group One, they found Laya 'crouching by the fence, trying to be as inconspicuous as possible... cowering there, trying not to cry, all alone in wretched fear'.[44] The Szpringers were, they thought, the only family group to remain entirely intact that day, deeming it a 'miracle' that the mother and her youngest child had not been sent to Auschwitz, and the father and older siblings to a slave labour camp, as was the pattern in so many other families. As Dora (later known as Doris) summarized it:

> For the next several days Bendzin was a city of tears. Mostly people just stayed in their homes mourning and praying. I would say that, at the most, only about one fourth of the people from our apartment complex returned to their homes the night of this devastating selection. The rest were on their way to Auschwitz or a slave labour camp.[45]

So many others were not as lucky as the Szpringer family, who at every turn during the subsequent course of events proved both remarkably resilient and remarkably fortunate.

Those unlucky enough to be chosen for deportation were either taken straight to the waiting train wagons—which had been lying in the sidings near Będzin station in preparation—or held for a day or two on the selection grounds or in the former Jewish orphanage, as well as two further buildings nearby, just across the road from the railway station.[46] As Lea Eisenberg recounts:

> All the people that were supposed to go with the transport were brought to an orphanage, there was a huge building in our city for orphans. This is where they brought the people for it was closer there to the railroad station, this is where they brought the people who were supposed to go to Auschwitz.[47]

Lea Eisenberg's brothers tried to bribe a policeman to get their mother and sister out of the orphanage. The policeman was willing to accept the bribe, but only for one of the two: he thought it 'too dangerous' to try to get two people out. Lea's 12-year old sister apparently refused to leave her mother, or perhaps the mother refused to abandon her daughter: so 'that was the last time I saw them'.[48]

There were many attempts at escape and rescue. Sam Goldofsky and his whole family went together to the Hakoach sports ground. His father was injured and still suffering from old wounds, which meant that he could not walk properly. He was held on the sports ground, while other members of the family were released and ran home. They waited, but their father did not come home; and they soon discovered that he was to be taken to a place where they were retaining people to be transported to Auschwitz. So at night Sam Goldofsky went back and sneaked in to the selection ground; he cut his fingers and buried his face, lying on the ground so the German guards would think he was dead. Subsequently, when a transport wagon was being loaded including his father, Goldofsky and his brother jumped onto

Figure 19. Orphanage today
The unmarked former Jewish orphanage that was used as a transit camp or 'Dulag' (*Durchgangslager*) to hold people prior to deportation. This is situated on the other side of the train tracks, close to the railway station.
Conrad Fulbrook.

the wagon in order to get their father off; they even succeeded in pushing him off the truck. But his mother and sister came out to see what was happening and were caught; Goldofsky managed to jump over a big gate and ran through a garden and into a different street. His sister and mother and father were all taken to the main collection point, the orphanage by the station. That night, Goldofsky and his brother went there to try to find their parents again. They found that their mother and sister had by now managed to get out using the sister's two ID cards showing they worked for the Germans; but that they were too late to rescue their father, who had already been taken to Auschwitz. Other members of the family too were taken; Goldofsky watched as their twin cousins were taken away to the train station to go to Auschwitz.[49]

Members of the youth resistance groups who had gathered together in the kibbutz, or 'farm', were very actively involved in attempts to rescue even people who were not known to them or their families. Jochanan Ranz was among the young people helping others to escape. They 'got into the orphan home working as kitchen helpers or garbage workers'. Then they devised strategies to confuse those on guard duty. As Ranz suggested, it was important first of all to get people 'out of the large rooms that they were in':

> So, if pots of coffee were brought by one person two persons were going back keeping both sides of the pot. The door guards hardly noticed the change as sometimes two kitchen helpers went up, sometimes one and the rush and traffic up and down was large.

The confusion was exacerbated by the general din: 'the crying and weeping of women and children' were 'indescribable'. There followed the problem of how to get the people out of the grounds of the orphanage. Again, they were lucky in that guards here seemed to pay little attention to detail:

> In the yard a German trooper was going up and down. Deep in the yard leaning on the fence was a small hill made of slag and garbage. The hill was nearly the height of the fence. While the guard went down the two people with garbage pails went up to the hill climbed on it and jumped over the fence. On the other side of the fence was liberty. This was the way to rescue friends and other people. Up to the hill always went two or three people, back one less.[50]

There were also other strategies: some children 'were rescued by taking them out in the bakers' van who brought bread'.[51] The degree of energy and courage on the part of those who had been involved in the kibbutz or 'farm' group was highly significant in saving individual lives at this time, while risking their own lives in the process. They also had considerable 'luck that there was just the always drinking SS man'.[52] But, for all their efforts, and however significant each individual rescue was for the people concerned, the numbers who could be saved were very few in comparison with the 4,700 who were deported to their deaths at this time.

According to the report by the Jewish Council of Elders, the 'evacuation of such a significant number of Jewish inhabitants had a shattering effect on the whole Jewish life in all areas, and this in general as well as private, economic and financial respects'.[53] It was particularly devastating for those whose families had been broken up by the selections and deportations:

> In the course of the evacuation many families were separated and as a result children without parents or relatives were left behind, who at present have no one to care for them. The children are exposed to hunger and cold as well as demoralization... Furthermore, in the course of the evacuation men were separated from their wives.[54]

This had knock-on effects: 'Workers' productivity and willingness to work have fallen significantly, since they are very concerned about both those members of their families who have been resettled and those who remain but without anyone to care for them.'[55] This report from the Jewish Council is accompanied by what read as very sad lists of the furs, woollen garments, gloves, jackets, trousers, and caps that had had to be handed over to the local authorities for redistribution, since their former owners would never wear them again.

In her diary entry, immediately after her account of her own escape, Rutka added one more detail:

> Oh, I forgot the most important thing. I saw how a soldier tore a baby, who was only a few months old, out of a mother's hands and bashed his head against an electric pylon. The baby's brain splashed on the wood. The mother went crazy. I am writing this as if nothing has happened. But I'm young, I'm 14, and I haven't seen much in my life, and I'm already so indifferent. Now I am terrified when I see 'uniforms'. I'm turning into an animal waiting to die. One can lose one's mind thinking about this.[56]

This was what had happened during those days in August 1942; these were just some of the experiences of the victims.

Those in charge of civilian administration could hardly have been uninformed about these events. The instructions issued to the local police authorities the day before the selections of the sports grounds began made it very clear that the usual curfew and 'Jew-ban' restrictions on the movement of Jews—restrictions for which the *Landrat* was responsible—had been lifted with effect from the morning of 12 August, to allow Jews to pass through the streets to the collection points. One of the initially designated collection points was to be the Police Riding School in Będzin.[57] Klausa returned on 6 August from a brief trip to Posen, where he had gone for discussions with his former colleagues in the Warthegau. In a letter to her mother on 8 August Alexandra comments that Udo was now going out riding early every morning with the Commander of the Police Riding School.[58] We cannot know what were the subjects of discussion on these newly instituted pre-breakfast rides, but practical arrangements for the coming days were very likely on the informal, un-minuted agenda.

Once the selections had started, it was impossible even for those who had no official role whatsoever, like Alexandra, not to see the violence taking place all around. In a letter to her mother on 12 August 1942, in the midst of her usual domestic updates, she commented: 'Today 15,000 Jews here were resettled out of town, it was so terrible that one would also have liked to leave the place immediately oneself. Russia is as nothing to this.'[59] I had initially wondered what direct knowledge—perhaps gleaned from Udo Klausa's experiences the previous summer, when he was involved in the invasion of Russia, or perhaps gleaned from her brother, who continued to serve as an officer on the eastern front—might have lain behind Alexandra's phrase 'Russia is as nothing to this'.[60] But I was soon put right on this by a member of Klausa's family: apparently the phrase was current among conservative circles who wanted to compare Nazism unfavourably with communism; communist violence in Russia was bad enough (as were earlier Russian pogroms), but the Nazis were, in the understanding of this expression among these circles at the time, supposedly even worse than anything that had ever happened in Russia. On this view, Alexandra was courageously expressing a degree of outrage that she could not contain, even despite the possibility of her letter being read and occasioning the disapproval of *NSDAP* authorities.[61]

Alexandra's attitude, at least as expressed in this letter, implies some sympathy with the victims ('terrible') but predominantly records regret that she had herself to be a witness to the violence; she does not explicitly query its purpose, nor seek either to justify or to challenge its necessity. The very next sentence in this letter matter-of-factly requests the address of a friend to whom Alexandra owes a thank-you letter for having sent her a brown dress. In effect, she clearly registered disquiet at having to see the brutality and violence; but somehow she 'did not see' what this actually amounted to; she witnessed, without actually bearing witness. In this, Alexandra's perceptions were very different from those who were the victims; and in this, she was arguably very ordinary, very similar to the multitude of other Germans who failed to 'see' what was actually going on all around them—even though she was so much closer to the epicentre of death than many others. Alexandra was clearly shocked, but did not want (or dare) to question further the purpose or destination of the 'resettlement' action. Whether or not this was because of fear of the consequences if she had openly written any more, the fact remains that, for whatever reasons (which we cannot at this stage probe with any certainty), the situation was such that a German in Alexandra's position played along with the official pressure not to enquire, not to 'know' or discuss too explicitly what was so obviously and clearly going on in front of their own eyes.

There is one further point worth noting about this brief comment in Alexandra's letter. The figure of 15,000 is astonishingly precise, rather than some more vague expression, such as 'thousands'. It would have been very difficult, if not impossible, for Alexandra to have gained an accurate head count, given the throngs of people and the overcrowded chaos on the Hakoach sports ground situated just across the road from her house. Moreover, in this area—unlike areas where the German authorities relied on local collaborators—no exact lists were drawn up of specific names; only overall target numbers were decided in advance.[62] It is possible that the figure of 15,000 had been mentioned at home, or discussed more widely among the circles of local administration.

Alexandra also provides us with some glimpse of the heightened activity in the *Landrat*'s home during that week of selections. There seem to have been a number of visitors, functionaries who perhaps had to be present at the sports ground (while their wives perhaps enjoyed a day in town) and who then required some hospitality before making their way home. As she notes, 'this evening two local functionaries [*Amtskommissare*] are coming with their wives for a meal'.[63] Whether or not they were there in an official capacity, there is likely to have been some talk at the dinner table about the events of the day. Her letter of 19 August comments on having had frequent visitors that week: coming to lunch, to tea, to dinner, or even staying all day, one of whom was from the regional government, and one was a district official.[64]

Is it really plausible that the *Landrat*, Udo Klausa, was the one person in the entire area who actually 'did not know' what was going on in the streets all around him—even despite morning rides with the Commander of the Police Riding School, and written preparations for lifting the curfew and 'Jew ban'; even despite selections and corralling and transports leaving daily over a period of several days, with shootings and deaths and thousands of distressed people collected not only in the Hakoach sports ground situated directly opposite his house, but also in the streets all around his home, at the orphanage across the tracks, and at the Będzin railway station, which lay on the direct route between his home and the *Landrat*'s office—and all this in an area where he had held direct responsibility for segregation and 'resettlement' before the latter became a euphemism for mass murder? Even though his wife wrote home to her mother about the events, on the very first day on which the selections started?

Whatever he actually 'knew', Klausa's post-war accounts were distinctly understated. Even given the undoubted vicissitudes of memory—which seem to have affected the former *Landrat* to a far greater degree than the few survivors of this selection process, whose memories are by contrast vivid and detailed—Klausa provides a far from comprehensive or accurate record of his likely knowledge and actions at the time.

A turning point?

Klausa reports, not only in his memoirs but also in his official statements for the Ludwigsburg investigations into crimes committed in the *Landkreis* of Będzin, that neither he nor the gendarmerie were involved in any antisemitic activity, and, furthermore, that in all the time he was physically present in the area he only ever once personally witnessed an incident in which Jews were being maltreated. As he put it to the Ludwigsburg investigators in December 1975:

> If it is put to me again that, according to the results of the investigation, there is indeed the suspicion that, even during the times when I was present in Bendsburg, actions took place in the *Landkreis* of Bendsburg against the Jewish population and other murderous actions, then I also cannot explain this fact. I can only explain the fact that I heard nothing of all this in that the police stationed in the *Landkreis* of Bendsburg had a line management that led past me. I am convinced that the gendarmerie that was under my responsibility had nothing to do with such actions.[65]

Klausa explained further that the Police President in Sosnowiec was responsible for the police actions in the more thickly populated urban areas of Sosnowiec and Będzin:

> This is why it is altogether explicable that I was not at all involved professionally in actions in Bendsburg and other localities in my district, which were not my responsibility as far as policing was concerned, and I also did not hear anything about such actions.[66]

The Ludwigsburg investigators had documentary evidence of the involvement of the gendarmerie of the neighbouring *Landkreis*, Olkusz (Ilkenau), in assisting deportation actions, under the orders of the Olkusz *Landrat*.[67] But Klausa persisted in claiming that his gendarmerie, under Mentgen, had never been involved in any way in actions against Jews or others.

But, despite Klausa's repeated assertions, there is clear evidence that the gendarmerie were not only involved—as we have already seen—in numerous individual incidents, as well as in running the Golonog forced labour camp, but also in assisting the deportation process of August 1942. They were particularly useful in rounding up the small communities of Jews who had been concentrated in a few villages of the Będzin district.

There are eyewitness testimonies recalling the participation of the gendarmerie. For example, Jakób Freiberger (born in Będzin on 24 December 1906) provides, in early post-war testimony, a detailed description of how members of the gendarmerie, many of them on motorcycles, surrounded and rounded up Jews in the villages around Będzin.[68] Freiberger estimated that at this time there were some 300–400 Jews living in the village of Grodziec, 100 in Bobrowniki, some 60 Jews in Sączów, and groups of between 30 and 100 in other hamlets. He recalled how at eleven o'clock on the morning of 13 August 1942, the day after the start of the sports ground selections, the gendarmerie came roaring into his own village on their motorbikes, surrounded groups of Jews and took them to the general collection point in the orphanage of Będzin, where, Freiberger estimated, some 6,000 Jews had already been gathered—probably an overestimate (official figures claim 'only' 4,700), but the impressionistic figure gives a good indication of the sense of overcrowding in the orphanage. Jakób Freiberger recalls that, at four o'clock in the afternoon of 13 August 1942, the gendarmerie finally handed over charge of the Jews from his village to the Gestapo and the German police, who took them directly to the station to be transported to Auschwitz. Another survivor, Felicja Scwarc, similarly provides early post-war testimony on the role of the gendarmerie controlling the whereabouts of Jews in her village and assisting in the run-up to the final arrests and deportation.[69] Although far later in terms of the vicissitudes of memory, elderly Polish residents also recall the round-ups in the villages by the gendarmerie. Wacław W., still a young boy at the time, remembers clearly the actions of individual members of the gendarmerie in the round-ups, recalling them by name, reputation for violence, and where they came from.[70]

Klausa does concede that he personally, if briefly, witnessed one incident that for him allegedly became a turning point precipitating a request to return as rapidly as possible to the front. He was, on his account, witness to the deportation of 'around 1,000 Jews' who were being dragged along in a 'miserable procession' (*Elendszug*) along the main road some 30 yards from his own house, situated on the side street directly opposite the post office and close to both the Hakoach sports ground and the railway tracks. In his memoirs Klausa recounts how he was sitting eating lunch when he noticed the unhappy and bedraggled crowd going by: 'They were flanked by their own Jewish police, who, at the slightest sign of rebellion, used wooden batons to hit anyone resisting. At the head of the procession were two German policemen.'[71] This suggests that those exerting physical violence were primarily members of the Jewish militia, with allegedly only very minimal German police presence who—unlike the Jewish militia with their batons—are portrayed as peacefully leading, rather than forcibly coercing, the group. Nevertheless, Klausa claims he was so concerned that, as he recounts, he immediately ran back into his house, picked up the telephone, and called Police President Alexander von Woedtke:

> I go back into the house and ring up the Police President of Sosnowitz, since, as already described, I do not have police powers in this area. 'Herr von Woedtke,—what is going on here?'—'Herr Klausa, don't you get yourself involved in this, orders from the Reichsführer SS [Himmler]: the Jews are all going to a Jewish republic in Russia.'[72]

The stories were apparently not well coordinated: von Woedtke told the Ludwigsburg investigators that he had thought the 'resettlement' measures were taking the Jews to Theresienstadt.[73]

Following a statement in almost identical wording to the Ludwigsburg investigators in 1975, Klausa added: 'Today I know that these transports were going to Auschwitz. At that time I did not know about this function of Auschwitz.'[74] It is difficult to imagine, looking at this formulation, what other 'function' of Auschwitz Klausa would have been prepared to admit he did know about, and indeed how he would have defended the legitimacy of any other 'function' of Auschwitz than gassing, which is presumably what he meant by 'this function'.

Having initially suggested that all he knew of the August action, or indeed of any action against Jews in the area, was the brief lunchtime glimpse of the procession guarded by Jewish militia, Klausa also does admit in the context of the criminal investigations that he had at some point seen Jews collected on the sports ground. But he again takes this opportunity to aver that: 'This is the only action of which I had any knowledge as an eyewitness . . . Other resettlement actions or actions of murder in Bendsburg and in the district of Bendsburg are not known to me.'[75] Klausa tells us in his memoirs that, although he believed the tale of the 'Jewish republic in Russia' at the time, he was nevertheless unsettled by the sight and determined to get out of the area once and for all:

> The very same afternoon I drove to Kattowitz to the military recruitment inspection office, in which by the way my... cousin... was the [General's] adjutant. I could talk with the General quite openly. I described what had happened and requested the fastest possible military call-up... The General showed full understanding for me, and perhaps ten days later I took my leave of the Regional President in order to join my troop.[76]

In the version for the Ludwigsburg investigation, Klausa phrases it somewhat more vaguely, but to the same overall effect: 'Just a few days after this action I left Bendsburg and also made arrangements for my family to move to relatives in northern Germany a short time later.'[77] There is an extraordinary collapse of the dating here: what was in reality a few crucial months—from mid-August to 1 December—becomes 'just a few days' as far as Klausa's own departure was concerned. What was in actuality a full further year in the area for his wife and children, until August 1943, becomes 'a short time later'.[78] There are also some misrepresentations of the processes by which these departures took place.

The story Klausa gave, of having so briefly witnessed just a fraction of the deportations that took place over a full week from 12 to 19 August 1942—a mere 1,000 Jews and 2 German policemen over one lunch hour is clearly a massive understatement—and then immediately offering his services to return to the army rather than remain party to what was going on in the area, is belied by the archival evidence, the actual sequence of events, and the contemporary letters written by his wife to her mother.[79] But it may stand as a form of condensed symbol of how Klausa felt; perhaps more plausible as an account of a dream than what actually took place.

What then actually happened at this time? It seems clear that Klausa already had a prior appointment for a medical examination, scheduled for the day before the sports ground selections took place. Whether or not he had accidentally witnessed a 'miserable procession' on this particular day and then decided to drive in to see the General in Kattowitz that very same afternoon—incidentally an unlikely sequence, since the selections only actually began in the early to mid-afternoon—he would have had to attend a medical examination the previous day in any event. This medical examination was simply because his period of sick leave had now run out, and was designed to resolve the question of whether Klausa was deemed physically fit to return to the army, now desperately short of manpower and bogged down in Russia.

Alexandra's letters are crucial in this connection. The letter of 12 August, in which she briefly describes the violent deportation action, begins with a longer discussion of Udo's health and his possible return to military service. As Alexandra tells her mother: 'Yesterday Udo was in Kattowitz, and let himself be [medically] registered as "fit to fight" [*kv*].' As she explains quite explicitly, 'he had to attend another medical investigation, since his "indispensable" status due to ill-health had run out'. From this it is absolutely clear that the prescheduled medical appointment took place on the day before the selections started: the designation of 'fit to fight' was a medical bill of clean health, terminating an official period of sick leave. This could hardly be interpreted, as Udo Klausa's later account suggests, as a sudden gesture of revolt and spontaneous request to be sent back to active military service as a direct consequence of unexpectedly witnessing a deportation on the day *after* the medical examination. But there was indeed some element of Udo's own will involved, at least as far as the presentation of symptoms of ill-health was concerned:

> He is personally quite clear that he is not really fit for active fighting, and he also doesn't want to get involved in the battle developing between the civilian and military authorities over the deployment of his valuable personage, but rather will just wait and see who turns out the winner. But... it is perfectly understandable that he didn't want to go blabbering on again to the doctor about this and that [*dass er dem Arzt nicht wieder etwas vorjammern wollte*], since on investigation he always appears totally healthy. At that time he was written off sick because he described his state to the doctor. Now he says, I can't start up all over again about lassitude, nerves, etc., no one would believe me, they would think it was just shirking. So he simply said that the cure had helped, he had recovered, and on that basis he was registered fit for war.—I am now in considerable suspense about what will happen.[80]

It is possible that, having passed the medical examination by keeping silent about his sense of continuing malaise, Klausa did subsequently go on to visit his cousin and request as fast a transfer back to the front as possible. If he did so, this had to be rooted in prior knowledge rather than sudden revelation of the now clearly criminal turn of events.

Having passed the medical with the kind of qualifications he had already discussed with his wife earlier in the summer, Klausa was now clearly keen to return to the army, if in a motorized capacity only. But he did not in fact return, as he claimed, 'just a few days' after witnessing the August deportation. There followed prolonged negotiations between the Kattowitz Regional Government and the military authorities, once again battling over who would retain his valued services. Klausa did not, in the end, leave for military service until 1 December 1942, and remained in full charge of the

Landkreis throughout the autumn months. There were, as we shall see, further developments during those months with which he would also probably have preferred not to have been associated.

It is hard to know what to make of Klausa's attempt to link his own horror at witnessing a line of deportees—even while professing ignorance of where they were being taken—with a supposedly principled and sudden, spur-of-the-moment offer of returning to the front, when the realities of a period of medical leave that had come to an end were somewhat different. There was clearly some degree of leeway here: Klausa could, presumably, have made more of continuing stomach symptoms and feelings of lassitude and thus be confirmed as still physically unfit to return to military service; he apparently chose not to. The symptoms could well have been psychosomatic: watching the selections between those chosen to remain alive in order to work, and those designated as on the tracks to the gas chambers of Auschwitz, taking place in a sports ground literally just over the garden fence, can hardly have been less than stomach-churning for a sentient human being. Klausa clearly did not have the constitution or sadistic mentality of a Dreier, a Kuczynski, or a Mildner. His 'nerves' had been plaguing him, and worrying Alexandra, not only in the preceding months but also in the weeks since his return from his rest cure, and in the run-up to the August action; his 'nerves' and clear sense of unease may well have been closely linked with the murderous enterprise going on all around, and with which he knew he was inextricably associated for as long as he remained in the area.

Klausa also knew far more about the process of selections on the sports ground than he was prepared to admit to the Ludwigsburg authorities. Ironically, we know this from another story that he was only too keen to recount: that of having tried to 'save a Jew'.

An attempt to 'save a Jew'

One story in Klausa's account in his memoirs is particularly puzzling. This was his story of trying to save the life of Laib Flojm, his factotum: part janitor, part gardener, part auxiliary help at the *Landrat's* office.

In some respects, this is not an unusual story: many West Germans after the war claimed some instance when they had tried to save an individual Jew from among the vast numbers of anonymous victims who had been sufficiently dehumanized in the Nazi world view as not to elicit such personal sympathy. Even some of the accused at the Auschwitz trial that opened in Frankfurt in December 1963 adopted this ploy to try to establish their credentials as having been, as they claimed, essentially on the right side of history but also a hapless victim of the system. But unlike many such stories, in this particular case it is possible to try to reconstruct the incident against what we actually know of the details of the time.[81]

There is no doubt that Klausa felt warmly towards Laib Flojm, whom he introduced in his memoirs in positive (if slightly patronizing) terms:

> As caretaker, gardener, boiler-man, also for deployment in the district administration, Laib Flojm turned up, a likeable, nice little Jew, with a haggard wife and two small children. He lived in the Jewish quarter and came every morning to deal with all manner of things.[82]

In the records of residents of Będzin, probably based on the German census carried out in the winter of 1939, the Flojm family are listed as resident at 4 Narutowicza Street.[83] Flojm (whose first name is here spelled Lajb), born on 25 January 1905, has his occupation given as 'choffeur' [*sic*]; clearly he was capable of many useful activities, including that of chauffeur. Alexandra too found Laib Flojm a great help, even as an effective childminder of her small son, who liked to play in the garden while Flojm was gardening, allowing her to concentrate on other tasks rather than having to keep a constant eye on her toddler.[84] In the residents' list, Flojm's wife Rywka (born 10 December 1903) is listed as a 'housewife', looking after their two daughters, Fajgla (born 15 February 1931) and Gitla (born 10 May 1933).

It is clear that Flojm was not merely one of what other Nazis had categorized as 'useful Jews' but one towards whom the Klausas appear to have felt some warmth, even if of a slightly patriarchal sort (as with other house servants), also giving him extra rations for himself and his family. It certainly seems very plausible that Klausa would be personally disturbed and concerned at Flojm's deportation from Będzin. Moreover, this sort of sympathy with an 'individual Jew' was quite widespread, even among those who agreed that in general Germany should be rendered 'Jew free'.

Despite his claim that he had already been reassured that the Jews were merely being 'resettled' in a 'Jewish republic' in Russia, Klausa was apparently willing, on his own account, to take what he saw as a major personal and professional risk to save not only Laib Flojm, but also Flojm's wife and children. This was etched in Klausa's memory in a way that other incidents in the lives of Będzin Jews were not; but the elements in his account are confused, and it is difficult to build a coherent picture of the exact sequence of events, which do not entirely add up to an internally consistent narrative. As in so many other areas of memory, there is clearly a large grain of psychological truth shrouded in a historical wrapping that cannot be entirely accurate in every detail:

> Flojm found himself with his wife and both his little children in the miserable procession already described, which at first, at least in part, was shut into the sports ground of Bendsburg. He succeeded in smuggling out a note in which he indicated, in a few key words, where he was and begged for help.[85]

Here, the sequence as far as Flojm was concerned appears to be backwards: the 'miserable procession' would presumably have been on its way either directly to the railway station or to the orphanage to await further transport in due course; the selection on the sports ground would have had to have taken place prior to, not after, this 'miserable procession'. If Flojm had indeed smuggled out a note to Klausa, who claims he rescued him from the sports ground, it must have been still during the selection process and Flojm could not, as described, have also been in the (subsequent) procession to the station. In any event, according to Klausa:

> So I threw myself into my *Landrat*'s uniform and went to the commanding SS officer at the entrance to the sports ground and demanded, appealing to my role, the release of Flojm. After a bit of back and forth this was then granted, and like dogs that have been thrashed the four came creeping out of the enclosure in order to stumble home.[86]

At this point, with apparently the best of motives, it would seem that Klausa himself took part in the sports ground selections: he appeared in his capacity as *Landrat* to request the release of someone deemed by the Germans to be an essential worker. He thus in effect played the same role as the representatives of the Schmelt organization selecting those who were useful for labour in the camps, and local employers such as Rossner and Braune who still wished to retain the workers in their local 'shops'.

Thus far, and whatever Klausa's personal motives and perhaps paternalistic feelings about Flojm, this was a role fully integrated into the official script for this 'action', which was designed precisely to select those deemed still useful for work, and to weed out those who were no longer capable of working for the Germans in one capacity or another. This also reveals that Klausa himself was personally present on the sports ground at some point while the selections were taking place. He must have had a very good overview of how things were organized and been aware of the precise criteria for selection for work rather than death, in order to ensure, in discussion with the SS, the release of 'his' particular Jew from the enclosure of those already selected for deportation.

The story that is told by Klausa as one of some personal courage in going to the sports ground could, up to this point, also be related far more cynically: as a story of participation as a German employer in the selection of those still useful for work, when one of his own workers was at risk of possible deportation. And no doubt, in order to secure Flojm's release Klausa would have had to act as though he were playing by the rules of the game, arguing for the essential nature of Flojm's work. Whatever Klausa may have felt inside, his behaviour was in effect more or less identical to that of other employers participating in the selections.

This and the next part of the story have to rely on speculation. We know that families were regularly separated in the selection process, with anyone clearly unfit for work being sent straight to the gas chambers. The Schmelt organization would certainly have had no interest in two small girls and their unwell mother. Had Klausa not intervened on Flojm's behalf on the sports ground, and had Flojm been selected as fit to work in a labour camp, it is very unlikely that Flojm's 'haggard wife' and two young children would have been in any group other than that headed for Auschwitz. The likelihood of Klausa officially getting them all released as essential workers is low, but possible, given his level of authority in the area.

The story then becomes more complicated, and here it is again not quite clear how things developed in practice. For Klausa goes on to suggest that, even having secured the official release of Flojm and his family, who were allegedly all allowed to 'stumble home' as a result of his intervention, they nevertheless needed again to seek refuge and protection:

> But there [in their home] they remained in danger. A little later they made themselves known to my house-manager Margosch and begged him for shelter. Margosch took them into the central heating system of my house and reported to me what he had done.[87]

This is odd; for, had all four members of the Flojm family, including the 'haggard' wife and the two small children, been officially released from the sports ground and permitted to return home, they would not at this point have had to seek a safe hiding place. Other families who were allowed to return home intact, such as the Szpringer family, simply tried to pick up the remnants of their lives again in the depressing wake of the selection without any immediate need to go into hiding.

It is possible that as a result of Klausa's intervention on the sports ground only Laib Flojm himself was officially released as fit to work. His wife and children had then perhaps managed to escape from the group being led to the railway station, perhaps diving down the side street by the post office to the *Landrat*'s home; in this case, these three would certainly have needed to seek refuge, and Flojm might well have taken them to the *Landrat*'s house. It is very unlikely that the Flojm family would have sought to hide in the *Landrat*'s villa, an extremely dangerous undertaking, had they been legitimately released from the selections (and indeed we know from the sources that Flojm himself had no further need to hide at this time). All of this is, however, a matter of speculation.[88] The fact remains that, whether or not the whole family or merely Laib Flojm himself had been officially released from the sports ground, they all ended up in the *Landrat*'s basement.

The end to this story is also rather ambiguous. Klausa's trusted colleague, Margosch, had first hidden the Flojm family. Margosch himself lived on the 'lowest floor' of the *Landrat*'s residence, and had easy access to the basement heating system, which the family factotum, Flojm, had been responsible for maintaining; they both therefore were very familiar with potential hiding places (although the *Landrat*'s house would be the last place anyone would think of looking for hidden Jews). Margosch at some point reported what he had done to the *Landrat*, whose own position as well as that of his family was at stake. This sequence is clear from Margosch's own account, written several years after the events he describes, as a character reference in support of Klausa when he was under legal investigation. Flojm, on Margosch's account, came first to him to seek help, and Margosch duly informed the *Landrat*. According to Margosch, Klausa then 'even went down to the cellar to say a few words to give Flojm some courage'. The Klausas also apparently provided the Flojm family with food during the days they spent there, until the 'action' was over and they could emerge.[89] Again, this suggests that the hiding incident did indeed take place during the relevant week in August, and that it was very probably the wife and children who were hidden rather than Laib Flojm himself, who had been officially released and who was in the event able to continue working in Będzin until the following summer.

The situation was not without risk. Being found to have hidden a family of Jews in his own home would probably have cost Klausa, as he was well aware, far more than just his job as *Landrat*:

> So then they lived for probably another five to eight days under my roof, hidden, looked after by us, in fear and terror, and I myself was greatly worried that this could be discovered. Since naturally hiding Jews and protecting them from 'resettlement' was a crime that would at the minimum have brought immediate dismissal from office and [being sent to a] concentration camp.[90]

We do not quite know how this story ended. We do not know how long the Flojm family remained hidden in the heating system of the *Landrat*'s villa before Margosch reported their presence to Klausa. We do not know who actually ousted them from their hiding place or under what conditions, although Klausa's account suggests that it was probably he who eventually told them when they had to leave. Klausa's misdating of his return to the army to late August (rather than the correct date at beginning of December) comes in useful here, since it allows him to suggest that both he and Flojm had to leave at virtually the same time, and were both relatively powerless in the situation. Klausa too was, on his own account, purportedly a victim of circumstances and thus unable to help the trusty Flojm any more: 'Flojm certainly did not escape his frightful fate. When I left for the troop, I said to him sadly that I could now no longer help him.'[91] Yet Flojm's deportation in fact took place around a year later than Udo Klausa suggests, and there was at this time no need for him to be hidden. From the archival sources it is clear that as late as 12 April 1943 Flojm was still officially listed as working for the *Landrat*'s office: he would thus have had no need to hide at any earlier date.[92]

The most likely interpretation of the story is therefore that, while in August 1942 Flojm was selected as a useful worker on Klausa's intervention at the sports ground, Flojm's wife and children—for whatever reason—remained at risk. Margosch then sought to hide them in the central heating system and subsequently informed Klausa. It is likely that it was Klausa who decided when they should be ousted from his basement, at the end of the 'action', when they no longer appeared to be in immediate danger of deportation. Since on Klausa's own account they stayed in the basement for some 'five to eight days', he was certainly aware that this 'action' consisted of far more, over a longer period of time, than the single 'miserable procession' during a lunch break that was all he was prepared to admit to having witnessed in the context of the Ludwigsburg investigations.

There is no further mention of Flojm's wife and children in the available records; not even any record of them arriving at Auschwitz, indicating in all probability that, like the vast majority of victims deemed incapable of work, they were instantly gassed on arrival rather than being registered and given a number. Flojm himself, however, clearly kept going through the winter and spring of 1942–3, officially employed by the *Landrat*'s office; but he does not seem to have survived the final ghetto clearance of the summer of 1943. There is no further record of his existence after this date.[93] In a letter of 5 August 1943, Alexandra complained about the way the garden had not been properly tended since Flojm had 'gone', and there was now little by way of fruit and vegetables for the summer, since, as she commented to her mother, she had originally planned to be away for August and return to Będzin only in October 1943, and had therefore not herself tended the garden.[94] This letter, incidentally, also contradicts Klausa's assertion that he had arranged for his wife and children to leave Będzin 'a short time' after the events of August 1942. From Alexandra's letters it is clear that she greatly disliked the area, and sought all manner of alternative places to stay for shorter or longer periods; but there was clearly no plan at this time to give up either the *Landrat*'s role or the villa on any permanent basis.[95]

There are many ways Klausa's own vagueness and apparent confusion in telling this story of 'trying to save a Jew' can be interpreted. He was clearly very concerned about the fate of Flojm and his family, and perhaps this personal connection brought home to him the full impact of Nazi racist policies. But, on the other hand, he was yet again caught by career considerations. Perhaps Klausa, for all his desire to help the family, took fright when he realized the personal danger he was in by virtue of their illicit presence in his house, and told Flojm's wife and children that they must leave before it was really safe for them to do so. To assuage the likely sense of guilt this might have provoked, he perhaps felt it easiest to end the story on a vague note, implying that he had done all that he could for them despite the personal risks involved, but that his own supposedly imminent departure for the army meant that he could no longer act to prevent theirs for deportation.

Whichever way one interprets it, the story is not quite as straightforwardly courageous as Klausa might have liked, and did not take place quite in the way he sought to present. It perhaps accurately reflects his own troubled feelings about the loss and subsequent murder of someone who had been a loyal servant of the family, as well as his wife and children, but the account is accurate neither in its details nor in the claimed wider moral of the story. The tricks of memory may account for some of the confusion; but this is probably compounded by an unwillingness explicitly to acknowledge the full facts of the situation at the time. It is rendered all the more significant by standing in clear contradiction to his claims to the legal investigation that he 'did not hear anything about such actions'.

There are several possible explanations of Klausa's consistent misdating of his departure from Będzin. It is likely that the truth lies in a combination of the following alternatives, which—given the ambivalence and evident difficulties in explicitly admitting, even to himself, let alone to the wider world, the actual implications of his own role as *Landrat* in the unfolding events in Będzin—are, at least psychologically, not mutually exclusive. But they may be posed as alternatives from the logic of later, perhaps overly rational, historical interpretations.

Either Klausa genuinely did not remember that he did not actually leave Będzin until the beginning of December 1942—a date that was only finally agreed in the course of the late autumn—and in his mind made such a close connection between witnessing the horrors of the August deportations and his own army medical that took place at around the same time that, the more he repeated it, the more he believed his own story of offering himself back to army service and leaving Będzin within a matter of days. It is quite possible that advance knowledge and prior realization of what the deportations really meant had strengthened his determination to pass the medical and to prove that he was capable at least of service in a 'motorized' capacity. In this case, there is a psychological truth to his story, irrespective of its factual inaccuracy with respect to the details. Mentally, it was in August that he 'left' his inner commitment to the role of *Landrat*, even though in practice he continued to exercise his official functions until 1 December 1942.

Or he was determined, in all the interrogations after the war, to construct what was effectively an alibi, and to disassociate himself from any responsibility for or even knowledge of what was to come. For the policies pursued by the municipal administration in the following months proved crucial to the implementation of the 'final solution'. Even though he had indeed finally left by the time these policies came into effect under his own nominated deputy—the supposedly 'utterly decent' Hans Felden of Czeladź—Klausa was still in full charge during the autumn of 1942, when the key decisions about the effective incarceration of the Jews in explicit preparation for the final ghetto clearance were made.

Whichever way we interpret Klausa's own account, the tangle he presents cannot stand as an accurate representation of his own knowledge and actions. But it is certainly revealing of the kinds of conflicts he faced, both in carrying out his official duties at that time and in developing an acceptable representation of his past at a later date.

11

Ghettoization for the 'Final Solution'

Over the following year, from August 1942 to August 1943, developments took place that, step by step, ended in the extermination of the vast majority of Będzin's Jews. Very few indeed survived to tell their tales: they were remarkably lucky in emerging alive at all, even if psychologically and physically scarred by their experiences in ways that many of them never overcame, however outwardly successful some of their later lives may have appeared.

The Klausa family too finally left Będzin: Alexandra and her children only in November 1943, after witnessing in August 1943 the final clear-out of the remaining Jews in the last ghetto, as Będzin was 'cleansed of Jews'; Udo Klausa, the *Landrat*, through returning to military service at the beginning of December 1942.

One of the oddest parts of Klausa's account, and the lynchpin of his whole story of innocence, has to do with the end of his and his family's time in Będzin. This is the claim that, once he sensed that he was 'innocently becoming guilty', he offered himself back for service at the front and left Będzin within a matter of days after the deportations of August 1942, arranging for his family to leave shortly thereafter. He consistently claimed—whether in testimonies given at different times for the Ludwigsburg investigations, or in his memoirs, even in dates under a photograph of himself and his local government colleagues in the *Landkreis*—that he left Będzin in August 1942. Neither this nor the claim about his family's departure shortly thereafter is true. Even if the sentiments informing this concertinaed chronology reflect his underlying unease at the unfolding extermination of the Jews of his area, the question remains of why he so actively and persistently sought to disassociate himself from any personal responsibility for what took place in the last three months during which he was still officially in charge of Będzin.

After August

There is some evidence that Klausa was initially relieved and relaxed after the great 'action' of August 1942 was over. In the midst of the week of actions, on 14 August—just two days after the selections had started, and when the first train transports were running down the tracks close to the *Landrat*'s house—Alexandra was complaining to her friend Frau von H. that Udo's condition continued to be frightful.[1] But in Alexandra's letter to her mother of Sunday, 23 August, with the 'action' now over, we hear of Klausa finally relaxing on a deckchair in the garden and chatting to his toddler son.[2] Although Klausa's condition was clearly still labile, Alexandra's letters no longer regularly contain the complaints about his nerves, comments that had repeatedly studded her letters to her mother for several weeks in July, following his return from his rest cure at the end of June.

The following evening, Monday, 24 August 1942, Klausa attended a dinner in Sosnowiec, along with senior figures in the regional government, including his immediate superior, Regional President Springorum, and other significant functionaries from the area, in order to host a five-person 'ministerial commission' from Berlin that had come to tour the area and assess developments. This two-day commission was treated to talks on a range of subjects, including a discussion of questions of racial population politics, planning, and the economy, as well as a report by a fellow *Landrat*, Eugen Hering of Saybusch (a district immediately south of the *Landkreis* of Bielitz in which Auschwitz was located), on the topic of 'the active cooperation of the general administration in resettlements'.[3] The file does not, unfortunately, include any details of what such cooperation in 'resettlement' actions might have consisted in, but it does confirm that *Landräte* were not merely officially informed but actively involved in such actions.

We can only wonder about what might have been talked about informally at the dinner, over a few glasses of wine, so soon after the selections carried out among some 50,000 Jews of the wider area. There can be no question about knowledge of the character and destination of the transports. Not only had Springorum already visited Auschwitz personally on several previous occasions: on 14 May, shortly after the first major deportation, and again in the company of Heinrich Himmler on 17 July, prior to the evening discussions in the Bracht villa that had led to Eduard Schulte's mission to bring the news to the world. Springorum was also fresh from another visit to Auschwitz on the very day before this dinner in Sosnowiec.

Just the previous day, Sunday, 23 September, Springorum had accompanied Gauleiter Bracht to a meeting in Auschwitz, where they had met Auschwitz Commandant Rudolf Höss, senior SS officials, and some technical experts from Berlin, as well as the local *Landrat* Ziegler and a subordinate functionary, *Amtskommissar* Butz. Not only Springorum but also the *Landrat* and even a quite junior functionary at this meeting were clearly part of the inner circle in which the killing programme and its practical implications for local government—public health, the danger of epidemics, and problems of ensuring a clean water supply—could be openly discussed. Knowledge of the existence of a policy of mass extermination was even obliquely recorded in the official minutes of the meeting: Gauleiter Bracht 'confided that he is aware of the Führer's order with respect to the special task that is currently in hand'.[4] At the Sosnowiec dinner the following evening, at which Springorum and other local functionaries, including Klausa, were reporting to the Berlin commission assessing developments in the area, there will no doubt have been similar discussions.

The August deportations had significant consequences for local administration in their wake. The *Landräte* of the area had to deal with the practical implications of the loss of large numbers of Jews from the local economy, as well as orderly disposal of the property and possessions that they had left behind. This was predicated on the knowledge that these Jews would never return to claim their belongings.

Klausa's regular monthly *Landrat* report of 3 October 1942, which he signed personally, included comments on the impact of the deportations on life in the town. He noted the ways in which shops were standing empty and the market had more or less closed down, while many factories were experiencing labour shortages:

> In this district too a total exhaustion of the reserves of the *labour force* is becoming evident... If previously there was a lack of space for shops and enterprises, now the opposite has become the case. Numerous shops are now standing empty. Some shops in the Jewish quarter (the Old Ring) are already being remodelled along German lines... In the same way the market has almost completely come to an end... The clothes and linen left behind by the Jews who were resettled have been collected by the Jewish Community and dealt with so that these can later be

distributed among the remaining Jews. There are supposedly considerable quantities involved.[5]

This short-term devastation of the town's activities was clearly the direct result of the deportation of so many of its inhabitants, although Klausa barely makes this connection explicit, even in his comment about the disposal of the clothing and linens of the Jews who had left without any suggestion of possible return.

There are perhaps hints of Klausa's unease in this and other contemporary sources—although again, were I not a family friend trying hard to see this from the family's perspective and seeking to understand why his family believed Klausa's version of events, I would probably never have noticed these. We see, for example, some conflicting and partially ambiguous signals in this report. On the second page, Klausa's phraseology with respect to the deportations is significant: 'At the end of August some 3,000 Jews were allegedly taken for resettlement. That means a certain easing of the pressure on housing. The *Landrat* was not engaged in the preparation and carrying out of the action.'[6] The use of the word 'allegedly' (*angeblich*) is interesting here, since Klausa is clearly trying to report this deportation as though he had not himself witnessed it, or at least had no official knowledge of the precise numbers involved. While the second sentence concedes its functional uses from the perspective of German local government, the third sentence provides further explicit distance between himself and any responsibility for the 'action'. There was no obvious reason why Klausa should have to include a comment such as this, and it probably therefore indicates a strong desire on his part to record, explicitly, his lack of responsibility for an action he knew to be criminal in nature. This self-distancing is perhaps as far as Klausa felt he could go in indicating any sort of disapproval.

It is notable, however, that such explicit self-distancing, even if somewhat more muted, is echoed also in the regular monthly report produced by Schönwälder, City Mayor of Sosnowiec:

In the reporting period the evacuation of Jews has continued to a limited extent. As far as I have been informed, around 6,000 Jews have been evacuated, so that the number of those Jews still present here is somewhat over 19,000 people.[7]

Schönwälder seems in his report to be trying to make it clear that he had himself merely been 'informed', and had not been an active participant in these 'evacuations'.

Neither Schönwälder nor Klausa went beyond these passing suggestions of distance. Before any contemporaries could begin to suspect Klausa of harbouring illicit sympathy for those subject to Nazi oppression, further features of Klausa's report immediately revert to what might be called the colonial racism mode. On the very same page, he embarks on praise of the work of the gendarmerie, and its leader, his trusted colleague Heinrich Mentgen:

> The *gendarmerie* is working in a very pleasing way in the district. The credit for this must go in the first instance to the district leader, who is of excellent character and has already been active in this area for a long time.[8]

This comment follows a series of discussions during the previous two months of the role of the gendarmerie in cooperation with the other police forces, in the course of which the role of the gendarmerie had been made abundantly clear.[9]

On 9 September Klausa had personally passed on an order of 13 August originally emanating from Himmler, the Reichsführer SS, to all local functionaries in their capacity as responsible for local policing, the local leaders of the gendarmerie, and to the district leader of the gendarmerie, to remind them to work together for common goals, particularly those of political significance:

> The greatest value must be laid on keeping the local police administrations constantly informed about all local matters of significance and all important activities of the gendarmerie; this is particularly the case for incidents of immediate or potential political significance.
>
> Signed Klausa.[10]

Commenting the following day on a further circular from Regional President Springorum to the *Landräte* of the region on this matter, Klausa added a note to the effect that in his district 'cooperation between the administration and the gendarmerie has always been smooth'.[11] There is in all of this no whiff of any inner hesitations and doubts about the policies or practices of Nazi rule, let alone any hint of internal opposition.

Moreover, Klausa's outer faithfulness to regime-sponsored racism remained fully in place. In relation to the supposedly 'particularly difficult' and as yet unresolved question of whether or not Poles should be made to wear a 'P' on their clothing, Klausa adds a clearly antisemitic argument to the pragmatic 'divide and rule' approach: 'Propagandistically, however, it is right to further precisely the variety of social, economic, and political currents among Poles, and in particular to sustain antisemitism, so that no united block develops.'[12] In Klausa's expressed view, therefore, being made to wear stigmatizing insignia in this area might conceivably begin to engender among Poles a degree of solidarity among themselves, which had up until now been missing; moreover, it was important to foster a sense of racial hierarchy between groups, and not to allow any common cause between Poles and Jews.

At the same time, the old battle between the army and regional government over whether Klausa should stay in his role of *Landrat* or return to military service continued, at a time of a rapidly growing shortage of men of an appropriate age, as the Russian campaign continually took its toll. Klausa himself complained of the fact that men were continually being taken away from his administrative staff for military service. As he put it: 'As of now, the imminent call-up of virtually all officials and employees of the year groups 1908 and younger will tear holes in this district that we will not be able to fill for the duration of the war.'[13] Interestingly, in an earlier list drawn up by Klausa commenting on administrative officials and colleagues with respect to their importance in the district, by far the longest entry is that for his loyal house manager, Ignatz Margosch, whose services were portrayed by Klausa as utterly indispensable.[14]

In the case of Klausa's own return to the army, the evidence is again more complex, with the characteristic battle flaring up once again between the civilian and military authorities over the deployment of Klausa in their respective spheres.

A letter of 4 September 1942 from Springorum on behalf of the regional government in Kattowitz to the relevant military authorities starts by commenting: 'I hear that Landrat Dr Klausa was, at the last military medical examination, found to be fit for war with the proviso that if possible he should be put in a motorized unit.'[15] Springorum goes on, however, to argue that this diagnosis is perhaps less than entirely sound, and that Klausa's evident enthusiasm for military service may have outweighed what he saw as a continuing physical malaise:

> According to my own observations, an improvement in his state of health is as little to be observed as a result of this rest cure as it was following the intestinal operation last year. I therefore strongly doubt whether Landrat Klausa will be at all up to more strenuous physical demands.

In these circumstances I consider myself obliged to request a further examination, in which the whole previous course of the illness is to be taken into account. It is beyond my capacity to determine how much the *Landrat*, who is passionate about military matters, has told the investigating doctor about the details of his illness, since in my opinion his external appearance alone lets even a lay person see that Landrat Klausa is not in full possession of his bodily strength.[16]

Klausa's medical examination—which had taken place on the day before the start of the sports ground selections—was, accordingly, revisited. But the military conscription authorities were determined to uphold the findings, confirming that a comprehensive examination had found no serious problem with Klausa's health. A letter from the military inspection authorities reiterated to Springorum on 18 September that the medical examination had been 'thorough' and that 'the medical finding of k.v. [fit for war] is *sustained*'. Furthermore, 'Dr Klausa belongs to the year group 1910 and must, according to current regulations, be called up'. However, they were prepared to leave time for further negotiations with the Reich Minister of the Interior with respect to a 'possible exception' in this case.[17] A note in the file followed to the effect that this had been further discussed and that, since the finding was that Klausa was fit to fight, they had to stick by it and this was the most they could do for the moment, pending further discussion.

The regional government in Kattowitz did not give up its attempt to retain Klausa's services, writing on 25 September 1942 to the Reich Minister of the Interior, at that time still Wilhelm Frick (Heinrich Himmler took over this post the following year), requesting a special exemption in this case. The letter included both the argument that Klausa was not as yet back to full health and that, furthermore, his services were desperately required in the light of the 'particular difficulties' associated with the area in which he held the post of *Landrat*. The possibility that Klausa had indeed played down the extent of his malaise was underlined in Springorum's comment that Klausa's 'perfectly understandable wish, at his age, to be able to serve again in the troop' had played a role in his comments in the medical examination 'about his physical condition'. Springorum added that 'I do not need to underline further the particular difficulties associated with the administration of an annexed district in the east'.[18] After much discussion, the military authorities finally permitted Klausa to stay in office for the time being, and stated that he should not be called up to the army before the end of

November 1942.[19] Alexandra's letters confirm that Klausa did finally leave for military service on 1 December 1942.

This process was rather long drawn out, and seems again to have had deleterious effects on Klausa's 'nerves'. As Alexandra put it in a letter of 14 September, 'Udo's state continues to be the same, very disagreeable, for him frightfully distressing and burdensome. Whether he will become a soldier again is not yet clear.'[20] It does appear as if Klausa was overemphasizing his fitness to return to the front; on the other hand, the army's need for manpower, despite the strong rival claims of regional government, was clearly urgent. At this distance, there is simply no way of telling whether Klausa did or did not have much leeway either way. He clearly did not want to be considered a 'shirker', and was strongly attracted by military pursuits. Since his teenage days, he had always had a hankering after military service; but even before the war, while still in his twenties, he had come to the view that he was physically too delicate for a career in the military, and had reverted to the career path of civilian administration; yet from the very start of the war, he had not wanted to miss out on military action or honours, and had been jealous of his contemporaries who were away at the front. It is also quite possible that Klausa's long-standing problems of 'nerves', and his evidently continuing physical malaise, were exacerbated by mounting unease about the murderous developments in which he was inextricably now involved; and that he was now increasingly keen to mask his symptoms in order to leave the area without risking any trouble with the authorities.

Whatever was going on in Klausa's mind (and body) at the time, it is clear that, after the war, he did not in any way want to be associated with what did actually take place under his continuing authority during the autumn of 1942. Developments included both the continuing exercise of force and individual killings of civilians carried out by members of the gendarmerie, for which Klausa might later be legally held to account, and also key strategic decisions about ghettoization, decisions that were made in the autumn of 1942 and that had ultimately fatal consequences for the Jews of Będzin the following summer. Whether intentionally or through a subconscious process resulting in an elision of memories and dates, Klausa appears to have been determined to pre-date his absence to before the date when the final decisions were taken on further ghettoization: decisions that no longer had merely unintended consequences, but were made for an expressly articulated purpose and made in full knowledge of the underlying reasons—namely, effective imprisonment pending the final deportations to death.

Fatal decisions

The imposition of a regime of terror continued through the autumn; and the gendarmerie, under Heinrich Mentgen's leadership, with Klausa's warm personal support as well as overall responsibility, continued to play a full role in assisting the other Nazi forces of repression. It is instructive to take a glance at some of the daily incident reports from Mentgen, in the light of Klausa's praise for the latter both at the time and later, and his own assertions that he knew of no acts of violence carried out in his *Landkreis* by the gendarmerie for which he was responsible.[21]

The daily reports (*Morgenmeldungen*) are full of incidents indicating the active role of the gendarmerie at the grass roots. On 20 September 1942, for example, Mentgen reported that fifteen people had been arrested under suspicion of having a stockpile of weapons, which they were supposed to reveal to the gendarmerie; two of those arrested had tried to escape and were 'shot while trying to escape' (*auf der Flucht erschossen*).[22] On 7 October 1942, an agricultural labourer by the name of Ludwig Lorenz was arrested on a charge of being in possession of 4 kilogrammes of ham or sausages and 10 kilogrammes of flour. He threw away the two packages he was carrying, resisted arrest, and tried to flee, but was shot in the back by a member of the gendarmerie by the name of Mathe.[23] On 4 November 1942 Mentgen reported that the gendarmerie were providing assistance in the coordinated search for 100 Russian prisoners of war who had broken out of Auschwitz.[24] On 17 November 1942 he reported on an incident the previous day in which four Jews who had managed to escape from the General Government—three men and one woman—were arrested by two gendarmes in the Losien area of the Będzin *Landkreis*. On being interrogated, they sought to escape; one of the gendarmes, Paul Grytz, shot dead the elder man, by the name of Kupferberg, while the other gendarme, Krehs, shot dead Kupferberg's son. Mentgen added that the gendarmerie was continuing its pursuit of the other two Jews.[25]

These cases reported by Mentgen illustrate the range of ways in which the gendarmerie was cooperating with other authorities in imposing the Nazi reign of terror: by arresting people on suspicion of hiding arms, for having foodstuffs beyond what was permitted in the rationing system, for escaping from Auschwitz, for simply being Jewish. In each case, the penalty for trying to evade Nazi force was death: being 'shot while trying to escape'.

The last case, that of Paul Grytz, was in fact investigated quite thoroughly by the Ludwigsburg authorities in the late 1960s. Grytz explained his hierarchy of command quite clearly: 'The gendarmerie post in Losien was part of the gendarmerie district of Bedzin (Bendsburg). My immediate superior was the gendarmerie captain and district leader Heinrich Mentgen based in the *Landrat*'s office in Bendsburg.'[26] When confronted with this case by the legal investigators, the former *Landrat*, Udo Klausa, claimed in his statement of 17 March 1969 that he had already left for military service in August 1942. He continued:

> Because of this I have no professional knowledge of the events that are the subject of discussion here. I was in communication by letters with my deputy. But he never told me anything about this...
>
> An order according to which Jews or Poles who were encountered could be shot dead 'while trying to escape' is not known to me. If this had been made known to me, I would certainly have noticed. It cannot have passed across my desk.[27]

Klausa's self-distancing here through the claim that he was at the time away at the front and not kept fully informed on matters relating to the gendarmerie in his area is manifestly untrue. These reports certainly 'passed across' his desk, even if later he had no memory of them. There can be no doubt on the archival evidence that Klausa was both physically present and in charge of the area at the time of the Losien murders, and highly appreciative of the way in which the gendarmerie was performing. Indeed, on file there is even a letter of 20 November 1942 from Klausa to the district leadership (*Kreisleitung*) of the *NSDAP* praising Mentgen and his work, which Klausa personally signed, using the Nazi 'Heil Hitler' salutation.[28]

Whether or not Klausa's distortions of dating and gaps in memory were intentional, they certainly again proved, as in the case of the Celiny incident in June 1940, very useful in this connection: the *Landrat*'s overall responsibility for these incidents was not pursued further by the Ludwigsburg authorities, who accepted without further investigation Klausa's assertion that he was absent on military service. Nor did they wonder about his claim of ignorance with respect to Auschwitz, which seems somewhat at odds with Mentgen's report on the gendarmerie's assistance in searching for escapees from that camp.[29] These are uncomfortable facts, and it may well be that Klausa himself did not want, more then twenty years later, to confront the full implications of the role he had held at the time.

There was another and more major policy development during this autumn too: one that it would have been even more difficult for Klausa to confront explicitly. This was the decision on the final move of the Jews of Będzin to a more readily guarded ghetto, specifically designed for purposes of effective entrapment prior to their final deportation to death. At this stage, death was not just an unintended consequence of ghettoization for those individuals who fell prey to sickness and starvation or fell foul of the authorities for one reason or another; it was the central reason for this final move. This third and last major phase of ghettoization in Będzin was explicitly designed as a form of transitional incarceration pending the final 'evacuation' of all the Jews of the area to their deaths in Auschwitz. And, as with the previous two phases of ghettoization, Klausa was physically present and in full charge of the administration when the key policy decisions were taken; but he was absent when the practical implementation of these decisions took effect on the victims. Again, Klausa sought through physical dissassociation and temporal distance from violent acts to ensure a degree of personal exoneration for the role he had actually played in developing a system in which such violence was possible.

There are chilling minutes of a meeting held in the municipal offices of Będzin at eleven o'clock on the morning of Saturday, 29 September 1942.[30] Present at this meeting were four people, all relatively senior representatives of their respective spheres, clearly there merely to discuss the details of implementation and not the overall direction of policy. (Purely in this sense, though obviously on a far smaller scale and at an infinitely lower level of the hierarchy, it is not dissimilar to the infamous gathering in January 1942 of 'second-rank' officials, meeting in a Berlin lakeside villa to discuss the implementation of the 'final solution', that has gone down in history as the Wannsee Conference.) Present on behalf of the Będzin municipal government was the *Stadtkämmerer*, which roughly translates as the Finance Director or City Treasurer, a post generally viewed as a second-in-command in German local government. On behalf of the *NSDAP* was the *Kreisstabsamtleiter*, Hirtbach, again something of a second-in-command post to the *NSDAP* district leader, or *Kreisleiter*. On behalf of the Gestapo was the officer responsible for Jewish affairs in the Kattowitz Gestapo headquarters, the much-feared Hans Dreier. Dreier's track record in the area and his prominent role in previous selections and deportations was by this time well known, as was that of his close associates, including Dr Mildner, Head of the Kattowitz Police and frequent visitor to Auschwitz overseeing the 'court' in which death sentences could be meted out at a rate of one a minute.[31] Dreier also brought along an unnamed colleague from the Gestapo.

This little group quite openly discussed the question of how to ensure that Jews could in future be corralled in a more closely controlled space for easier round-up and deportation, given the widespread knowledge about Auschwitz and the view that the trick relating to ID card renewals that had been perpetrated on them in August would never work again. The new purpose of ghettoization for easier capture of the Jews at the time of the next deportation was quite explicitly stated by Dreier and recorded in the minutes. There can be no question that the representatives of both the *NSDAP* and the municipal authorities at this meeting knew, just as clearly as the Gestapo, precisely what issues they were dealing with, and what the proposed 'solution' was to consist in. As the report of this meeting, drawn up by a municipal official, noted:

> In terms of the local preparation for further evacuations it is considered that the Jews should be brought together as much as possible in one section of town... The preparations shall be undertaken in such a way that no disquiet arises among the Jews.[32]

The municipal authorities were then charged with the practical task of organizing the concentration of Jews in one particular area of town in order to facilitate their planned roundup:

> In view of this position, for the town would come first of all the question of organizing the collection of those Jews still remaining here in a particular section of town. The related resettlement of Poles would also play a considerable role in this. There was general agreement that these tasks would not be easy to solve.[33]

The meaning could hardly be made clearer: any further 'evacuation' would be fiercely resisted by the Jews; plans therefore had to be made in advance to achieve effective incarceration, precisely for the purpose of preparing for the next deportation. It should be noted that the word I have here translated as 'resettlement' with respect to the Poles is *Umsiedlung* (movement around) not, as now characteristically used in relation to the Jews, *Aussiedlung* or *Evakuierung* (movement out, evacuation). These delicate distinctions and euphemistic connotations cannot be adequately conveyed in the English translation, but the differentiated code was clear to those participating in this meeting. Local government was explicitly party to and intrinsically involved in planning for easing the process of deportation to death.

It is also notable that the authorities were still thinking in terms of separating out those Jews who were deemed to be 'economically useful', who were to be held until later, from those designated for immediate murder. As the notes of this meeting recorded, explicitly registering the key distinction between those who were still economically productive and those designated for immediate 'evacuation': 'First of all there should be a census of those Jews employed in the factories. Through this census the number of those who come into consideration for evacuation could be ascertained.'[34] The municipal authorities were, over the coming months, closely engaged in the process of gaining a remarkably precise head count of those Jews still held by their German employers to be essential to the functioning of their enterprises.

The civilian administration of Będzin was therefore in full and explicit awareness, at this juncture, of the fact that this final stage of ghettoization was directly geared towards incarceration pending 'evacuation' and the rendering of Będzin totally 'cleansed of Jews' (*judenrein*). This last was indeed a phrase in general use at the time, echoed repeatedly and independently by numerous survivors across the world, even echoing in oral history interviews carried out some half a century later. For the word to have stuck in the minds of survivors as far afield as Australia, the United Kingdom, the United States, and Canada, when the phrase was not necessarily part of the global Holocaust 'culture industry' with its primary focus on the death camps, suggests its extremely widespread currency in everyday usage at that time.[35]

The location chosen by the authorities for the final ghetto prior to 'cleansing' Będzin of Jews was a poor area known as Kamionka, situated on the other side of the railway tracks—conveniently on the same side of the tracks as the former orphanage where Jews were held while waiting for transports. A further section of this newly designated ghetto area was known as 'Little Środula' (Środula Dolny). Over the coming months Poles had to be moved out, and all Jews moved in, but in such a way as not to arouse suspicion.

Matters were made slightly easier in one respect by making the Jews 'self-sufficient'—after a manner—by forcing them to rely on their own resources and distribution channels for what food they were still allowed to have. As Klausa noted in his report of October 1942: 'All *Jewish food shops* have been closed. The distribution of foodstuffs now takes place through larger distribution points that the Jewish Community has itself set up.'[36] But there was not a great deal of food to be distributed. The Reich Minister for Food and Agriculture took a decision to cut rations for Jews even further, with effect from 19 October 1942, to near starvation levels. Jews were clearly now deemed to be barely worth feeding for very much longer.

Himmler had already on 19 July 1942 issued a directive that all Polish Jews were to be 'resettled'—either actually exterminated or waiting in a 'collection camp'—by December 1942.[37] No Jew was to remain in any kind of labour in the General Government after that point. This was a 'target' that was in the event not met and was subsequently reiterated by Himmler for completion in 1943. Himmler's goals, here relating to the Jews held in the General Government under Hans Frank, seem to have applied to Jews in Eastern Upper Silesia too, where a similar if slightly more extended time-scale appeared to be operating. And the shifting climate of policy and ultimately murderous goals percolated down in some form to the municipal authorities responsible for such a large Jewish population, however much the plans were wrapped in the euphemism of 'evacuation', since the planned implementation involved the active cooperation of local government in facilitating preparations for the round-ups.[38] Far from reacting against such developments with horror, civilian administrators seem not merely to have gone along with these measures, but on occasion also actively to have welcomed such policies in the light of mounting local problems.

The municipal authorities were acutely aware of the growing issues relating to disease and malnutrition, with wider consequences and risks for public health, directly arising from the combination of German policies. The City Mayor of Sosnowiec, Schönwälder, reported, for example, that there was an increasing shortage of labour in the area, with the recent 'evacuation' of some 6,000 Jews and the accelerating pace of removal of Poles to forced labour in the heart of the 'old' Reich.[39] This had knock-on effects for Germans—who were even complaining about shortages of goods such as cigarettes and chocolate, a comment on their lifestyle and expectations at a time when those whom they subjugated were literally starving. Labour shortages and low productivity would, in Schönwälder's view, be made dramatically worse by the decision to cut Jewish food rations. Thus, from this perspective, a 'final' solution appeared ever more urgent.

It is worth quoting from this analysis at length. Schönwälder first discussed the plans to develop a discrete ghetto in the northern suburb of Środula, which would require the displacement of some 7,000–8,000 Poles from already impoverished streets that could therefore 'not come into question' as residential areas for Germans. This could, with a little difficulty, be achieved. But the issues to do with the knock-on effects of near starvation remained a major concern:

As a result of a new direction from the Reich Minister for Food and Agriculture, the Jews will, from 19 October this year, only receive food in very limited quantities. Jews are prohibited from receiving any meat, eggs or foodstuffs on special distribution that are in short supply.[40]

This meant that 'ever more Jews will have to drop out of employment . . . and as carriers of disease, who owing to severe malnutrition will no longer have any resistance to illness, will endanger the German population to a quite considerable extent'. Typhus was already 'gaining ever more victims among Poles and Jews'.[41] The 'solution' was, however, in the Nazi world view not the obvious humanitarian one of ensuring adequate food supplies for the starving Jewish population. Rather, Schönwälder raised the question of whether 'a further evacuation of the Jews should be carried out' that might in fact be the best 'solution' to these mounting problems. By now, it was more than clear what 'evacuation' actually meant.

Unlike in previous years, when the danger of the spread of epidemics from the impoverished Jewish quarters to the wealthier German population had also been mentioned as a serious concern, there was now a short route to 'solution': the total extermination of the Jewish population, which had by now, as a direct result of the German policies, been reduced to real and not merely metaphorical 'carriers of disease' and hence posed a genuine 'danger' to the health of the German body politic. All further developments in the linked ghetto areas of Sosnowiec and Będzin ran more or less in unison—as had previous 'actions', deportations, and incidents such as the public hangings—with this overall situation and radical goals as the guiding themes.

Ghettoization as transitional incarceration

The fatal decisions having already been taken, Klausa finally left to rejoin the army on 1 December 1942, although he was able to return to visit his family on occasion. On 14 January 1943, while Klausa was still in a military training establishment in Liegnitz and not as yet actively engaged in military combat, Alexandra wrote to Frau von H. that there seemed at last to be some improvement in his condition:

Udo was here for three days and now he is still in Liegnitz; I so much hope that he will stay there for a good long time, because he does seem to be recovering with this lifestyle and feels his strength returning slowly.[42]

But the Jews of Będzin did not have the option of leaving for better conditions elsewhere. As a direct result of Nazi policy decisions, their situation now worsened radically and rapidly.

In the course of the winter and spring of 1942–3 the ghetto areas were established in the impoverished slum districts and partially rural area (now more or less reverted to scrub land) between Będzin and Sosnowiec. The two main ghetto areas could be mutually accessed, with Środula Dolny ('Little Środula') situated between Środula to the south, and Kamionka to the north, thus effectively filling in the area between the two closely neighbouring towns in this industrial conurbation. In an early post-war account, Pawel Wiedermann claimed that this meant a complete population turnover, with two or three Jewish families being moved into every tiny house or apartment where previously only one very poor Polish family had lived in what were already cramped circumstances.[43] The overcrowding was horrendous.

The movement of Sosnowiec Jews to Środula began in November 1942. The designated area was first viewed by a group made up of both local government officials and representatives of the Jewish community in October, and the first Jewish families were moved there on 17 November 1942. By the end of December some 740 families with 3,000 people were resident there; by mid-March, this had risen to 14,000; hundreds more were somehow crammed in, with their numbers periodically being augmented by arrivals from elsewhere, and thinned by continuing raids taking groups of Jews still capable of work off to labour camps, until the move had been completed by 1 April 1943.[44]

Similar moves took place on the Będzin side of the inner-city border, although, as Wiedermann noted in his early post-war account, 'living conditions in Kamionka and Little Srodula were even worse' than in the Sosnowiec ghetto areas.[45] As the report on a meeting between the Będzin Mayor, Kowohl, and Dreier from the Kattowitz Gestapo, as well as two other officials, makes clear, the Germans themselves envisaged the need for Jews to build temporary shelters since insufficient housing was available; and they confirmed that the area was to be surrounded by a secure fence.[46] The Jews were effectively to be corralled in. It was also clear to many Jews that this new move was likely only to be temporary, given both the nature of the accommodation and the lack of food supplies.

The Szpringer family, who had survived the August 1942 selection intact, had been living along with their cousins, the Felsensztein family, in a cramped apartment in the old town of Będzin. Of the original seven Szpringers, only five were still in Będzin: Issa Szpringer was in a labour camp in Russia; and by now Dora had been deported to a German labour camp. Her brother, Moishe Szpringer, provides a very clear account of the experience of the remaining five members of the family on being moved out of their already overcrowded quarters in the original ghetto area in the centre of town:

In January of '43, notices were posted around the city ordering that all Jews had just three days to evacuate Bendzin proper, and relocate in an area called the Kamionka, a rural area between Bendzin and Dambrowa. The Kamionka would now be the 'Bendzin Ghetto'. Agents of the Judenrat had the task of assigning living space to all the Jews forced to move to Kamionka. Of course, housing in this rural locale was woefully inadequate for all of the displaced people. Many families were simply assigned an open plot of land, where they fashioned a makeshift 'home' by stretching sheets, or whatever they could scrounge, over furniture and poles. This provided them with a little privacy and some minimal protection from the weather.

Fortunately, Father managed to get us assigned to an empty stable that stood behind a two-storey house.

The stable was divided into two parts: one side for cows and the other side for horses. Father took the horse side for our family because it was taller and had a hayloft overhead. Cousin Issa [Felsensztein] and his family moved into the cow side.[47]

Between them, the two families set to work to make these quarters as habitable as they could, furnishing them with the few possessions they had managed to bring with them and that would fit inside. Surviving photographs of this area show streets where piles of cupboards, tables, and bedsteads are simply piled up outside in courtyards or on the street, many families having discovered too late that this last move was not one designed to give them any space for comfort, or indeed even for minimal and adequate spaces in which to sleep. One of the Szpringer brothers, Yossel, was particularly good as 'a plasterer and jack-of-all-trades', skills that now came in very useful in trying to turn the stables into a more habitable space. But, as Moishe Szpringer comments, 'we were well aware that the Germans had other plans for us; it was just a matter of when'.[48]

Conditions with respect to food, drink, and sanitary arrangements in the ghetto area were bordering on disastrous; but there seemed no means of escape. Water had to be collected from a well, and carried back to the place of habitation by balancing two buckets from the ends of a yoke carried across the shoulders, like oxen. Gunter Faerber, who had less than a year previously bid farewell at the Będzin railway station to his grandmother from Beuthen, on her way among one of the first groups to be gassed at Auschwitz, was by this time aged 14 but still physically very small. He recalls that the old well was full of rubble; because of his size he was sent down the well to clear out the rubble, until he got down to the water. After that someone could work a hand pump and they could then fill the water buckets. In Faerber's house, six families lived in three rooms. One of the people they lived with was a man by the name of Oppenheimer, who reportedly had done a lot of trade and had many connections with Germans, including wealthy Germans in banking circles, 'and even he couldn't arrange for himself to get out'. Faerber's parents too had connections in Germany, including influential friends who were high-ranking civil servants; they hoped in this way to gain permits to move to Switzerland. 'My parents have tried, and a lot of people have tried to get out, and my parents still had the money, or the gold, they could have bribed people, but very few people, I don't know of any who succeeded to get out.'[49]

One person who did manage to get out of this ghetto area alive was Mindzia Tenenbaum. Now aged 10, Mindzia had already lost her mother, and then her elder sister, to the work camps. In the ghetto, she lived with the remaining members of her family, and some relatives who had joined them:

> there was one room with bunk beds . . . I wanted my brother [Idek] to lie there and hold my hand. I was frightened, every night I cried myself to sleep. But my grandmother from Sosnowiec, she was there in ghetto with us. And my father David, he was very much afraid for his parents, because there were rumours when he came back from work that elderly people, and young children, they said that they don't have a chance to survive, but the young ones that can work, and capable of working, there's no problem, they're going to go to work and it will be fine. At that point he was worrying about his parents and me. He still wouldn't let me go to [the family's Polish former maid] Cecilia, he couldn't believe it will come to that. So he built a little basement and there was a closet . . .[50]

Every day Mindzia and her brother Idek had to hide in this little closet; Idek would close the closet and they lay there all day, every day, in the

Figure 20. Two girls in the Będzin ghetto, 1942–3
Two young girls in a relatively deserted street in the ghetto. The furniture piled up in the street is indicative of the overcrowding; many families were squeezed into small houses, with insufficient room for the furniture they had brought with them from their former homes. This photo would have been taken when all able-bodied adults were out on forced labour duties.
United States Holocaust Memorial Museum, courtesy of Arnold Shay (Abram Szyjewicz).

basement until their father came home from work and pulled it open and took them out.

One day Mindzia and her brother found themselves stuck in their small hiding place. Later, they found out why their father had not returned to let them out:

> My father was taken away, from work, they sent him away ... and at that point we knew that my father will not come back any more. There were pogroms every day at work and they just sent away people, and sirens every night because they came into the house, into the room, and they would take children away and older people, and they just sent away and we didn't know where. There was no newspaper, there was no radio, there was no news.[51]

Mindzia's older sister was now insistent that Idek should take Mindzia to their Polish friend and former maid, Cecilia, who had continued to supply them with additional rations even after they had been moved out of the old quarters in the centre of town, and who might be willing to hide her. Mindzia's grandfather protested, saying it was against his son's wishes, and that the family should remain together; he kept praying for guidance. But eventually the sister gave the two children a piece of bread, and told them to make their escape:

It was at night, we start running, running, running towards barbed wires and Idek somehow he knew that there was place where Cecilia dig a deep hole in the earth, and she cover it with stones, because she used to help us, she didn't care if she will be caught, she didn't care to survive war without her family, and we were her family, she only cared to help us. So she would put flour, bread, potatoes whatever she could to the big hole and would cover it with branches, with stones, and someone from the family would go there . . . and digged out and took this nourishment that we survived on. There was little, little food.[52]

So Idek took Mindzia to this place, covered her with branches, made her wait while he ran to a gate in the fence and dug a big hole, then came back for her. She recalls that she was shaking terribly 'and so we ran to the other side, there were SS with dogs, screaming, shouting, dogs . . .'. It was daylight already, so they hid in a bush and covered themselves with branches, with Idek comforting her. Then, as she recalls: 'Early in the morning we were lucky, I don't know how the miracle happened, I really don't know . . .'. They managed to evade detection and got to Cecilia's apartment, consisting of 'one small little bedroom and one small little kitchen', under the attic of a large tenement building on one of the central streets leading to the railway station, Modzrejowska 81. Cecilia came down on her way out to work, found Idek and Mindzia there, and told them it would be too dangerous to take them both up at once. Idek's hands were bleeding and he had to hide them in her shawl while they were talking. Cecilia took him down to the basement and told him to wait there while she took Mindzia up to the attic, with Mindzia crying all the time. Cecilia promised she would go back and get her brother and bring him up when it was safe to do so, after she had returned from work later in the day. But, as Mindzia recalled, every day there were 'pogroms and people running', and police and dogs, 'and they warned that anybody who will keep a Jew, the whole family will be hanged, nobody had the courage to do anything'. Idek never was brought up to the attic; Mindzia constantly waited, desperately hoping, but she never saw her brother again.

The atmosphere for those remaining in the Będzin ghetto over the following months is captured in the notebook of Rutka Laskier.[53] Her diary consists of notes written between 19 January 1943 and 24 April 1943, with one fragment that may have been written the previous August, although it discusses the experience of winter. Much of her 'notebook' is taken up with discussion of friends, and particularly her growing interest in one particular boy, Janek. Previously a pupil at the highly academic Fürstenberg High School—which was closed by the invading Germans in 1939—Rutka, like her contemporary Anne Frank writing a diary while in hiding in Holland, was also interested in literature and in self-expression. Rutka's perceptions, not so much of the perpetrators themselves as of the effects of the Nazi occupation on the victims, are remarkably insightful. On 5 February 1943, Rutka queried the existence of God:

> The little faith I used to have has been completely shattered. If God existed, he would have certainly not permitted that human beings be thrown alive into furnaces, and the heads of little toddlers be smashed with the butt of guns or be shoved into sacks and gassed to death... Those who haven't seen this would never believe it... Or the time when they beat an old man until he became unconscious, because he didn't cross the street properly.[54]

The following day, she noted the effects on herself: 'Something has broken in me. When I pass by a German, everything shrinks in me, I don't know whether it is out of fear or hatred.'[55] On 1 March 1943 Rutka wrote:

> I must pull myself together and not wet my pillow with tears. Because of whom or what am I crying? Because of Janek, certainly not. Then because of whom? Probably because of freedom. I am sick and tired of these grey houses, of the steady fear seen in everybody's faces. This fear clutches on to everyone and doesn't let go.[56]

In a final and ambiguous fragment following the last 'diary' entry of 24 April 1943, written on a page referencing the earlier date of 11 August 1942—it was the last day before the 12 August selections—Rutka wrote of winter in the ghetto:

> Big flakes of snow... Nevertheless, the usual children's cries of joy announcing the arrival of winter are not heard on the streets. For most of the ghetto's inhabitants, the winter is a nightmare of terrible poverty and hunger. Everywhere people are standing in line, lines for potatoes, coal, bread. Children dressed in worn-out clothes stretch out their hands to those passing by. These children are the most predominant symbol of the grey ghetto. The parents have been deported, and the children were left abandoned to their destiny, to go astray in the streets. The people's faces express sadness and worry. Suddenly there is a scream, a police officer pushed an elderly person, he fell and his head hit the road. The white snow was absorbed with the purple red blood. Over there, a woman is crying, her husband has been imprisoned, who knows if she'll ever see him again...

. . . The 'shop' [workshop] workers pour out onto the streets. Young hungry girls, pale-faced, anaemic . . .[57]

These descriptions portray people clinging onto life, aware of the fact that they too are probably ultimately doomed to die, 'gassed to death' or thrown into the 'furnaces' of which even a 14-year-old girl in the ghetto was well aware at this time.

The Jewish Council was of little help at this time. In early 1943, in precisely the months during which Rutka was writing this diary, Merin was continuing his previous policy: effectively cooperating in delivering Jews to the slaughter. One speech of his, delivered in early 1943 in the *Judenrat* courtyard in the Środula ghetto, has been reported almost verbatim. This suggests Merin may, perhaps, have been losing his grip on sanity as well as clearly suffering from delusions about the extent of his power:

I warn you . . . I am in a cage, confronted by a raging hungry lion. I stuff flesh down his throat, human flesh, my brothers' and sisters' flesh . . . Why? Because I am trying to keep the lion in his cage, so that he doesn't get out and trample and devour every one of us at once . . . No one will dissuade me from this course! . . . I tell you that I shall continue to gorge the lion with my brothers' and sisters' flesh! . . . I shall fight all those men who would disrupt my work . . . I shall not let youth distract me from my bloodstained labour . . . No! . . . I shall fight them with all the means at my disposal, and let history judge me![58]

Even so, while some were apparently mollified by Merin's words and his attempts to curb the worst excesses of the Jewish militia, others remained radically critical of his actions and continued their attempts at resistance.

Circles of young people, including those who had managed to gain false papers and remain on the 'Aryan side', continued to engage in plans for resistance. There were continuing contacts with Polish partisan groups—sadly betrayed by a Pole who, posing as a partisan, was in fact informing for the Gestapo—and with the Jewish resistance in Warsaw.[59] Some Jews obtained weapons and trained themselves and others in their use, as well as encouraging people to make use of scissors, knives, and any other implements readily at hand, in order to prepare for an armed fight against the Germans. Some committed acts of sabotage, or produced anti-German leaflets that could be stuffed into the army uniforms and boots that they were making in the 'shops', to be found by German soldiers at the front. In the ghetto members of the resistance established a form of kibbutz in a large building used as a laundry, and sought to maintain contacts with an emissary of the World Organization of Jews in Geneva, Natan Schwalb. Even at this stage there were continuing conflicts over strategy and tactics with Merin: relationships had been further soured by the fact that, when anti-war leaflets were found in the boots and army uniforms manufactured by Jews in the workshops, Merin personally arranged for the arrest and handover of two of the most active members of the resistance groups, Dunski and Minz, to the Gestapo.[60]

The largest resistance activity at this time was, however, that of making preparations to hide: personal survival was in itself, in some views, the single most significant form of resistance to the German policy of exterminating the Jews of Europe. Not only members of the resistance groups but families and individuals everywhere in the ghetto built what they called 'bunkers': hiding places under false floors in large cupboards, behind false walls at the backs of cellars, under trapdoors or in disguised holes in the ground in yards and gardens, in parts of the rafters of attics—wherever there was some small and enclosable space into which a few bodies could be squeezed, in the hope that they would not be found in a cursory search by German troops rounding up people for deportation. Such hiding places could be quite elaborate, with air-holes, pipes, or other means to obtain fresh air from outside; but none was designed for more than a few hours of hiding, with no kind of water, food supply, or sanitary facilities. These were designed as temporary bolt-holes to evade immediate discovery on a quick raid, not as strategic bases for a long haul in hiding.

Slowly, over the spring of 1943 all the Jews employed in German workplaces were named, listed, and counted up by the municipal authorities, and employers persuaded to find other ways of meeting their workplace needs. Many employers, including Rudolf Braune, sought to argue that their employees were essential members of the workforce, and vital to the German war effort—arguments that were ultimately of little avail.[61] On 30 April 1943 the Jewish Council produced figures to the effect that there were now just 18,670 Jews left in Będzin, of whom 13,182 were working, and 5,488 were children or others who were not working.[62] They also calculated that some 3,800 Będzin Jews were working in slave labour camps elsewhere. On 12 May 1943 the summary report of the municipal authorities claimed that, without any emotional considerations involved, the only conclusion could be that Jews were central to German economic productivity and could not be displaced from the workplace without harming German interests.[63] But national policy was running in a different direction. On 21 May 1943 a telegram from Ernst Kaltenbrunner, now Himmler's second-in-command and Heydrich's successor as head of the Reich Security Main Office (RSHA), referred to the 'orders of 20.2.1943' and ordered a Reich-wide 'evacuation' by 30 June 1943 at the latest of all Jews, including those who were 'still in work ... without any consideration of declining production', although those in the Schmelt camps were to be the subject of separate discussions between Eichmann and the Kattowitz authorities.[64] Over the summer of 1943, the Jewish population almost completely disappeared from the face of Będzin; they were not to be any part of the town's future.

On 19 June 1943 Moses Merin was called to a meeting with members of the SS, along with his principal assistant and secretary in the *Judenrat* headquarters, Fanny Czarna, as well as his brother Chaim Merin and two other senior Jewish Council members. Far from this being a routine meeting to discuss the details of further collaboration in the machinery of mass murder, Merin was now himself summarily sent to Auschwitz, along with his committee colleagues, and murdered.[65] With the planned extermination of the entire remaining Jewish community, there was no longer any need for collaboration with Merin or the Jewish Council to assist in selecting and weeding out the old, the young, and the weak.

Judenrein

The 'final clearance' of the ghetto of Będzin started on 22 June 1943. Tusia Herzberg recalls:

> In the night of 21–2 June 1943 the German police and members of the order police went into the Jewish homes and pulled the Jews out and brought them to a square in the ghetto. There a selection took place, that Dreier carried out... The whole square was surrounded by Gestapo people...[66]

Jochanan Ranz remembered the night vividly:

> About 4 a.m. different formations of SS Police, SA and many Gestapo officials surrounded and entered the Ghetto... The people got up and hid in their bunkers, whoever had one. The Germans went from house to house and drove out the people they met, beating with their clubs those who didn't dress up so quick. They didn't spare anybody, women or children, old or young. People unable to walk out were shot immediately then...[67]

Those driven out of their homes now included those workers from the Rossner shops who had thought they were safe, and members of the Jewish militia and other collaborators who had assumed they alone would survive by virtue of their usefulness to the Germans. In the summary of Ranz:

> For the Nazis all Jews were equal. And all should be exterminated only one earlier one later. After the Nazi-figured plan they only had to help kill one another. Now the Nazis could show their real face, they were no more obliged to play in promises. The large majority of Jews in Upper Silesia were already dead in Auschwitz. The remaining were in a Ghetto behind the town. The Nazis were no more afraid that their extermination will make a noise in the town, as the Germans in the town didn't like the tragic crying of women and children being killed. That could spoil their afternoon mood.[68]

This was intended as the final round-up, the final 'cleansing' of the Jews of Będzin: making Będzin *judenrein*, 'cleansed of Jews'.

Even despite the removal of the ghetto to the other side of the railway tracks, the scenes were still witnessed and still occasioned distress among the 'Germans in the town'. Alexandra's lengthy letter to her mother on 2 July 1943 includes extensive complaints: she was experiencing difficulties with retaining her maids (with Minna trying to leave, she would have to make do with just Rosa, unless she could have Erna back, but even so this would not suffice); her own plans to spend four months of the summer elsewhere had been thwarted; and the lack of fresh garden produce was compounded by difficulties in obtaining fresh food now that the formerly thriving market in town had completely closed down. As she summarized her situation:

> But it's probably now quite general, that one has virtually nothing but vexation [*Ärger*] . . . First of all, there is nothing to eat, not a scrap of vegetables to be bought; in the garden there's not much going on either . . . So I don't know what we are to live off!

Alexandra also registers her discomfort in having to witness the horrendous scenes relating to the deportation of the entire Jewish community, a process which had just begun:

> Added to that, all hell has broken out in Bendsburg, all Jews are being resettled [*ausgesiedelt*] at the moment, and the whole misery is there to see on the streets. Perpetually some Jews are fleeing, there is constant shooting, everywhere dead Jews are lying around, everywhere there is turmoil. We have now received one battalion of soldiers, also Waffen-SS. I'm sure nothing will happen to us, but one simply can't avoid seeing all this, and the constant shooting drives one quite mad.[69]

Many Jews had been shot between 22 and 26 June, before the massive final clearance operation 'succeeded' in August. An estimated 6,000 Jews were transported to Auschwitz from Będzin and Sosnowiec over these few days.[70]

Alexandra's letter of 2 July 1943 was written several weeks before the even more bloody 'clearance' of the ghetto, an undertaking that took, not the few days that had initially been catered for (also literally, in terms of police rations) by von Woedtke, but a full two weeks given the strength of Jewish resistance. A series of repeated requests for prolonged reprovisioning of personnel, including the participation of members of the Police Riding School Bendsburg (with whose chief Udo Klausa had been enjoying pre-breakfast rides the previous summer, just before the 1942 deportations), indicate just how unexpectedly protracted the final clearance proved to be, in face of fierce resistance on the part of the Jews.[71] But professional assistance was available from further afield. Survivors recall how closely the final clearance of the ghetto was linked to the Auschwitz organization of the machinery of death: as one recalled, 'members of the SS camp personnel from Auschwitz also took part in the resettlement actions in Bendzin and Sosnowitz'.[72]

The final ghetto clearance had been planned meticulously in advance, with the purpose of the total destruction of the Jewish community of the area. The German authorities had not only terminated all employment arrangements that included Jewish workers, but were also envisaging already setting up a museum of Jewish life for the posthumous, 'Jew-free' Będzin. A letter of 27 July 1943 from the mayor of Będzin to the municipal housing office, for example, noted that a Jewish library 'consisting of a good half dozen languages' had been 'secured', which was 'indicative of the international character of Jewry'. He therefore requested 'that this should be kept for the intended Jewish Museum of the town'.[73] But the Jews were not prepared to be turned into the dead objects of museum culture without considerable resistance.

Many Jews remained in their carefully prepared hideouts and 'bunkers' without food, water, sanitation, for as long as they could possibly manage. There are innumerable tragic stories of individual experiences—all with personal twists and variations, with moments of intense danger and tragedy, with moments of extreme luck and of desperation. Infants were suffocated in order to prevent the noise of crying that would have betrayed and hence sacrificed the lives of others; the elderly and sick died through lack of water and food, through exhaustion and misery. Some were discovered by the thorough and brutal searches of the Germans, who shot into every conceivable corner and hiding place; others were discovered only when one member of a group in hiding eventually risked going out in search of water for fear they would all die of thirst. Some managed to get by through drinking their own urine, on occasion filtered through a rag. Some even managed to find food—potatoes are mentioned—in scary night-time foraging, and food was even on occasion provided by well-meaning Polish neighbours, who risked being shot if discovered. People sat in suffocating darkness, listening to the shooting, the shouting, the screams, and the crying of those who were being forcibly removed from their makeshift homes and bolt-holes. There were tears as families were separated, tears as loved ones were brutally beaten or shot before their eyes, as people knew this was the end. One survivor commented that 'the screams and the noises were extremely loud, if you lived five kilometres away you would have heard it'.[74]

Some, particularly members of the Jewish youth groups who had been preparing for a revolt over many months, now engaged in armed resistance and even succeeded in killing some of the Germans. One of these was Frumka Plotnicka, who had been sent by the Warsaw Jewish resistance movement to encourage similar groups in Będzin in the autumn of 1942. She died in the bunker of a resistance group in Kamionka on 3 August 1943; her sister had already been killed on 20 April 1943.[75] Many continued fighting to the bitter end, even on the trains to Auschwitz, as Jochanan Ranz recounts:

> from one train the Nazis didn't let the people out, but opened the doors and shot in with machine guns killing them all. They did this because the train was mutinous on the way, many jumping off and one SS guard was killed. The troopers were afraid of a possible desperate resistance before the gas-chambers.[76]

And some 2,800 people were killed 'while trying to escape' (*auf der Flucht erschossen*), in the terms of the well-worn Nazi euphemism. One of these was a relative of Arno Lustiger, shot by Dreier.[77]

It was estimated that a total of between 30,000 and 35,000 Jews were deported from the linked ghettos of Będzin and Sosnowiec at this time.[78] A very few—perhaps in the hundreds—did survive this brutal clear-out. Minimal 'selections' were still carried out—again, primarily by Dreier and Kuczynski, with the assistance of others—in a square in the ghetto before being taken to the railway station. The selection scenes were immensely bloody, with shooting of anyone who sought to run from the group that had been sentenced to death.[79] A few were selected for forced labour even at this late stage, and were retained in a small labour camp to 'clean up' the ghetto after it had been emptied. A handful of Jews who had survived the clearance in hiding were later caught or even chose to attempt survival by joining work gangs, including for Rossner's workshops. In November 1943 the last Jews of Będzin were transported to Auschwitz, leaving a mere 150 Jews to assist in the final clearance of the debris.[80] This last little group was then deported to Auschwitz at the end of 1943. Members of the civilian administration, including Sosnowiec City Mayor Schönwälder, were closely involved in this ghetto clearance and in collecting up any remaining possessions, as were local industrialists such as Rudolf Braune.

Those Jews who were sent to labour camps stood a slightly higher chance of remaining alive than if they had been sent straight to Auschwitz. Arno Lustiger's family, for example, had been rounded up and forced into the Kamionka ghetto in 1943, but then evaded the August deportations by hiding in a bunker in the ironware works formerly owned by Lustiger's uncle and situated near the railway station. Friendly Polish railway workers had tipped them off that 'on the tracks around Bedzin hundreds of railway carriages were standing waiting for their "load"'.[81] Later, Arno Lustiger was deported to work in subsidiary labour camps in the huge Auschwitz complex; unlike his father, he was sufficiently young and strong to survive the multiple privations, starvation rations, and overwork, and managed to crawl through to the death marches and the end of the war.

Gitel Donath too survived the *Judenrein* action, and was in a labour camp for cleaning up the Środula ghetto before the planned final deportations of this clean-up crew to Auschwitz. Her brother Chaim was shot dead while in the camp, but she and her sister Pearl managed to escape from, of all places, the Sosnowiec police station itself while they were being held there awaiting deportation to Auschwitz; somehow, they figured out to the exact second when the guard would have just passed by and it would for a fractional moment be safe to leap from the kitchen window to the derelict ground behind and run for the cover of a deserted house nearby. For some days the two sisters roamed between what they had thought to be a safe haven in the house of a Pole by the name of Kowalski, who lived some way outside Będzin, and, when told to leave this house, back again to hide in deserted houses in the Środula ghetto. Here, new Polish owners were already taking over the now empty premises, cleaning them up, and moving in. The

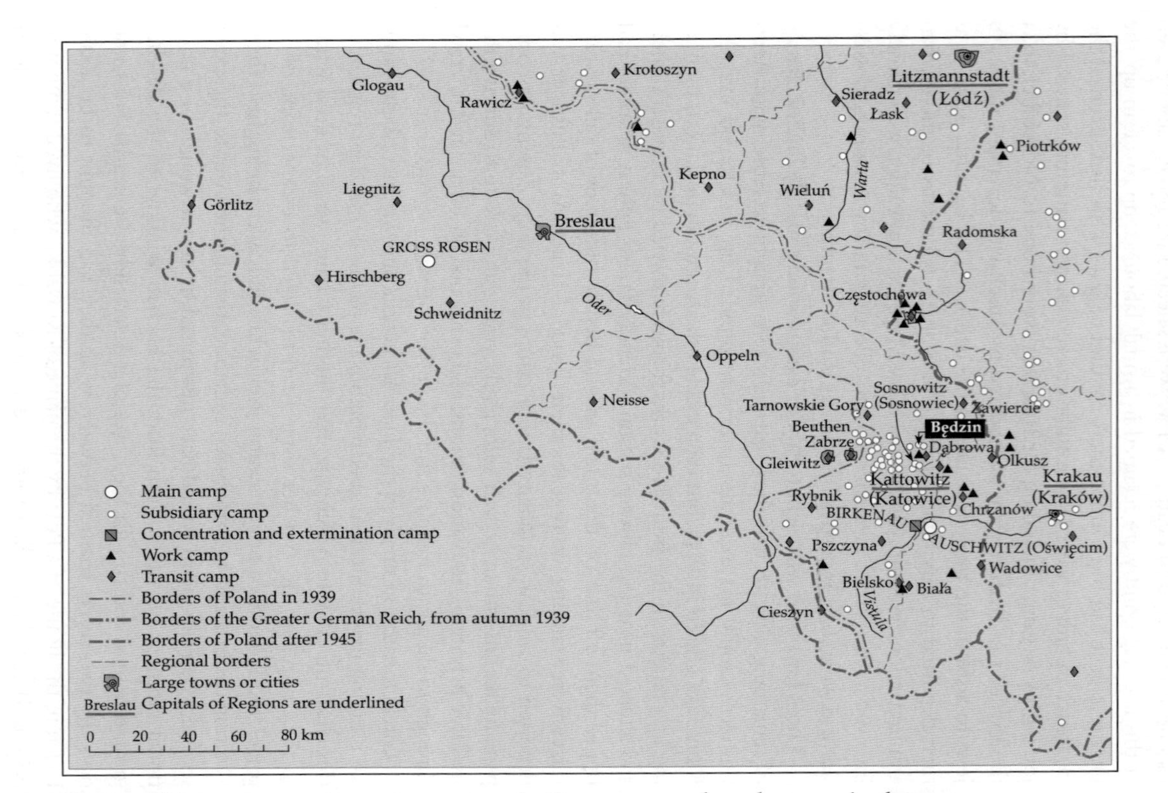

Map 4. Major concentration camps, extermination camps, and work camps in the area

sisters were weak with terror, hunger, and exhaustion, and plagued by fear of Polish antisemitism and the ever-present threat of betrayal. As Donath put it: 'We were afraid to knock on any door. It was horrible. We felt like we were surrounded and vulnerable to attack by wild animals. Prejudice against Jews made it risky even to enter a Polish bakery to buy a piece of bread.'[82]

Fears of being found out to be Jewish by Poles was widely prevalent: many survivors recount that Poles had a 'nose' for Jews, and could 'sniff' when someone was speaking even perfect Polish but with Jewish intonation and mannerisms. Their gait and bearing, too, often betrayed them. Survivors recount how hard they found it to walk as though not afraid, to walk boldly and upright and not instinctively flinch, shrink, or turn to run on seeing army uniforms.

Perhaps the boldest of all—on occasion almost foolhardily so—were the Szpringers.[83] The five members of the Szpringer family remaining in Będzin had constructed one of the most elaborate 'bunkers' in the roof of their stable, and, squeezed together and in acute discomfort, had survived the ghetto clearance entirely undiscovered. They then managed, with false identity papers that one of the sons had forged, first to pass themselves off as Poles on a two-week holiday in Jelesnia, a popular resort in the mountains south of Będzin. They took different lodgings and in various ways obtained sufficient food to subsist—the daughter Laya, for example, was fixed up with a job helping a local farmer and lived with this family—until it was no longer safe for them to be in the area for such an apparently extended 'holiday'. Later, once the traditional Polish holiday season was over, they managed to forge further papers suggesting that one or another had been laid off for a longer period from their workplace because of shortage of materials, a not uncommon occurrence in Polish industry at this time. In the meantime, while some of the family remained hidden for stints in their former hiding place in the stable roof in Kamionka, and others slept rough or stayed under cover in different ways, Moishe and Jusek (Jossel) roamed between Kattowitz and Dąbrowa, trying to avoid Będzin itself, where they would be easily recognized by former neighbours, searching for a longer-term means of survival. This depended also on trying to maintain a relatively clean appearance as someone who was not living rough; they used public facilities whenever possible to ensure a minimal standard of hygiene, preferably at odd hours late in the evening when few others were around. On one occasion, while using the public urinals in Kattowitz railway station (always a risky undertaking for someone who was circumcised), they were shocked to find standing next to them the ethnic German, a man by the name of Theo Lalushna, who had first taken over their shop when it was initially expropriated, before it was subsequently taken over by a far less well-disposed Romanian. Fortunately, Lalushna was not merely surprised to see them alive and at large, but also willing to help rather than denounce them instantly. Lalushna's first piece of advice was to avoid the restaurant where Moishe had been in the habit of eating, revealing that—unknown to Moishe—the Gestapo headquarters were in the very same building; he then assisted them in obtaining false papers via his sister, whose husband was in the German Army and away fighting at the front. All the while, they had to combine strategies of sliding around under cover of darkness, sleeping rough, and yet remaining well-kempt and maintaining appearances so as not to betray their vagrant status; passing off, when using public transport or on well-populated streets, as legitimate Polish citizens going about their business; seeking always to be on the alert and yet trying not to look as though inwardly they were in constant fear and trembling that any false move or bad luck could instantly bring their lives to an end.

Similar experiences of close encounters, repeated near misses, periodic captures, arrests, and escapes, occasional sheer good luck and the incredible fortune of meeting a human being prepared to risk all to help save lives, are told in many other survivors' accounts. Shmuel Ron, for example, and some members of the resistance group of which he was part, were looked after, sometimes for just a few days and in Ron's case for months at a time, by a Polish woman in Kattowitz who made her primary living as a prostitute who offered her favours even to high-ranking Germans.[84] Many survivors recount individual instances when a Polish family—often just one member, such as the farmer's wife—was willing to let them sleep in a barn overnight, on condition they would be away by daybreak and not risk discovery by other members of the family, who it was said would inevitably denounce them to the German authorities. But longer-term practical assistance was quite exceptional, and in many cases rooted in previous close personal relationships; the vast majority of 'ethnic Germans' and Poles were inclined to be hostile, suspicious, unwilling to enter into the extraordinarily risky business of assisting Jews in their attempts to evade detection and survive. It has to be remembered that survivors' stories represent merely the tiniest fraction of most Jews' experiences: for the vast majority, even survival of the ghetto clearance of summer 1943 sooner or later ended in death.

In the late summer of 1943, my godmother Alexandra also finally left Będzin for the safety of an estate of aristocratic friends and relatives in East Prussia. Her situation had been becoming increasingly uncomfortable over the summer months and particularly during the final period of the ghetto clearance. Alexandra had initially been planning only a temporary summer break, staying with relatives again. But her plans did not initially work out. As she put it in a letter of 5 August 1943:

> In the garden there is a lot of work and little that is edible. Since Flojm has gone, no one has really had any time to do anything about it, so now there is a lot that needs catching up. And I had not reckoned on needing food from the garden in August, not until October... There is also nothing to buy—so one just doesn't know what one is supposed to have!

Moreover, conditions all around in Będzin at this time were increasingly unbearable, as Alexandra registered when making social visits to the always more 'Germanized' areas around Kattowitz and Tarnowitz: 'I met up with Elisabeth and Köttgen... Everyone is appalled that we are back here, since the conditions here are unimaginable for anyone at a distance!' But, much as Alexandra would have liked to move out permanently, this could only be effected 'by giving up the house here, which for political reasons is apparently not possible'.[85]

Considerations for the safety of the *Landrat*'s wife should the Russians arrive, given the changing fortunes of the war, were uppermost in Klausa's mind in making the arrangements for his family's departure to relatives in Döhrings, in East Prussia:

> Since at that time I could already clearly predict that the war was lost and would have an unhappy ending for Germany. I could predict that the Russians would invade eastern Germany. It was just a question of how far they would get, that was not clear. In any case, the wife of the *Landrat* of Bendsburg would not be able to flee in time. It would be easier to succeed in this as Frau Klausa from Döhrings.[86]

Just as Klausa himself was still deemed to be only temporarily away from the *Landrat*'s office on military service pending the 'final victory' (*Endsieg*), with a deputy appointed in his place for the meantime, so Alexandra's departure was not to be represented as a permanent move; giving up the villa entirely would have been deemed defeatist and politically unwise. Yet it is also clear, on Klausa's own account, that his family's final departure was not quite the political act of defiance that he had suggested when he erroneously claimed he had arranged for his wife and children to leave Będzin after witnessing the first major deportations a whole year earlier.

By the summer of 1943, when Alexandra and her growing young family finally left the 'villa of the Jew Schein', the population of Będzin had, on Klausa's own figures, been virtually halved from 54,000 to around 27,000. The Klausas' experiences had been a long way from their initial hopes and expectations when Klausa had first taken on the coveted post of *Landrat*. Now, as a result of German aggression and a war that was taking an 'unhappy' turning for Germany, it was Alexandra who would have to try to 'flee in time' for fear of possible retributions against the *Landrat*'s wife. From what we know of the rapes and murders committed by Russians when they did finally manage to turn the tides of war and enter onto German soil, and in the light of the success of Alexandra's eventual well-organized flight to the west, this was good planning, But it was not quite the story of implicit moral and political protest that Udo Klausa had sought to portray in other contexts.

12

Final Thresholds

'Auschwitz' has widely come to stand as shorthand for the mass murder of the European Jews, as well as Gypsies and other groups persecuted by the Nazis. Auschwitz was, as many people put it, the *anus mundi* or 'anus of the world', as one survivor, Wieslaw Kielar, even chose to entitle his memoirs.[1] Even Nazis who assisted in and were to a degree repelled by its gruesome goals and operations used this term at a relatively early date, as Johann Paul Kremer, a physician and member of the SS, noted in his diary entry of 5 September 1942:

> This afternoon was present at a special action in the women's camp ('Moslems')—the most horrible of all horrors. *Hschf.* Thilo, military surgeon, is right when he said today to me we were located here in '*anus mundi*'. In the evening at about 8 p.m. another special action with a draft from Holland. Men compete to take part in such actions as they get additional rations then—1/5 litre vodka, 5 cigarettes, 100 grammes of sausage and bread.[2]

A photograph exists of SS Oberscharführer Heinz Thilo on the infamous ramp at Birkenau, actively participating in the selections of those deemed unfit for work and headed straight for the gas chambers.[3] And, for all his strong reactions to witnessing the undressing and gassing of some 800 totally emaciated women—who had reached the stage of physical starvation and psychological collapse that occasioned, in camp parlance, the label of *Muselmänner* or 'Moslems'—Kremer was able to record the details of his own provisions with some satisfaction and precision. In his diary entry of the following day, he notes: 'Today an excellent Sunday dinner: tomato soup, one half of chicken with potatoes and red cabbage (20 grammes of fat), dessert and magnificent vanilla ice-cream.'[4] A moment of revulsion and possible empathy with at least the female victims of murder was clearly not enough to spoil his own appetite.

The extermination camp at Birkenau was responsible for the largest number of deaths in a single location by gassing. And the experiences of those who survived were among the worst imaginable, even unimaginable. The difficulties of representation are manifest; even survivors possessed of extraordinary gifts of creativity are hard put to find adequate modes of expression for their experiences and their suffering.[5] There is a reason why people wondered whether it would ever be possible, in Theodor Adorno's oft-quoted phrase, to 'write poetry after Auschwitz'. For historians, there is even a danger that too 'adequate' an 'explanation' could suggest a degree of awful logic or reason to the extermination; the enormity and unthinkable character of the crime almost demands that it should be left as ultimately inexplicable, beyond any historian's capacity to collate an adequate account of motives, circumstances, conditions, causes, however possible it is to provide a 'chronology', a full narrative of details arranged in date order.

Moreover, the connections with the massive slave labour system of the I. G. Farben Buna works at Dwory, and with some forty other sub-camps employing slave labour across a very wide geographical area, mean that 'Auschwitz' epitomized the Nazi policies not only of extermination by gassing but also of extermination through exploitation of slave labour. Its location at the heart of a major industrial centre, within the expanded borders of the Greater German Reich, raises further questions about the ways in which civilians interacted with the slave labourers passing through their midst, the ways in which the news spread, and the ways in which people 'chose not to see'.

In the most acute form, 'Auschwitz' raises questions relevant for all of that which very soon became known as the Jewish 'catastrophe', or *Shoah*. It is, rightly, held to epitomize the abyss to which Nazi policies led.

But at the same time, 'Auschwitz' can be used as evasion. When crystallization becomes reduction—when anything outside the gates of Auschwitz becomes 'not really' the 'Holocaust'—then a great deal of (generally self-) exculpation can take place on the part of those who were involved in upholding the system and making this possible. It can also, in a quite different direction, lead to a potential 'hierarchy of victims': on one such scale, for example, it is sometimes implicitly suggested that only those who bear the tattooed number on their arm 'really' know about suffering, and even then those who gained this number at an external labour camp do not 'really' know what 'Auschwitz itself' really means; those who survived in hiding or exile are not 'really' victims—and so on. These are iniquitous and inappropriate comparisons leading to the logical absurdity that only those who actually died in the gas chambers 'really' knew what 'Auschwitz', and hence the worst victimhood, was about. Primo Levi's insight that survivors cannot speak for the experiences of the dead has a ring of truth, but it is a truth that can be taken in entirely the wrong directions.

We have to be aware of what is implied by 'Auschwitz' from many angles, many perspectives: for the abyss that it was, and for the wider context; as a horrendously concentrated but by no means defining instance of the murderous racism of the Nazi regime—a racism that had been evident from the moment Hitler came to power in 1933, and even before, but that took off into what was euphemistically called the 'final solution' only as the war proceeded. A focus on 'Auschwitz' as the epitome of an always evil regime is entirely justified, but it is important to resist the temptation to narrow our focus to solely this particular concentration of brutality and death—for to do this can imply a downplaying of the suffering and terror of so many, and can assist in the exoneration of those who upheld the wider system that made Auschwitz possible.

Auschwitz and beyond

A highly concentrated nexus of brutality and death it certainly was, and the Jews of Będzin and surrounding areas soon experienced this in all the ways possible. While the vast majority were murdered immediately on arrival, eyewitness accounts of survivors still give us some inkling of their experiences.

Mordecai Lichtenstein deposited his testimony within a matter of days after the war had come to an end. He had been deported from Będzin, along with many members of his extended family, on 1 August 1943 during the final major ghetto clearance. Following a one-hour journey in the cattle trucks to Auschwitz, the transport arrived in the sidings near the main railway station (the extended tracks directly into Birkenau had not yet been constructed). Here, a limited 'selection' immediately took place:

> We were dragged out of the trucks and SS men, bellowing, and beating us with clubs and truncheons, drove us to a siding. Here the women were immediately segregated from the men, parcels had to be thrown on the ground, and the SS started to select the strong and healthy-looking from the feeble ones. Elderly persons, the feeble-looking ones, and children, were made to jump into 10 or 12

lorries, which were waiting. Anyone who would not jump quickly was beaten in the most brutal way, crying children and babies were seized by the SS and their heads bashed against the lorry, or sometimes taken by one foot, like poultry, the head hanging down, and killed by a blow with a club. The sight of these weeping children, with their tear-stained cheeks even more rosy in the summer sun, slaughtered or stunned on the spot, like ducks, broke my heart.[6]

Of the transport of some 3,000 people with whom Lichtenstein arrived, only some 450 were selected to remain alive for the time being. Those who arrived the following day were even less fortunate, as Lichtenstein recounted:

The whole group that was brought from Bendzin on the day following my arrival, was at once loaded on to the lorries and driven straight to the gas chambers... The SS raiding a dug-out in which Jewish members of the underground movement had gone into hiding, threw hand grenades into this strongly defended shelter, whereupon the Jews answered with shots. One or two SS men were supposed to have been killed. For that the chief of Gestapo in Kattowice, Dreier—the other Gestapo official dealing with Jewish affairs was Dr Mildner—ordered the wholesale extermination of this batch of prisoners.[7]

As another prisoner at Auschwitz recalls of those brought from Będzin and Sosnowiec, 'with these deportations, as was widely talked about at the time, it came to terrible scenes'.[8] Many transports coming to Auschwitz from areas further away across Europe went relatively unsuspectingly into the gas chambers, having been led to expect that following their 'showers' there would be fresh clothes and a meal. But this was not the case with those arriving from Będzin and Sosnowiec, who, living in such close proximity to the camp, had long known what awaited them.[9] And many of them, undeterred by the defeat of their attempted uprising in the ghetto, had come prepared for one last show of resistance. As one former prisoner recalled, writing up her experiences while they were still relatively fresh in her mind a year after the end of the war:

At about the same time the rest of the Jews from Bendsburg O/S [Upper Silesia] arrived at the camp. Up until then they had been privileged and had been assured that they were indispensable and that nothing would happen to them. There were dentists, apothecaries, lab technicians, a few business people, and the Jewish Community. As they came off the train, something happened that had never happened before. They opened fire on the SS with pistols they had brought with them. Unfortunately only one SS man was killed and my boss Quackernack got a bullet in the leg. They were immediately mowed down by machine guns.[10]

The transport from Będzin that did not even get as far as the gas chambers but, because of resistance, was shot on the spot, while still in the train and on the ramp, was unprecedented in the history of Auschwitz.

What life was like for those who were 'spared' the gas chambers and remained in Auschwitz as living skeletons can only be sensed through the accounts of some who managed to survive. In the well-known literary works of survivors such as the French writer Charlotte Delbo, the Viennese-born literary scholar Ruth Klüger, and the Italian chemist Primo Levi, and in the numerous and generally less well-known memoirs, paintings, and drawings of so many others, we gain some inkling of what it meant to inhabit a still sentient human body, often perilously close to death through thirst, starvation, exhaustion, managing to keep alive through unique individual combinations of age and prior physical condition, psychological determination, quick-wittedness, sheer and inexplicable good luck, and a degree of physical and psychological support from others.[11] There is by now an extensive literature exploring the different experiences of prisoners placed into different categories—the Jews were always treated worse than, for example, political prisoners—and those who were selected to work in different areas. Positions within the camp hierarchy could make all the difference between relative privilege, the chance of getting through another day, or week, or month, and immediate death. Even so, being at the constant mercy of the whims of tormentors meant that nothing was ever certain except suffering, illness and an ever-present sense of imminent mortality.

For some, the only 'way out' was to choose one's own moment of death—whether by running against the electric wires, or even when actually on the way to execution. Mala Zimetbaum, for example, who had managed to escape with Edek Galinski, got as far as the Slovakian border before being caught and returned to Auschwitz. Sentenced to public hanging, while in full view on her way to the scaffold she pulled out a razor blade she had managed to obtain and hide in her clothing, cut her wrists, and hit the accompanying SS man in the face with her bloody fist, before dying; this was seen as a sign of bravery and resistance for those who were there to watch.[12] Most of those not designated instantly for the gas chambers, however, eked out their days in a constant battle to survive for longer than the average three-month life expectancy of Auschwitz prisoners who were slave labourers.

We can gain some sense of the experiences of the few Będzin survivors through their written accounts, testimonies, and oral history interviews. Here, the experience of just one must stand for many. Josef Baumgarten had, at the age of about 15, been put to work in a factory in Będzin. He was unaware of what happened to his parents, who at some point were simply taken away to a labour camp. He and his siblings had tried as best they could to survive in the ghetto, effectively orphaned like so many other youngsters; at some point during this period his sister was taken to Birkenau; then, he thinks in October 1942, he himself and his remaining two brothers were taken. These young people were not part of one of the major selections but were one of the many smaller interim 'raids': they were simply taken from their house at night, walked to the railway station, put into one of the box cars and held there overnight before the transport left the following day.

In Baumgarten's recollection, it then took 'ages' to get to Auschwitz; on arrival, the 'smell was unbelievable ... but you try to tell these people when they come in ... and they wouldn't want to give [their child] up'.[13] Baumgarten's little brother was about 6 years old: as he put it, the Nazis just took him and put him on a truck 'and that was the last time I saw my little brother'. His older sister who was also in the camp after a while became ill, and she was also taken to the crematorium. His other brother gained the dubious short-term status of a member of a *Sonderkommando*: 'his job was to burn people', and this brother told Baumgarten exactly what they were doing. Baumgarten's own first job at Auschwitz was to 'help sort people' on arrival:

> as a transport came in from Europe, we tried to open up the box cars, let these people out, and ... sometimes I went over to some Jewish woman, give me your baby, give me your son, otherwise you're going to go to the crematorium, and they wouldn't believe it, because which mother wants to give up her own child ... there was a band playing ... and further away you saw a sky full of flames and they were burning and nobody would believe, so they just didn't want to give up their children ...

Later Baumgarten was sent in a group of some fifteen boys as a 'special detail' to the 'hospital' in Auschwitz: it was 'research, we didn't know what type of research they gonna do ... they shaved us and told us we were going to have surgery ... Polack told us gonna be okay, they going to take out one testicle ...'. There was no pain relief, they just put 'some kind of cream on it'. The surgery was, he thought, carried out by Dr Mengele, but he 'didn't say anything at all to me'. In fact, we know from contemporary records that, on 15 October 1943, Horst Schumann conducted a sterilization procedure by intense radiation, following which Baumgarten's left testicle was removed by Wladislaw Dering, assisted by Sobieszczański.[14] Dering was a Polish 'prisoner doctor', an 'ethnic German' who identified increasingly with the Auschwitz staff rather than prisoners, and was eventually released for his cooperation in Auschwitz procedures.[15] The addition of an inaccurate detail in Baumgarten's account—inserting Mengele's name—reflects the fact that as a young prisoner at the time he had no idea who was dealing with him, and added as a possibility the name of the most notorious Nazi doctor. This is quite typical of the vicissitudes of oral history interviews carried out after a considerable time lapse, with the vague contours of memory augmented by subsequently acquired details; but the emotions conveyed are clearly authentic and the personal consequences of the procedure beyond doubt. Baumgarten was 'very frightened, nothing I could do, just do what they told me to do... with the surgery... I could see everything...'. After surgery the area started to burn; he was given a couple of stitches and sent back to barracks. He could not walk the following day, the burning sensation worsened. Trying to survive the effects of this brutal surgery, Baumgarten thought he would soon end up in the crematorium, but after a week he was taken back to camp. The group of boys talked to each other about what had been done to them: while he had had one testicle cut off, other boys had lost both, and yet others had all sorts of variations on these operations. This interview was the first time that he had ever publicly mentioned this operation. He had always kept it secret, 'because I always kept it secret to myself, maybe I'm ashamed, I don't know why I didn't tell anybody... I just kept it to myself, and this is the first time I mentioned it... to see what I went through'. When asked by the interviewer, 'do you still feel ashamed of it now?' Baumgarten responded: 'not really'.

Baumgarten's brother, who had been in the *Sonderkommando*, once took the punishment of twenty-five lashes on his behalf when he had been caught stealing potatoes. For stealing these potatoes, Baumgarten had been made to stand in the freezing cold between the two electric fences for two hours with a potato in his mouth. He had thought he would die of freezing, but no longer cared whether he lived or died since he felt so bad; having not died of cold and exposure during the two hours, he was then sent back to camp for the twenty-five lashes; but his brother took this additional punishment in his place. Baumgarten recalls that 'one night I went in to him' and heard that he was planning a group of five to escape. His brother asked him what he should do, and Baumgarten responded that his brother should do what he wanted: 'don't worry about me, maybe you will survive the war if you escape.' But the next day all five escapees were brought back, and shot dead in front of camp; Baumgarten had to watch his oldest brother, aged 21, being shot dead: 'and I just cried and cried and cried'; this was 'the last time I saw him . . .'.[16]

Baumgarten summarized the two years or more that he spent in Auschwitz–Birkenau as follows: 'You just tried to survive day in and day out and just think one of these days the war will be over.' He did not talk much to others; some prisoners 'talked about old times, and what's going to happen to us, and where's my parents, where's my sister'. The Russian prisoners 'had some outside connections, got treated a bit better than we did, POWs they treated a little bit better'. As far as Jews were concerned, 'you had to steal, otherwise you wouldn't survive'. After the war he weighed 90 lbs, which he considered quite an achievement under the circumstances: 'with me it wasn't so bad because of the type of job what I had, because the people coming in from Europe, they left all kinds of groceries . . . so we got along pretty good when a transport came in . . .'. His only real contacts were with people from his home town of Będzin. But in essence, as he repeatedly emphasized, he 'just tried to survive'; he was scared, and tried as best he could to stay away from guards and SS. He had lost both his brothers and his sister, and also had no news from outside. He alone was left alive in Auschwitz; he knew another sister had been taken to a labour camp somewhere, but all he knew about with any certainty were those who were already gone, already dead; he had heard somehow that his parents had died, so from his family there was only one remaining sister about whose fate he knew nothing. At this point, all he could do was try to stay alive: 'Well the main thing was the food, you didn't think about anything, just tried to get something in your stomach, this was your main concern, to survive.'

Once again highly unusual in their experiences, the Szpringer family, who had survived the ghetto clearance in hiding, remarkably survived this period too in a variety of ways. Between them, the Szpringer family went through virtually every variant of survival apart from being directly in an extermination camp such as Auschwitz itself.[17] Dora, in a slave labour camp, was set to work on munitions production; her first surprise, on arrival, was the fact that women here seemed to come in three garish colours. She too very soon changed colour, turning green on working with the green powder that she was made to process; this was slightly less toxic than the powder that turned other women bright red. Her own survival she put down to periodic changes of workplace, the green powder alternating with less dangerous and disagreeable work, and occasionally acquiring extra rations, including, remarkably, one day being given a piece of bread by a German woman from outside the camp who clearly felt agonized by the condition of the inmates. Dora was also given a sense of hope, essential in the struggle to keep going, when one of her brothers managed to smuggle a message in to her that other members of the family were still alive; previously demoralized and close to despair, she then felt determined to make it through somehow to the end of the war.

Five other members of the Szpringer family, on false papers, eventually made it to the region of Magdeburg in Germany, where they passed the remainder of the war years pretending to be Poles, working as forced labourers on farms. While some of them became adept at talking and acting as though they were Polish Catholics, it was difficult at times. In church, they could follow the example of others in terms of kneeling, standing, and sitting at the right times, as well as mumbling their way through prayers, and making the sign of the cross. Laya nevertheless had considerable difficulty understanding what she was meant to be doing in the privacy of the confessional, risking arousing potentially fatal suspicions on the part of the priest; and her father, on first crossing the threshold of a Catholic church, reportedly looked as though he thought the heavens would open and not the Nazis but God would strike him dead in wrath. It was difficult even passing off as a Pole as far as uncouth behaviour was concerned: one of the sons was accused of speaking in too educated a manner, and not drinking and swearing as a Polish lad was expected to do. The mother's features were deemed to be too Jewish in appearance to be able to evade recognition, and she spent the closing months of the war posing as ill, remaining in bed all day and going outside only at night. Unfortunately, the experiences of five years of privation and hiding took their toll, and she lived for only a few months after the end of the war—just long enough to find out that the whole family had indeed survived, as brother Issa returned from Russia and Dora was released from the labour camp in Poland where she had barely managed to cling on to life. But the experiences of the Szpringer family were highly exceptional.

A few highly courageous individuals not only sought their own self-preservation, but continued trying to rescue as many as they could. Shmuel Ron and others worked in groups trying to smuggle people out to Palestine or elsewhere.[18] Another person very active in rescue attempts was Leon Blat.[19] He arranged for Jewish girls who happened to be blonde and could pass as 'Aryan' to try to spread news of what was happening. Having himself managed to escape the ghetto clearance in August 1943, he travelled as far as Vienna and Hungary, preparing and facilitating escape routes for others and identifying reliable helpers, but, following a series of arrests and narrow escapes, eventually returned to Sosnowiec. At the end of his strength, and in a state of complete resignation, he was unexpectedly helped by a Pole: 'A Pole by the name of Dabrowski, whom I knew from earlier, met me while I was in this frightful state, took me to live in his apartment, fed me back to health and gave me courage again.'[20] Following more travels (including Budapest again) and organization of further escape routes for others, he was finally caught and sent to Auschwitz, where again he sought unsuccessfully to organize resistance and escape. Finally, he escaped from a death march and survived.

Some Jews from the Będzin area managed against all the odds to survive within the town itself, never being taken to Auschwitz or a labour camp. This was more likely in the case of female children, such as Erin Einhorn's mother, or Mira Binford, both hidden by Polish families when still very young.[21] It was clearly far easier to pass off a girl than a boy as non-Jewish. Binford's documentary film tells the story of herself and two other child survivors—the three of them making up around a quarter of the total of perhaps a dozen children who survived the destruction of the Będzin Jewish community.

One other child survivor was Mindzia Schickman, who, as we have seen, was hidden by their faithful family friend, a young Polish woman by the name of Cecilia Krzeminska.[22] As with others, Mindzia's terror, long-lasting in its effects, should not be played down in any later 'hierarchy of victims'. She was, as a child hidden in an attic, terrified and well aware of the risk she was posing to her beloved Cecilia. Every day there were 'pogroms and people running, and police and dogs', and her own and Cecilia's lives were constantly in the balance: 'they warned that anybody who will keep a Jew, the whole family will be hanged, nobody had the courage to do anything'. She was constantly hoping and waiting for her brother Idek to arrive; but he never came. She sometimes stood on a table to look out of the top window of the attic down at the street: 'Many times I took the table to the top window, a tiny little opening, and I wanted to look down, and I saw young children dressed up, laughing, walking, and I was just hoping one day one day I would be able to go out...'. Cecilia kept hoping the family would all come back, telling Mindzia that they must survive, that Idek and her parents would return: 'we have to have the courage, we have to have the strength.' But the situation was far from safe: 'People knew on the street . . . some people were guessing, thinking, that maybe she hides me, and two women, neighbours, they always knock on the door in the evening, so she put me under the bed or she put me in her closet.'

Even despite her own lack of adequate food supplies, Cecilia was determined to look after Mindzia as best she could: 'She would give me the potato and [she would only] eat up the skin from the potato, her life was me.' Despite all this care and love, from an ordinary Polish woman risking her life out of affection and friendship, Mindzia was continually terrified: 'But at night the pogroms they were so frightening, they were so scary . . . it was just just unbelievable. I wanted to live, I didn't want to, when I saw what they are doing to small children, we had to watch people getting punished for things they didn't even do it.' She had seen enough acts of terror even before she had gone into hiding: 'We were not allowed to close our eyes, we had to stay there and watch the people being hanged.' But the sights of continuing terror were only too evident from her attic window, from a building on the main street that led directly to the square in front of the railway station. Mindzia could clearly see people being 'evacuated', 'it was like at the station, when we looked down . . . it was a terrible situation, I climbed up on a table and chair and there were wagons full of people, it was very bad . . . Every night there were SS because people ran away.'

Mindzia was not safe even in Cecilia's apartment. In the communal part of the attic there were, however, large barrels of sour pickles and sauerkraut, relating to the business of another resident of the building, as well as laundry hung up to dry. One night, when a member of the SS came through the building searching, Cecilia hid Mindzia in a barrel that she had emptied of pickles, putting laundry over the top and ensuring there was a hole through which she could breathe. The SS man came in and searched; but she was lucky, because, after looking into two barrels, he 'said oh, that smells good, and he would like very much to know if that's it'. There then followed a conversation in which Cecilia assured him she would never hide a Jew and the SS man reminded her that such an offence carried the death penalty.

Fearing further and more thorough searches, Cecilia said she must hide her elsewhere. She took Mindzia by train at night, covered with a large blanket, to a farm in the country and told the family a story about having no man in the house and not enough food and being unable to feed her child. Mindzia was initially taken on as a help to the farmer's family: working in the field, and looking after their young baby. But they soon became suspicious when she clearly did not know the prayers on attending church with them. Moreover, the farmer began to abuse her physically, drunkenly coming to assault her when she was asleep in the barn, beating her and threatening her, and treating her 'like a Jew has no right to live'. One morning the farmer's wife showed her where the train was and told her she would not survive any longer with them, 'because if he is going to find out that I'm not gentile he's going to kill me with his own bare hands'. She escaped back to Będzin, terrified, and made her way back to Cecilia's attic and the relative safety of the barrel of pickles.

Cecilia's next attempt at finding a safer place was in Czeladź, with a man who knew her father. He was very much afraid, but agreed to hide her in his attic for a few days so long as his wife did not find out. At this point Mindzia became very ill with typhus; he allowed her to stay a few more days, mostly sleeping or crying: 'I didn't have no strength, I was too weak to worry about my life or anything, it didn't matter . . . I guess I wasn't strong enough to think, I had high temperature, I was sick . . .'. One day Cecilia came 'and she said the area had quietened down, she wants me home'. By now it was late 1944, there were bombing raids as the war came ever closer to Germany. People were ordered to take shelter in the basement, including Cecilia, but of course she could not take Mindzia with her: 'So I was under the bed, shaking and crying . . . and I was just scared, and I was very happy when it was over and she came upstairs, and this went on and on.'

Mindzia trusted Cecilia and 'knew that I can depend on her'. But 'it wasn't easy to go through all the torture . . . I was so scared, I was so frightened'. For all the love and affection Cecilia provided, 'I was a frightened little girl'. And looking out of the window at the outside world, she could see not only the faces of those for whom life seemed to be going on as normal, children playing in the streets, but also what was happening to virtually her entire community: 'From the attic you could see the trains, people crying, and running and bullets, and it was a terrible terrible way of survival. And living with such anxiety and fear, it was almost impossible to go through . . .'.

These are just a few of the experiences of that minority who survived and were later able to recount what they had been through. There were different forms of terror, not all directly related to the torture and deaths in Auschwitz, but all unleashed by the Nazis' determination to 'cleanse' Będzin, and Europe, of Jews.

The Auschwitz uprising

Resistance could be in small acts—keeping a child alive, hiding her in a barrel of pickles; giving an unknown slave labourer a piece of bread—and in large collective actions, which have, as the saying goes, 'gone down in history'. One such, in which Będzin Jews played a significant role, was the blowing-up of a crematorium in Auschwitz–Birkenau.

By the summer of 1944, and despite the difficulties of accessing accurate news about what was going on in the outside world, inmates of Auschwitz were increasingly aware that the end of the war was in sight. Plans were developed to organize an inner-camp resistance, which should be coordinated with an external attack on the camp to be mounted by partisans. The idea was to mount this resistance when external help was close at hand, and the SS were—as the prisoners predicted—about to try to destroy all the inmates; the idea was to fight back, kill as many SS guards as they could, cut the wires of the women's camp and surrounding locations, and assist as many as possible to escape. Initially the plan was that this uprising should take place in the early summer of 1944, but the opportunity passed.[23]

The plans were discussed with the greatest of secrecy among resistance circles within the camp. Prisoners involved in these plans conferred with only one or two others, one of whom in turn acted as a go-between with other groups; no one, if tortured, could be at risk of betraying many people, genuinely not knowing further names. The groups included both Polish political prisoners, and Jews. In the men's camp, key conspirators included Israel Gutman and Jehuda Laufer, who had contacts with the women in the Union Munitions Works.

Among the latter were Sala Garncarz's friend and former protector, Ala Gertner from Sosnowiec, and fellow-prisoners, Regina Sapirstein and Roza Robota from Będzin. Roza Robota had personal links to members of the *Sonderkommando* charged with pulling out the dead bodies from the gas chambers and loading them into the furnaces of the crematorium. Ala Gertner had, on arrival in Auschwitz in August 1943, first worked in the area known as 'Canada' (standing for a land of plenty), where the clothing and possessions of those designated for the gas chambers were sorted; in the autumn of 1943 she was transferred to work in the Union Munitions Works.[24] Here, she seems to have been engaged in lively discussions with members of resistance groups, including still fiercely active Zionists as well as political prisoners. Among those women also involved were two sisters who had originally come from Warsaw, Anna (Hanka) and Esther (Estusia) Wajcblum, who were aware of the resistance activities that had led to the Warsaw Uprising.[25] Ala Gertner had the bunk next to Anna's, and talked her through the plans for revolt. It did not take long to convince her: as Anna, who had been active in the Hashomer Hatzair movement in Warsaw, later commented:

> I survived the Warsaw ghetto, and I felt guilty. Nobody in Auschwitz, unless they came from the Warsaw ghetto, knew about what happened there. We, too, decided that we were not going to let ourselves be taken without a struggle.[26]

The two Wajcblum sisters worked in different rooms in the Union Munitions Works, processing gunpowder and preparing ammunition for the Germans. Regina Sapirstein was in charge of the *Pulverraum*, or gunpowder room. There were nine women working in the *Pulverraum* in total; a few of them were able, over the course of many months, to steal and secrete tiny quantities of the gunpowder. One of these women, Rose Meth, later recounted how she started stealing gunpowder in March 1944, by mixing in a little cast-off reject powder (*Abfall*) with good powder to fill in some of the little holes in the parts they were making (a part that would ignite the bomb, called *Verzögerung*), and then saving the same quantities of good power.[27] Quantities were overseen by their guard and all had to be measured very carefully before it was checked; some of the completed parts were randomly tested to ensure there was no sabotage, so it was difficult to be certain that this mixing of discarded and new powder would go unnoticed. Regina Sapirstein had, however, figured out the rough pattern to the 'random' checks made by the German supervisor, one Meister von Ende, and then placed the defective parts carefully on the tray in parts that she thought were unlikely to be checked. The good gunpowder, thus saved, was hidden in scraps of material. Estusia took the powder from Rose Meth, stored it under the false bottom of a tin used to collect waste, and then gave it to someone else; Rose did not herself know the names of others involved at that time.

The next link in the smuggling was in fact Estusia's sister, Anna Wajcblum: she devised a self-imposed task—on which she was never challenged—of making a regular circuit of factory offices carrying two metal boxes, in one of which she genuinely collected rubbish from the gunpowder room for disposal, and in the other of which she collected the little bundles of gunpowder from Estusia, which she took back to her workplace in a nearby office. From there, secreted in small scraps of material tied up as little bags (known as 'Beuttel' or 'Boitl') and stuffed into their underwear, Anna Wajcblum, Ala Gertner, and others were then able to smuggle the bags of gunpowder from their daily shifts in the Union Munitions factory back to their barracks in Auschwitz. If the women were stopped and searched on the long trek back to their quarters after leaving work—as happened at random but frequent intervals—these little bundles could easily be dropped, the black gunpowder ground into the ash of the pathway, the remaining rags simply looking like innocuous rubbish.

In this way, Anna and others smuggled out quantities of explosives, which Ala and Roza then managed to get across from the women's camp to the members of the *Sonderkommando* involved in preparing the revolt. The latter used discarded shoe polish tins, and twisted material to make wicks, thus constructing quite serviceable handmade grenades.

For all the care with which the revolt had been planned over the preceding months, it did not in the event go as the prisoners had hoped. On the morning of 7 October 1944, members of one *Sonderkommando* were informed that they were about to be 'deported'—a euphemism for murder, since this was the inevitable fate of these groups after they had performed their duties for three or four months. A semi-spontaneous revolt now broke out: prisoners decided that, if they had to die, they would go down fighting. A revolt among those working in Crematorium III (IV) broke out, uncoordinated with resistance groups in other *Sonderkommandos* and crematoria.[28] At least three and perhaps as many as four SS officers were killed, including Corporals Rudolf Erler, Willi Preeze, and Jozef Purke; perhaps a dozen others were seriously injured, and two people were apparently tipped alive into the ovens.[29] In the melée, well over 200 prisoners managed to escape through the back fence; later, they were all rounded up, returned to Birkenau and executed. About 250 prisoners involved in the uprising were killed straightaway; a further 200 inmates who had not escaped were subsequently killed when guards found that 12 escaped prisoners were still missing; these 12 were later also found and killed. During the course of this revolt grenades were thrown, and Crematorium III (IV) was blown up: it never came back into action, its ruins serving as a symbol of the courage of those who sought to exert even a small degree of agency over the manner of their own inevitable deaths.

Arrests and interrogations of others suspected of involvement in the uprising followed during the succeeding weeks. Anna Wajcblum's sister,

Estusia, was among those kept in confinement and eventually condemned to death, as were Ala, Roza, and Regina. For weeks the women were tortured, in the hope that more names of the resistance would emerge; Rose Meth recalled that, when they were first released, 'their bodies looked like raw liver'.[30] Despite being reduced to near corpses, they maintained silence. It was only through use of a fellow-prisoner turned spy who wooed her affections and won her confidence that rather more was eventually gained from Ala. Even so, the names of the male prisoners with whom they had conspired were never revealed by these women, nor the names of other women in the gunpowder smuggling chain; many of these co-conspirators were in fear for weeks that they would soon share the fate of those arrested, but they were never betrayed.[31] As Mala Weinstein, another woman involved in the smuggling, later put it: 'I owe my life to their courage.'[32] And, despite finding tell-tale traces of the distinctive gunpowder in the ruins of the crematorium, no wider network was ever discovered and no further prisoners could be implicated in the plot and the eventual death sentence.

While in confinement awaiting execution, Estusia Wajcblum wrote to her sister from her basement cell—a letter that her sister Anna clung onto for as long as she could, and in words that she memorized by heart. Anna in turn wrote these words down as soon as she could after liberation, while recuperating at a camp in the Ardennes, Belgium, in July 1945. She recalled:

I remember your last letter as if it were today:

I hear the footsteps of the prisoners banging on the ground above my head, the murmur of people returning after a long day of work to the Block *to rest. Through the bars of my window, the stingy grey ray of light tries to break in, the ray of sunset broken by shadows of many pairs of passing feet.*

The familiar sounds of the camp—the screams of the Kapos, *the screams for* czaj, *for soup, for bread, all those hated sounds now seem so precious to me and so soon to be lost. Those outside of my window still have hope, but I have nothing; everything is lost for me. Not for me the glad tidings of forthcoming salvation, not for me the* czaj, *the* Appel, *everything is lost and I so want to live.*[33]

Last words were also smuggled out from Roza Robota. Israel Gutman managed to find a *kapo* who arranged, illegally, for Roza's old friend Noach to visit her one night when the *kapo* had made the SS guard drunk. Roza was reportedly for the most part unconscious, but Noach finally managed to rouse her sufficiently to talk to him and even write a note for the others:

Noach brought us a note from Roza—a last farewell. She wrote to us about how hard it was to take leave from life; but we had nothing to fear, she would not betray us. She had only one request of us: in case any of us did one day manage to reach freedom after all, they should take revenge. The note was signed with the Hashomer Hatziar greeting: *Chasak we'emaz* (be strong and brave).[34]

The four women were executed by hanging on 5 or 6 January 1945.[35] Members of both the night shift and the day shift were forced to watch the hangings of these four women; two in the morning, two in the evening, as the shifts were on their respective returns from work. These were the last such hangings to take place in Auschwitz; the death marches began a little over ten days later.

The hangings were visually captured in a striking drawing by Ella Shiber. Born in 1927 in Berlin, Shiber had a Polish-born mother and a German father who, like so many Jewish Germans of his generation, had fought in the First World War and loved his native Germany. Shiber and her family were expelled from Germany in 1938 because of her Polish mother, and went to Będzin, her mother's native town.[36] They had survived the ghetto clearance by hiding in August 1943, but were captured later and deported to Auschwitz. The hangings made a profound impression on Shiber, at that time still a teenager, only 17 years old:

Straight and proud they walked through our ranks with their eyes fixed on the gallows. I have never seen such young people march to their death with such calm and composure. Just a few days earlier Ala showed us her right hand which had a missing finger. 'You see, Elly, from this hand they tore my baby Rochele away from me, and for screaming so much they cut off a finger. I fought for my child but they were stronger.' She described other horrors to me—babies cut up or their backs broken and thrown into garbage cans, all in front of their crazed mothers' eyes... She swore to fight these terrible criminals to her dying day. And now we stand and watch Ala Gertner and her comrades walk towards the gallows, soon to join little Rochele. Her executioners were *Hauptsturmfüher* Hössler, Margot Drechsler, Hasse, and others.[37]

The deaths of these women affected many others too. One of their co-workers, Ilse Michel (née Berlowitz), who was not herself involved in the plot, put it as follows: 'Words are too empty to describe the heroic act of those who were involved. While we clung to life, hoping for liberation, those men and women risked their lives for the future of others.'[38] Rose Rechnic, at the time in Bergen–Belsen, heard only after liberation about the death of her aunt, Regina Safirstein, and was shattered to find that she was now definitely the last and sole member of her family to be left alive, now almost wishing she too was dead; but later she realized quite how proud she could be of her aunt's participation in this massive act of resistance.[39]

The death of her sister Estusia affected Anna Wajcblum, still in Auschwitz in early January 1945, very badly: 'The day after Estusia's execution . . . I suddenly realized that the world would go on without her, that her death wouldn't make any difference to anybody. I lost my mind; I became a living corpse; I did not care if I lived or died.'[40] But the end of Auschwitz was then only a matter of days; and, with the support of another prisoner, Anna Wajcblum somehow dragged herself as a living corpse through the death march and eventual liberation.

Ultimate borders

In a sense, for Klausa too 'Auschwitz' appeared as the 'final threshold', the ultimate crossing of the moral boundaries, with the infamous archway entrance of Birkenau marking the gates to the real kingdom of evil.

Klausa claimed in his memoirs that he had heard about Auschwitz, or perhaps about what was 'really going on' in Auschwitz, only relatively late in the war, when by chance he met a former school comrade on a train. The old schoolfriend was wearing SS uniform, allegedly shocking Klausa (or so he represents it in his memoirs). On being asked by Klausa what his job entailed, the friend reportedly whispered back that Klausa should not ask; it was 'frightful'. Klausa uses this story to demonstrate, once again, his own innocence and supposed ignorance of the worst depths of the Nazi regime. Such 'train stories' are a relatively typical way of conceding that one had in fact known 'something' rather than 'nothing', but only indirectly, at second hand, registering with a degree of belated shock and clear self-distancing from having borne any responsibility.

Even if we try to take Klausa's version of this story at face value (however implausible this may seem), his mode of expression is illuminating. As Klausa put it of his former schoolfriend: 'I am sure he did nothing wrong. I assume he had to stand in a watchtower and shoot if a prisoner escaped. He quite certainly had nothing to do with the actual task of execution in Auschwitz.'[41] It is difficult to imagine what, in Klausa's understanding, the 'actual task of execution' then really consisted in, if shooting at anyone trying to escape this place of mass murder, this 'anus of the world', was not considered to be doing something 'wrong'. And who, if participation in evil really were restricted purely to those assisting in the functioning of the gas chambers and crematoria, would then be held 'actually' responsible? Perhaps only the members of the *Sonderkommandos* who did the dirty work of physically assisting the condemned into the 'shower blocks' and then subsequently pulling out the bodies and putting them into the furnaces—but not the SS guards on the watchtowers whose task it was to imprison also these, who would in turn soon become victims of the same process?

In any event, it is remarkable that some forty years after the war, in retirement in the affluent western Federal Republic of Germany, Klausa could still be resorting to the essentially Nazi notion that it was in some way intrinsically legitimate to shoot someone trying to escape: echoing the old phrase, 'shot while trying to escape' (*auf der Flucht erschossen*), used so many times when innocent people were killed as they sought to escape Nazi brutality, or killed when they had been found after escape and brought back to Auschwitz.

Klausa's qualms and doubts had arguably already begun in the course of 1942, when he had himself realized what 'Auschwitz' meant, and not, as he claimed in his memoirs, some two years later in a supposed chance encounter on a train in July 1944. As he put it in one of his defence statements, made on 16 December 1975: although he allegedly did not at that time know where the transports were being taken, nor was he then aware of what he called 'this function' of Auschwitz, nevertheless 'it was clear to me that a crime was in train here. And I wanted to have nothing to do with this crime.'[42]

Wherever Klausa actually drew the line of where 'evil' really began, of significance here is the fact that he seems to have baulked at the final stage of the persecution of the Jews: their extermination by gassing, if not by shooting 'while trying to escape' (let alone as a result of enforced impoverishment and ghettoization). This is very likely a quite typical syndrome; and it is for this reason that an excessive concentration on the ultimate terror of 'Auschwitz'—while entirely justified in itself—can also inadvertently aid in the post-war camouflage of those who had actually facilitated the Nazi system of racist persecution all the way up to, but not including, this 'final threshold'.

The story has a further odd twist; Klausa shores up his assertions about his former schoolfriend's alleged innocence by adding: 'Besides, I heard after the war that he had after all succeeded in getting away from Auschwitz and getting to the front.' Moreover, 'he survived and was probably also not pestered' about his role before 1945.[43] There are striking echoes here of Klausa's own story: that this friend 'succeeded' in getting away from the ultimate place of evil and going instead to the front; and that he survived and was never accused or prosecuted after the war.

This story as a whole functions, then, as what literary scholars call a *mise-en-abîme*, a text within a text, a miniature story mirroring the story as a whole: nearby, in some supposedly legitimate way assisting but not actually a culpable participant in a site of evil; escaping from the site of evil to the military front, represented as entirely honourable; never being prosecuted or found guilty after the war—all, in a concentrated form, suggesting a pattern or composite package intended to convince others of one's innocence.

The cynical view would say that this partial admission of knowledge combined with a simultaneous self-distancing, this determination to profess a degree of fractured ignorance and yet proven innocence, was a post-war self-representation with which Klausa—and innumerable other former Nazis—could comfortably live. Not being brought to account by the German courts, which were notoriously tardy and lenient in their investigation and prosecution of those involved in the machinery of the Nazi state, was held to be definitive proof of innocence. Of course, in the strictly legal sense, all are innocent until proven guilty; but that of course depends on individuals facing a fair trial, rather than evading justice and misrepresenting their past.

Klausa was far from alone in this pattern of post-war self-representation. Many of Klausa's colleagues in the Będzin and Sosnowiec area professed that they, too, had nothing to do with and had known little or nothing of what was 'really' going on in the area: the Ludwigsburg files are full of similar kinds of testimony from members of the civilian administration and individuals involved in economic exploitation of Jewish labour. People protested that they had never seen, heard, or in any sense participated in anything untoward going on around them. None of the three who had, whatever the differences in their respective roles, worked so closely together to agree and implement policies of ghettoization—Sosonowiec Police Chief von Woedtke, Sosnowiec City Mayor Schönwälder, and Będzin Landrat Klausa—seemed after the war to want to accept that they bore any responsibility for the ghettoization of the Jews or even knew anything much about the bloody ending of the ghettos they had created.

The former City Mayor of Sosnowiec from 7 January 1940 to 26 January 1945, Franz-Josef Schönwälder, made a statement to the Ludwigsburg investigation on 11 June 1960, at the age of 63, at which time he was a practising architect in Wesel. He alleged he had been on holiday in the summer of 1942, when on his account the one and only action against Jews in his area might have taken place; and he claimed that he had therefore known nothing about and had nothing to do with any maltreatment of Jews in his area:

> Up until summer 1942 no deportations of Jews took place. In the summer of 1942 I went on holiday. After my return I heard that in the meantime in the space of three days all the Jews apart from a work troop of around 1,200 men and women had been deported, and as far as I knew taken to Theresienstadt and Auschwitz. The reason given for deportation was that if the Jews were collected together in a larger camp, they could more easily be taken to work. What happened to them I don't know.[44]

Conveniently forgetting his own role in the ghettoization of the Jews, and indeed also the ghetto clearance of the following summer, 1943, Schönwälder went on to assert:

> I knew nothing of any maltreatment of Jews in Sosnowitz. The Jews were completely excluded from our communal administration. They were under their own Jewish administration, which in turn received its direction from the office for deploying Jewish labour under the leadership of the SS Oberführer Schmelt.[45]

Thus any miseries of life in the ghetto were represented as, essentially, the problems of the Jews' own ghetto administration, and of the SS.

A similar pattern is evident in the statements made by the former Sosnowiec police chief, Alexander von Woedtke. In his testimony of 8 March 1960, when he was living in retirement in Göttingen, von Woedtke tries to shift some of the responsibility onto Schönwälder, while at the same time partially exonerating him:

> I would like to mention that Herr Schönwälder as the City Mayor of Sosnowitz had to carry the major burden of this moving of Jews. This action went without a hitch; it did not come to any excesses... I... know that he [Schönwälder] was in fact a National Socialist, but was not a persecutor of Jews. Since Herr Schönwälder took his duties seriously, he was in part responsible for Jews.[46]

Von Woedtke also lays the blame for Jewish living conditions squarely on the Jews themselves, omitting any mention of the ways in which German administration was actually responsible for their appalling situation: 'I would like to mention that the Jews in Sosnowitz had their own administration and their own militia.'[47] Von Woedtke does concede the participation of police forces under his command in what he suggests was a purely 'administrative' role in 'clearing' the ghetto in the short time available, which occasioned some 'difficulties': 'The clearance of the ghetto had to take place in such a short time that I had difficulties with my police tasks of keeping order.'[48] But he suggests that it was not his police forces, but rather those of the State Police headquarters in Kattowitz, who were actually responsible for any 'political' aspects of this action:

> I would like to emphasize that my office had only to fulfil police duties with respect to order and administration, in contrast to the political tasks of the State Police headquarters, which was subordinate to the Reich Security Main Office.[49]

Curiously, however, even members of the State Police headquarters in Kattowitz professed to have 'known nothing about it', being away in other locations 'for months' (as Walter Baucke claimed), or claiming that (in the words of Franz Gawlik): 'I cannot say anything about the resettlement of the Jews, because I had nothing to do with it . . . Besides, there were no Jews any more in Kattowitz, but only in Sosnowitz still, where there was a big ghetto.'[50]

Others involved in various lower-level capacities in the area had similar gaps in memory and made similar attempts to shift responsibility onto others. Rudolf Braune, the former Nazi businessman who had taken over Jewish concerns that had been expropriated, and who had participated both in selections and in the ghetto clearance, was aged 52 and living as a successful businessman in Hamburg in 1961. Over the course of the summer and autumn of 1961 he gave intermittent statements, repeatedly breaking off or postponing meetings with the legal authorities; he too now claimed he had known nothing and witnessed little, even though he had allegedly tried to protect 'his' Jews from deportation.[51] Johannes Karl Hähnel, a former postal services worker (*Postbeamter*) and now a 'refugee from Upper Silesia' (in post-war West German representations, then, one of the many 'German victims') living in the southern Bavarian resort of Lenggries in the foothills of the Alps, testified in 1960 that he knew that around 6,000 Jews from Olkusz (Ilkenau) were deported to Auschwitz. But, according to his testimony, this had taken place at a time when he himself happened to be absent on unspecified other duties elsewhere. He also claimed that on his return he did not actually register the fact that the Jews were no longer there, because even before their deportation they had not been allowed out of their houses and ghetto area anyway, so their absence made little impact on him.[52] Theodor Clausen, a former senior municipal inspector and registrar in Sosnowiec, and living in Munich at the time of his testimony, claimed that he had never seen anything 'of actions against Jews or of their resettlement', nor had he ever witnessed any deaths or maltreatment of Jews or Poles in the town, because his office lay on the other side of town, some 2–3 miles away from the ghetto, and because he worked 'until late in the evening in his office'.[53] Johan Weißfloch, a former criminal investigator in Sosnowiec, had similarly neither seen nor heard of any actions against the Jewish population, because his activities concentrated primarily on 'the in-coming post and the news service'.[54]

Even Heinrich Mentgen, Klausa's much-praised former head of the gendarmerie in the *Landkreis* of Będzin, had seen nothing, knew nothing, and could remember nothing. He too had allegedly been away—attending his son's wedding in either 1942 or 1943, he could not remember which year—when, so his driver supposedly informed him on his return, all the Jews of Będzin had been deported. He was taken to see the still evident bloodstains at the railway station, but had, he claimed, never witnessed anything himself.[55] He was never challenged on where he had been during the 'other' year—1943 or 1942—when his son was not actually getting married but in which another major deportation had taken place, nor on what he had been doing during all the months in between.

In short, those who had been involved in running the German system in a wide variety of capacities in the area later professed that they had seen and heard nothing at all while an estimated 85,000 people in total were deported in stages out of the towns, villages, and surrounding localities and through the ghettos of Będzin and Sosnowiec on their way to labour camps and the gas chambers of Auschwitz. These Germans all claimed, however implausibly, that they had been working late, were engaged in other duties, away on holiday, attending a son's wedding—or, in Klausa's case, had 'disappeared' to the front—at the time of any violent incident or deportation that they might have been expected to have witnessed; and they had supposedly only at a later date gleaned—at second hand, by being told—something of what had allegedly taken place. For all the differences of detail, the general pattern of these stories is remarkably similar: engagement in purely routine and respectable administrative duties; absence from the area when someone else did something wrong; later partial insights gained through hearsay, snippets, and clues.

Whatever the reason for these post-war cover-ups, people like von Woedtke, Schönwälder, and Klausa clearly had been more involved in events in the area than they were willing to admit. The cynical view, then, might see these apparent gaps and distortions in memory as in line with an unofficial post-war consensus that the best legal defence strategy was simply a blanket denial of any relevant knowledge. Whether this pattern of self-representation was coordinated actively among former colleagues who were still in personal contact with one another (as we know at least some of them were), or by talking to people of similar experiences, views, and outlooks, or independently and almost subconsciously, as part of a general manner of talking and a 'climate of the times' in post-war West Germany, is not easy to judge.

A more charitable view might say that distinctions can nevertheless still be made on the basis of the contemporary evidence. Udo Klausa, in particular, had not been as proactive in pursuing antisemitic policies, deploying incendiary language, and taking the initiative to quite the same extent as von Woedtke and Schönwälder; his was a more muted racism, going along with policy and effectively implementing directives, but not driving it forward to quite the same degree. Moreover, his absences on military service were not as brief as their periods of holiday or attendance at a wedding; he had genuinely been absent for longer periods of time, even if not for quite as long as he later claimed. He had perhaps been internally more opposed to developments than these colleagues, and had felt more uneasy about what it was he was inevitably being caught up in while remaining in his role in the area. He therefore perhaps did not feel he personally had anything to cover up, and was not prepared to engage in a fuller discussion of his role, finding it easier to claim absence from the scene by a somewhat elastic treatment of his dates of military service. Possibly he had, by this time, even come to believe his own frequently repeated story, and was even perhaps genuinely confused about dates. He had in any event, as far as we can tell, barely registered the effects of Nazi policies on the victims and the misery all around him at the time, thus quite easily failing to 'remember' them later. None of this exonerates him for his conformist behaviour or reduces its tragic consequences, however. To suggest he was not a fanatic Nazi is not to suggest he did not faithfully carry out Nazi policies to the end. The situation is simply that any form of antisemitism in these circumstances, however supposedly 'moderate' rather than 'fanatic', could have fatal consequences for the victims. It was not inner qualms but behavioural conformity that mattered.

This story has many ramifications for our understanding of 'how Auschwitz was possible', in terms of both mentalities and the consequences of behaviour. Partially caught in the system himself—although in a very privileged position, with many options still open to him, unlike the victims of Nazism—Klausa was, in this more charitable view, to some degree internally immobilized.[56] He was, and had been since his youth, committed to serving his state in civilian administration, and fighting for his fatherland in wartime. Once he did finally and very belatedly realize what the former really meant in practice—which was a very long way down the road, but a road along which he was accompanied by many others—Klausa was possibly trapped in an emotional and political impasse. He later asserted that he dared not speak out, that 'one had to be terribly wary'; and he was clearly not willing to risk the lives and well-being of himself and his family by any outward resistance, however discomfited he may have been by growing awareness of the murderous character of the system that he served. Suffering from 'nerves', he was clearly unable to articulate, either then or later, any explicit opposition to what was going on, or even to acknowledge quite what he knew; he perhaps even did not want to 'know' what he knew. On this interpretation, his only strategy was to ensure that, despite his continued physical malaise, he managed to pass the scheduled army medical examinations, persuade the authorities that he was fit for military service, and eventually return to the army, pretending, arguably as much for his own psychological health and career as for avoidance of prosecution, that he really had 'known nothing about it'. This is at least one possible reading of the evidence.

But there are other perspectives that do not cast in him in quite such a sympathetic light. Whatever Klausa's private feelings and reactions at the time, it is undoubtedly the case that he did not baulk at any stage in terms of his own actual behaviour and his faithful fulfilment of his official role along the way, which ultimately made Auschwitz possible: he played his allotted part in the system throughout, and faithfully implemented the racial policies of stigmatization, segregation, containment, and ghettoization. His energetic, committed, and intelligent contribution to the administration of the area was highly prized by Springorum, his immediate superior in Kattowitz, to such a degree that the Kattowitz government did their utmost to prevent Klausa's return to military service. Had there been any evidence of foot-dragging or ambivalence on Klausa's part, the struggle over his retention in civilian government is unlikely to have been as protracted and vigorously pursued as it was, even in the autumn of 1942. Nor, with the exception of 'his' Jew, Laib Flojm, did Klausa appear at any stage to have shown any visible concern for the suffering caused to fellow human beings by Nazi policies up to this point—until, several decades after the events he portrayed, he sought to evoke a sense of sympathy for the victims of Nazi policies in his memoirs, even while failing to remember much of their history or his own role in it. If there were inner glimmerings of such sentiments at the time, they failed to show up in the archival records and had no impact on his superiors' positive evaluation of his service.

It is certainly the case that even in Klausa's long post-war efforts to understand this period of history, and even in the light of an undoubted learning process and democratization of outlook, the omissions are striking. He seemed ultimately to be unable to face up to or register the consequences of his own role for the victims of Nazi policies. His memoirs of his time in Będzin omit all awareness of the violence inherent in the system and the multiple tragedies caused by the policies he implemented. There is no evidence of any sense of personal guilt or remorse.

These differences in interpretation are not impossible to reconcile. The story of inner conflicts and ambivalence is harder to prove, and largely reliant on indirect sources produced in the constraints of wartime, such as Alexandra's letters, and on transmission within the family of stories by and about a man they loved and respected; the story of outer conformity, with all the tragic consequences, is by contrast far more readily recounted on the basis of the archival evidence. Both interpretations could well be true, in principle, despite all the glaring factual errors and striking omissions in Udo Klausa's own account of his past; but the former interpretation, that of the 'decent' man who was not 'really' a Nazi, amounts, if recounted on its own, to very much less than half the picture. It is the outcomes of actions, not any well-hidden inner ambivalence, that had historical effects. To ignore the consequences of the actions of even someone with inner doubts is not to face up adequately to the past.

It is in part because of the behaviour of people like this highly educated lawyer and professional civil servant—who appears only to have become queasy about his own involvement in the system once he realized what was to be the next destination in the chain, the final outcome of ghettoization—that it was ultimately possible for those at the front line of violence to put the Holocaust into practice. Klausa's case is perhaps located at a rather unique position in the spectrum, having held a role of responsibility in civilian administration in a district so close to the gas chambers of Auschwitz; but it is also a very ordinary example, in the sense that the same determination to have 'known nothing about it' was very widespread. This failure of imagination, this unwillingness to see or register what was actually going on, was a precondition for the successful functioning of the system and hence, eventually, for the machinery of extermination.

For the facilitators of Nazi rule in this province, the denial of any knowledge of 'Auschwitz' (or 'this function of Auschwitz') as a final threshold of evil could potentially serve as a convenient means of self-exculpation. From the post-war perspective of these facilitators, all that was then needed were brief alibis and tales of absence at crucial times, sometimes combined with hints of fragmentary hearsay. The vast majority of those questioned by the West German legal authorities and answering along these lines were subsequently able to live out their retirements in a degree of peace and affluence, untroubled by uneasy memories.

Mordecai Lichtenstein, an Auschwitz survivor who after liberation left for England, ended his deposition of May 1945 with the following comments:

> Before I left Poland I wanted to see Bendzin for a last time. I wish I had not returned to this once flourishing Jewish town which has now become a ghost town. Of 30,000 Jews living there five and a half years ago, only 160 were registered on February 15th, 1945 and I assume that even these figures are too high...
>
> Now I am here [in London]... I am free, but I cannot feel happy. My parents-in-law were gassed, my younger brother, his wife and their little daughter gassed, my brother-in-law Moses hanged, and his wife and daughter died from typhus in the women's camp. I lost sight of my second brother and my brother-in-law Wolf during the shooting [on the death march], and I do not know whether they have survived that assault. Worst of all, however, I do not know anything about my wife's fate...
>
> I am very grateful for the hospitality this country has offered me, but whether a man of my experience will ever be able to enjoy life again, that remains to be seen. At the moment I cannot believe it.[57]

13
Afterwards and After-Words

For the first couple of years after the war, Klausa lay low, being in an Allied automatic arrest category and fearing lengthy incarceration. Once denazification measures had passed into German hands, however, he was able to surface again, and deployed family connections to ensure that he gained the coveted classification of 'exonerated'—a quite remarkable outcome for a long-standing *NSDAP* member who had held such a significant position in the political hierarchy.[1] Thereafter, like so many other former Nazis, Klausa became a loyal and committed civil servant in the Federal Republic of Germany: a convinced democrat, a well-respected administrator, and an upstanding citizen; intelligent, charming, energetic.

The fact that Klausa himself was never brought to court—despite lengthy legal investigations into crimes committed in the Będzin area, coordinated by the Ludwigsburg Central Office—is very typical. So many of his colleagues in civilian administration, whose names are sprinkled throughout the bulky files in Ludwigsburg, and members of the police forces, SS, and others who were brutally involved in physical implementation of front-line violence, went on, like Klausa, to perfectly respectable careers in post-war Germany.[2]

'Going back': returns, repressions, and remembrance

There were many patterns of post-war life among those victims of Nazi persecution who managed, against all the odds, to survive: but common to many was a brief return to their former home town, sometimes to search for relatives and friends, sometimes just to see it one last time before leaving their former homeland and starting a new life in an entirely foreign country.

These experiences have been written about many times, and each has its own individual inflection, but there are some striking similarities among the tales of the Będzin survivors. As Arnold Shay sadly put it, at the start of his memoirs entitled *From Bendzin to Auschwitz: A Journey to Hell*:

Bendzin Jewry flourished in poverty and under Polish anti-Semitism, and we brought pride and civility to the cities we lived in.

Now Bendzin as we knew it is no more, and will be no more...

Why any Jew stayed after the war in Bendzin, and for that matter anywhere in Poland, is beyond my comprehension...

All of Poland is one big Jewish cemetery. The grounds are soaked with Jewish blood.[3]

And it was not only the bad memories and the blood of so many friends and relatives; it was also the reception survivors experienced when they did seek to return to their homes after the war.

After liberation, for example, Josef Baumgarten went first to a Displaced Persons camp in Frankfurt; here, he heard that his last remaining sister had actually managed to survive the labour camps. When he had sufficiently recovered, he returned to Będzin in 1945, but found his home town less than welcoming:

There was nobody there, the house we used to live, there was a Polack living there, and people, I mean, most of them were gone, that I was brought up with them, and I just couldn't see staying in Poland, there's nobody to talk to, you know, and what I'm going to do, I mean, I'm 19 years old, what I'm going to do in Poland...[4]

The locals in Będzin were unwilling even to talk to him. He went back to his own former home:

I just went back to see for myself the house where we used to live...I looked through the window and this Polack gave me a dirty look, he says what are you doing looking through my window, and I walked away and that's the last time I saw the house where we used to live.

At this point in the interview, Baumgarten became quite emotional. Even now, he admits: 'I spend a lot of time asking why me, why not my parents, why not my sisters, why did I survive what I went through, and the answer is, I just don't know.' He came to the USA to get a new life, 'because I lost everything, just get out...I couldn't wait to get out'.

Many others echo these early post-war experiences. Yetta Kleiner recalls that, when she went back to Poland in 1945, 'we came and didn't find another paradise, it was the Russians occupied Poland and they were still killing Jews'.[5] The Poles too, she remembers, were just as hostile as before the war. She went back to her former house, the house where she had been born, wanting just to see it, but a woman at the door said to her 'we have no Jews, we want no Jews' and would not let her in. She concluded that 'there was no future for us, we never wanted to be there...the way they greeted us, very inhumane, the ones that knew you'. Although she initially managed to settle in Germany, there too she felt that she 'couldn't live among them'; she persuaded her husband—a survivor of Warsaw, Majdanek, Auschwitz, and slave labour in a coalmine—that, even though he was doing well in his new business, she would not be able to stay. They emigrated to Canada.

Some had managed to survive the war in hiding, still in the Będzin area, but even they were fearful of coming out into the open again as Jews, and did not remain there for very long afterwards. Mindzia Schickman, despite having been hidden and protected by a Polish woman, was terrified to admit her Jewish identity following the end of the war, and recalled her difficulties with persuading herself that she was genuinely free to live and exist as a Jew.[6] One day the rumour spread that the war had come to an end. Her protector and Polish 'mother', Cecilia, went out to work as usual, and Mindzia thought she would once again see the sunshine and feel what it meant to be free:

> I went outside, onto the street, I didn't believe, I didn't believe I have the right to be there, I felt like, Jewish people they don't have rights, for whatever reason, we have to sacrifice our lives...I wasn't ready to sacrifice my life just because I am a Jew, not ready to die after what I went through, I wanted to live more than ever, my hope it was so bright, I knew that my family will be dead, but nevertheless...

When she went back upstairs, Cecilia had returned 'and apparently [the] war wasn't over'. Mindzia was now terrified that someone would have recognized her: and 'again the sirens and again the terrible fear of bombing and again...all the torture, all the suffering, all the fear, but the will to live, and the hope, I never lost it'. Once the war really was over, her fears did not cease: 'I was so afraid, I was so terrified to admit that I am Jewish...'. She thought that maybe God would punish her one day, but 'I just wanted to play with other children and to be free and to have the right to see the sunshine and the trees and the snow. I guess I love life, life itself.' Cecilia signed her up for school, and Mindzia took Cecilia's surname, Krzeminska, posing as her daughter. She dared not admit her real name to anyone, or the fact that she was Jewish: 'I was afraid that I will not be accepted, I will have to hide . . . I was so afraid, it took years, years . . .'. Even well into adult life, married and living in Canada, Mindzia suffered from screaming, crying, and sweating at night from appalling nightmares, such that her husband had to wake her. She had constant stomach trouble, and for long periods of time could not eat normally: 'I just couldn't go through all that again.' After her terrifying childhood experiences of the forcible moves, the ghettoization, the violence, and the loss of so many members of her family, Mindzia's years of being hidden merely in order to survive—hiding from a regime that held that simply being Jewish was sufficient grounds for persecution and death—had taken a terrible, lifelong toll on her.

On two occasions Udo Klausa, too, returned with a few members of his family—by now adult children and their partners—to see Będzin. Alexandra does not seem to have accompanied them on these visits, possibly more because of her chronically poor physical health than out of any unwillingness to be reminded again of the violent scenes around the railway station that she, and Mindzia, had observed from such close geographical and such radically different emotional perspectives. On the occasion of the second visit, which took place in May 1989, the family record of the trip—a combination of travelogue and photographs—noted Udo Klausa's reactions to the places they visited in the course of their journey to Będzin via former family residences in Silesia, including Klausa's home town of Leobschütz, and eventually on to Kraków. These notes included the comment, still using the old 'Germanized' name for Będzin, that 'the most dismal impression was given by Bendsburg'.[7] Under a photo of one of the central streets, a street that had been rendered 'Jew free' under Klausa's administration, the inscription was written: 'Bendzin: the main street. In the brief German period it wasn't *this* hideous!'

Reading this, and even allowing for the undoubted effects of a failing communist economy on increasingly dilapidated housing in an old industrial town, one has to wonder whether Klausa had ever really faced up to his part in 'cleansing' the streets of Będzin, or had ever really registered just what this had meant for the tens of thousands of former Będzin citizens who were Jewish. The victims of Nazi 'Germanization' policies had been ousted from their homes in what had once been a thriving town, a vibrant centre of Jewish cultural, social, and religious life widely known as the 'Jerusalem' of the region. The experiences of these former Jewish inhabitants, the character of the world that had been taken away from them and the way they had in turn been taken from the world, certainly did not figure much in Klausa's memoirs, nor seem to dent his own claim to innocence. Perhaps some awareness hovered, hinted at in his repeated concern that he did not want to become 'innocently guilty'; but the uneasy hovering could be quelled only by a concomitant downplaying of his own awareness of what was going on all around, and what the consequences of his own actions really were.

For survivors, too, it was not always easy to develop an explicit account with which they could comfortably live. Arno Lustiger, living in West Germany after the war, did not want to be reminded of this painful past; for a long time he doubted that people would believe him anyway; and he did not want to burden his two daughters with the weight of this past, feeling that it was enough that he had been robbed of his own childhood and youth by the Nazis. In the 1960s, he attended some hearings at the Auschwitz trials in Frankfurt, and was horrified at the lack of respect with which survivors were treated by lawyers for the defence of those on trial for war crimes. It was only on the occasion of the fortieth anniversary of the liberation of Auschwitz, on 27 January 1985, when he was asked to give a speech at the commemoration ceremonies in Frankfurt, that Arno Lustiger finally broke his silence.[8] One of his daughters, the writer Gila Lustiger, has recorded just how belatedly she managed to glean further details of her father's experiences.[9]

This pattern was not necessarily typical of all: many survivors spoke very openly straight after the war; many complained that it was not that they had in some way kept silent, but rather that, for many years, they failed to find a receptive audience beyond their own circles. For whatever reasons, a broader confrontation with the past seems to have been possible only in an altered climate many decades later; and in some respects a full confrontation could never take place, for a wide variety of reasons.[10]

It took a relatively long time for Będzin, too, to enter an era of memorialization of its Jewish past. While Auschwitz became a museum very soon after the war, and went through a series of iterations and controversies (from celebration of communist resistance over the post-war decades under communist rule to belated recognition of its significance as the ultimate site and symbol of Jewish suffering once the Iron Curtain was no more) areas nearby were largely ignored as sites of memory. The little hamlet of Celiny was prompted into memory of the suffering of thirty-two people at the hands of the gendarmes in June 1940 only thirty years or so later, when the Ludwigsburg investigators started requesting material relating to that incident; their memorial was erected in the mid-1970s. Plaques and memorials in the town of Będzin began to be erected only in the 1980s, with the return of Arno Lustiger, accompanied by his Catholic cousin, Cardinal Jean-Marie Lustiger, an acquaintance of the Polish-born Pope Jean Paul II: Catholic connections and Catholic heroism in helping to rescue Jews fleeing the burning synagogue in September 1939 assisted in the assimilation of these memories into the remembrance culture of the town. A number of memorials were erected, regular ceremonies held, streets and squares renamed; the square on which the former *Landrat*'s office was located has now been renamed Jean-Marie Lustiger Square after Arno Lustiger's cousin.

Only as immediate conflicts of interest over ownership of property and use of space faded, as personal animosities, mutual suspicions, and painful registration of acquaintanceship and loss began to heal over, was it possible for the municipality of Będzin to begin to think of taking the initiative in marking significant places and engaging in rituals of remembrance. By the first decade of the twenty-first century, such exploration and signification of the town's Jewish heritage were finally fully under way. Forgotten Jewish prayer rooms were uncovered and prepared for potential tourists; gatherings of survivors and their families were hosted; the diary of Rutka Laskier was published and celebrated as Będzin's 'Anne Frank'; schoolchildren were encouraged to learn about the past of their now entirely Polish home town.[11] Often the original impetus for such memorialization still came from outside: it was, for example, the Zaglembie Jewish World Organization and the 'Jona' Foundation (Centre of Jewish Culture) that provided the initiative for opening the Heroes' Ghetto Square in Kamionka-Warpie in 2004, with a monument unveiled in the presence of David Peleg, Ambassador of Israel, and former Jewish inhabitants of the town and ghetto.[12] But the municipal authorities, and other local interest groups and individuals, energetically picked up the project, often clashing with one another in their enthusiastic pursuit of conflicting ways of disinterring and preserving the remnants of what the Nazis had tried to destroy. This was the case, for example, with the fragments of Jewish gravestones discovered in the overgrown sidings and disused railway tracks near Będzin's railway station, redeployed when the former 'new' Jewish cemetery was taken over after the war by a trucking and cement works.[13] It was the case, too, with discussions over ways to mark the Jewish burial grounds. But it was noticeable all the same that the old Jewish cemetery, tucked down the dark, steeply sloping hillside at the back of the castle, was falling into ruins and weeds, uncared for, untended, even as a young photographer committed to the preservation of history was producing artistic photographs of the Jewish cemeteries in honour of the former Jewish citizens of Będzin.[14] By contrast, the neighbouring Catholic burial ground, still very much in use and seemingly ever expanding, stretched across a series of fields, decorated throughout by fresh flowers lovingly tended by local families.

In some ways, the reconciliation between the current Polish inhabitants of the town and the ghosts of the past seemed a belated attempt to make up for the highly fractured, often deeply hostile, relationship between the former Jewish and Polish communities during the Nazi era. Yet, for anyone with some knowledge of what had gone on at that time, the pattern of memorialization may seem slightly displaced, ill at ease, combining (as memorialization inevitably always does) current concerns with highly selective re-presentation and emphasis on some aspects while entirely ignoring or downplaying others. The more I got to know about events in Będzin during the German occupation, the more surprised I was about places that had, at the time I was exploring the area, no memorial at all. One such is the old Jewish cemetery on Zawale Street, where the public hangings had taken place to such frightening effect in April 1942. Another, even more surprising, is the former Hakoach sports ground, transformed into a bus terminus, where the August 1942 selections had taken place. One might have thought that, set into a paving stone or a wall of a bus shelter, at least a small plaque could have commemorated the 15,000 or so people who were gathered here for selection between life and death, and the further 8,000 collected in the sports ground down near the river. Similarly, there is no plaque on the former Jewish orphanage, just on the other side of the railway tracks, where so many of the 4,700 who were condemned to death in August 1942, as well as innumerable 'transports' before and afterwards, were held against their will while waiting for lorries and cattle wagons to be lined up at the station. Nor is there any kind of memorial to the first major ghetto area in the centre of the town, around the former marketplace—half of which is now in any event obliterated by the broad post-war highway running below the castle and the Catholic church.

No one really wants to live in a ghost town, or to be reminded daily of gruesome events that, while vividly alive in the memories of those who lived through them—more in some people's minds than others—now seem to younger generations to have taken place a very long time ago, in quite another era. And in some respects, in terms of healing the wounds and scars of an appalling past, silencing or sidelining that past can be a helpful precondition for living a life more worth living in a later present. The significance of this silence varies massively, of course, depending on who is keeping silent and for what reasons: there is a world of difference between the painful wounds that those who suffered have no desire to reopen, and the uncomfortable nagging of a possibly troubled conscience of a former facilitator or beneficiary of Nazi rule. But, seventy years and more after the event, these kinds of consideration are no longer operative. And, as forms of collective as well as individual identity are ever more open to choice and negotiation, the old fault lines of exclusion and animosity are no longer relevant in quite the way they once were.

Even so, individual experiences more than half a century after the clearance of Będzin at times suggest that the past lingered on among subsequent generations. Josef Baumgarten returned again in 1994, now with his elderly sister, to the house where they had been born:

> There was a little old lady, she must have been about 80 years old, comes out... I looked at her and she was very nice to me, and she took us in for some coffee... and she [told us she] was the lady who used to come on Saturday and light the fire and put on the light, but I don't remember, and she told us that she knew my parents, you know, and I took my sister also back to Auschwitz, to the camp where I was, I broke down, because it was really emotional, for my sister because she had never really been in a concentration camp, she had been in a labour camp...

Feeling some sense of at least partial closure, they then

> went back to my home town again, to Będzin. The next day as we walked by again in this same street, there used to be an old, not old, a hotel for older people you know, and the Poles they remodelled it to condominiums, whatever, as we walked by there in the afternoon, myself, my sister and my brother-in-law and my girlfriend, there were four Poles, maybe 15, 19 years old, as we walked by they waved their arms and they said 'Heil Hitler' to us. So we felt really bad, because what we went through, and coming back to Poland, we had the feeling again, but we didn't talk to them, we just walked by... I would never believe it, but it's still antisemitic.

Baumgarten's unhappy conclusion was that, once again, he 'just tried to get out... that's Poland'.[15]

Others with Będzin family connections, having heard such stories, came to visit with this sort of expectation, but often had far more favourable experiences on visiting in the early twenty-first century. Erin Einhorn, for example, was the American-born daughter of a woman who had been hidden by a Polish family. Despite the delicacy of the negotiations with both the Polish legal system and the particular individuals—one of whom had saved her mother's life—now living in what had once been her family home, Einhorn had something of a mixed experience. On balance, she was persuaded that, despite tourist kitsch and tackiness in Kraków, and a degree of suspicion in Będzin and elsewhere, modern Poland was both hospitable to and supportive of Jewish culture once again.[16] Poland had certainly gained something of a mixed reputation over centuries: the land where Jews for hundreds of years were able to settle and flourish; the land of ambivalently bloodthirsty, fearful, self-serving, or greedy collaboration with the Nazis on antisemitic policies if nothing else; and yet also the land with the largest number of those deemed by Yad Vashem to have earned the award of Righteous among Nations for having assisted Jews to survive the Holocaust. The fractured relations, constantly evolving memory cultures and sensitivity of debates about Jews and Poles in communist and post-communist Poland, do not allow of any easy generalizations.[17]

On my own visits to Będzin I found huge willingness among local people to talk about their memories. It was as if, in some ways, stories that had lain gathering dust—neither repressed, nor regularly resuscitated and rehearsed—could finally burst out of the floodgates before those who lived through this period had passed away. There was also considerable interest among those whose parents or other relatives had been dramatically affected by the Nazi occupation. To a very much lesser extent, there was a willingness to engage with the town's past among teenagers for whom this really was just 'history', and not even a history with which they felt any personal connection at all, particularly if their families had been forcibly resettled to Będzin from areas of eastern Poland taken over by Russia with the border changes after the war.

Yet key aspects of this past could barely be found in the architecture or everyday life of this post-Nazi, post-communist, post-industrial town, now little more than a nondescript satellite of the newly flourishing Katowice, and bearing little trace of the former richness of Jewish life that was so comprehensively destroyed by the Nazi policies of 'Germanization'. And, while the victims are now memorialized, there is a strange absence of any visible narrative concerning those responsible for the early stages and preconditions of their ultimate destruction. This is not a site on the scale of

Auschwitz; nor were the facilitators of expropriation and ghettoization perpetrators in quite the same way as those at the top of the Nazi regime, giving the orders, or those engaging in physical acts of brutality and murder; yet they too were part of this past, and should be included in its history. The 'ordinary Nazis' have to be written back in. And here, this essentially very typical story—unfolding with differences of detail, dates, personalities, particular local events, and policies, but to depressingly similar effects all across Poland under Nazi rule—has wider implications.

Understanding 'ordinary Nazis'

There are many different ways in which the term 'Nazi' can be understood: involvement in the Nazi movement and more general support for aspects of Hitler's policies varied across a huge spectrum of organizational memberships, attitudes, and viewpoints, and among people in different situations and at different times. There was wide variation not only among 'Nazis' in the formal sense of *NSDAP* membership, but even among those deemed to be, for one reason or another, 'fanatical' Nazis, or among enthusiastic supporters of the Führer who never actually joined the *NSDAP*. For some Germans, foreign policy successes and economic well-being took priority over 'racial' policies; for some, the war and patriotism in service of the fatherland could be a source of self-mobilization even to the very, and very bitter, end; for many, faith in the charismatic Führer was always a central energizer and comfort; but, for many others, matters were far more mixed, views more ambivalent, even as in their outward behaviours they remained formally obedient and apparently committed to the regime.

There is no simple definition of what can be meant by 'Nazi', let alone an 'ordinary Nazi', and I do not propose to suggest any essentialist definition here: the very range and ambiguity, the multifaceted palette of changing attractions, fears, and temptations, the varying and changing degrees of ambivalence and complexity, are in themselves striking characteristics of participation in Nazi rule during those twelve years.

But in the very basic sense of turning a blind eye to the consequences of racist policies—policies that they were not responsible for designing, but that they actively assisted in implementing—the functionaries, facilitators, and beneficiaries at the grass roots do deserve rather closer attention than they have generally received. They were not the initiators of policy, the movers and shakers at the top; they were not caught as pawns or cannon fodder below. Perhaps, for these groups, the label 'ordinary Nazis' can for the time being serve as a symbol of how Nazism was able to wreak such horrendous effects in practice, as policies designed by others were translated, intentionally or otherwise, into an ever more radical system of racism in practice, a system ultimately paving the way for what became a deadly reality for so many victims.

There are also many ways in which the term 'decent' can be understood. Himmler even deployed it in his infamous Posen speeches of October 1943, claiming that the SS could 'remain decent' in face of and despite their terrible secret; despite the fact that, for the alleged benefit of the future of the German 'race', they were murdering even innocent women and children.[18] His speech seems to have been in part designed to reassure his audience about the validity of a path that seemed on the face of it even to such committed Nazis so terrible, at the same time as implicating them in the knowledge of and hence shared responsibility for the murderous enterprise. For many Germans, and not only Germans, to be 'decent' (*anständig*) was a virtue in itself, with far more innocent meanings. It would take a quite separate investigation to explore the meanings of the term 'decent' across the spectrum of prevalent world views at the time.

I have no doubt that Udo Klausa held himself to be perfectly 'decent' in his dreams of becoming, like his father before him, a loyal servant of the state, a *Landrat* faithfully providing leadership in his own little domain. But nor can there be any question that, as Klausa claimed, he was 'only' engaged in some anodyne, apolitical, innocent form of 'administration', an absolutely impossible notion in this highly volatile, constantly evolving, but always radical situation. 'Germanization' policies were central to the task of local government in this area; and the role of *Landrat* was a key position at the front line of the expanding Nazi racial empire. The production of 'Jew-free' cities in the Reich for the enjoyment of the German 'master race' was an explicit goal of Nazi occupation policies from the outset; and policies for realization of this goal rapidly came to shift from the always brutal and often fatal policies of humiliation, stigmatization, expropriation, exploitation, and ghettoization, in what might be seen as an extreme form of 'colonial racism', into the 'final solution' of deportation to extermination—for which all the previous policies had helped, even if unwittingly, to prepare the ground.

Perhaps Klausa did suffer from 'nerves' when involved in this enterprise. But it is notable that Alexandra's comments on his health considerations and his 'nerves', as well as his oscillations between civilian and military service to the Reich, long pre-date the shock of the August 1942 selections. The evidence for his own version of his story is veiled and opaque. If Klausa had growing inner doubts about the Nazi project, and particularly about the role of administration in the annexed territories, he never expressed them explicitly: neither at the time nor later. If his commitment to Catholicism caused any potential hitches on his career ladder, it does not seem to have stopped him from acting in the ways demanded of him; indeed, he possibly conformed all the more strenuously in order to override any possible disadvantages of being a Catholic. Thoughts and behaviour may on occasion have run in conflicting directions: it would be surprising if this were not the case; and it is the tragedy of this period, after all, that so many Germans went along with the Nazi regime for so long and, despite their conformist and supportive behaviour at the time, nevertheless after the war professed to have 'always been against it' (in the standard catchphrase, *immer dagegen*). Despite his admission to have been an early supporter of at least some aspects of Nazism, and despite his claims to disenchantment relatively early on, there is not a whiff of any real sense of guilt or personal responsibility in Klausa's later self-representations.

Only once did Klausa comment in his memoirs that 'today one does ask oneself if it was even right to serve this system in one way or another under the circumstances of that time. But that would lead too far here.'[19] Klausa did not himself take the occasion to pursue this thought further. It is not my place to suggest an answer on his behalf, glaringly obvious though such an answer must seem to anyone living in the post-Holocaust world—and already obvious even to those who, like my mother while still only a teenager in the spring of 1933, recognized the iniquities of Hitler's regime from the very start.

I find myself in a difficult position here. The task of the historian is to explore, understand, and explain; not to mount a legal case (whether for the defence or the prosecution), or pronounce moral judgements, or pursue political agendas. In this case, however, I am writing not only as a professional historian, but also as someone who is personally and emotionally involved in the exploration. One part of me wants to yell back at Udo Klausa, posthumously; to scream that, without him and countless other functionaries with similar views and in similar positions, Hitler could never have wrought such mass destruction; that it is outrageous that Klausa could have got away with all this and have led such a successful and prosperous life after the war while so many had suffered and died as a result of his faithful fulfilment of his role as *Landrat*; that it is both sad and maddening that my mother's renewed friendship with her former schoolfriend was built on an effective silencing and denial of so much evil.[20] But another part of me wants to protect family friends, the surviving members of Klausa's family, from having so belatedly to engage with what seem to me the full horrors of the consequences of their father's mentality and actions; this part of me wants to avoid the inevitable difficulties involved in filling in some of the omissions in Klausa's account, challenging the fictions he constructed, contextualizing the myths he could live with after the war, and which allow his family to honour and respect him. All the same, I cannot go as far as members of his family would like. Even allowing for the fact that what the archives reveal is far from everything, I can see no evidence whatsoever of Klausa having tried in practice to temper or alter the direction of Nazi policies, and much to suggest that he behaved in ways that more than satisfied his superiors. According to his son, Udo Klausa's real value to the regional government was in his superior administrative abilities and not in any particular commitment to or enthusiasm for specifically anti-Jewish policies, in which he was less than actively involved.[21] Yet even 'mere administration' in such a context and system was intrinsically deeply compromised and inevitably effected on racial lines. To suggest that this can be separated from the 'really' reprehensible actions of physical violence and deportations is, it seems to me, simply to be trapped in repeating the blinkered views of the generation that made Nazism possible. Nor did Klausa seem even aware of the extent of his own complicity, remembering little in any detail of the Jewish plight or his role in exacerbating it. He expressed no apparent sense of personal responsibility, let alone any sense of regret, shame, guilt, or moral qualms about his role, even in his later, essentially self-justifying memoirs. His principal aim seems to have been to assert his innocence. But I do have some understanding for the family's uncomfortable situation in facing up to this past, and for their attempt to interpret Klausa's past in ways consistent with their intimate knowledge of him as a person.

The realities are not always easily accessible, and I have tried to give Klausa's side of the story as much of a hearing as I could—certainly far more of a hearing than most people would ever think a Nazi functionary could deserve—while also suggesting that the facts often conflict with, challenge, or go way beyond the picture as portrayed by Klausa himself. Perhaps both versions of the story are in some sense true; the inner doubts that gave rise to Klausa's own later version of his story, and the outer conformity that left the archival debris and the traces of historical action. There is, however, a sense in which giving too much credence to convenient fictions can amount to collusion in covering up the past; and giving too much weight to inner doubts can downplay the actual consequences of conformist behaviour. So ultimately the role of historian, trying to explore the wider picture, has to predominate.

However complex and ambiguous, there are some things that can be said on this matter; and people do have degrees of freedom and can make choices about how to act—with far more leeway in some elevated and relatively powerful positions, such as Klausa's, than in others where people are heavily constrained and repressed by the system, as most obviously in the case of the Jews. However much I would like to have persuaded myself otherwise, I cannot help but conclude that, whatever Klausa's perhaps ambivalent inner feelings, the way he actually behaved had horrendous historical consequences; and hence to have played any such role in this system was morally wrong. We can look at his role as, in effect, a tragic combination of careerism, courage, cowardice, and callousness. Careerism, because he pursued a perfectly valid ambition of state service, which would under many other historical circumstances have been entirely reputable; a degree of courage, because there do seem, certainly in the course of 1942 and perhaps much earlier, to have been glimmerings of recognition on his part of the fundamentally evil character of the regime he served, thus tipping the balance of the medical evidence in favour of a return to the army while not yet completely physically fit; cowardice, because he never dared to speak out at the time, and never quite faced up to the truth in his later self-representations, distorting dates and forgetting or omitting details in an effort to present his case for innocence and ignorance; and also an undoubted degree of callousness, because again and again he ratified and implemented racist policies in his administrative role with absolutely no regard for the long-term consequences for the victims, and even an apparent unawareness of their suffering as a direct effect of the policies he upheld.[22] This lack of awareness continued across the post-war decades: Klausa's memoirs and other self-representations portray a personal past almost entirely without violence, almost entirely without victims.

I am aware that I write in what might be seen as mutually conflicting personal roles here: as the daughter of a refugee from Nazi Germany, who had lost close childhood friends and relatives to the Holocaust; as the god-child of the *Landrat*'s wife and continuing friend of the family, who may quite understandably feel ill at ease with an account so deeply contextualizing the *Landrat*'s role; and as a professional historian trying to weave together the multiple strands of a many-sided tale. I am aware of the different pressures of these conflicting perspectives: the *Landrat*'s family, for example, may have been relieved to find he 'did nothing wrong' by way of actively engaging in specific criminal acts of physical brutality (at least in his civilian role), yet the far less comfortable implication of this analysis is that, as Klausa himself intimated, to serve the system at all at that time was in itself inevitably wrong. Whether intentionally or otherwise, such conformity up to a very late point facilitated consequences of a character and on a scale for which words such as appalling, horrendous, seem utterly inadequate. This must surely be widely recognized in a world 'after Auschwitz', a world still marked by ideologically inspired acts of violence and genocide.

There is, therefore, a more general conclusion that can be drawn from this story. It draws attention to the nature of the system, to the structures of power, as well as to the ways in which these shape and are in turn shaped by people's actions; it draws attention to the unintended long-term consequences of serving such a system; for it was not Klausa's individual motives, but rather the fact that he was so easily both mobilized and constrained by the system to act in certain ways, even as he grew increasingly aware of the murderous consequences, that is at the heart of this story. His availability for mobilization was undoubtedly rooted in the particular milieu and the particular period in which he grew up and came to maturity: he was stamped by a set of assumptions about class and 'racial' superiority, and formed by a conservative nationalist milieu; he was brought up with a strong sense of both duty and obedience to the state. However such orientations may have been inflected also by his Catholic upbringing, Klausa was able to pursue a career within a system that others saw as evil from the outset. The mobilization of sections of the cohort of which he was a part, the 'war youth generation' who were too young to have fought in the First World War, played a key role in the development and functioning of the Third Reich.[23]

We will never know with any certainty the nature of Klausa's inner doubts, of which he left precious little externally verifiable evidence. Even his post-war assertions in his memoirs are repeatedly tinged with Nazi phrases and formulations; this was clearly a formative world view from which, even long after he had recognized just where it had led, he struggled to escape. But, whatever the possibly growing inner distance, it would seem that up until the late 1930s or early 1940s—1942 at the latest—he continued to act as he did out of a combination of career ambition, lack of respect for (or even apparent awareness of) the victims, blindness to the consequences of racism, and a continual unwillingness to stand up against the prevailing political tide—whether Nazi or, after the war, democratic.[24] These are attributes Klausa shared with so many others. His self-exoneration strategies, even decades later, often bear more than a little trace of Nazi mentalities, although also an occasional hint of self-doubt and of empathy with the victims, while distancing himself from ever having had anything to do with their plight. Most of all, as he put it, however one felt inside, one should never betray the slightest hint of opposition in public: 'At that time one had to be terribly wary' (*Man musste sich damals ganz schrecklich vorsehen*)—an assessment certainly borne out by the experiences of those who did engage in active opposition.[25] Klausa seems, then, to have struggled to continue his career while internally making a distinction between his own commitment to 'mere administration', and the ever more extreme racial policies initiated by others but in which he was himself unwillingly becoming increasingly involved. This appears to have created an unbearable tension for him; the only resolution was to seek some means of personal removal from the situation.

Klausa was probably typical of many hundreds of thousands of low- and middle-level functionaries and facilitators of the racist policies of the Third Reich. The attempt to understand the mentalities and practices of such functionaries is one route among many to understanding the preconditions for mass murder. For without the actions of many perfectly decent and ordinary civilian administrators like Klausa, the Jews of Eastern Upper Silesia would never have been brought to a position in which it would be, relatively, so easy for the 'final perpetrators' and 'actual executioners' to carry out the last and lethal stages in the mass extermination of the Jews. In a way, then, Klausa's story is illustrative both of how so many would-be 'decent' Germans could so readily become 'ordinary Nazis', and how, after the war, so many who had faithfully served the Third Reich could live so easily with their past.

Klausa's wife Alexandra, who was later to become my godmother, was not a 'person of contemporary history', and should, at least according to the professional guidelines displayed in the archives, play no real role in this account. Yet I cannot help but feel that her responses are also an integral part of understanding the fate of the Jews of Będzin, and her husband's role in this fate. It is Alexandra's letters to her mother and to her family friend that provide the only compelling contemporary insights we have into Udo Klausa's continual state of 'nerves'; it is on the evidence of her letters that we can gain some awareness, even if only to a limited extent, of the strain he seems to have been under. Without her letters, this side of the story would escape from view almost entirely. But it is also from her letters that we can begin to understand a little more clearly the nature of the unthinking racism that was so prevalent at the time. My godmother was very clear about what it was that she was seeing all around, and yet at the same time she seemed to have an impermeable barrier between herself and the screaming, fighting, and dying victims. It is almost as if the boundaries of her moral universe, the boundaries of the community with which she felt any kind of empathy, were drawn so narrowly that personal discomforts, as well as a concern to allay any fears her mother may have had about her own safety, seem to have predominated. Clearly there was some difficulty in writing openly in wartime, and quite possibly Alexandra was far more shocked by what she saw than she would ever commit to writing. But this has to remain speculation. What we do know is that she saw, and yet was able to describe in such a way that prevented her from acting against what was going on, whether for fear of the consequences of more explicit critique or for other reasons. There can be no question of the standard defence of 'we knew nothing about it', at least not as far as those being shot dead in the streets all around her were concerned. Was Alexandra, as the wife of a Nazi functionary, simply being guarded in the ways in which she expressed herself, feeling unable to say more or express her real feelings in a letter written in wartime? This does seem highly likely, and is the interpretation favoured by members of the family who knew her best. But there are also more uncomfortable possibilities, ones that may not apply to Alexandra but almost certainly do apply to others in her position. Did the notion of Jews as human beings entitled to live peacefully in their own home town, without being so forcefully 'resettled', simply not exist in the minds of some of these Germans? Or was the ultimate goal, a 'Jew-free' German Reich, sufficient in their eyes to justify the violent and clearly murderous means, particularly if one did not personally have to witness what was going on and how the 'cleansing' of Jews from their home town was being effected in practice? Was this seen simply as part of a 'racial war', since in any war there are bound also to be casualties, however distasteful it may be to have to witness this at first hand?

Certainly there is little hint in Alexandra's letters of any sense of outrage or concern on behalf of the victims—and, given the context of writing, we could hardly expect this. The one explicit (rather than veiled, ambiguous) exception is her description of the events of August 1942. This brief outburst is to some extent similar to expressions of German outrage at the visible violence of the pogrom of November 1938; yet those who were appalled by specific incidents of violence remained apparently unaware of or unconcerned by the long-term suffering of those condemned to a 'social death' during the peacetime years, and the deterioration in conditions during the phases of impoverishment, stigmatization, expropriation, and eventually ghettoization, before complete physical extermination became the 'final solution'.[26] The other significant exception is Alexandra's apparent willingness to take the considerable personal risk of helping Laib Flojm and his family, hiding them and feeding them for several days at the time of the deportation action in August 1942 (although again it is difficult to assess this, given the lack of contemporary sources). This, too, is to some extent typical of the possibility of having empathy with one particular individual, someone known personally, while overlooking the character of the system as a whole over a period of years, and its impact on so many more who remained anonymous. More generally, both Alexandra and Udo continued to support the Church in an anti-Christian state, again a feature widely shared by Germans (and where for many the injunction to neighbourly love did not extend to include Jews).[27] In competing evaluations, we face the question of balance: weighing up moments of unease, moments of sympathy, against continued participation in the Nazi system and public conformity in the interests of self-preservation. This is, arguably, the most widespread conundrum faced by 'Aryan' Germans of this political and social status in this period.

The harsh response to what appears to be moral insensitivity, a response so easy to enunciate at this safe distance from the events, would be to rage against the inaction of a woman in a clearly privileged position, and against the apparent careerism of her husband, whose claimed courage in returning to military service in a state of continuing ill-health was matched by what could be deemed a degree of cowardice in failing ever to deviate visibly from fulfilling his duties in both civilian and military service of the Nazi state, and in failing ever fully to face up to his past. Passing remarks about looking for a job in the economic sphere suggest a degree of unease, but not enough to result in taking effective action or abandoning long-prized career plans. Class was not a barrier to action; the circles of the educated bourgeoisie and the aristocracy had plenty of opportunities available to them for simply shifting to another occupation, of 'inner emigration', even well before we come to speak of any resistance and mobilization against Hitler; in July 1944 some of them finally came to act, belatedly, and without success. And neither youth nor gender can be appealed to here in defence of my godmother. At the age of 26 when she finally left Będzin in the late summer of 1943, Alexandra was a full five years older than Sophie Scholl had been when, just over four months earlier, she had been put to death on 22 February 1943 at the age of 21 for her resistance to the Nazi regime. Sophie Scholl had been able to perceive the fundamental immorality of Nazism even from her distant vantage point in the University of Munich, in a southern region of Germany, Bavaria, a quiet backwater far away from the eastern front. My godmother had apparently not been able to register it fully, even though she lived in the very epicentre of the Holocaust, resident a mere marathon's distance away from Auschwitz. Or perhaps she had been able to register it, but had not found any way to articulate her feelings in this context, and had not known how to react in practice; and, like her husband, had sought only to escape from the scene without any idea of how to prevent the escalation of this monumental crime. Perhaps I should not even ask about this, or raise these questions, living as I do in far more comfortable historical circumstances; and perhaps my response should be tempered by greater understanding of her perspective and practical difficulties in translating any inner qualms into effective actions. Nevertheless, Alexandra's ambivalent responses alongside continued outward conformity can perhaps help us to understand the reactions of so many at this time—reactions that did, in effect, make both the social death and the physical murder of millions of people a horrendous reality.

Even with the growth of approaches to the 'history of everyday life' there is an odd asymmetry here. We can explore the ever more horrendous everyday life of the victims—their sheer survival tactics—but are requested to respect the privacy of those who were not 'persons of contemporary history': to respect the privacy of lives behind the garden fence, as it were.[28] Yet this very segregation between 'persons of contemporary history' and those who may conveniently be designated innocent bystanders begs the most fundamental questions: inaction and conformity may be historically highly significant in certain circumstances. When I first confronted this story, I was filled with outrage about the significance of 'failing to see', and failing to speak out. Had my godmother really not been able to see, metaphorically, over the garden fence—even though the house in which she was living had, before she moved in, been expropriated from a Jewish couple who later died in the gas chambers; even though the physical garden fence in question separated her by a matter of literally only a few yards from the sports ground where thousands of Jews were gathered for 'selections' and the old, young, and weak sent to Auschwitz; and even though her own janitor and gardener, Laib Flojm, a man who had at one time happily played with her toddler behind this very same garden fence, was ultimately, along with his family, among those sent for gassing? Even though my godmother had written to her own mother at the times of the deportations about the horrific scenes she had witnessed, the shooting all around, and the deaths on the streets, mentioning the precise numbers of Jews affected? Even though the scenes she was witnessing at the railway station were much the same as the scenes witnessed by a terrified Mindzia, peeping fearfully out of her attic window in a tenement building situated only a block or so away from the *Landrat*'s villa? Was it really possible 'never to have known anything about it', effectively reducing 'it' to the extermination facilities at Auschwitz, even at these incredibly close quarters? What did 'not knowing' really mean in such a context? Trying to put together the pieces of the story, I initially became very angry—an anger that no doubt has been shared by countless others exploring personal connections in this period. How dare Alexandra's husband Udo make so much of the attempt to save 'their' Jew, Laib Flojm, when they both appeared blind or indifferent to the fate of so many thousands of others with whom they had no such personal connection, and when Udo even praised Mentgen's work and saw no problems with shooting Jews 'while trying to escape'? Is my godmother's apparent incapacity to register the significance of what she undoubtedly saw with her own eyes—effectively an 'eyewitness' while yet failing to 'bear witness'—in itself a crucial clue, helping us to understand both how the Holocaust was possible and how so many Germans lived with the knowledge afterwards? And did she effectively try to erase all memory of this after the war, and evade any confrontation with this past, particularly after her own struggles to escape from the oncoming Red Army and with her own regrets about the loss of the ancestral Prussian heritage—as she too became a 'victim' of the consequences of Hitler's war?

But such a response, such an evaluation, may be too harsh. There is little sense now in raging against the respects in which my godmother's reactions, like those of her husband, were in fact so very typical and so widespread among similar quarters at this time—nor, incidentally, of trying in some way to 'excuse' them by appealing to this typicality, or even deploying the moments of unease as a means of honouring their continuing 'decency' and inner resistance despite outward conformity. It is more useful simply to register the wider historical significance of what were in fact very ordinary responses. Indifference to the fate of those demeaned and debased in practice, and ultimately deemed sufficiently 'other' to be beyond a universe of common empathy; unwillingness to register that one did really 'know' the murderous character of their fate, reducing the relevance of any knowledge to the 'gas chambers'; concern for one's own well-being and the safety of oneself and one's family—these attitudes and mindsets were so very common, so very widespread among Germans, that my godmother's non-responses are simply illustrative, and thus also form an integral part of a wider explanation of how the Holocaust was possible.

One thing is, for me personally, nevertheless remarkable in this story. Despite all that my godmother had witnessed during the war, and despite the vehement political disagreements and the lengthy physical separation between my godmother and my mother, who had emigrated in the mid-1930s, the two rapidly picked up their former friendship again after the war; and they sustained a close emotional bond—symbolized by my mother asking Alexandra to act as my godmother—until their respective deaths many decades later. The lingering warmth born of an intense teenage friendship overcame the gulf that one might have expected between adults who had lived in such different political worlds. Or nearly overcame it; at least helped to paper over any potential fissures.

I am strongly aware of just how much this continuing friendship always meant to my mother; but I suspect that it was at some emotional cost on both sides, with an unwillingness ever explicitly to open up areas where there might be serious difficulties in understanding or wide differences of opinion. On Alexandra's part, this probably meant an avoidance, whether consciously or otherwise, of any serious discussion of Nazism with my mother; for my mother, it meant a limitation of conversation to a relatively superficial level, something she worried about at times, while with other former schoolfriends she addressed—frequently, explicitly, and at length—those political and historical questions with which she was always actively and deeply concerned. There was, I sense, an implicit understanding about the need to avoid sensitive areas that might potentially endanger a friendship that mattered so much—and it certainly mattered massively as far as my mother was concerned. For my mother, Alexandra was not only an incredibly important link back to memories of the happy times together at school that had terminated so abruptly in 1933; Alexandra was also someone for whom my mother felt a deep personal fondness that overrode all differences of politics. So the latter had to be left out of the equation in order to preserve the former.

In this Alexandra too was probably fairly typical of a whole generation of Germans who after the war claimed that they had 'known nothing about it'—implicitly or explicitly restricting what was meant by 'it' to knowledge of the gas chambers, and partially or entirely failing to register the fundamental inhumanity of the regime, and their own largely unthinking roles as carriers of racist practices in everyday life, from the outset. This founding myth of post-war Germany played a significant historical role in integrating many people into the new democracy, allowing energy to focus on building up anew from the ruins while turning their backs on some of the more sensitive aspects of the past. On a small and personal level, this reflected the reintegration of so many former Nazis at a wider political and national level. I suspect that the price of silence was one that both my godmother and my mother, if she had then known what I now know, would have felt was worth paying for the pleasures of many years of renewed friendship. But, occasionally, I do wonder how my mother might have responded to Udo Klausa, had they ever engaged in serious, full, and open discussion of his professional contributions, in his role as *Landrat*, to the project of the 'Germanization' of Będzin on behalf of the Nazi state.[29] In any event, I am glad that my mother and my godmother never discussed this in depth, if at all, in their lifetimes; I doubt that their friendship could have withstood it. It is in many cases only members of subsequent generations, living in wholly different environments, who are able to reflect back with less personal involvement on the experiences of their parents and grandparents.

Even so, it is difficult to escape entirely an emotional involvement in this past. Hidden legacies for subsequent generations pose highly complex questions, in general terms, that cannot be explored further here. It will, however, be apparent to any reader of this book that different interpretations of the same empirical evidence are perfectly possible. On some interpretations, the glass is metaphorically half-full, while for others it is half-empty; and it is in part a matter of perspective as to which half seems to carry most weight in the overall evaluation. In this case, Udo Klausa's son Ekkehard Klausa is most acutely aware of the unbearable constraints of the situation from the perspective of his parents, and of their own inner unease but practical incapacity to find alternative courses of action, or to find means of enunciating and acting on this unease, and their refuge finally in escape, even at considerable personal risk. I am more acutely aware of the consequences for the victims of continued behavioural conformity among Nazi functionaries and others, whatever their sense of distance and inner doubts—which also seem to have allowed them to survive the Third Reich with a good conscience, apparently not plagued by the lifetime anguish and sense of guilt that is prevalent among so many Jewish survivors. In writing this book, my early rage has transmuted into a greater sense of understanding for the position of the Klausa family; but the fact remains that in this story of perfectly decent Germans who had no personal desire to be involved in such violence against Jews there are wider lessons to be learned about how the Holocaust was in fact possible.

Historical perspectives

For decades after the war there were, and still are, heated debates about what the victims—as well as others, far better placed to act—might have done differently. Were the Jewish Councils short-sighted and sometimes self-serving collaborators? Did Jews go 'like lambs to the slaughter'? Should members of *Sonderkommandos* be shunned and condemned, were the *kapos* in the concentration camps in effect as evil as those in whose system they held a privileged place, and yet in which they too were trapped? What should one make of the behaviour of those prisoners who survived by virtue of, for example, stealing bread from others in a weaker position than themselves; ensuring that not their name, but that of another less fortunate inmate, was on the list of those to be deported or gassed; stealing or engaging in bribery and corruption, trading in sexual favours, and other behaviours that in other circumstances seem immoral? Is it even appropriate to ask such questions? Why should some survivors be plagued by feelings of 'survivor guilt', whereas the vast majority of those who had tormented them or were responsible for their incarceration appeared to have no sense of guilt at all? Why did not the outside world, including Jews in Palestine, more actively heed the cries of help and more effectively come to the aid of those trapped in Nazi-occupied Europe? Why was Auschwitz not bombed, once it was within the Allies' reach? Why did Poles, even members of Polish underground resistance groups, so often betray individual Jews, and not cooperate with or further assist Jewish resistance groups? Much of post-war 'Jewish' Holocaust historiography (whether or not written by people who were themselves also Jewish) ran along these and similar lines, effectively continuing bitter controversies that had emerged already during the period of Nazi domination.[30] The agency and everyday lives of Jewish communities and individuals were always of interest, and have constituted a growth area over the last few decades, but generally within frameworks that take for granted the 'German' context.

Meanwhile, what could very broadly be called the historiography of 'Germany' (again, whether or not written by historians who had any personal connections with Germany) has tended to focus on questions surrounding the character and motives of 'perpetrators', a net cast ever more broadly with the passing of decades; the character of 'resistance', again a notion changing in definition and evaluation with period and place of discussion; as well as, increasingly, controversies over the roles of 'ordinary Germans'. In such histories, 'Jews' appeared largely as passive victims—destroyed communities, statistics of corpses, or percentages of survivors—who played little role as agents in the accounts of policy formation and implementation.

Historians have only recently begun to bring these two strands of this hugely complex story together, and even then one side or the other often appears only in an essentially illustrative, rather than fully integrated, role in the account: illustrating the effects of German actions, bearing witness to the tragic consequences of Nazi policies, but frequently playing little role in the energizing motor of the account.

Moreover, there have been further gaps in a cast list where the key roles, of necessity, are populated by obvious perpetrators and power-holders, on the one hand, and handfuls of resistance fighters alongside the vast masses of largely nameless, faceless victims, on the other. Somewhere in between these poles of activists and the largely uninvolved lie what may be called, for all the differences and distinctions within each of these broad groupings, 'ordinary Nazis' and 'ordinary Jews': those who were caught up in the system, neither actively fighting for nor against, largely unaware of where their actions were leading. This system, from the moment of the Nazi invasion of Poland onwards, was one of immense and evident brutality and inhumanity, yet, for the first two years of German occupation, few could have predicted that it would lead to mass murder on quite the scale that it did in the course of 1942.

The incapacity to predict, on the part of the victims, that what was already so terrible, so stamped by terror and fear, could develop into something infinitely worse and ultimately fatal, and the difficulties of even knowing how best to escape, respond, or resist, rendered them effectively trapped under the superior force of German rule. The incapacity to predict, on the part of ordinary Nazis, members of the civilian administration imposing German rule, was accompanied by a wilful refusal to acknowledge the intrinsic inhumanity of this rule even well before it became only too clear that it was the prelude to and precondition for the eventual policies of organized murder. 'Turning a blind eye' to the direct consequences of the policies of humiliation, expropriation, exploitation, impoverishment, degradation, containment, ghettoization, and effective imprisonment might then be followed by a degree of shock that such policies had prepared the ground and made the final round-up so much easier. Members of the civilian administration could then more readily try to ignore their own role in creating the preconditions for mass murder; they could try to evade recognition of their own role as a key link in the causal chain leading up to genocide. But the prior treatment of the victims had undoubtedly rendered them easier prey. Jews whose will and physical health had been broken—weakened by maltreatment, terrified because terrorized—were far more easily led into the waiting train wagons of Będzin and down the track to the gas chambers of Auschwitz–Birkenau than were those who were still young, strong, and somehow possessed of continuing determination to fight, escape, survive. There were also many instances of quick thinking and sheer good luck that assisted those few who did ultimately manage to survive, at least physically, this reign of terror.

These stories, often told in almost complete isolation from each other—Jewish victimhood and heroism, on the one hand, German policies and practices, on the other—have to be brought together if we are even to begin to understand a fuller picture. There is no point, if we are really trying to understand this past, in repeating the blinkered views—blinkered, it should be said, for very different reasons—of the different sides who barely knew each other. Victims of Nazi policies were largely aware only of the direct actions of the Jewish militia, the Jewish Council, and the front-line agents of brute force, particularly in the shape of the Gestapo and the SS, but also the ordinary police forces, including the gendarmes. The agents of civilian administration were well out of sight, and not well known or remembered by the victims. The lack of an adequate overview on the part of the Jews was a direct result of their enforced isolation and the imposed mediating levels of the Jewish Council and Jewish militia.

Members of the civilian administration, for their part, seem not to have wanted to 'know' about the consequences of Nazi polices, or to concede that there was anything intrinsically inhumane about the system that they sustained. A sense of German 'racial' superiority and an unquestioned antisemitism were simply part of their accepted world view, and empathy for victims—unless there was some close personal relationship with a particular individual—was in very short supply. For the most part, the civilian administration had little to do with direct physical acts of brutality; these could be seen as the responsibility of 'others', the 'real Nazis'. Both psychologically and for pragmatic reasons, it was most convenient after the war to assert that administrators had neither known about nor had anything to do with the machinery that led to Auschwitz. The 'real Nazis' were always someone else, generally in the anonymous collective form of the SS.

Yet such separation of oneself from the 'real Nazis' was merely a useful myth, regarding both the system as a whole, and its details. Udo Klausa, in his role as *Landrat*, was directly responsible for the gendarmerie, who in turn carried out 'retribution' killings (as in Celiny); managed a small labour camp (in Golonog); on a routine basis rounded up anyone suspected of being Jewish and still at large, or found having more food than the starvation rations to which they were 'entitled'; and routinely shot dead anyone who 'sought to escape' (as in Mentgen's reports to Klausa in the autumn of 1942). But it is psychologically easier to ignore the direct human consequences of such actions if one is at one remove, not witnessing them personally. Reports of these activities certainly 'passed across the desk' of the *Landrat*; as did the policy directives from Heydrich, Himmler, and others, which passed through Regional President Springorum's office in Kattowitz, and were passed on in turn via the *Landrat* to the mayors of the three towns and the local functionaries in the smaller communities of his *Landkreis*. Back across the *Landrat*'s desk passed the notes and reports from the latter, recording with satisfaction how the Jews in their respective areas had been moved, contained, crowded together, prevented from travelling on public transport, prevented from straying into areas now forbidden to them; how they were being forced to observe the curfew, and wear the star; how they were prevented from obtaining adequate food, or arrested and hanged if they did; eventually, how one by one all the communities of the area were progressively made 'Jew free', even as the ghetto areas of Będzin and Sosnowiec were swelling with massive overcrowding, cramming two or three families into a room in areas that had formerly been the poorest of Polish slums, and where diseases started to spread to such an extent that it alarmed the municipal authorities—but only with respect to the possible effects on the health of neighbouring Germans.

The *Landrat* allegedly did not 'see', did not 'know', anything of this. If we are to set the balance of the evidence against the picture portrayed in Klausa's memoirs, these reports went 'across his desk' and through his office, but not across his mind and through his conscious awareness of the human implications of the policies he was responsible for administering. This apparent failure to register the human realities at the time is reflected in seeming later gaps of memory, and in corresponding omissions in his self-representations. There are different possible interpretations here: either, because of an underlying 'colonial racism', Klausa really did not register the brutal inhumanity of the system in which he was so centrally involved, and did not notice the character and consequences of ghettoization and forced labour; or, later, he underplayed and omitted these aspects in order to suggest that 'mere administration' at that time was as anodyne as it subsequently appeared in the Federal Republic of Germany. This certainly was a convenient myth with which to live. It seems only to have been when policies reached the point of deportation to death in Auschwitz, or 'exterminatory racism', that Klausa appears to have fully registered the intrinsically murderous character of the system he was serving—and, even allowing for the medical complications occasioning further delays in extricating himself and returning to the army, it was a very late departure after the final decisions had already fallen into place.

Although the general goals were clear from the outset—the construction of an almost entirely German area, with Poles in a servile status and Jews nowhere to be seen—the measures taken to achieve these goals were, in this area as elsewhere, piecemeal and cumulative in character. Many civilian administrators later claimed to have been entirely unaware of the developing policy of mass murder in the extermination camps; they appeared not to realize, or to want to realize, that this was a possible if not necessary culmination of the policies that they had themselves been pushing along, all the way up until the final moment when the Jews were taken by the Gestapo and SS out of their hands and forced towards the gas chambers. If this was not an outcome intended by the civilian administrators of the area, it was certainly one that they had in large measure made possible by laying the practical foundations: the increasing geographical concentration and effective imprisonment, as well as physical and psychological subjugation of the Jews. We can concede that Klausa, as *Landrat*, may have been perfectly honourable in his intentions and ambitions, and as blind as so many other Germans to the ultimate impact of his quite typical form of antisemitism—an antisemitism that simply regarded the Germans as superior, blinding him and others to the sufferings of fellow human beings who did not seem to register in this racist moral universe. This antisemitism was not murderous in intent, but it was so in the outcomes of the actions made possible by such a mentality. We also, therefore, cannot avoid looking at what such blinkers made possible in practice at the time, and at the lingering consequences for those involved, consequences that, in some respects, are reverberating even today.

We have, now, to put these different sides of the story together to understand how events could unfold in the way that they did. We cannot tell it only from the unwillingly constricted perspectives of the victims—perceiving, recounting, and remembering the fate of members of the Jewish communities and the brutal actions of their immediate oppressors—or from the ideologically blinkered perspectives of the facilitators, and in particular of the 'decent' Germans, including those in the civil service who sought to distance themselves from the fanaticism of those they portrayed as the 'real' Nazis, and who failed ever really to register the eventual consequences of their actions. If historians continue to tell these as separate tales, they merely remain trapped in the divides that were created by the times and that allowed that tragedy to unfold in the first place.

It is too easy to say that both victims and civilian facilitators of Nazi rule were caught in a wider system in which they had little freedom of manœuvre. This is certainly true of the victims, the direct targets of Nazi racial policies; it is not the case with the administrative functionaries responsible for implementation of Nazi rule at the grass roots, even if they played no role in designing these policies and began to have doubts about where such policies were leading. There is, of course, a clear difference between those perpetrators from the Gestapo, the SS, and the ordinary police forces on whom so much attention has been focused—men who shot and killed, smashed out the brains of babies, threw orphans in sacks onto lorries, and forced thousands of people onto cattle wagons headed for the gas chambers of Auschwitz—and the grey-suited civilian administrators who sought to pursue an ordinary career in state service. But analysis of those conventionally designated as perpetrators has to be complemented by an understanding of Hitler's facilitators. Their roles in the system, the effects of their actions on the victims, were brutally inhumane from the outset. And, in systematically degrading and constraining the victims of Nazi policies, in destroying their physical and psychological capacity for resistance or escape, Hitler's facilitators also—whether willingly or unwillingly—ultimately helped pave the way for genocide.

It is impossible to convey the full magnitude of the events and the multitude of experiences of those living through these times. We can only gain glimpses, collate fragments, and try to develop some sense of the enormity of what went on in this antechamber of Auschwitz. Anyone confronting and seeking to understand this past must be only too well aware of the inadequacies of any historical account.

Yet some general conclusions can be drawn about the wider significance of the case of Będzin. It can help to explain how the Holocaust was made possible by the actions of so many, yet actually intended by so few; and how some people could later claim that they had 'always been against it' with varying degrees of honesty, while their behaviour at the time had in fact propelled the dynamism of Nazism on to the murderous conclusion that was Auschwitz and all that this stands for.

Notes

CHAPTER 1. LEGACIES OF VIOLENCE

1. Reminiscences of the band by a former student of Fürstenberg school, Arno Lustiger (born Będzin, 1924), interview, Frankfurt, 8 May 2008.
2. Irena G. (born 1928), interview, Będzin, 9 Aug. 2008.
3. See, e.g., Michael Roth, *Herrenmenschen: Die deutschen Kreishauptleute im besetzten Polen—Karrierewege, Herrschaftspraxis und Nachgeschichte* (Göttingen: Wallstein Verlag, 2009).
4. The German plural of *Landrat* (roughly pronounced 'Lant-rraaht') is *Landräte* (roughly pronounced 'Lant-rrayter'). I have retained the German terms and spellings throughout; there is not a good or obvious English equivalent, and to try to anglicize the plural as 'Landrats' would sound too much like a reference to rodents leaving a sinking ship.
5. On the wider area including Auschwitz, see the excellent study by Sybille Steinbacher, *'Musterstadt' Auschwitz: Germanisierungspolitik und Judenmord in Ostoberschlesien* (Munich: K. G. Saur, 2000).
6. For an overview of the unfolding 'final solution of the Jewish question', as the Nazis euphemistically termed it, see particularly Saul Friedländer, *Nazi Germany and the Jews*, ii. *The Years of Extermination* (London: HarperCollins, 2007).
7. Chełmno is, in German, Culm or Kulmhof. The Polish name Łódź is pronounced, roughly, 'woodsch' or 'wootsh'; in German, it was known as Litzmannstadt.
8. Bundesarchiv Ludwigsburg, Zentrale Stelle der Landesjustizverwaltungen zur Aufklärung nationalsozialistischer Verbrechen (henceforth ZSt, BArch), B 162/7720, Pawel Wiederman, 'Plowa Bestia' [The Blond Beast] (Munich, 1948), here fo. 14. On France, see, e.g., Friedländer, *Nazi Germany and the Jews*; and Julian Jackson, *France: The Dark Years, 1940–1944* (Oxford: Oxford University Press, 2001).
9. See, e.g., the debates surrounding Jan Gross's study of *Neighbors: The Destruction of the Jewish Community in Jedwabne, Poland, 1941* (Princeton: Princeton University Press, 2001).
10. On the notion of 'working towards the Führer', see particularly Ian Kershaw, '"Working towards the Führer": Reflections on the Nature of the Hitler Dictatorship', *Contemporary European History*, 2/2 (1993), 103–18.

11. Figures summarized in Steinbacher, *'Musterstadt' Auschwitz*, 116–18. Czeladź is roughly pronounced 'chay-latsh' or 'chay-ladge'. Dąbrowa is roughly pronounced (and sometimes spelled) as Dombrowa, with the 'ą' pronounced as 'om' and the 'w' having a 'v' sound in English.
12. Udo Klausa, 'Rasse und Wehrrecht' in Falk Ruttke and Erich Ristow (eds), *Recht und Rechtswahrer: Beiträge zum Rassegedanken*, ii (Stuttgart und Berlin: W. Kohlhammer Verlag, 1936).
13. See, e.g., the repeated, vociferous critique by Lothar Gothe, as summarized in his article (which contains a few factual inaccuracies with respect to Klausa's career) on 'Der Landschaftsverband Rheinland und seine psychiatrischen Anstalten: Eine dunkle Vergangenheit', *Sozialistische Zeiting* (July 2011) <http://www.sozonline.de/2011/06/der-landschaftsverband-rheinland-und-seine-psychiatrischen-anstalten> (accessed 2 July 2011).
14. Archiv des Landschaftsverband Rheinland (henceforth LVR), Dr Wolfgang Werner, 'Vorwort: Zur Person', *Nachlass Klausa* (Findbuch), p. iv, for some time available on the Internet as Wolfgang Franz Werner, Portal Rheinische Geschichte, 'Udo Klausa (1910–1998), Direktor des Landschaftsverbandes Rheinland' <http://www.rheinische-geschichte.lvr.de/persoenlichkeiten/K/Seiten/UdoKlausa.aspx>. Following critiques (including discussions in which I was involved), this version of Klausa's life was removed from the website in Aug. 2011, pending further research. A cached version may now be accessed at <http://webcache.googleusercontent.com/search?q=cache:9ptoDCOAzrUJ:www.rheinische-geschichte.lvr.de/persoenlichkeiten/K/Seiten/UdoKlausa.aspx+udo+klausa+lvr&cd=1&hl=de&ct=clnk&gl=de> (accessed 7 Sept. 2011). A short summary of Klausa's post-war achievements is posted at <http://www.kommern.de/app/Presse_quick/Archiv.asp?NNr=6484> (accessed 7 Sept. 2011).
15. LVR, Klausa 400, Udo Klausa, 'Erlebt—Davongekommen. Erinnerungen', vol. i. 'Erlebt—Überlebt, 1910–1948' (1980).
16. There is by now a large literature on these areas, which cannot be cited in full here; but see, e.g., Harold Welzer, Sabine Moller, and Karoline Tschuggnall, *'Opa war kein Nazi': Nationalsozialismus und Holocaust im Familiengedächtnis* (Frankfurt am Main: Fischer Taschenbuch Verlag, 2002).
17. Ekkehard Klausa, '"Deine gehorsame Tochter Alexandra"—"Deine kesse Alex". Teil I: Auszüge aus Briefen von Alexandra von Schweinitz-Klausa an ihre Mutter und ihre Freundin 1927–1947, Teil II: aus Briefen von 1950–1967', private family archive.
18. Letter from Alexandra to her mother, 12 Aug. 1942, private family archive. This letter has also been reproduced, under a pseudonym, with an amended figure of 1,500 and an inaccurate date of May rather than Aug. 1942, in Ute Benz (ed.), *Frauen im Nationalsozialismus: Dokumente und Zeugnisse* (Munich: Beck, 1993), 225. These errors reproduce errors in the way the letter was initially typed up in the family compilation; the date and figure are quite clear in the handwritten original in the private family archive. See further Chapter 10.

CHAPTER 2. BĘDZIN BEFORE 1939

1. The aunt who survived Auschwitz now lives in England, but was unwilling to be interviewed because her memories remain too painful and she avoids talking about this period of her life as far as possible. Her niece, tending the bar in Będzin, could not have been more helpful in talking to us about the town's past and facilitating contacts with neighbours, on the several occasions I visited with members of my family and an interpreter, Marta Szymska.
2. The name of the Henckel von Donnersmarck family has become well known through the film *The Lives of Others*, about the GDR and its State Security Service, or Stasi, made by the West German film-maker Florian Henckel von Donnersmarck.
3. T. Hunt Tooley, *National Identity and Weimar Germany: Upper Silesia and the Eastern Border, 1918–1922* (Lincoln, NB: University of Nebraska Press, 1997). See also Sybille Steinbacher, *'Musterstadt' Auschwitz: Germanisierungspolitik und Judenmord in Ostoberschlesien* (Munich: K. G. Saur, 2000), ch. 1. Estimates of population numbers in Będzin after the German invasion vary because the Jewish population fluctuated, being periodically swollen by Jews ousted from their homes elsewhere and repeatedly decimated by removals for forced labour.
4. Steinbacher, *'Musterstadt' Auschwitz*, 121.
5. For a brief sketch of the pre-war social structure, see Avihu Ronen, 'The Jews of Będzin', in Kersten Brandt, Hanno Loewy, and Krystyna Olesky, *Before They Perished: Photographs found in Auschwitz* (Oświęcim: Auschwitz–Birkenau State Museum, 2001), 16–27.
6. Brandt, Loewy, and Olesky, *Before They Perished*; see also Ann Weiss, *The Last Album. Eyes from the Ashes of Auschwitz–Birkenau* (2nd edn; Philadelphia: Jewish Publication Society, 2005). There are some discrepancies in the accounts of how the photographs may have survived.
7. Again, the spellings vary. I have generally spelled these and comparable words without a gap after the 'Ha' except in quotations or names where the usage is different.
8. Arno Lustiger, *Sing mit Schmerz und Zorn: Ein Leben für den Widerstand* (Berlin: Aufbau Verlag, 2004), 14.
9. Emanual Wajnblum, *My Destiny* (Melbourne: published by E. Wajnblum and Swinburne University Design Centre 1998), 19–20.
10. Yad Vashem, VT-1924, Leah Melnik (born 1908), interviewed by Miriam Avezer, 10 June 1998, pp. 14–15.
11. See, generally, François Guesnet, *Polnische Juden im 19. Jahrhundert: Lebensbedingungen, Rechtsnormen und Organisation im Wandel* (Cologne: Böhlau, 1998).
12. On Cyrele Schein, see Arnold Shay, *From Bendzin to Auschwitz: A Journey to Hell* (Hanover, MA: Christopher Publishing House, 1996).
13. Yad Vashem, VT-1924, Leah Melnik, p. 15.
14. Ibid. 7.
15. Ibid. 16.
16. Minka Pradelski, *Und da kam Frau Kugelmann* (Munich: btb-Verlag, 2007).

17. David Kane, USC VHA, Interview Code 7942. Born Będzin, 29 July 1928; interviewed Long Beach, FL, USA, by Robert Clary, 25 Oct. 1995.
18. Zofie Kosobowicz-Rydel, interview, Będzin, 14 Feb. 2009.
19. Yad Vashem, VT-1924, Leah Melnik, p. 45.
20. Ibid. 5.
21. Ibid. 15.
22. Marion Landau, USC VHA, Interview Code 28646. Born Będzin, 28 Jan. 1918; interviewed Raleigh, NC, USA, by Stephen di Rienzo, 20 Apr. 1997.
23. Ibid.
24. David Kane, USC VHA, interview.
25. Ibid.
26. Marion Landau, USC VHA, interview.
27. Ibid.
28. Josef Baumgarten, USC VHA, Interview Code 10509. Born Będzin, 7 July 1925; interviewed San Diego, CA, USA, by John Kent, 22 Dec. 1995.
29. Yetta Kleiner, USC VHA, Interview Code 288. Born Będzin, 5 Mar. 1928; interviewed Toronto, Ontario, Canada, by Anita Jacobson, 28 Nov. 1994.
30. Elias Burstyn, USC VHA, Interview Code 6969. Born Będzin, 14 Sept. 1921; interviewed Arcadia, CA, USA, by Dana Schwartz, 20 Sept. 1995.
31. Josef Baumgarten, USC VHA, interview.
32. Elias Burstyn, USC VHA, interview.
33. David Kane, USC VHA, interview.
34. Yetta Kleiner, USC VHA, interview.
35. Morris Danziger, USC VHA, Interview Code 11570. Born Będzin, 19 May 1915; interviewed Cedarhurst, NY, USA, by Marian Weisberg, 29 Jan. 1996.
36. Samuel Bradin, USC VHA, Interview Code 20726. Born Dąbrowa Górnicza, 1 May 1929; interviewed Suffern, NY, USA, by Martha Frazer, 8 Oct. 1996.
37. Jacques Ribons (né Jakub Rybsztajn), USC VHA, Interview Code 3718. Born Strzemieszyce, 15 Aug. 1927; interviewed West Hills, CA, USA, by Masha Loen, 5 July 1995.
38. Mania Richman, USC VHA, Interview Code 730. Born Chrzanów (a town near Katowice, mistakenly identified as Kraków on the VHA site), 12 June 1922; interviewed New York, by Kathy Strichlic, 25 Jan. 1995.
39. Rosa Rechnic, USC VHA, Interview Code 2566. Born Będzin, 15 Jan. 1926; interviewed Hallandale, FL, USA, by Gard Norberg, 12 May 1995.
40. Ibid.
41. Karoline Chajkiewicz, interview, 10 Aug. 2008.
42. Henryk Smogór, interview, Będzin, 14 Feb. 2009.
43. *Rutka's Notebook, January–April 1943* (Jerusalem: Yad Vashem, 2007), 9–11.
44. See further Chapter 12.
45. Milla Tenenbaum (née Mindzia Schickman, born in Chorzów; lived first in Dąbrowa then Będzin), USC VHA, Interview Code 33627. Born Chorzów, 28 Sept. 1932; interviewed Toronto, Ontario, Canada, by Fran Starr, 16 Sept. 1997.

46. Ibid.
47. Wajnblum, *My Destiny*, 21.
48. Yad Vashem, VT-1924, Leha Melnik, pp. 15–16.
49. Ibid.

CHAPTER 3. BORDER CROSSINGS

1. See, e.g., Marion Kaplan, *Between Dignity and Despair: Jewish Life in Nazi Germany* (Oxford: Oxford University Press, 1998).
2. In a controversial article, Ekkehard Klausa has in fact developed the notion of 'antisemitism lite' to describe this kind of racism, which arguably fell short of the more virulent forms that might have sought to justify policies of extermination; see Ekkehard Klausa, 'Ganz normale Deutsche: Das Judenbild des konservativen Widerstandes', in Johannes Tuchel (ed.), *Der vergessene Widerstand: Zu Realgeschichte und Wahrnehmung des Kampfes gegen die NS-Diktatur* (Dachauer Symposien zur Zeitgeschichte, 5; Göttingen: Wallstein Verlag, 2005), 183–207.
3. Emanual Wajnblum, *My Destiny* (Melbourne: E. Wajnblum and Swinburne University Design Centre, 1998), 32.
4. See the description of the German troops entry in Adam Dziurok, 'Zwischen den Ethnien: Die Oberschlesier in den Jahren 1939–1941', in Klaus-Michael Mallmann and Bogdan Musial (eds), *Genesis des Genozids: Polen 1939–1941* (Darmstadt: Wissenschaftliche Buchgesellschaft, 2004), 221–33, at p. 222.
5. For illuminating illustrations of German anti-Polish feelings in this area, see the 1930s account (under a pseudonym) of Edgar Polonius, *Ost-Oberschlesien als Polens Kolonie: Ein Appell an die Kulturvölker* (Breslau: Wahlstatt Verlag, 1933); and, worryingly echoing the overtones of the contemporary German sources used, the account written half a century later by Frank Keitsch, *Das Schicksal der deutschen Volksgruppe in Ostoberschlesien in den Jahren 1922–1939* (Dülmen: Laumann-Verlag, 1982).
6. See the Diagram III.II.I 'Call-up of Age-groups 1883–1929 for Active Military Service', in Militärgeschichtliches Forschungsamt (ed.), *Germany and the Second World War* (Oxford: Clarendon Press, 2000; orig. German 1998), v, pt 1, 831.
7. Militärgeschichtliches Forschungsamt (ed.), *Germany and the Second World War*, v, pt 1, 830–45.
8. The 'Wanted Persons Lists' collated in a *Sonderfahndungsbuch*, issued to *Einsatzgruppen* as part of the so-called Operation Tannenberg. See also Alexander Rossino, 'Nazi Anti-Jewish Policy during the Polish Campaign: The Case of the Einsatzgruppe von Woyrsch', *German Studies Review*, 24/1 (Feb. 2001), 35–53, at pp. 37–8.
9. Bundesarchiv Berlin (BArch), R/58/7001, Tagesbericht für die Zeit vom 8.9, 20:00 Uhr, bis 9.9, 8:00 Uhr, Bl. 26.
10. Boder archive, Udel Stopnitsky, interview, 12 Sept. 1946, spool 122.

11. Rosa Rechnic, USC VHA, Interview Code 2566. Born Będzin, 15 Jan. 1926; interviewed Hallandale, FL, USA, by Gard Norberg, 12 May 1995.
12. Wiener Library, 068-WL-1631, M. Lichtenstein, 'Eighteen Months in the Oswiecim Extermination Camp', Jewish Survivors' Report, Documents of Nazi Guilt, no. 1, p. 1. Lichtenstein's testimony was carefully checked for authenticity at the time. Lichtenstein was born in Będzin in 1912, had attended the Jewish grammar school (*Gymnasium*), and was a well-educated person, speaking Yiddish, German, Polish, Russian, and Hebrew.
13. M. Gilbert, *The Holocaust* (London: Collins, 1986), 87.
14. Wajnblum, *My Destiny*, 34.
15. Ibid. 35–6.
16. Morris Danziger, USC VHA, Interview Code 11570. Born Będzin, 19 May 1915; interviewed Cedarhurst, NY, USA, by Marian Weisberg, 29 Jan. 1996.
17. Sam Goldofsky (original given name Chaim Schlomo), USC VHA, Interview Code 29363. Born Będzin, 28 Jan. 1928; interviewed Fort Lee, NJ, USA, by Miriam Horowitz, 29 May 1997.
18. Josef Baumgarten, USC VHA, Interview Code 10509. Born Będzin, 7 July 1925; interviewed San Diego, CA, USA, by John Kent, 22 Dec. 1995.
19. Abraham Froch (né Frochcwag), USC VHA, Interview Code 92. Born Będzin, 20 Feb. 1927; interviewed Calabasas, CA, USA, by Merle Goldberg, 8 Sept. 1994.
20. Irene Gdesz, interview, 9 Aug. 2008; and Karoline Chajkiewicz and Regina Kuligowska, interviews, Będzin, 10 Aug. 2008.
21. Henryk Smogór, interview, Będzin, 14 Feb. 2009.
22. Ibid.
23. Rosa Rechnic, USC VHA, interview.
24. Karoline Chajkiewicz and Regina Kuligowska, interviews, 10 Aug. 2008.
25. Arno Lustiger, interview, Frankfurt, 8 May 2008; also Zofie Kosobowicz-Rydel, interview, Będzin, 14 Feb. 2009.
26. ZSt, BArch, B 162/7725, fo. 21, Himmler to von Woyrsch, 3 Sept. 1939; also quoted in Helmut Krausnick and Hans-Heinrich Wilhelm (eds), *Die Truppe des Weltanschauungskrieges: Die Einsatzgruppen der Sicherheitspolizei und des SD 1938–1942* (Stuttgart: Deutsche Verlags-Anstalt, 1981), 51; and Nuremberg Documents NOKW-1006.
27. I am very grateful to Robert Gerwarth for this information, based on his research in Heydrich's personal papers; personal communication, Trinity College Dublin, 26 Feb. 2009.
28. See also Klaus-Michael Mallmann, Jochen Böhler, and Jürgen Matthäus, *Einsatzgruppen in Polen: Darstellung und Dokumentation* (Darmstadt: Wissenschaftliche Buchgesellschaft, 2008).
29. BArch, R/58/7001, Einsatzgruppe z.b.V., Bl. 42.
30. Mieczysław Zawadzki, quoted in Arno Lustiger, 'Die Stadt Będzin', unpublished typescript. I am very grateful to Arno Lustiger for making a copy of this available to me.

31. BArch, R/58/7001, Tagesbericht für die Zeit vom 8.9, 20:00 Uhr, bis 9.9, 8:00 Uhr, Bl. 26, and Tagesbericht für die Zeit vom 9.9.1939, 20:00 Uhr, bis 10.9, 8:00 Uhr, Bl. 31.
32. ZSt, BArch, B 162/7718, 'The Jewish Agency for Palestine. Political Department. Records of War Criminals. Instigators and Perpetrators of Crimes against Jews', p. 60.
33. Ibid. 60.
34. ZSt, BArch, B 162/7725.
35. Rossino interprets the *Einsatzgruppen* attacks in this light, suggesting they did not prefigure later genocidal murders but rather were in a line of continuity with the violence perpetrated by the SD and SS since the measures taken to expel Polish Jews from the Reich in Oct. 1938; see Rossino, 'Nazi Anti-Jewish Policy during the Polish Campaign'.
36. See Jochanan Ranz, *In Nazi Claws: Bendzin 1939–1944* (New York: no publisher, 1956). (I have on occasion corrected a few idiosyncratic spellings and what I assume to be typographical errors in selected passages from Ranz's book.)
37. Rosa Rechnic, USC VHA, interview.
38. Arno Lustiger, interview, Frankfurt, 8 May 2008.
39. For detailed accounts of the experiences of Lustiger's family, see Arno Lustiger, *Sing mit Schmerz und Zorn: Ein Leben für den Widerstand* (Berlin: Aufbau Verlag, 2004); and Basil Kerski and Joanna Skibińska (eds), *Ein jüdisches Leben im Zeitalter der Extreme: Gespräche mit Arno Lustiger* (Osnabrück: fibre Verlag, 2004).
40. LVR, Klausa 400, 'Erlebt', 142.
41. See further John Horne and Alan Kramer, *German Atrocities: A History of Denial* (New Haven and London: Yale University Press, 2001); and Alan Kramer, *Dynamic of Destruction: Culture and Mass Killing in the First World War* (Oxford: Oxford University Press, 2007).
42. For further discussion and more detailed references, see Mary Fulbrook, *Dissonant Lives: Generations and Violence through the German Dictatorships* (Oxford: Oxford University Press, 2011), ch. 5.
43. Rossino, 'Nazi Anti-Jewish Policy during the Polish Campaign', 42–3.
44. BArch, R/58/7001, EK II, 14.9.39, 8:00 Uhr, Bl. 69.
45. See Krausnick and Wilhelm (eds), *Truppe des Weltanschauungskrieges*, 54–5.
46. As one scholar has put it: 'The proliferation of officially sanctioned violence and the simultaneous relaxation of legal constraints presented the opportunity for German troops to act summarily against Poland's civilian population and as a result reprisals soon gave way to atrocities' (Alexander Rossino, *Hitler Strikes Poland: Blitzkrieg, Ideology and Atrocity* (Kansas: University Press of Kansas, 2003), 143). See also Isabel Hull, *Absolute Destruction: Military Culture and the Practices of War in Imperial Germany* (Ithaca, NY, and London: Cornell University Press, 2005).
47. Wolfram Wette, *Die Wehrmacht: Feindbilder, Vernichtungskrieg, Legenden* (Frankfurt am Main: S. Fischer Verlag, 2002), 105.

48. Archivum Państwowe w Katowicach, Starosta Powiatu Będzinskiego, 771/91, fo. 1: covering letter from the Chef der Zivilverwaltung Kattowitz, 27 Sept. 1939, with fos 2–3: 'Verordnung. Betr. Errichtung einer besonderen Polizeiverordnung für das ostoberschlesische Industriegebiet.'
49. For purposes of simplicity, from now on 'Poles' and 'Jews' will be used to refer to 'gentile' Poles, and Polish Jews, respectively.
50. Archivum Państwowe w Katowicach, Starosta Powiatu Będzinskiego, 771/91, 'Verordnung über die Errichtung staatlicher Polizeiverwaltungen in Kattowitz u. Sosnowitz. vom 6. März 1940', fos 12–13.
51. Archivum Państwowe w Katowicach, Ältestenrat der jüdischen Kultusgemeinde in Dombrowa O/S, 1600/3, fo. 1, Der Leiter der Aeltestenräte der jüdischen Kultusgemeinden in Ost-Oberschl., Bulletin Nr. 1. Sosnowitz, den 15 Sept. 1940.
52. In the memoirs of contemporaries, usage varies, with the phrases Jewish Community and Jewish Cultural Community also often being used interchangeably, if somewhat inaccurately, with Jewish Council.
53. This sketch is based on Philip Friedman, 'The Messianic Complex of a Nazi Collaborator in a Ghetto: Moses Merin of Sosnowiec', in Ada June Friedman (ed.), *Roads to Extinction: Essays on the Holocaust*, intro. by Salo Wittmayer Baron (n.p.: Jewish Publication Society of America and Conference on Jewish Social Studies, 1980; first published in Hebrew in 1953), ch. 13, pp. 353–64.
54. Wajnblum, *My Destiny*, 44.

CHAPTER 4. THE MAKING OF A NAZI *LANDRAT*

1. Ian Kershaw, '"Working towards the Führer": Reflections on the Nature of the Hitler Dictatorship', *Contemporary European History*, 2/2 (1993), 103–18.
2. For the area of the General Government, see now Michael Roth, *Herrenmenschen: Die deutschen Kreishauptleute im besetzten Polen—Karrierewege, Herrschaftspraxis und Nachgeschichte* (Göttingen: Wallstein Verlag, 2009). See also Wolfgang Stelbrink, *Der preußische Landrat im Nationalsozialismus: Studien zur nationalsozialistischen Personal- und Verwaltungspolitik auf Landkreisebene* (Münster: C. H. Beck, 1998); and, for an earlier period of history, Lysbeth W. Muncy, 'The Prussian *Landräte* in the Last Years of the Monarchy: A Case Study of Pomerania and the Rhineland in 1890–1918', *Central European History*, 6 (1973), 299–338.
3. See, e.g., Catherine Epstein, *Model Nazi: Arthur Greiser and the Occupation of Western Poland* (Oxford: Oxford University Press, 2010).
4. See, e.g., Christopher Browning, *Ordinary Men: Reserve Police Battalion 101 and the Final Solution in Poland* (New York: HarperCollins, 1992).
5. There is a large literature on these issues, too great to be surveyed in a note. For further discussion, see Mary Fulbrook, *Dissonant Lives: Generations and Violence through the German Dictatorships* (Oxford: Oxford University Press, 2011).

6. Kerstin Freudiger, *Die juristische Aufarbeitung von NS-Verbrechen* (Tübingen: J. C. B. Mohr (Paul Siebeck), 2002), 417, discusses the 'subjective theory' in terms of which the bourgeois 'functional elites', in particular, tended to be exonerated, since they were assumed to have remained 'decent' as far as their inner views were concerned, even while performing their official roles.
7. LVR, Klausa 400, Udo Klausa, 'Erlebt—Davongekommen. Erinnerungen', vol. i. 'Erlebt—Überlebt, 1910–1948' (1980), 74.
8. Ibid.
9. Ibid.
10. See BArch 1050088525, letter from Udo Klausa (No. 1,9411,466) to 'Reichsschatzmeister der NSDAP München', Berlin, 31 Jan. 1935, for details of his *NSDAP* application.
11. LVR, Klausa 400, 'Erlebt', 74.
12. Ibid. 75 ff.
13. See BArch SA/4000002271 for details of Klausa's membership of the SA, in which organization he held the rank of *Obersturmführer* (First Lieutenant); and BArch ZA VI 265.A.14 for evidence of his application to join the SA in Dec. 1932, having already been heavily engaged in paramilitary activities in the Silesian–Polish borderlands since 1925; for his own account, see LVR, Klausa 400, 'Erlebt', 78 ff.
14. LVR, Klausa 400, 'Erlebt', 80.
15. LVR, Klausa, 402, Udo Klausa, 'Wann wird der Hass überwunden?—Gespräch zwischen Siegern und Besiegten', July 1945, pp. 8, 10–11.
16. Ibid. 9, 8.
17. Sebastian Haffner, *Geschichte eines Deutschen: Die Erinnerungen 1914–1933* (Munich: Deutscher Taschenbuch Verlag, 2002), translated into English under the title *Defying Hitler: A Memoir.*
18. See more generally for this notion Michael Wildt, *Generation des Unbedingten: Das Führungskorps des Reichssicherheitshauptamtes* (Hamburg: Hamburger Edition, 2002), and Fulbrook, *Dissonant Lives.*
19. Walther Hubatsch (ed.), *Grundriß der deutchen Verwaltungsgeschichte 1815–1945*, iv. *Schlesien*, compiled by Dieter Stüttgen, Hemut Neubach, and Walther Hubatsch (Marburg (Lahn): Johann-Gottfried-Herder-Institut, 1976), details for Dr Walter Klausa as *Landrat* of Leobschütz (pp. 221–4) and Groß-Strehlitz (pp. 251–4), as well as photographs 94 and 95.
20. For both Schulenburg hagiography and more realistic accounts, see, e.g., Ulrich Heinemann, *Ein konservativer Rebell: Fritz-Dietlof Graf von der Schulenburg und der 20. Juli* (Berlin: Siedler Verlag, 1990); Albert Krebs, *Fritz-Dietlof Graf von der Schulenburg: Zwischen Staatsraison und Hochverrat* (Hamburg: Leibniz Verlag, 1964); Sybille Steinbacher, *'Musterstadt' Auschwitz: Germanisierungspolitik und Judenmord in Ostoberschlesien* (Munich: K. G. Saur, 2000), 107 ff.
21. LVR, Klausa 400, 'Erlebt', 168, 192–3, 221–4,
22. Udo Klausa, 'Rasse und Wehrrecht'.

23. Ekkehard Klausa, personal communication, 6 Nov. 2011.
24. Ekkehard Klausa, personal communication, 6 Nov. 2011; see also LVR, Klausa 387, Ekkehard Klausa, 'Zur Entstehungsgeschichte von Papas Schrift "Rasse und Wehrrecht": Die dritte Dimension', 1991.
25. Udo Klausa, 'Rasse und Wehrrecht', 15.
26. Ibid. 25.
27. LVR, Klausa 387, 'Eidesstattlicher Unbedenklichkeitsschein (sog. "Persilschein") für Udo Klausa von Graf Baudissin'; Ekkehard Klausa, personal communication, 6 Nov. 2011.
28. BArch ZA VI 265.A.14, Reich Interior Ministry, Berlin, 3 Oct. 1939.
29. BArch ZA VI 265.A.14, Akten betr. den Regierungs-Referendar Udo Klausa, letter, 25 Oct. 1939.
30. On Greiser, see further Epstein, *Model Nazi*.
31. On 'uncrowned king' and 'father', see, e.g., Stelbrink, *Der preußische Landrat*, 1.
32. *Reichskunde für junge Deutsche* (Darmstadt: Winklers Verlag, Gebrüder Grimm, 1943), 93.
33. See further Michael Alberti, *Die Verfolgung und Vernichtung der Juden im Reichsgau Wartheland, 1939–1945* (Wiesbaden: Harrassowitz Verlag, 2006), 65; Isabel Heinemann, *'Rasse, Siedlung, deutsches Blut': Die Rasse- und Siedlungshauptamt der SS und die rassenpolitische Neuordnung Europas* (Göttingen: Wallstein Verlag, 2003), 187–303; Epstein, *Model Nazi*. Epstein translates *Landrat* as 'sub-district magistrate'; at least for a UK-based English speaker, this has all the wrong connotations, since these county chief executives were not 'magistrates' in the legal sense in which the term is used in the UK.
34. See Martin Broszat, *Nationalsozialistische Polenpolitik 1939–1945* (Stuttgart: Deutsche Verlags-Anstalt, 1961), 51–2; Diemut Majer, *'Non-Germans' under the Third Reich: The Nazi Judicial and Administrative System in Germany and Occupied Eastern Europe, with Special Regard to Occupied Poland, 1939–1945*, trans. Peter Thomas Hill, Edward Vance Humphrey, and Brian Levin (Baltimore and London: Johns Hopkins University Press, in association with the Washington Holocaust Memorial Museum, 2003), esp. 199–200, 215.
35. Letter from Alexandra to Frau von H., Posen, 14 Dec. 1939, private family archive.
36. Ibid.
37. BArch ZA VI 265.A.14, reference by August Jäger, 31 July 1940.
38. Letter from Alexandra to Frau von H., Kladno, Bohemia, 20 Sept. 1939, private family archive.
39. Letter from Alexandra to Frau von H., Gersdorf, 21 Oct. 1939, private family archive.
40. Letter from Alexandra to Frau von H., Posen, 25 Nov. 1939, private family archive.
41. Alberti, *Die Verfolgung und Vernichtung*, 58. For the general context of policies in the Wartheland at this time, see Epstein, *Model Nazi*.

42. See Epstein, *Model Nazi*.
43. LVR, Klausa 400, 'Erlebt', 139–40, 144.
44. Ibid. 143.
45. BArch R 70 Polen/198, fo. 2.
46. Ibid., fo. 3.
47. Ibid., fo. 5.
48. Ibid. Later parts of this file include reports from the *Landräte* on developments in their areas of responsibility.
49. Archivum Państwowe w Katowicach, 117/826, Oberpräsident Kattowitz, fo. 195.
50. Archivum Państwowe w Katowicach, 117/826, Oberpräsident Kattowitz, letter from Reich Minister of the Interior Wilhelm Frick to senior regional officials, 8 Dec. 1939, fos 226–7.
51. Ibid.
52. Ibid.
53. BArch ZA VI 265.A.14, Akten betr. den Regierungs-Referendar Udo Klausa, letter, 25 Oct. 1939. Ekkehard Klausa suggests that his father would have done anything to get away from the political conditions in the Warthegau at this time, and that personal reasons alone would not have been sufficient to have driven him to request any kind of alternative employment in this way. Ekkehard Klausa, personal communication, 6 Nov. 2011.
54. BArch ZA VI 265.A.14, Akten betr. den Regierungs-Referendar Udo Klausa, Vom 16. Oktober 1933 bis—, note of 7 Nov. 1939.
55. LVR, Klausa 400, 'Erlebt', 141.
56. BArch R 1501/133703, Akten betr: Das Landratsamt des Kreises Bendzin ['zin' then crossed out and 'sburg' written over it] vom Dez. 1939 bis Okt. 1944, Reich Interior Ministry, Nr/II c 605/39, letter, Berlin, 15 Dec. 1939, headed 'SOFORT! (Noch heute!)' [*Immediately!* (Today!)].
57. BArch R 1501/133703, letter from Regional President, Kattowitz, to Reich Interior Ministry, 9 Jan. 1940 (Berlin NW40, Königsplatz 6), p. 2.
58. BArch R 1501/133703, letter from Kattowitz, 29 Jan. 1940.
59. BArch R 1501/133703, letter from Liegnitz, 17 Apr. 1940, pp. 1–2.
60. BArch ZA VI 265.A.14, note from Fründt, 13 Feb. 1940.
61. Ibid.
62. BArch ZA VI 265.A.14, letter from Pfundtner to Gauleiter Wagner, Breslau, 20 Feb. 1940.
63. BArch ZA VI 265.A.14, note, 15 Feb. 1940.
64. BArch ZA VI 265.A.14, letter from Fründt, 11 Mar. 1940.
65. BArch ZA VI 265.A.14, note from Regional President, Kattowitz, 1 Apr. 1940.
66. On lower-level functionaries in the General Government, see, e.g., Roth, *Herrenmenschen*.
67. Alexander Hohenstein (pseudonym), *Wartheländisches Tagebuch 1941/42* (Munich: dtv, 1963), 17. The name Hohenstein was a pseudonym used when the diary was published by the Institute for Contemporary History in Munich.

68. Letter from Alexandra to Frau von H., Berlin, 16 Mar. 1940, private family archive.
69. Letter from Alexandra to Frau von H., Repten, 6 Nov. 1940, private family archive. Ekkehard Klausa interprets this remark as further evidence of relatively early disquiet about the position. Personal communication, 6 Nov. 2011.
70. LVR, Klausa, Bd 130, 'Vorfahrenliste' collated by Udo Klausa, pp. 3–5.
71. Among the many mines of the Myslowitz area was the Fürstenburg mine, which eventually became a subsidiary labour camp of Auschwitz. In this particular mine one of my mother's closest childhood friends, with whom as a teenager she had avidly discussed Thomas Mann's novels while on walks through Berlin's Tiergarten Park, died some three months after his deportation to Auschwitz and selection for slave labour. The contrast in the emotional connotations of the 'same' landscape can be striking.
72. LVR, Klausa 400, 'Erlebt', 147.
73. Ibid. 164.
74. Ibid. 145.
75. Ibid. 143.
76. See further pp. 259–64.
77. LVR, Klausa 400, 'Erlebt', 147.
78. Ibid. 145.
79. Ibid. 145.
80. Ibid. 149.
81. Steinbacher, *'Musterstadt' Auschwitz*, 108. The only exception to this overlap of personnel in the newly annexed territories was in Danzig–West Prussia.
82. See the evaluation based on detailed investigation of his role during this period in this area in ibid., 107. See also Ulrich Heinemann, *Ein konservativer Rebell: Fritz-Dietlof Graf von der Schulenburg und der 20. Juli* (Berlin: Siedler Verlag, 1990), 54–65. Heinemann notes (p. 274, n. 100) that the self-serving memoirs of former Nazi civil servants were collected in the BArch Koblenz by one Dr Hans Hopf, who was himself a former functionary and director of the *Abteilung 'Deutsches Volkstum' of the Abteilung Bevölkerungswesen und Fürsorge* in Warsaw from 1940: thus both the memoir-writers and the archivist who collected the memoirs had a strong interest in distancing both themselves and von der Schulenburg from Nazism; this collection amounts to 'one giant whitewashing facility', according to one source. For an earlier, more sympathetic, if not actually hagiographic reading, see Albert Krebs, *Fritz-Dietlof Graf von der Schulenburg: Zwischen Staatsraison und Hochverrat* (Hamburg: Leibniz Verlag, 1964).
83. LVR, Klausa 400, 'Erlebt', 144.
84. Hannes Heer and Klaus Naumann (eds), *Vernichtungskrieg: Verbrechen der Wehrmacht 1941–1944* (Hamburg: Hamburger Edition, 1995); Hannes Heer, *Vom Verschwinden der Täter: Der Vernichtungskrieg fand statt, aber keiner war dabei* (Berlin: Aufbau Taschenbuch Verlag, 2004).
85. LVR, Klausa 400, 'Erlebt', 143.

86. Ibid.
87. ZSt, BArch, B 162/7718, fo. 138.
88. LVR, Klausa 400, 'Erlebt', 151.
89. Cf. J. Noakes and G. Pridham, *Nazism*, ii (Exeter: Exeter Studies in History, 1995).
90. Archivum Państwowe w Katowicach, Regional Government, Kattowitz, 119/703, fos 17–18. Only the *Landrat* of Gleiwitz, long a part of the long-standing state of Prussia, was an 'old hand': the *Landrat* of Gleiwitz, Erich Heidtmann, had been born in 1880 and had served in the First World War. All of the other ten *Landräte* in the area were members of the 'war youth generation', born in the decade 1900–10. Klausa, born in 1910, was the youngest of these, but not by very much; the *Landrat* of Krenau had been born in 1908, the *Landrat* of Saybusch in 1906, the *Landrat* of Pless in 1903, the *Landrat* of Ilkenau in 1902, the others all in 1900. All but one of them had children; with the exception of Heidtmann, whose children were by then young adults, the vast majority of the total of thirty-six children were aged between 2 months and 10 years; only three were already teenagers.
91. Letters from Alexandra to my mother, 19 Sept. 1935 and 13 Nov. 1935, private family archive. My mother's letters to Alexandra have not been preserved, but the likely tone of her response is evident from Alexandra's conciliatory and apologetic reply.
92. An alleged mentality of 'exterminatory anti-Semitism' is central to the controversial thesis of Daniel Jonah Goldhagen, *Hitler's Willing Executioners* (New York: Knopf, 1996).

CHAPTER 5. AN EARLY QUESTION OF VIOLENCE

1. Kerstin Freudiger, *Die juristische Aufarbeitung von NS-Verbrechen* (Tübingen: J. C. B. Mohr (Paul Siebeck), 2002), 33.
2. For an early attempt to engage with the question of guilt from a philosophical perspective, see Karl Jaspers, 'Die Schuldfrage', originally delivered as lectures in 1945 and first published in 1946, repr. in Karl Jaspers, *Die Schuldfrage. Für Völkermord gibt es keine Verjährung* (Munich: Piper, 1979).
3. There are very many examples of this kind of dropping of friendships. See Mary Fulbrook, *Dissonant Lives: Generations and Violence through the German Dictatorships* (Oxford: Oxford University Press, 2011), ch. 4.
4. See esp. Bernhard Schlink, *Guilt about the Past* (London: Beautiful Books, 2010).
5. ZSt, BArch, B 162/19654, report of a meeting with Edward Stauber, Hanover, 12 July 1961, fo. 202.
6. LVR, Klausa 400, Udo Klausa, 'Erlebt—Davongekommen. Erinnerungen', vol. i. 'Erlebt—Überlebt, 1910–1948' (1980), 142.
7. On which see further, e.g., Chapters 6 and 7.

8. Archivum Państwowe w Katowicach, Polizeipräsident Sosnowitz, 807/331, Lagebericht Sosnowitz, 9 June 1940, fo. 153.
9. Ibid.
10. Ibid., fos 153–4.
11. Geheimes Staatsarchiv Preussischer Kulturbesitz (henceforth GStAPK), HA XVII Rep. 201e. Ost 4 Reg. Kattowitz Nr. 14, Politische Lageberichte sowie Kurzberichte über die bisherige Aufbauarbeit der Landräte, Bd 1 Landrat des Kreises Bendzin/Bendsburg, 1939–Sept. 1942; *Landrat*'s Report of 31 Mar. 1940, p. 4.
12. Ibid., p. 2.
13. Ibid., pp. 2–3.
14. For similar careers alternating between periods as 'desk perpetrators' and military action, see Michael Wildt, *Generation des Unbedingten: Das Führungskorps des Reichssicherheitshauptamtes* (Hamburg: Hamburger Edition, 2002); see also, for a larger sample with similar patterns, Michael Mann, 'Were the Perpetrators of Genocide "Ordinary Men" or "Real Nazis"? Results from Fifteen Hundred Biographies', *Holocaust and Genocide Studies*, 14/3 (2000), 329–66.
15. Letter from Alexandra to her mother, 18 June 1940, private family archive.
16. BArch ZA VI 265.A.14, Reich Interior Ministry, 19 June 1940.
17. Letter from Alexandra to her mother, 11 July 1940, private family archive.
18. Letters from Alexandra to her mother, 23 and 24 July 1940, private family archive; LVR, Klausa 400, 'Erlebt', 165 ff.
19. A letter from Regional Government, Kattowitz, to Berlin dated 22 Oct. 1940 confirms that Klausa picked up his responsibility for the administration of the county of Bendzin 'on the 14th of this month' (BArch ZA VI 265.A.14).
20. Letter from Alexandra to her mother, 17 July 1940, private family archive.
21. ZSt, BArch, B 162/7721, p. 20.
22. Ibid. 21–2.
23. Ibid., testimony of Ignacy Widera, fo. 21.
24. Ibid., testimony of Antoni Morawiec, fo. 26.
25. Ibid., testimony of Ignacy Widera, fo. 22.
26. Józef G., interview, Celiny, 10 Aug. 2008.
27. Antonine, Kazimierz, and Zbigniew K., interviews, Sączow, 10 Aug. 2008.
28. Wacław Widera (Ignacy Widera's son), interview, 15 Feb. 2009; he was a young boy, 8 or 9 years of age, at the time of the killings, but at the time of the interview still vividly remembered the stir that the incident caused in this little community.
29. Wacław Widera, interview, 15 Feb. 2009.
30. Kazimierz and Zbigniew K., interviews, Celiny, 10 Aug. 2008.
31. ZSt, BArch, B 162/2196; ZSt, BArch, B 162/7723, Klausa's statement, Staatsanwaltschaft Dortmund, 16 Dec. 1975, pp. 210–13.
32. LVR, Klausa 400, 'Erlebt', 144.
33. Cf., e.g., letter from Alexandra to her mother, Repten, 7 June 1940, private family archive.

34. Letter from Alexandra to her mother, Repten, 12 June 1940, private family archive.
35. Archivum Państwowe w Katowicach, Regional Government, Kattowitz, 119-6335, Kattowitz, 18 Dec. 1940, fo. 94; BArch ZA VI 265.A.14, Reich Interior Ministry, 19 June 1940.
36. BArch ZA VI 265.A.14, letter from the Reich Interior Ministry, 19 June 1940, announcing: 'Der mit der Verwaltung des Kreises Bendzin im Regierungsbezirk Kattowitz beauftragte Regierungsrat Dr Klausa wird für den Wehrdienst freigegeben.' Letter from Springorum, Regional President, Kattowitz, to the Reich Interior Ministry, 9 Mar. 1942, 'Betrifft: Endgültige Ernennung des Landrats Udo Klausa in Bendsburg', confirming: 'Regierungsrat Udo Klausa ist seit dem 21. März 1940 mit der Verwaltung des Landratsamtes in Bendsburg beauftragt und hat diese Tätigkeit am 1. Juli 1940 unterbrochen, um Wehrdienst zu leisten.'
37. ZSt, BArch, B 162/2196, deposition, 17 Mar. 1969.
38. Information about the telephone line given by Wacław Widera, who had lived in this house before it was taken over for use as the Tapkowice gendarmerie headquarters. Wacław Widera, interview, Tapkowice, 15 Feb. 2009.
39. Ekkehard Klausa is of the view that, had his father in fact been contacted for authorization, there would have been a file note to this effect (personal communication, 6 Nov. 2011). Unfortunately, however, the relevant report on the incident, written the following day and referred to in the regular end-of-month *Landrat*'s report, is missing from the files; this question therefore cannot be answered on the basis of contemporary evidence (see further below, n. 40).
40. GStAPK, HA XVII Rep. 201e. Ost 4 Reg. Kattowitz Nr. 14, Politische Lageberichte sowie Kurzberichte über die bisherige Aufbauarbeit der Landräte, Bd 1 Landrat des Kreises Bendzin/Bendsburg, 1939–Sept. 1942; *Landrat*'s Report, 27 June 1940, p. 2. This report was signed by Klausa's deputy, Asssessor Rahn, although Klausa was formally in charge of the *Landkreis* from 21 June to 1 July. The report of 7 June, to which he refers, is unfortunately not to be found in the file.
41. Kazimierz K., interview, 10 Aug. 2008.
42. Sylwina D. and Zofia N., interviews, 15 Feb. 2009.
43. Archivum Państwowe w Katowicach, 807/336, Morgenmeldungen, 6 June 1940, fo. 10.
44. Boder archive, testimony of Jacob Schwarzfitter, 'Voices of the Holocaust' <http://voices.iit.edu/> (accessed 18 May 2010).
45. ZSt, BArch, B 162/7724, testimony of Josef Lipa, fos 116–18, at fo. 118.
46. Boder archive, testimony of Jacob Schwarzfitter.
47. ZSt, BArch, B 162/7724, testimony of Henryk Otuch, fos 114–15.
48. Ibid., fo. 115.
49. ZSt, BArch, B 162/7723, p. 190, Benjamin Weizmann interview.
50. Ibid. 197.

51. ZSt, BArch, B 162/7724, testimony of Piotr Kluczewski, fo. 108.
52. See further, e.g., Martin A. Conway, *Autobiographical Memory: An Introduction* (Milton Keynes: Open University Press, 1990), 101.
53. ZSt, BArch, B 162/19653, testimony of Samuel Kucharski, 7 May 1960, fo. 158.
54. LVR, Klausa 400, 'Erlebt', 7–36, for a general depiction of the atmosphere in which he grew up.
55. Letter from Alexandra to her mother, 28 Aug. 1940, private family archive.
56. Ibid.
57. Letter from Alexandra to Frau von H., Repten, 29 Aug. 1940, private family archive.
58. LVR, Klausa 400, 'Erlebt', 143.
59. Confirmed in discussion with Arno Lustiger, 8 May 2008, whose father served alongside her on the Będzin City Council. On her philanthropic activities, see further Arnold Shay, *From Bendzin to Auschwitz: A Journey to Hell* (Hanover, MA: Christopher Publishing House, 1996), 49–51. A sketch of Cyrele Schein by Abram Liwer may be found in Hebrew in *Pinkes Bendin: A Memorial to the Jewish Community of Bendin (Poland)* (1959), available in English as 'Cyrele (Cesia) Szajn—The Mother of the Orphans', trans. Ricky Benhart (née Schikman) <http://www.jewishgen.org/Yizkor/bedzin/bed169.html#Page172> (accessed 27 Feb. 2008).
60. Ibid.
61. Yad Vashem database <http://www.yadvashem.org/> (accessed 19 Apr. 2009).
62. Letter from Alexandra to her mother, 28 Oct. 1940, private family archive.
63. Letter from Alexandra to her mother, 31 Mar. 1941, private family archive.
64. LVR, Klausa 400, 'Erlebt', 143.
65. Letter from Alexandra to her mother, 12 Apr. 1941, private family archive.
66. Letter from Alexandra to her mother, 17 Apr. 1941, private family archive.
67. Klausa mentions rather vaguely in his memoirs that parts of the area he was to take over had 'already belonged to Prussia' in 1795–1807; whether this is intended as some form of justification for invasion, reconquest, and attempted 'Germanization' of this area a century and a half later is unclear. LVR, Klausa 400, 'Erlebt', 141.
68. Ekkehard Klausa points out that such evidence could hardly be expected to exist in the archival records of Klausa's administration.

CHAPTER 6. 'ONLY ADMINISTRATION'

1. LVR, Klausa 400, Udo Klausa, 'Erlebt—Davongekommen. Erinnerungen', vol. i. 'Erlebt—Überlebt, 1910–1948' (1980), 151.
2. See Götz Aly and Susanne Heim, *Architects of Annihilation: Auschwitz and the Logic of Destruction*, trans. A. G. Bunden (London: Weidenfeld and Nicolson, 2002; orig. German 1991).

3. ZSt, BArch, B 162/19653, testimony of Nadzia Kochen (née Czarnes), Munich, 11 Jan. 1961, fo. 120; testimony of Paul Feder, Munich, 25 Jan. 1961, fo. 125(b).
4. This contrasts markedly with the proliferation of *Stolpersteine*, literally 'stumbling stones', on the streets of Berlin, commemorating former Jewish inhabitants who were deported and murdered.
5. See Gordon J. Horwitz, *Ghettostadt: Łódź and the Making of a Nazi City* (Cambridge, MA: Harvard University Press, 2008); Catherine Epstein, *Model Nazi: Arthur Greiser and the Occupation of Western Poland* (Oxford: Oxford University Press, 2010).
6. See in detail Sybille Steinbacher, *'Musterstadt' Auschwitz: Germanisierungspolitik und Judenmord in Ostoberschlesien* (Munich: K. G. Saur, 2000), 116–18; see also ZSt, BArch, B 162/1608, Abschrift von Mgr Matan Eliasz Szternfinkiel, Kattowitz, 1946, pp. 2–3.
7. Archivum Państwowe w Katowicach, Ältestenrat der jüdischen Kultusgemeinde in Dombrowa O/S, 1600/3, Bulletin Nr. 1. Sosnowitz den 15 Sept. 1940, fo. 1.
8. LVR, Klausa 400, 'Erlebt', 141.
9. Ibid. 142.
10. GStAPK, HA XVII Rep. 201e. Ost 4 Reg. Kattowitz Nr. 13, Lageberichte in politischer und polizeilicher Hinsicht sowie über die wirtschaftliche Lage seitens der Oberbürgermeister der Städte Beuthen, Gleiwitz, Hindenburg, Kattowitz, Königshütte und Sosnowitz 1940–42, Der Oberbürgermeister der Stadt Kattowitz, 1.Okt. 1940, fo. 41.
11. *Kattowitzer Zeitung*, 286, 16 Oct. 1940 (BArch Zeitungsarchiv Ztg 2215 MR).
12. See Steinbacher, *'Musterstadt' Auschwitz*, 268–71.
13. For Arlt's later attempt at legitimating his own views and former activities, see Fritz Arlt, *Polen-, Ukrainer-, Juden-Politik im Generalgouvernement für die besetzten polnischen Gebiete 1939 bis 1940. In Oberschlesien 1941 bis 1943 und im Freiheitskampf der unterdrückten Ostvölker. Dokumente, Äußerungen von Polen, Ukrainern und Juden; Richtigstellungen von Fälschungen, Erinnerungen eines INSIDERS* (Lindhorst: Wissenschaftlicher Buchdienst Herbert Taege, 1995). This self-defensive account was written partly in response to criticism of his role in Aly and Heim, *Architects of Annihilation*.
14. *Kattowitzer Zeitung*, 274/72, Fri., 4 Oct. 1940 (BArch Zeitungsarchiv Ztg 2215 MR).
15. Ibid.
16. Ibid.
17. *Kattowitzer Zeitung*, 283, Sun., 13 Oct. 1940 (BArch Zeitungsarchiv Ztg 2215 MR).
18. *Kattowitzer Zeitung*, 287, 17 Oct. 1940 (BArch Zeitungsarchiv Ztg 2215 MR).
19. *Kattowitzer Zeitung*, 290, 20 Oct. 1940 (BArch Zeitungsarchiv Ztg 2215 MR).
20. *Kattowitzer Zeitung*, 335, 4 Dec. 1940 (BArch Zeitungsarchiv Ztg 2215 MR).
21. LVR, Klausa 400, 'Erlebt', 144.

22. See, e.g., LVR, Klausa 308, vol. ii, 'Bescheinigung' of Mgr Albert Büttner, Kirchliche Hilfstelle, Frankfurt/Main Süd, 4 July 1946.
23. Archivum Państwowe w Katowicach, Starosta Powiatu Będzinskiego, 771/69, circular of 14 Apr. 1942 to the Bürgermeister and Amtskommissare, signed by Klausa, fo. 10.
24. LVR, Klausa 400, 'Erlebt', 143. See also Chapter 4.
25. LVR, Klausa 400, 'Erlebt', 143.
26. For the official responsibilities of the *Landrat* in close cooperation with the police forces, see in detail the documents reprinted in Wybór Żródeł, *Położenie Ludności w Rejenci Katowickiej w Latach 1939–1945. Documenta Occupationis Teutonicae XI* (Poznań: Instytut Zachodni, 1983), sect. II, 'Aussiedlung der polnischen und Ansiedlung der deutschen Bevölkerung'.
27. See LVR, Klausa 308, vol. ii, affidavits by Pfarrer Josef Pawelle (?—partially illegible signature), Gedächtnisprotokoll, 11 Feb. 1974, and Mgr Albert Büttner, Kirchliche Hilfsstelle Frankfurt/Main Süd, 'Bescheinigung', 4 July 1946. On the possibilities of church worship, and the support provided officially by the regional government, see, e.g., the documents reprinted in Żródeł, *Położenie Ludności w Rejenci*, 14–16, 17–19, where the major policy concern appears to have been whether religious instruction and practice could be held in the Polish language rather than German, given the wider context and desire to excise particularly the local dialect of 'water-Polish' (*Wasserpolnisch*) among the local population as part of 'Germanization' measures.
28. LVR, Klausa 400, 'Erlebt', 151.
29. See the recent work of Dan Michman, *The Emergence of the Jewish Ghettos during the Holocaust* (Yad Vashem and Cambridge: Cambridge University Press, 2011). This book was published only after I had completed this typescript, but the argument is entirely in accord with my interpretation here, and provides a broader and long-term context for these remarks.
30. See further Chapters 8 and 11.
31. Archivum Państwowe w Katowicach, 771/111, Der Landrat des Kreises Bendsburg: Juden, Vorschriften, Korrespondenz, Polizeiliche Verordnungen betr. Juden, From the Landrat to the 'Herren Amtskommissare der Gemeinden, die nicht zum Bezirk des Herrn Polizeipräsidenten in Sosnowitz gehören Bendzin', 25 May 1940, fo. 6. The *Landrat*'s areas of police responsibility are here listed as: Bobrowniki, Grodziec, Lagischa, Losien, Wojkowice-Koscielne, Sonczow, and Strzemieschütz (including Golonog, Zombkowice, and Strzemieszyce-Male).
32. Archivum Państwowe w Katowicach, Polizeipräsident Sosnowitz, 807/331, fo. 161.
33. Ibid., fo. 147.
34. Ibid., Lagebericht of 24 June 1940, fo. 167.
35. Ibid., fo. 168.

36. Archivum Państwowe w Katowicach, 771/111, fo. 7.
37. Archivum Państwowe w Katowicach, Polizeipräsident Sosnowitz, 807/331, fo. 150
38. Archivum Państwowe w Katowicach 771/111, Kattowitz Rundschreiben Nr. 10, 'Ausschaltung der Juden aus dem öffentlichen Verkehr', 14 Dec. 1940, fos 41 ff.
39. Archivum Państwowe w Katowicach 771/111, Rundschreiben Nr. 11, Kattowitz, 30 Jan. 1941, fo. 49.
40. David Apfelbaum, USC VHA, Interview 47699. Born Olkusz, 25 Feb. 1920; interviewed Melbourne, Australia, by Max Wald, 27 Oct. 1998.
41. ZSt, BArch, B 162/19659, testimony of Hirsch Barenblatt, fo. 6.
42. Ibid.
43. GStAPK, HA XVII Rep. 201e. Ost 4 Reg. Kattowitz Nr. 13, Lageberichte in politischer und polizeilicher Hinsicht sowie über die wirtschaftliche Lage seitens der Oberbürgermeister der Städte Beuthen, Gleiwitz, Hindenburg, Kattowitz, Königshütte und Sosnowitz 1940–42, Der Oberbürgermeister der Stadt Sosnowitz, 1 Oct. 1940, fos 102–9.
44. GStAPK, HA XVII Rep. 201e. Ost 4 Reg. Kattowitz Nr. 14, Politische Lageberichte sowie Kurzberichte über die bisherige Aufbauarbeit der Landräte, Bd. 1 Landrat des Kreises Bendzin/Bendsburg, 1939–Sept. 1942, report of 29 Nov. 1940 signed by Klausa, pp. 6–7. Ekkehard Klausa has pointed out that it could be hardly expected that his father would express any humanitarian considerations in the kinds of bureaucratic documents to be found in the archives, and that in this system it was only possible to argue against Nazi measures on 'pragmatic' grounds (personal communication, 6 Nov. 2011). However, proposing to go ahead with ghettoization in the two locations where this would be relatively simple, and to proceed in a more piecemeal fashion by ousting Jews from their homes on the better streets in areas where complete relocation was less practicable, hardly seems to me to qualify as an example of arguing 'against' Nazi racial measures of expropriation and resettlement; rather, it is a matter of seeking how best to effect these policies in practice, in the light of local conditions and related considerations.
45. Archivum Państwowe w Katowicach, Regional Government, Kattowitz, 119/2785, letter from von Woedtke to Springorum, 14 Dec. 1940, fo. 2.
46. Archivum Państwowe w Katowicach, 771/111, Der Landrat des Kreises Bendsburg: Juden, Vorschriften, Korrespondenz, 'Betrifft: Gesonderte Unterbringung der jüdischen Bevölkerung in den Städten Sosnowitz, Bendzin, Dombrowa und Czeladz', fo. 51.
47. Ibid., fos 51–2.
48. Ibid., fo. 54.
49. Letter from Alexandra to Frau von H., 6 Nov. 1940, private family archive.
50. Ekkehard Klausa, 'Streiflichter aus dem Landratsamt', drawing on documents from the Katowice archive. I am very grateful to Ekkehard Klausa for allowing me to read his unpublished typescript.
51. Letter from Alexandra to Frau von H., 4 Feb. 1941, private family archive.

52. Archivum Państwowe w Katowicach, Regional Government, Kattowitz, 119/2785, Vermerk of 7 Mar. 1941, Regional President, fos 8, 9.
53. Ibid., letter from the Aeltestenrat, 14 Mar. 1941, fos 10–11.
54. For the experiences of SS families living around Auschwitz, see Gudrun Schwarz, *Eine Frau an seiner Seite: Ehefrauen in der 'SS-Sippengemeinschaft'* (Hamburg: Hamburger Edition, 1997), 115 ff.
55. GStAPK, HA XVII Rep. 201e. Ost 4 Reg. Kattowitz Nr. 15, 'Landrat. Vertraulich! An den Herrn Regierungspräsidenten in Kattowitz. Betr.: Lagebericht. Bezug: Verfügung vom 5.3.1941–I Pol.489/39-Mitberichterstatter: Regierunsgassessor Schultz, Dated Bielitz, 10 Apr. 1941', pp. 1–2. See also Sybille Steinbacher, *Auschwitz: A History* (London: Penguin, 2005; orig. German 2004), 63.
56. Jakob Rosenbaum, USC VHA, Interview Code 26400. Born Oświęcim, 17 July 1925; interviewed Palm Desert, CA, USA, by Michelle Citron, 18 Feb. 1997.
57. Quoted in Steinbacher, *'Musterstadt' Auschwitz*, 268.
58. Archivum Państwowe w Katowicach, Regional Government, Kattowitz, 119/2785, letter from the Aeltestenrat, 4 June 1941, fo. 16.
59. Ibid., fos 16–17,
60. Alexander Hohenstein (pseudonym), *Wartheländisches Tagebuch 1941/42* (Munich: dtv, 1963), entry of 18 Jan. 1941, pp. 60–71.
61. Available for viewing at <http://www.youtube.com/watch?v=ZI–exb-0GqI> (accessed 20 Jan. 2011).
62. Archivum Państwowe w Katowicach, Regional Government, Kattowitz, 119/2785, fos 18–19.
63. Ibid., fo. 19.
64. Ibid., fo. 20.
65. There are mentions and descriptions of these ghettos in a variety of secondary works, particularly in connection with Merin's role. The major work supported by the United States Holocaust Memorial Museum, Geoffrey P. Megargee and Martin Dean (eds), *Encyclopedia of Camps and Ghettos, 1933–1945: Ghettos in German-Occupied Eastern Europe*, intro. by Christopher R. Browning, ii (Bloomington: Indiana University Press, 2012), had not appeared at the time of my writing. See also Gustavo Corni, *Hitler's Ghettos: Voices from a Beleaguered Society* (London: Hodder, 2002).
66. Yetta Kleiner, USC VHA, Interview Code 288. Born Będzin, 5 Mar. 1928; interviewed Toronto, Canada, by Anita Jacobson, 28 Nov. 1994.
67. Rosa Rechnic, USC VHA, Interview Code 2566. Born Będzin, 15 Jan. 1926; interviewed Hallandale, FL, USA, by Gard Norberg, 12 May 1995.
68. Marion Landau, USC VHA, Interview Code 28646. Born Będzin, 28 Jan. 1918; interviewed Raleigh, NC, USA, by Stephen di Rienzo, 20 Apr. 1997.
69. Ibid.
70. Helen Balsam, USC VHA Interview Code 9105. Born Będzin, 16 Dec. 1927; interviewed Riverdale, GA, USA, by Martha Frazer, 21 Nov. 1995.

71. Milla Tenenbaum (née Mindzia Schickman, born in Chorzów; lived first in Dąbrowa then Będzin), USC VHA, Interview Code 33627. Born Chorzów, 28 Sept. 1932; interviewed Toronto, Ontario, Canada, by Fran Starr, 16 Sept. 1997. When talking of her memories of childhood I refer to her by her maiden name rather than her adult name (unlike in the cases of other survivors), since her account is so strongly imbued with the experiences and perceptions of childhood.
72. Ibid.
73. Helen Balsam, USC VHA interview.
74. David Apfelbaum, USC VHA interview.
75. Marion Landau, USC VHA, interview.

CHAPTER 7. MEANS OF SURVIVAL

1. See, e.g., the anonymized excerpts of letters published in Ute Benz (ed.), *Frauen im Nationalsozialismus: Dokumente und Zeugnisse* (Munich: Beck, 1993).
2. David Apfelbaum, USC VHA, Interview Code 47699. Born Olkusz, 25 Feb. 1920; interviewed Melbourne, Australia, by Max Wald, 27 Oct. 1998.
3. Boder archive, Abraham Kimmelmann interview <http://voices.iit.edu/index.html> (accessed 25 Apr. 2008).
4. Wiener Library, 068-WL-1631, M. Lichtenstein, 'Eighteen Months in the Oswiecim Extermination Camp', Jewish Survivors' Report, Documents of Nazi Guilt, no. 1, pp. 1–2.
5. Boder archive, Abraham Kimmelmann interview.
6. Boder archive, Abraham Kimmelmann interview.
7. Archivum Państwowe w Katowicach, Polizeipräsident Sosnowitz, 807/331, Lagebericht of 24 June 1940, fo. 168.
8. GStAPK, HA XVII Rep. 201e. Ost 4 Reg. Kattowitz Nr. 14, Politische Lageberichte sowie Kurzberichte über die bisherige Aufbauarbeit der Landräte, Bd. 1 Landrat des Kreises Bendzin/Bendsburg, 1939–Sept. 1942, Report of 1 März 1940 signed by Grotjan, p. 5.
9. Ibid.
10. Ibid. 6.
11. Ibid., 'III. Wirtschaftliche Lage', p. 5.
12. Archivum Państwowe w Katowicach, Polizeipräsident Sosnowitz, 807/330, 1. Polizeirevier, Lagebericht of 8 Oct. 1940, fo. 8.
13. Ibid.
14. Archivum Państwowe w Katowicach, Polizeipräsident Sosnowitz, 807/330, 'Entwurf' of a Lagebericht from Sosnowitz, Schutzpolizei- Abschnittskommando V, S.Ak.V(So) 1a 6280, 11 Oct. 1940, fo. 27.
15. Archivum Państwowe w Katowicach, Polizeipräsident Sosnowitz, 807/330, Bendzin, 8 Oct. 1940, fos 21–3.
16. Archivum Państwowe w Katowicach, Polizeipräsident Sosnowitz, 807/330, Sosnowitz, 42. Polizeirevier, Lagebericht of 8 Oct. 1940, fo. 10.

17. Henrietta Altmann, USC VHA, Interview Code 5639. Born Bedzin, 1 Mar. 1922; interviewed Armidale, VIC, Australia, by Brenda Brain, 1 Nov. 1995.
18. Ibid.
19. Archival film of the ghettos in Dąbrowa Górnicza and Będzin <http:// www. youtube.com/watch?v=Z1-exb-0GqI> (accessed 7 July 2011).
20. Arno Lustiger, *Sing mit Schmerz und Zorn: Ein Leben für den Widerstand* (Berlin: Aufbau Verlag, 2004), 18; see also Sybille Steinbacher, *'Musterstadt' Auschwitz: Germanisierungspolitik und Judenmord in Ostoberschlesien* (Munich: K. G. Saur, 2000); and an English-language summary in Steinbacher, 'In the Shadow of Auschwitz: The Murder of the Jews of East Upper Silesia', in David Cesarani (ed.), *Holocaust: Critical Concepts in Historical Studies* (London: Routledge, 2004), 110–36.
21. Wolf Gruner, *Jewish Forced Labour under the Nazis. Economic Needs and Racial Aims, 1938–1944*, trans. Kathleen M. Dell'orto (Cambridge: Cambridge University Press, 2006), 229.
22. Archivum Państwowe w Katowicach, Regional Government, Kattowitz, 119/2783, letter from Springorum, Regional President, Kattowitz, 21 Nov. 1940, fo. 1.
23. Ibid., fo. 2.
24. Ibid.
25. Henrietta Altmann, USC VHA, interview.
26. GStAPK, HA XVII Rep. 201e. Ost 4 Reg. Kattowitz Nr. 14, Politische Lageberichte sowie Kurzberichte über die bisherige Aufbauarbeit der Landräte, Bd. 1 Landrat des Kreises Bendzin/Bendsburg, 1939–Sept. 1942, report of 29 Nov. 1940, p. 6.
27. Ibid. 6–7.
28. LVR, Klausa 400, 'Erlebt', 159.
29. Jerzy Frąckiewicz, 'Das Nebenlager Lagischa', *Hefte von Auschwitz*, 9 (1966), 109–19.
30. Ann Kirschner, *Sala's Gift: My Mother's Holocaust Story* (New York: Free Press, 2006), 13.
31. Ibid. 35.
32. Ibid. 37.
33. Ibid. 40–1.
34. Ibid. 43.
35. Ibid. 53.
36. Morris Danziger, USC VHA, Interview Code 11570. Born Będzin, 19 May 1915; interviewed Cedarhurst, NY, USA, by Marian Weisberg, 29 Jan. 1996.
37. For the range and variety of labour relations, wages, and 'rental' of Jewish labour, see Gruner, *Jewish Forced Labour under the Nazis* , ch. 8, 'The SS Organisation Schmelt and the Jews from Eastern Upper Silesia, 1940–1944', pp. 214–29; and Stephan Lehnstaedt, 'Coercion and Incentive: Jewish Ghetto Labor in East

Upper Silesia', *Holocaust and Genocide Studies*, 24/3 (Winter 2010), 400–30. There are legal complications relating to the categorization of forced labour at this time in relation to the question of compensation.

38. Archivum Państwowe w Katowicach, 771/111, Juden, from Gendarmerie-Posten I Golonog, Gend.-kreis Bendsburg, Reg.-Bez. Kattowitz, to the *Landrat* in Bendsburg, dated Golonog, 18 Apr. 1942, fos 18–19.
39. Archivum Żydowskiego Instytutu Historycznego (ŻIH), Warsaw, 301/942, testimony of Boruch Wadowski, no date, *c.*1946. (Folio numbers for the ŻIH follow the archive file foliation, not the pagination on the pages.)
40. See further Chapter 10.
41. LVR, Klausa 400, 'Erlebt', 151.
42. Rosa Rechnic, USC VHA, Interview Code 2566. Born Będzin, 15 Jan. 1926; interviewed Hallandale, FL, USA, by Gard Norberg, 12 May 1995.
43. See, e.g., ZSt, BArch, B 162/7715, fo. 49; testimony of Hirsch Barenblatt, fo. 6.
44. Danuta Czech, *Auschwitz Chronicle 1939–1945* (London: I. B. Tauris, 1990), 50; Peter Witte et al. (eds), *Der Dienstkalender Heinrich Himmlers 1941/42* (Hamburg: Hans Christians Verlag, im Auftrag der Forschungsstelle für Zeitgeschichte in Hamburg, 1999), 123, entry of Sat., 1 Mar. 1941, 'Besichtigung KL Auschwitz'.
45. Elias Burstyn, USC VHA, Interview Code 6969. Born Będzin, 14 Sept. 1921; interviewed Arcadia, CA, USA, by Dana Schwartz, 20 Sept. 1995.
46. Abraham Froch (né Frochcwag), USC VHA, Interview Code 92. Born Będzin, 20 Feb. 1927; interviewed Calabasas, CA, USA, by Merle Goldberg, 8 Sept. 1994.
47. Rosa Rechnic, USC VHA, interview.
48. Archivum Państwowe w Katowicach, Polizeipräsident Sosnowitz, 807/337, fos 45, 53, 55, 61, 65.
49. Ibid., fo. 96.
50. Ibid., fos 120, 128, 129, 132, 137, 139.
51. Archivum Państwowe w Katowicach, 807/316, Polizeipräsident Sosnowitz, fo. 26.
52. Ibid., fo. 28.
53. Ibid., fo. 44.
54. See, e.g., Z. Wojciechowski, K. M. Pospieszalsi, and K. Sosnowski (eds), *Documenta Occupationis Teutonicae*, i–iii (Poznań: Wydawnictwo Instytutu Zachodniego, 1945), 37–205.
55. See, e.g., the ration cards in ŻIH, Warsaw, 212/13, Vorstand der Jüdischen Interessenvertretung in Bendsburg 1939–43, e.g. fo. 86.
56. Archivum Państwowe w Katowicach, Polizeipräsident Sosnowitz, 807/330, 44. Polizeirevier, Czeladz, 8.10. 40, fo. 17.
57. Boder archive, Abraham Kimmelmann interview.
58. Helen Balsam, USC VHA Interview Code 9105. Born Będzin, 16 Dec. 1927; interviewed Riverdale, GA, USA, by Martha Frazer, 21 Nov. 1995.

59. Henrietta Altmann, USC VHA, interview.
60. Samuel Bradin, USC VHA, Interview Code 20726. Born Dąbrowa Górnicza, 1 May 1929; interviewed Suffern, NY, USA, by Martha Frazer, 8 Oct. 1996.
61. Gunter Faerber, USC VHA, Interview Code 41847. Born Lipiny, Swietochlowice, 25 Aug. 1928; interviewed Birmingham, UK, by Corinne Oppenheimer, 7 May 1998.
62. Ibid.
63. Helen Balsam, USC VHA interview.
64. Wiener Library, 068-WL-1631, Lichtenstein, 'Eighteen Months', pp. 1–2.
65. Boder archive, Abraham Kimmelmann interview.
66. Archivum Państwowe w Katowicach, 807/316, Polizeipräsident Sosnowitz, Rundschreiben of 26 Feb. 1942, fo. 154. Mildner was born in Silesia in 1902, and had the typical dual-track career of members of the war youth generation: a trained jurist, also a member of the *NSDAP* and SS.
67. See, e.g., ŻIH Warsaw, 212–2, Vorstand der Jüdischen Interessenvertretung in Bendsburg 1939–1943, fos 8, 10-11.
68. ZSt, BArch, B 162/7723, fo. 63. In fact the word *Kat* means 'executioner' in Polish, and was quite probably not the real name of this man.
69. Wiener Library, 068-WL-1631, Lichtenstein, 'Eighteen Months', pp. 1–2.
70. ZSt, BArch, B 162/19656, testimony of Szalom Herzberg, Ramat Gan, 19 Nov. 1961, fo. 30.
71. ZSt, BArch, B 162/19659, testimony of Miriam Liwer, Tel Aviv, 26 Dec. 1961, fos 47–8.
72. Arno Lustiger, interview, 8 May 2008.
73. Lustiger, *Sing mit Schmerz und Zorn*, 32–3.
74. Ella Liebermann-Shiber (born Berlin 1927; died Israel 1998); see her *On the Edge of the Abyss* (Western Galilee: Ghetto Fighters House, 1992).
75. Archivum Państwowe w Katowicach, 771/142, reports on suicides sent from the Gendarmerie to the *Landrat* of Będzin, fos 28, 66–8.
76. Archivum Państwowe w Katowicach, 771/142, fo. 21.
77. Ibid., fo. 71.
78. ZSt, BArch, B 162/7724, fo. 15.
79. Ibid., letter of 1 Aug. 1989 from the Central Office, summarizing the cases (forty-seven years later), p. 3.
80. ZSt, BArch, B 162/7723, p. 94.
81. Ibid. 99.
82. Ibid. 101.
83. Ibid. 106.
84. Ibid. 115–16.
85. Ibid. 185.
86. Ibid. 123.
87. Ibid. 125.
88. Ibid. 179.

89. Ibid. 118.
90. See further pp. 204–13.
91. ZSt, BArch, B 162/7723, p. 125.
92. Ibid. 94.
93. Ibid. 126.
94. Ibid. 99.
95. Ibid. 115–16. It is possible that these two witnesses were actually related, perhaps as uncle and nephew rather than father and son, given the slight difference in the spelling of the family name and the gap between their birth dates.
96. Ibid. 197.
97. Ibid. 104.
98. See further Chapter 8.
99. *Kattowitzer Zeitung*, 252, Tues., 15 Sept. 1942 (BArch Zeitungsarchiv Ztg 2215 MR).
100. *Kattowitzer Zeitung*, 259, Tues., 22 Sept. 1942 (BArch Zeitungsarchiv Ztg 2215 MR).
101. *Kattowitzer Zeitung*, 261, Thurs., 24 Sept. 1942 (BArch Zeitungsarchiv Ztg 2215 MR).
102. *Kattowitzer Zeitung*, 266, Tues., 29 Sept. 1942 (BArch Zeitungsarchiv Ztg 2215 MR).
103. *Kattowitzer Zeitung*, 276, Fri., 9 Oct. 1942 (BArch Zeitungsarchiv Ztg 2215 MR).
104. See further Chapter 8.
105. Boder archive, Abraham Kimmelmann interview.
106. Josef Baumgarten, USC VHA, Interview Code 10509. Born Będzin, 7 July 1925; interviewed San Diego, CA, USA, by John Kent, 22 Dec. 1995.
107. Milla Tenenbaum (née Mindzia Schickman, born in Chorzów; lived first in Dąbrowa then Będzin), USC VHA, Interview Code 33627. Born Chorzów, 28 Sept. 1932; interviewed Toronto, Ontario, Canada, by Fran Starr, 16 Sept. 1997.
108. Jochanan Ranz, *In Nazi Claws: Bendzin 1939–1944* (New York: no publisher, 1956), 34–5.
109. Lea Eisenberg, USC VHA, Interview Code 47578. Born Będzin, 17 Jan. 1925; interviewed West Palm Beach, FL, USA, by Saerina Tauritz, 11 June 1998.
110. Ibid.
111. Ranz, *In Nazi Claws*, 20–8.
112. GStAPK, HA XVII Rep. 201e. Ost 4 Reg. Kattowitz Nr. 14, Politische Lageberichte sowie Kurzberichte über die bisherige Aufbauarbeit der Landräte, Bd. 1 Landrat des Kreises Bendzin/Bendsburg, 1939–Sept. 1942, report of 31 May 1940, 'III. Wirtschaftliche Lage', p. 5.
113. Lustiger, *Sing mit Schmerz und Zorn*, 19.
114. Shmuel Ron, *Die Erinnerungen haben mich nie losgelassen: Vom jüdischen Widerstand im besetzten Polen* (Frankfurt am Main: Verlag Neue Kritik, 1998), 40–1.

115. Ibid. 37 ff.
116. Siegmund Pluznik recounts his story in Arno Lustiger (ed.), *Zum Kampf auf Leben und Tod! Das Buch vom Widerstand der Juden 1933–1945* (Cologne: Kiepenheuer and Witsch, 1994), 149–54.
117. Ranz, *In Nazi Claws*.
118. Ibid. 66.
119. Lustiger (ed.), *Zum Kampf auf Leben und Tod!*, 145.
120. Samuel Bradin, USC VHA, interview.
121. Ibid.
122. Lustiger, *Sing mit Schmerz und Zorn*, 19.
123. See Isaiah Trunk, *Judenrat: The Jewish Councils in Eastern Europe under Nazi Occupation* (New York: Macmillan, 1972); and Philip Friedman, 'The Messianic Complex of a Nazi Collaborator in a Ghetto: Moses Merin of Sosnowiec', in Ada June Friedman (ed.), *Roads to Extinction: Essays on the Holocaust*, intro. by Salo Wittmayer Baron (n.p.: Jewish Publication Society of America and Conference on Jewish Social Studies, 1980; first published in Hebrew in 1953), ch. 13.
124. Kirschner, *Sala's Gift*.
125. Emanual Wajnblum, *My Destiny* (Melbourne: E. Wajnblum and Swinburne University Design Centre, 1998), 44.

CHAPTER 8. ESCALATION, 1941–1942

1. Letters from Alexandra to Frau von H., 6 Nov. 1940 and 4 Feb. 1941, private family archive. See also pp. 139–40.
2. Archivum Państwowe w Katowicach, Regional Government, Kattowitz, 119–6335, fos 94, 95.
3. BArch ZA VI 265.A.14, letter from the Regional President, Kattowitz, to the Reich Interior Ministry, 21 Jan. 1941.
4. Archivum Państwowe w Katowicach, Regional Government, Kattowitz, 119–6335, fos 102, 104. Ekkehard Klausa suggests that his father 'may have found ways' of achieving his desire to return to the army by intervening directly with either his regiment or the Military Recruitment Office (personal communication, 6 Nov. 2011). As far as I am aware, there is no contemporary evidence of any such behind-the-scenes attempt to influence military decisions, although this scenario is in principle possible.
5. BArch ZA VI 265.A.14, letter from the Regional President, Kattowitz, to the Reich Interior Ministry, 18 Feb. 1941.
6. BArch ZA VI 265.A.14, letter from the Regional President, Kattowitz, to the Wehrersatz-Inspektion, Berlin, 18 Feb. 1941.
7. Archivum Państwowe w Katowicach, Regional Government, Kattowitz, 119–6335, fo. 110.

8. BArch ZA VI 265.A.14, letter from the Reich Interior Ministry, Berlin, to the Wehrersatz-Inspektion, Berlin, 26 Feb. 1941. Udo Klausa's son, Ekkehard Klausa, believes that Udo Klausa was seen as so vital to the *Landkreis* not because of his role in anti-Jewish policies but rather because of his superior adminstrative abilities in a broader sense, including ensuring increased production of eggs and milk from Polish farms through use of incentives rather than force, devising means of feeding horses according to their workload, and his unparalleled capacity to master growing mountains of bureaucratic paperwork with ever fewer staff in the *Landrat*'s office. Ekkehard Klausa, personal communication, 21 Jan. 2012.
9. Archivum Państwowe w Katowicach, Regional Government, Kattowitz, 119–6335, fo. 108.
10. See LVR, Klausa 400, Udo Klausa, 'Erlebt—Davongekommen. Erinnerungen', vol. i. 'Erlebt—Überlebt, 1910–1948' (1980), as well as the extensive extracts from this and other accounts in Jochen Löser (ed.), *Bittere Pflicht: Kampf und Untergang der 76. Berlin-Brandenburgischen Infanterie-Divison* (Osnabrück: Biblio Verlag, 1986).
11. There is an extensive literature in this area. See, e.g.: Omer Bartov, *Hitler's Army: Soldiers, Nazis, and War in the Third Reich* (Oxford: Oxford University Press, 1991); Omer Bartov, *The Eastern Front, 1941–45: German Troops and the Barbarisation of Warfare* (2nd edn; Houndmills: Palgrave, 2001, orig. 1985); Ray Brandon and Wendy Lower (eds), *The Shoah in the Ukraine: History, Testimony, Memorialization* (Bloomington and Indianapolis: Indiana University Press, 2008); Ernst Klee, Willi Dreßen, and Volker Rieß (eds), *'Schöne Zeiten': Judenmord aus der Sicht der Täter und Gaffer* (Frankfurt: Fischer Verlag, 1988). For discussion and further references, see Mary Fulbrook, *Dissonant Lives: Generations and Violence through the German Dictatorships* (Oxford: Oxford University Press, 2011), ch. 5.
12. Cf. Father Patrick Desbois, *The Holocaust by Bullets: A Priest's Journey to Uncover the Truth behind the Murder of 1.5 Million Jews* (Houndmills: Palgrave Macmillan, 2008); Timothy Snyder, *Bloodlands: Europe between Hitler and Stalin* (New York: Basic Books, 2010).
13. Ekkehard Klausa, personal communication (in conversation, n.d., *c.* Apr. 2006). On the Wehrmacht Ausstellung, see Hannes Heer and Klaus Naumann (eds), *Vernichtungskrieg: Verbrechen der Wehrmacht 1941–1944* (Hamburg: Hamburger Edition, 1995); and Hannes Heer, *Vom Verschwinden der Täter: Der Vernichtungskrieg fand statt, aber keiner war dabei* (Berlin: Aufbau Taschenbuch Verlag, 2004).
14. Klausa's symptoms are interpreted as at least in part psychosomatic by Ute Benz (ed.), *Frauen im Nationalsozialismus: Dokumente und Zeugnisse* (Munich: Beck, 1993), 89.
15. Letter from Alexandra to Frau von H., 9 Feb. 1942, private family archive.
16. See pp. 82–6.
17. Quoted in Ekkehard Klausa, 'Bendzin—Bendsburg', unpublished typescript. See the original decision that there should be a minimum two-year probationary

period in BArch ZA VI 265.A.14, Akten betr. den Regierungs-Referendar Udo Klausa, Fründt, Abschrift Berlin, 11 Mar. 1940.

18. BArch ZA VI 265.A.14, reference by August Jäger, 31 July 1940.
19. Letters in private family archive; see, e.g., letter from Alexandra to her mother, 29 July 1942, and see further pp. 225–6.
20. Archivum Państwowe w Katowicach, 771/111, Der Landrat des Kreises Bendsburg: Juden, Vorschriften, Korrespondenz, fo. 61.
21. Ibid., fos 88–94.
22. Ibid., fos 107–8.
23. Archivum Państwowe w Katowicach, 771/111, Der Landrat des Kreises Bendsburg: Juden, Vorschriften, Korrespondenz, 'Katt 14. Okt 1941—Betrifft Kennzeichen der Juden', fos 83–4.
24. Archivum Państwowe w Katowicach, 771/111, Amtskommissar, Amtsverwaltung Sontchow, 19 Sept. 1941, fo. 119.
25. Archivum Państwowe w Katowicach, 771/111, Amtskommissar der Gemeinde Strzemieszyce, 17 Sept. 1941, fos 120–1.
26. Archivum Państwowe w Katowicach, 771/111, fo. 124.
27. Archivum Państwowe w Katowicach, 771/111, *Landrat* on 11 Nov. 1941, fo. 125.
28. Archivum Państwowe w Katowicach, 771/111, Sontschow, 17 Dec. 1941, fo. 129.
29. Wacław Widera, interview, 15 Feb. 2009.
30. Archivum Państwowe w Katowicach, 771/111, Amtskommissar of Strzemieszyce, 29 Dec. 1941, fo. 132.
31. Archivum Państwowe w Katowicach, 771/111, Grodziec, 4 Dec. 1941, fos 133–4.
32. Archivum Państwowe w Katowicach, 771/111, Zombowitz, fo. 135.
33. Archivum Państwowe w Katowicach, 771/111, Kattowitz, fo. 137.
34. Archivum Państwowe w Katowicach, 771/111, fo. 141.
35. Archivum Państwowe w Katowicach, 771/111, e.g. Heydrich, fos 150–2.
36. Archivum Państwowe w Katowicach, 771/111, fo. 141 ff.
37. Ibid., fos 156 ff., 162.
38. Archivum Państwowe w Katowicach, Regional Government, Kattowitz, 119/2780, fos 95, 96.
39. Ibid., fos 95–6.
40. Ibid., fols. 100–4, for the draft letter to Himmler; fos 142–7 for Schmelt's criticisms of von Woedtke.
41. Archivum Państwowe w Katowicach, Polizeipräsident Sosnowitz 807/317, fo. 238; see also the sketch map of the Czeladź ghetto at the back of this file, fo. 295.
42. Ibid., fo. 239.
43. Archivum Państwowe w Katowicach, Regional Government, Kattowitz, 119/2785, fos 35–6, 37–8.

44. Ibid., fo. 30.
45. Ann Kirschner, *Sala's Gift. My Mother's Holocaust Story* (New York: Free Press, 2006), 121–2.
46. Ibid. 119–20.
47. Ibid. 125.
48. Avraham Susskind's account, in Ann Weiss, *The Last Album: Eyes from the Ashes of Auschwitz–Birkenau* (2nd edn; Philadelphia: Jewish Publication Society, 2005), 172–3. He erroneously dates the hanging to 1941 rather than 1942. Although the details in his memory may have been hazy by the time he gave this account, the underlying moral of the story is beyond question.
49. Ibid. 173.
50. ZSt, BArch, B 162/7722, testimony of Eugenia Dancygier, fos 23–4.
51. ŻIH, Warsaw, 301/2721, testimony of Icek Waksman, protocol N. Szternfinkiel, Będzin, 9 Sept. 1947; 301/2730, testimony of Mojźesz Szwarc, protocol N. Szternfinkiel, Będzin, 19 Sept. 1947.
52. See pp. 171–9.
53. Archivum Państwowe w Katowicach, 807/316, Polizeipräsident Sosnowitz, fos 158 ff.
54. Ibid., fo. 169.
55. Ibid., report of 13 Apr. 1942, fo. 172.
56. Ella Liebermann-Shiber, *On the Edge of the Abyss* (Western Galilee: Ghetto Fighters House, 1992); see also pp. 171–9, although not all survivors were quite sure when the hangings they witnessed had actually taken place, so it is not always possible to link them with certainty to any particular occasion.
57. Archivum Państwowe w Katowicach, 807/316, Polizeipräsident Sosnowitz, fo. 170.
58. Samuel Reifer (born in Chrzanów, 5 Nov. 1921), testimony <http://polishjews. org/shoahtts/026one.htm> (accessed 3 May 2011).
59. Alexander Hohenstein (pseudonym), *Wartheländisches Tagebuch 1941/42*, (Munich: dtv, 1963), 214–27.
60. ZSt, BArch, B 162/7723, pp. 99, 115–16.
61. See pp. 174–6. Ekkehard Klausa takes an absence of explicit mention of his father in the police documents discussing the practicalities of the event to provide evidence that Udo Klausa was not in fact present, and does not consider the comparison with the Hohenstein case to be valid (personal communication, 6 Nov. 2011).
62. BArch ZAVI 265.A.14, letter from the Senior President (Oberpräsidenten) in Kattowitz, signed by Springorum, to the Reich Minister of the Interior, 9 Mar. 1942.
63. BArch ZAVI 265.A.14, letter from the Senior President (Oberpräsident) of the Province of Silesia, Kattowitz, to the Reich Minister of the Interior, 21 Mar. 1942.
64. BArch ZAVI 265.A.14, letter from the Reich Minister of the Interior, Berlin, 22 Apr. 1942.

65. BArch ZA VI 265.A.14, 'Vorschlag zur Ernennung des Regierungsrates Udo Klausa zum Landrat 12. Mai 1942', stamped in name of the Führer, 15 May 1942.
66. Irene G., interview, 9 Aug. 2008.

CHAPTER 9. TOWARDS EXTERMINATION

1. On the wider phenomenon of the post-war claim that 'we never knew anything about it', see, e.g., Frank Bajohr and Dieter Pohl, *Der Holocaust als offenes Geheimnis: Die Deutschen, die NS-Führung und die Alliierten* (Munich: C. H. Beck, 2006); Bernward Dörner, *Die Deutschen und der Holocaust: Was niemand wissen wollte, aber jeder wissen konnte* (Berlin: Ullstein, 2007); Peter Longerich, *'Davon haben wir michts gewusst!' Die Deutschen und die Judenverfolgung 1933–1945* (Munich: Siedler Verlag, 2006).
2. See, e.g., Archivum Państwowe w Katowicach, Polizeipräsident Sosnowitz, 807/317, Der Sonderbeauftragte des Reichsführers SS für den fremdvölkischen Arbeitseinsatz in Oberschlesien, Sosnowitz, 1 Nov. 1940, fos 8–9.
3. Wiener Library, 053-EA-0919, ref. P.III.h.No. 445 (Auschwitz), testimony of Samual Hutterer, p. 1.
4. ZSt, BArch, B 162/19659, fo. 31.
5. Alexander Hohenstein (pseudonym), *Wartheländisches Tagebuch 1941/42* (Munich: dtv, 1963), entry of 28 Dec. 1942, p. 201.
6. A Regina Faerber, presumably Gunter Faerber's grandmother, is included on a list probably originally compiled by the Gestapo in 1942, available at the United States Holocaust Memorial Museum (USHMM) and Yad Vashem, and collated by Peter Lande for JewishGen, Inc. and the Yizkor Book Project; see <http://ellisisland.jewishgen.org/Yizkor/bytom/Bytom1.html#F> (accessed 11 Mar. 2011). A major deportation of Jews from Beuthen to Auschwitz took place on 15 Feb. 1942; see Danuta Czech, *Auschwitz Chronicle 1939*–1945 (London: I. B. Tauris, 1990), 135.
7. Gunter Faerber, USC VHA, Interview Code 41847. Born Lipiny, Swietochlowice, 25 Aug. 1928; interviewed Birmingham, UK, by Corinne Oppenheimer, 7 May 1998.
8. Czech, *Auschwitz Chronicle*, 135 (and footnote correcting details from a previous edition). See also Aleksander Lasik, Franciszek Piper, Piotr Setkiewicz, and Irena Strzelecka, 'Central Issues in the History of the Camp', *Auschwitz 1940–1945*, trans. William Brand (Oświęcim: Auschwitz-Birkenau State Museum, 2000), i. 61.
9. Czech, *Auschwitz Chronicle*, 146.
10. Filip Müller, *Eyewitness Auschwitz: Three Years in the Gas Chambers* (Chicago: Ivan R. Dee, 1999), 35 ff; also described in detail in Claude Lanzmann's film *Shoah*.
11. Müller, *Eyewitness Auschwitz*, 35–9.

12. Czech, *Auschwitz Chronicle*, 165.
13. Archivum Państwowe w Katowicach, 807/316, Polizeipräsident Sosnowitz, fo. 193.
14. Peter Witte et al. (eds), *Der Dienstkalender Heinrich Himmlers 1941/42* (Hamburg: Hans Christians Verlag, im Auftrag der Forschungsstelle für Zeitgeschichte in Hamburg, 1999), on 20 Apr. in Friedrichsruh, with Arthur Greiser, on which date there is a note 'no extermination of the Gypsies' (*keine Vernichtung der Zigeuner*), p. 405; on 25 and (twice) on 26 Apr. in Berlin, pp. 410–11; on 28 Apr. and 30 Apr. in Munich, pp. 412–13; on 2 May and again twice on 4 May in Prague, pp. 415, 417–18; see also Peter Longerich, *Heinrich Himmler: Biographie* (Munich: Siedler, 2008), 582–3.
15. ZSt, BArch, B 162/1608, Auszugsweise Abschrift von Mgr Natan Eliasz Szternfinkiel, p. 3.
16. See Natan Eliasz Szternfinkiel, *Zagłada Żydów Sosnowca* [*The Extermination of the Jews of Sosnowiec*] (Katowice: Wydaw. Centralnej Żydowskiej Komisii Historycznej w Polsce, 1946), 34.
17. ZSt, BArch, B 162/7720, Pawel Wiedermann, 'Plowa Bestia' [The Blond Beast] (Munich, 1948), fo. 6.
18. Czesław Madajczyk, *Die Okkupationspolitik Nazideutschlands in Polen 1939–1945* (Berlin: Akademie Verlag, 1987; shortened version of original Polish published in Warsaw, 1970, under the title *Politika III Rzeszy w okupowanej Polsce*), 373.
19. ZSt, BArch, B 162/7720, Pawel Wiedermann, 'Plowa Bestia', fo. 6.
20. ZSt, BArch, B 162/19659, testimony of Hirsch Barenblatt, fo. 7.
21. *Time Magazine*, 22 Mar. 1963; *Jewish Telegraphic Agency, Jewish News Archive*, 12 July 1963. I am very grateful to Dan Porat for correcting my first impressions and providing me with additional details.
22. Sybille Steinbacher, *'Musterstadt' Auschwitz: Germanisierungspolitik und Judenmord in Ostoberschlesien* (Munich: K. G. Saur, 2000), asserts that *Landräte* were routinely informed about impending deportations; and in neighbouring areas we have evidence of the local gendarmerie being mobilized to assist the Gestapo, SS, and regular police forces in the operation.
23. ZSt, BArch, B 162/1608, fo. 10.
24. See, e.g., Ute Benz (ed.), *Frauen im Nationalsozialismus: Dokumente und Zeugnisse* (Munich: Beck, 1993), 179.
25. Archivum Państwowe w Katowicach, 771/19, Landrat Bendzin, Klausa, fos 1–2 and telegram.
26. Letter from Alexandra to her mother, 28 June 1942, private family archive.
27. Letter from Alexandra to her mother, 2 July 1942, private family archive.
28. Letter from Alexandra to her mother, 29 July 1942, private family archive.
29. In his memoirs, Klausa first relates a story indicating his opposition to the 'euthanasia' programme, and then introduces his account of the August deportation as follows: 'The worst experience, however, that occasioned my immediate departure for the front . . .' (LVR, Klausa 400, Udo Klausa,

'Erlebt—Davongekommen. Erinnerungen', vol. i. 'Erlebt—Überlebt, 1910–1948' (1980), 162). There is no mention either in his memoirs or in any of his Ludwigsburg statements of any knowledge of earlier deportations.

30. ZSt, BArch, B 162/7723, testimony of Chaim Michal Silberberg, fo. 179.
31. ZSt, BArch, B 162/19659, testimony of Miriam Liwer, Tel Aviv, 26 Dec. 1961, fo. 43.
32. Arbeitsgruppe der ehemaligen Häftlinge des Konzentrationslagers Auschwitz beim Komitee der Antifaschistischen Widerstandskämpfer in der Deutschen Demokratischen Republik (eds), *Dokumentation zum Auschwitzprozeß I. G Farben Auschwitz. Massenmord über die Blutschuld der I. G.Farben* (n.d., *c.*1964), Document 28, letter written and signed by Dürrfeld of the Leuna Werke, 26 May 1942, 'Betrifft: Abgrenzung des Einflußgebietes der SS gegen Stadt' and also 'Gestellung von Häftlingen', p. 42.
33. See Longerich, *Heinrich Himmler*, 591–2.
34. Walter Laqueur and Richard Breitman, *Breaking the Silence: The Secret Mission of Eduard Schulte, Who Brought the World News of the Final Solution* (London: Bodley Head, 1986).
35. LVR, Klausa 400, 'Erlebt', 149; see also Chapter 4.
36. Rudolf Höss, *Autobiography of Rudolf Höss*, repr. in *KL Auschwitz Seen by the SS*, trans. Constantine Fitzgibbon (Oświęcim: Publications of the Państwowe Muzeum w Oświęmcu, 1972), 117. Höss wrote his memoirs during his confinement in Poland in 1946 prior to his death sentence and execution in Apr. 1947; they are fascinating in many respects, but not always reliable with respect to details and particularly dates.
37. Pery Broad, 'Reminiscences of Broad', in *KL Auschwitz Seen by the SS*, trans. Constantine Fitzgibbon (Oświęcim: Publications of the Państwowe Muzeum w Oświęmcu, 1972), 170–1.
38. Höss, *Autobiography*, 116.
39. Laurence Rees, *Auschwitz: The Nazis and the Final Solution* (London: BBC Books, 2005), 207–8.
40. Broad, 'Reminiscences of Broad', 59.
41. Ibid. 172–3.
42. Höss, *Autobiography*, 116.
43. Ibid. 122.
44. Ibid.
45. Broad, 'Reminiscences of Broad', 182–3.
46. Bernd C. Wagner, 'Gerüchte, Wissen, Verdrängung: Die IG Auschwitz und das Vernichtungslager Birkenau', in Norbert Frei, Sybille Steinbacher, and Bernd C. Wagner (eds), *Ausbeutung, Vernichtung, Öffentlichkeit. Neue Studien zur nationalsozialistischen Lagerpolitik* (Munich: K. G. Saur, 2000), 231–48, here p. 236.
47. Stephan Wachwitz, *An Invisible Country*, trans. Stephen Lehmann (Philadelphia: Paul Dry Books, 2005; orig. German 2003), 5–6.

48. Discussed in more detail in Mary Fulbrook, *Dissonant Lives: Generations and Violence through the German Dictatorships* (Oxford: Oxford University Press, 2011), 209–12.
49. GStAPK, HA XVII Rep. 201e. Ost 4 Reg. Kattowitz Nr. 15, 'Vertraulich! An den Herrn Regierungspräsidenten in Kattowitz. Bielitz, 30 Sept. 1942, Betrifft: Lagebericht für die Monate Juli, August, September 1942', p. 8.
50. ZSt, BArch, B 162/7718, fos 93–6.
51. ZSt, BArch, B 162/7718, fo. 99.
52. Hadasseh Rosensaft, *Yesterday. My Story*, intro. by Elie Wiesel (New York and Jerusalem: Yad Vashem and the Holocaust Survivors' Memoirs Project, 2004; Series Editor David Silberklang), 18.
53. Shmuel Ron, *Die Erinnerungen haben mich nie losgelassen: Vom jüdischen Widerstand im besetzten Polen* (Frankfurt am Main: Verlag Neue Kritik, 1998), 41 ff.
54. Ibid. 44.
55. Ibid. 45.
56. See Philip Friedman, 'The Messianic Complex of a Nazi Collaborator in a Ghetto: Moses Merin of Sosnowiec', in Ada June Friedman (ed.), *Roads to Extinction: Essays on the Holocaust*, intro. by Salo Wittmayer Baron (n.p.: Jewish Publication Society of America and Conference on Jewish Social Studies, 1980; first published in Hebrew in 1953), ch. 13, pp. 353–64.
57. See the overview in Saul Friedländer, *Nazi Germany and the Jews*, ii. *The Years of Extermination* (London: HarperCollins, 2007), and Walter Laqueur, *The Terrible Secret: Suppression of the Truth about Hitler's 'Final Solution'* (Boston and Toronto: Little, Brown, 1980). I have reproduced some selections from the remarkably accurate reports in the British press during the latter half of 1942 in Fulbrook, *Dissonant Lives*.
58. See Himmler's Posen speeches in Bradley Smith and Agnes Peterson (eds), *Heinrich Himmler: Geheimreden 1933 bis 1945* (Berlin: Propyläen Verlag, 1974); and Höss, *Autobiography*.

CHAPTER 10. THE DEPORTATIONS OF AUGUST 1942

1. Archivum Państwowe w Katowicach, 807/316 Polizeipräsident Sosnowitz, Bendsburg, 20 Aug. 1942, Betrifft: Sonderaktion gegen Juden, fos 224–31.
2. Archivum Państwowe w Katowicach, 807/316 Polizeipräsident Sosnowitz, Bendsburg, 20 Aug. 1942, Betrifft: Sonderaktion gegen Juden, fo. 227.
3. Ibid., fo. 225.
4. ZSt, BArch, B 162/19656, Tusia Herzberg (fos 10–27, born 1921 Będzin, Laborantin, two occasions: 16 Nov. 1961, 28 Nov. 1961), fo. 16.
5. Hadasseh Rosensaft, *Yesterday: My Story*, intro. by Elie Wiesel (New York and Jerusalem: Yad Vashem and the Holocaust Survivors' Memoirs Project, 2004; Series Editor David Silberklang), 27, 21.
6. Archivum Państwowe w Katowicach, 807/316, Polizeipräsident Sosnowitz, 'Betrifft: Sonderaktion gegen Juden' report of 20 Aug. 942, fos 224–5.

7. *Rutka's Notebook, January–April 1943* (Jerusalem: Yad Vashem, 2007), 25–6. On p. 27 the editors of Rutka's notebook mistakenly state that the Hakoach sports ground was in Sosnowiec; this is indicative of the lack of the memorial marking of the site, which is now a somewhat run-down bus terminus near the Będzin railway station.
8. Ibid. 26.
9. David Kane, USC VHA, Interview Code 7942. Born Będzin, 29 July 1928; interviewed Long Beach, FL, USA, by Robert Clary, 25 Oct. 1995.
10. ZSt, BArch, B 162/19659, testimony of Michael Lasker, Tel Aviv, 24 Dec. 1961, fo. 33.
11. *Rutka's Notebook*, 26. SS Obersturmführer Friedrich Kuczynski (born1914; put to death in Poland probably on 22 Feb. 1949; some sources state 1948) was responsible for Jewish affairs in Sosnowiec and Będzin.
12. See, e.g., ZSt, BArch, B 162/19659, testimony of Miriam Liwer, Tel Aviv, 26 Dec. 1961, fo. 46.
13. ZSt, BArch, B 162/19656, Tusia Herzberg (fos 10–27, born 1921 Będzin, Laborantin, two occasions: 16 Nov. 1961, 28 Nov. 1961), fo. 13.
14. Ibid., fo. 16.
15. ZSt, BArch, B 162/7722, testimony of Eugenia Dancygier (née Fajner), fos 23–4.
16. See, e.g., Bella Guttermann, *A Narrow Bridge to Life: Jewish Forced Labour and Survival in the Gross-Rosen Camp System, 1940–45* (New York and Oxford: Berghahn Books, 2008), 59.
17. ZSt, BArch, B 162/7718, fo. 119.
18. ZSt, BArch, B 162/19656, testimony of Szalom Herzberg, 19 Nov. 1961, fo. 29.
19. Ibid., fo. 34.
20. Ibid., fo. 35.
21. Ibid.
22. ZSt, BArch, B 162/7722, testimony of Alexander Gattmon (formerly Guttman), 19 June 1974, fo. 179.
23. Ibid.
24. Ibid.
25. Ibid.
26. ZSt, BArch, B 162/19656, Tusia Herzberg (fos 10–27, born 1921 Będzin, Laborantin, two occasions: 16 Nov. 1961, 28 Nov. 1961), fo. 14. Herzberg, who had never seen Schroeder, thought he was a 'policeman'; she clearly remembered stories about his dog.
27. ZSt, BArch, B 162/7722, testimony of Miriam Liwer (née Kaminer), 22 June 1974, fo. 194.
28. ZSt, BArch, B 162/7722, testimony of Chaim Michal Silberberg, fo. 211.
29. Some survivors list only three groups (those released, those held for work camps, those sent directly to the gas chambers); it may be that these were the most salient categories from their perspective, and that in the chaos on the ground it was not always clear that the Nazis were operating with four categories.

For an outline of the procedure in one of the Sosnowiec sports grounds, see Rosensaft, *Yesterday: My Story*, 21–2.

30. *Rutka's Notebook*, 28.
31. Ibid.
32. Jochanan Ranz, *In Nazi Claws: Bendzin 1939–1944* (New York: no publisher, 1956), 52–3.
33. Ibid.
34. ZSt, BArch, B 162/7722, testimony of Alexander Gattmon (formerly Guttman), 19 June 1974, fo. 178.
35. Ranz, *In Nazi Claws*, 54.
36. Henrietta Altmann, USC VHA, Interview Code 5639. Born Będzin, 1 Mar. 1922; interviewed Armidale, VIC, Australia, by Brenda Brain, 1 Nov. 1995.
37. Ibid.
38. Lea Eisenberg, USC VHA, Interview Code 47578. Born Będzin, 17 Jan. 1925; interviewed West Palm Beach, FL, USA, by Saerina Tauritz, 11 June 1998.
39. Zosia Baigelman, USC VHA, Interview Code 7119. Born Dąbrowa Gornicza, 7 Apr. 1928; interviewed California, USA, by Merle Goldberg, 8 Jan. 1996.
40. Gunter Faerber, USC VHA, Interview Code 41847. Born Lipiny, Swietochlowice, 25 Aug. 1928; interviewed Birmingham, UK, by Corinne Oppenheimer, 7 May 1998.
41. Doris Martin (with Ralph S. Martin), *Kiss Every Step* (privately published, 2009), 62). Note that she firmly recalls only three groups.
42. Ibid. 64.
43. Ibid. 65.
44. Ibid.
45. Ibid. 66.
46. See, e.g., ZSt, BArch, B 162/19659, testimony of Miriam Liwer, Tel Aviv, 26 Dec. 1961, fo. 47.
47. Lea Eisenberg, USC VHA, interview.
48. Ibid.
49. Sam Goldofsky, USC VHA, Interview Code 29363. Born Będzin, 28 Jan. 1928; interviewed Fort Lee, NJ, USA, by Miriam Horowitz, 29 May 1997.
50. Ranz, *In Nazi Claws*, 54–5.
51. Ibid. 55.
52. Ibid. 55–6.
53. Archivum Państwowe w Katowicach, Ältestenrat der jüdischen Kultusgemeinde in Dombrowa O/S, 1600/3, 'Der Einfluss der Evakuierung auf das jüdische Leben in O/S', fos 20–1.
54. Ibid.
55. Ibid.
56. *Rutka's Notebook*, 39.
57. Archivum Państwowe w Katowicach, 807/316, Polizeipräsident Sosnowitz, 11 Aug. 1942, fo. 214.

58. Letter from Alexandra to her mother, 8 Aug. 1942, private family archive.
59. Letter from Alexandra to her mother, 12 Aug. 1942, private family archive. An incorrect date of 12 May 1942, and an incorrect figure of 1,500 (not 15,000) Jews deported, are given in the (anonymized) published extracts from these letters in Ute Benz (ed.), *Frauen im Nationalsozialismus: Dokumente und Zeugnisse* (Munich: Beck, 1993), 225.
60. Cf. the interpetation in Mary Fulbrook, *Dissonant Lives: Generations and Violence through the German Dictatorships* (Oxford: Oxford University Press, 2011), 217, where the details and dating of the relevant letter are based on the inaccurate printed version in Benz (ed.), *Frauen im Nationalsozialismus*, 225. I had not at that point compared this excerpt with the correct date and details in the original letter in the private family archive.
61. I am very grateful to Ekkehard Klausa for pointing this out to me (personal communication, 20 Sept. 2011).
62. Franciszek Piper, *Auschwitz 1940–1945*, iii. 'Mass Murder', trans. William Brand (Oświęcim: Auschwitz-Birkenau State Museum, 2000), 21–2.
63. Letter from Alexandra to her mother, 12 Aug. 1942, private family archive.
64. Letter from Alexandra to her mother, 19 Aug. 1942, private family archive.
65. ZSt, BArch, B 162/7723, fos 212–13.
66. Ibid.
67. ZSt, BArch, B 162/7723, Bürgermeister of Ilkenau to Herrn Regierungspräsident/Stabsoffz. d. Sch.P., 16 June 1942, reporting: 'Auf Anordnung des hiesigen Landrats sind die Gendarmeriekräfte bis zum 15. Juni 1942 zum Abtransport der Juden, sowie zur Überwachung des geräumten Gebietes der Dienstabteilung zugeteilt worden.'
68. ŻIH, Warsaw, 301/2711, testimony of Jakób Freiberger, protocol N. Szternfinkiel, Katowice, 19 Aug. 1947.
69. ŻIH, Warsaw, 301/2722, testimony of Felicja Scwarc, protocol N. Szternfinkiel, Katowice, 9 Sept. 1947.
70. Wacław Widera, interview, Sączów, 15 Feb. 2009.
71. LVR, Klausa 400, 'Erlebt', 163.
72. Ibid.
73. ZSt BArch, B 162/1608, von Woedtke, testimony of Mar. 1960, fo. 129.
74. ZSt, BArch, B 162/7723, Klausa's statement, Staatsanwaltschaft Dortmund, 16 Dec. 1975, p. 212.
75. Ibid.
76. LVR, Klausa 400, 'Erlebt', 163.
77. ZSt, BArch, B 162/7723, Klausa's statement, Staatsanwaltschaft Dortmund, 16 Dec. 1975, p. 212.
78. See further pp. 299–300.
79. Klausa subsequently mentions the sports ground in connection with the story of trying to save Laib Flojm, but not as part of his own 'turning-point story' entailing a sense of shock and desire to leave the area.

80. Letter from Alexandra to her mother, 12 Aug. 1942, private family archive.
81. For the differences between West and East German accounts in this respect, see Lutz Niethammer, Alexander von Plato, and Dorothee Wierling, *Die volkseigene Erfahrung* (Berlin: Rowohlt, 1991). For an example of stories that cannot readily be checked against the evidence, see Harold Welzer, Sabine Moller, and Karoline Tschuggnall, *'Opa war kein Nazi': Nationalsozialismus und Holocaust im Familiengedächtnis* (Frankfurt am Main: Fischer Taschenbuch Verlag, 2002).
82. LVR, Klausa 400, 'Erlebt', 143.
83. ŻIH, Warsaw, 212/9, Records of the Aeltestenrat der Jüdischen Kultusgemeinde in Bendsburg O-S., fo. 118.
84. Letter from Alexandra to her mother, 2 July 1942, private family archive.
85. LVR, Klausa 400, 'Erlebt', 163.
86. Ibid.
87. Ibid. 63–4.
88. Ekkehard Klausa suggests that I have here developed a determinedly 'negative' and implausible interpretation (personal communication, 6 Nov. 2011); but I advance this interpretation merely in order to try to make sense of an otherwise self-contradictory story, one that is simply not consistent with what we know from other evidence would be plausible at this time.
89. LVR, Klausa 308, 'Zeitgeschichte und wie man sich in sie verstricken kann', vol. ii, affidavit by Ignatz Margosch, Düsseldorf, 25 June 1968.
90. LVR, Klausa 400, 'Erlebt', 164.
91. Ibid.
92. ŻIH, Warsaw, 212/13, fo. 53, gives the last mention of Laib Flojm as employed by the *Landrat*'s office.
93. Ekkehard Klausa was told in the mid-1980s by a prominent Będzin survivor, Sigmund Strochlitz, who lived in the USA, that he thought Laib Flojm might have been seen in Israel after the war; but I have not been able to find any corroboration of this claim, and there is much to suggest that it is highly improbable. It is unlikely that, following deportation in 1943, Flojm was among the few who went on to the labour camps, since he would in this case have been tattooed with a number, and there is no such record in the lists. Nor is there any other record of his existence after 1943. I am extremely grateful to William Connelly of the United States Holocaust Memorial Museum (USHMM) for searching all the available databases via the USHMM Namesearch engine, as well as checking with the International Tracing Service (ITS), and confirming that there are 'no records whatsoever for any persons named Flojm (or its likely variants) from Bedzin' apart from the records up to 1943 that I have already cited (email from William Connelly, 16 Sept. 2011). Disappearance without a trace in this way suggests that instant gassing was eventually Laib Flojm's fate too, like that of his wife and daughters some months earlier.
94. Letter from Alexandra to her mother, 5 Aug. 1943, private family archive.
95. See further pp. 299–300.

CHAPTER 11. GHETTOIZATION FOR THE 'FINAL SOLUTION'

1. Letter from Alexandra to Frau von H., 14 Aug. 1942, private family archive. I am grateful to Ekkehard Klausa for drawing this letter to my attention, and providing the quotation in his communication of 6 Nov. 2011.
2. Letter from Alexandra to her mother, 23 Aug. 1942, private family archive.
3. Archivum Państwowe w Katowicach, Regional Government, Kattowitz, 119/10630, fo. 46.
4. Archivum Państwowe w Katowicach, Rejencja Katowcije, Regional Government, Kattowitz, 119/2909, Niederschrift über die Besprechung in Auschwitz am 23.9.1942 betr. K.L. Auschwitz, Berlin 26 Sept. 1942, fo. 100. This comment and the wider purpose of the meeting is discussed further in Mary Fulbrook, *Dissonant Lives: Generations and Violence through the German Dictatorships* (Oxford: Oxford Uiversity Press, 2011), 209–11.
5. GStAPK, HA XVII Rep. 201e. Ost 4 Reg. Kattowitz Nr. 14, Politische Lageberichte sowie Kurzberichte über die bisherige Aufbauarbeit der Landräte, Bd. 1 Landrat des Kreises Bendzin/Bendsburg, 1939–Sept. 1942, pp. 5–6.
6. Ibid. 2.
7. GStAPK, HA XVII Rep. 201e. Ost 4 Reg. Kattowitz Nr. 13, Der Oberbürgermeister der Stadt Sosnowitz. 6 Oct. 1942, fo. 127, p. 3.
8. Ibid., pp. 2–3.
9. See Archivum Państwowe w Katowicach, Starosta Powiatu Będzinskiego, 771/91, fos 139 ff.
10. Archivum Państwowe w Katowicach, Anordnungen des Herrn Landrat, 771/813, fos 20–1, Bendsburg, 9 Sept. 1942, *Landrat*, fo. 20.
11. Archivum Państwowe w Katowicach, Starosta Powiatu Będzinskiego, 771/91, 'Vermerk' of 10 Sept. 1942, fo. 143, p. 2.
12. GStAPK, HA XVII Rep. 201e. Ost 4 Reg. Kattowitz Nr. 14, Politische Lageberichte sowie Kurzberichte über die bisherige Aufbauarbeit der Landräte, Bd. 1 Landrat des Kreises Bendzin/Bendsburg, 1939–Sept. 1942, p. 10. Ekkehard Klausa interprets this as a 'typical attempt to argue against a Nazi measure with a Nazi argument' (personal communication, 6 Nov. 2011)—but again, whatever the possible inner motives, the speech act itself serves simply to legitimate and reinforce racist thinking.
13. See, e.g., ibid., p. 2.
14. Archivum Państwowe w Katowicach, Regional Government, Kattowitz, 119–6335, 'Sperrliste für Wehrbezirkskommando Kattowitz', prepared by Udo Klausa on 16 Apr. 1942.
15. Archivum Państwowe w Katowicach, Regional Government, Kattowitz, 119–6335, letter from Wehrersatz-Inspektion, Kattowitz, to Regional President, Kattowitz, 4 Sept. 1942, fo. 118.
16. Ibid., fo. 119.
17. Archivum Państwowe w Katowicach, Regional Government, Kattowitz, 119–6335, letter from Wehrersatz-Inspektion, Kattowitz, to Regional President, Kattowitz, 18 Sept. 1940, fo. 120.

18. Archivum Państwowe w Katowicach, Regional Government, Kattowitz, 119–6335, letter on behalf of Springorum to the Reich Minister of the Interior, Berlin, 25 Sept. 1942, fos 122–3.
19. Archivum Państwowe w Katowicach, Regional Government, Kattowitz, 119–6335, letter from Generalleutnant u. Inspekteur, Wehrersatz-Inspektion, Kattowitz, 20 Oct. 1942, fo. 127.
20. Letter from Alexandra to her mother, 14 Sept. 1942, private family archive.
21. See, e.g., LVR, Klausa 400, Udo Klausa, 'Erlebt—Davongekommen. Erinnerungen'. vol. i. 'Erlebt—Überlebt, 1910–1948' (1980). See also pp. 92–3.
22. GStAPK, HA XVII Rep. 201e. Ost 4 Reg. Kattowitz/2, Morgenmeldungen bzw. Ereignismeldungen über politische Vorfälle in Oberschlesien seitens des Kommandos der Schutzpolizei bzw. des Kommandeurs der Gendarmerie für die Zeit vom 2. Mai bis 30. Mai 1940 und 15. August 1942 bis 6. Dezember 1943, report of 20 Sept. 1942, fo. 26.
23. GStAPK, HA XVII Rep. 201e. Ost 4 Reg. Kattowitz/2, Morgenmeldungen bzw. Ereignismeldungen über politische Vorfälle in Oberschlesien seitens des Kommandos der Schutzpolizei bzw. des Kommandeurs der Gendarmerie für die Zeit vom 2. Mai bis 30. Mai 1940 und 15. August 1942 bis 6. Dezember 1943, Morgenmeldung Nr. 11, 8 Oct. 1942, fo. 33.
24. Ibid., Morgenmeldung Nr. 28, 4 Nov. 42, fo. 42.
25. Ibid., Morgenmeldung Nr. 34, 17 Nov. 1942, fo. 44.
26. ZSt, BArch, B 162/2196, fo. 65.
27. Ibid., fo. 73.
28. Archivum Państwowe w Katowicach, Starosta Powiatu Będzinskiego, 771/91, fo. 151, p. 2.
29. Ekkehard Klausa states that his father did not deny knowledge of Auschwitz as a 'normal' concentration (rather than extermination) camp—from which therefore it would presumably be acceptable to pursue fleeing prisoners of war—and that he simply did not know about the gas chambers (personal communication, 6 Nov. 2011). The significance of Udo Klausa's representation of his knowledge or otherwise of what he calls 'this function' of Auschwitz, and his implict restriction of all that is evil to the gates of the gas chambers, is discussed further in Chapter 12.
30. GStAPK, HA XVII Rep. 229. BA Ost 12 St. Bendsburg/1.
31. On Mildner and the Auschwitz summary court, see, e.g., Pery Broad, 'Reminiscences of Broad', in *KL Auschwitz Seen by the SS*, trans. Constantine Fitzgibbon (Oświęcim: Publications of the Państwowe Muzeum w Oświęmcu, 1972), 139–98.
32. GStAPK, HA XVII Rep. 229. BA Ost 12 St. Bendsburg/1, report of 29 Sept. 1942.
33. Ibid.
34. Ibid.
35. Cf., e.g., the concepts used in many USC Shoah Foundation interviews. The question of the relationships between later discourses in the media and

individual frameworks of self-representation goes beyond the scope of the present discussion.

36. GStAPK, HA XVII Rep. 201e. Ost 4 Reg. Kattowitz Nr. 14, Politische Lageberichte sowie Kurzberichte über die bisherige Aufbauarbeit der Landräte, Bd. 1 Landrat des Kreises Bendzin/Bendsburg, 1939–Sept. 1942, report of 3 Oct. 1942, p. 7.
37. Repr. in Yitzhak Arad, Israel Gutman, and Abraham Margaliot (eds.), *Documents on the Holocaust*, trans. Lea Ben Dor (Bison Books, 1999; orig. Jerusalem: Yad Vashem, 1981), 275–6.
38. Unfortunately the relevant Gestapo files from the Kattowitz area appear to be entirely missing from the archive. Although some series of other files are incomplete owing to the vicissitudes of preservation, including the reuse in impoverished post-war Poland of the back sides of the paper mountains left by the efficient wartime German bureaucracy, it would seem more likely that the Gestapo files were systematically destroyed at the end of the war in a last-minute effort to dispose of clearly incriminating evidence.
39. GStAPK, HA XVII Rep. 201e. Ost 4 Reg. Kattowitz Nr. 13, Der Oberbürgermeister der Stadt Sosnowitz, 6 Oct. 1942, fo. 126, p. 1.
40. Ibid., fo. 127, p. 3.
41. Ibid., fo. 127, pp. 3–4.
42. Letter from Alexandra to Frau von H., 14 Jan. 1943, private family archive.
43. ZSt, BArch, B 162/7720, Pawel Wiedermann, 'Plowa Bestia' [The Blond Beast] (Munich, 1948).
44. Ibid., fos 7–9.
45. Ibid., fo. 10.
46. Archivum Państwowe w Katowicach, Akta Miasta Bedzina 773/1194, report of 15 Apr. 1943 on the Stadkämmerer meeting of 8 Apr. 1943, fos 12–13.
47. Doris Martin (with Ralph S. Martin), *Kiss Every Step* (privately published, 2009), 75–6.
48. Ibid. 76–7.
49. Gunter Faerber, USC VHA, Interview Code 41847. Born Lipiny, Swietochlowice, 25 Aug. 1928; interviewed Birmingham, UK, by Corinne Oppenheimer, 7 May 1998.
50. Milla Tenenbaum (née Mindzia Schickman, born in Chorzów; lived first in Dąbrowa then Będzin), USC VHA, Interview Code 33627. Born Chorzów, 28 Sept. 1932; interviewed Toronto, Ontario, Canada, by Fran Starr, 16 Sept. 1997.
51. Ibid.
52. Ibid.
53. *Rutka's Notebook, January–April 1943* (Jerusalem: Yad Vashem, 2007). This paragraph, and some other parts of this chapter, are also published as part of a chapter in Andrea Löw, Anna Hájková, and Doris Bergen (eds), *Schriftenreihe der Vierteljahrshefte für Zeitgeschichte*, 106 (Munich: Oldenbourg, 2013).

54. *Rutka's Notebook*, 35.
55. Ibid.
56. Ibid. 50.
57. Ibid. 57.
58. Quoted in Philip Friedman, 'The Messianic Complex of a Nazi Collaborator in a Ghetto: Moses Merin of Sosnowiec', in Ada June Friedman (ed.), *Roads to Extinction: Essays on the Holocaust*, intro. by Salo Wittmayer Baron (n.p.: Jewish Publication Society of America and Conference on Jewish Social Studies, 1980; first published in Hebrew in 1953), ch. 13, p. 362.
59. See the near contemporary account by David Liwer, *Ir Hametin—Hashmadat Hayehudim be'ezor Zagblembie (Town of the Dead—The Extermination of the Jews of the Zaglembia Region)*, trans. A. Sz. Sztejn (Tel Aviv, 1946); trans. into English by Ada Holtzman, in honour of Lance Ackerfeld, pp. 123–9. Section on 'Defence' <http://www.jewishgen.org/yizkor/zaglembia1/zag1-123.html> (accessed 6 Sept. 2011).
60. Arno Lustiger (ed.), *Zum Kampf auf Leben und Tod! Das Buch vom Widerstand der Juden 1933–1945* (Cologne: Kiepenheuer and Witsch, 1994), 143–60.
61. Archivum Państwowe w Katowicach, Akta Miasta Bedzina 773/1194, fo. 21.
62. Ibid., fo. 13.
63. Ibid., fos 62–3.
64. ZSt, BArch, B 162/19683, telegram from Ernst Kaltenbrunner, 21 May 1943, fos 242, 244.
65. Friedman, 'Messianic Complex', 363; see also ZSt, BArch, B 162/7715, fo. 52.
66. ZSt, BArch, B 162/19656, Tusia Herzberg (fos 10–27, born 1921 Będzin, Laborantin, two occasions: 16 Nov. 1961, 28 Nov. 1961), fo. 19.
67. See Jochanan Ranz, *In Nazi Claws: Bendzin 1939–1944* (New York: no publisher, 1956), 69–70.
68. Ibid. 71–2.
69. Letter from Alexandra to her mother, 2 July 1943, private family archive; also in Ute Benz (ed.), *Frauen im Nationalsozialismus: Dokumente und Zeugnisse* (Munich: Beck, 1993), 227.
70. ZSt, BArch, B 162/7715, fo. 51. See also David Liwer, 'Bedzin in her Destruction', excerpts from the book *City of the Dead*, trans. Lance Ackerfeld (Tel Aviv: Teverski, 5707, 1946/7), <http://www.jewishgen.org/yizkor/bedzin/bed342.html> (accessed 9 Mar. 2008); also M. Gilbert, *The Holocaust* (London: Collins, 1986), 340, 598.
71. ZSt, BArch, B 162/19658, fos 54–61.
72. Wiener Library, 054-EA-1011, ref. P.III.h.No. 1174a (Auschwitz), p. 7.
73. ZSt, BArch, B 162/7720, letter from the Bürgermeister of Będzin to the Housing Office, 27 July 1943, fo. 28.
74. Abraham Froch (né Frochcwag), USC VHA, Interview Code 92. Born Będzin, 20 Feb. 1927; interviewed Calabasas, CA, USA, by Merle Goldberg, 8 Sept. 1994.

75. Lustiger (ed.), *Zum Kampf auf Leben und Tod!*, 148–9; Ranz, *In Nazi Claws*, 88–90.
76. Ranz, *In Nazi Claws*, 78.
77. ZSt, BArch, B 162/19659, testimony of Hirsch Barenblatt, fos 3, 15å.
78. ZSt, BArch, B 162/7715, fo. 52.
79. See, e.g., ZSt, BArch, B 162/7718, testimony given by a survivor on 9 Aug. 1946, fo. 80.
80. ZSt, BArch, B 162/7715, fo. 52.
81. Arno Lustiger, *Sing mit Schmerz und Zorn: Ein Leben für den Widerstand* (Berlin: Aufbau Verlag, 2004), 34.
82. Gitel Donath, *My Bones don't Rest in Auschwitz: A Lonely Battle to Survive German Tyranny* (Montreal: Kaplan Publishing, 1999), 182 ff., 211.
83. Martin, *Kiss Every Step*.
84. Shmuel Ron, *Die Erinnerungen haben mich nie losgelassen: Vom jüdischen Widerstand im besetzten Polen* (Frankfurt am Main: Verlag Neue Kritik, 1998).
85. Letter from Alexandra to her mother, 5 Aug. 1943, private family archive.
86. LVR, Klausa 400, 'Erlebt', 165.

CHAPTER 12. FINAL THRESHOLDS

1. Wieslaw Kielar, *Anus Mundi: Five Years in Auschwitz* (Harmondsworth: Penguin, 1982; orig. Polish 1972; trans. from the German edn by Susanne Flatauer). See also Yad Vashem, VT-1924, Leah Melnik (born 1908), interviewed by Miriam Avezer, 10 June 1998, pp. 33–5.
2. Johann Paul Kremer, Diary, repr. in *KL Auschwitz Seen by the SS*, trans. Constantine Fitzgibbon (Oświęcim: Publications of the Państwowe Muzeum w Oświęmcu, 1972), 215–16.
3. Reproduced in *KL Auschwitz Seen by the SS*, 216.
4. Kremer, Diary, in *KL Auschwitz Seen by the SS*, 216–17.
5. See for renowned examples Charlotte Delbo, *Auschwitz and After*, trans. Rose C. Lamont; intro. Lawrence Langer (New Haven and London: Yale University Press, 1995); Primo Levi, *If this is a Man*, trans. Stuart Woolf (London: Everyman's Library, 2000; orig. 1947).
6. Wiener Library, 068-WL-1631, M. Lichtenstein, 'Eighteen Months in the Oswiecim Extermination Camp', Jewish Survivors' Report, Documents of Nazi Guilt, no. 1, p. 3. Lichtenstein's testimony was given to the Jewish Central Information Office in May 1945, shortly after his arrival in London, and was carefully checked for authenticity at the time.
7. Ibid. 4.
8. Wiener Library, 054-EA-1011, ref. P.III.h.No. 1174a (Auschwitz), p. 7.
9. Cf. Raul Hilberg, *The Destruction of the European Jews* (updated edn; New Haven: Yale University Press, 2003; orig. 1961), iii. 972–3.
10. Jenny Spritzer, *Ich war Nr. 10291* (Darmstadt: Darmstädter Blätter, 1980; orig, 1946), 78.

11. Delbo, *Auschwitz and After*; Ruth Klüger, *weiter leben* (Munich: dtv, 1992); Levi, *If this is a Man*; Ella Liebermann-Shiber, *On the Edge of the Abyss* (Western Galilee: Ghetto Fighters House, 1992).
12. Recounted by Raya Kagan in Arno Lustiger (ed.), *Zum Kampf auf Leben und Tod! Das Buch vom Widerstand der Juden 1933–1945* (Cologne: Kiepenheuer and Witsch, 1994), 223–7.
13. Josef Baumgarten, USC VHA, Interview Code 10509. Born Będzin, 7 July 1925; interviewed San Diego, CA, USA, by John Kent, 22 Dec. 1995.
14. Surgical diary of 'Block 21' (*Operationsbuch Auschwitz*), Auschwitz documentation centre 18.968. I am extremely grateful to Paul Weindling for providing this reference for me. See also the (as yet unpublished) database in progress on 'The Victims of Unethical Human Experiments and Coerced Research under National Socialism', compiled by Paul Weindling, Anna von Villiez, Marius Turda, Aleksandra Loewenau, and Nichola Hunt, in which details of more than a dozen other victims from Będzin are included.
15. On Dering, see Robert J. Lifton, *The Nazi Doctors: Medical Killing and the Psychology of Genocide* (New York: Basic Books, 2000), 246–9.
16. At this point, Baumgarten broke down in tears, and the interviewer had to make a pause in the interview.
17. Doris Martin (with Ralph S. Martin), *Kiss Every Step* (privately published, 2009).
18. Shmuel Ron, *Die Erinnerungen haben mich nie losgelassen: Vom jüdischen Widerstand im besetzten Polen* (Frankfurt am Main: Verlag Neue Kritik, 1998).
19. Blat's account can be found in Lustiger (ed.), *Zum Kampf auf Leben und Tod!*, 154–60.
20. Ibid. 158.
21. See Erin Einhorn, *The Pages in Between: A Holocaust Legacy of Two Families, One Home* (New York: Simon and Schuster, 2008), and Mira Binford's film, *Diamonds in the Snow* (1994).
22. Milla Tenenbaum (née Mindzia Schickman, born in Chorzów; lived first in Dąbrowa then Będzin), USC VHA, Interview Code 33627. Born Chorzów, 28 Sept. 1932; interviewed Toronto, Ontario, Canada, by Fran Starr, 16 Sept. 1997.
23. For overviews, see: Józef Garliński, *Fighting Auschwitz: The Resistance Movement in the Concentration Camp* (Glasgow: Fontana/Collins, 1976); Henryk Świebocki, 'The Resistance Movement,' in *Auschwitz 1940–1945*, iv, trans. William Brand (Oświęcim: Auschwitz–Birkenau State Museum, 2000); and Eric Friedler, Barbara Siebert, and Andreas Kilian (eds), *Zeugen aus der Todeszone: Das jüdische Sonderkommando in Auschwitz* (Lüneberg: zu Klampen, 2002).
24. On Ala Gertner's time in Auschwitz, see Ann Kirschner, *Sala's Gift: My Mother's Holocaust Story* (New York: Free Press, 2006), 185–93.
25. The following account is based on the memoirs of participants who survived, including Anna Heilman, *Never Far Away: The Auschwitz Chronicles of Anna Heilman*, ed. Sheldon Schwartz, intro. by Dieter K. Buse and Juergen C. Doerr

(Calgary, AB: University of Calgary Press, 2001); Lore Shelley (comp., trans., ed.), *The Union Kommando in Auschwitz: The Auschwitz Munition Factory through the Eyes of its Former Slave Labourers*, foreword by Dori Laub, afterword by Israel Gutman (Studies in the Shoah, 13; Lanham, MD, New York, and London: University Press of America, 1996); Brana Gurewitsch (ed.), *Mothers, Sisters, Resisters: Oral Histories of Women who Survived the Holocaust* (Tuscaloosa, AL, and London: University of Alabama Press, 1998).

26. Anna Heilman (née Wajcblum), in Gurewitsch (ed.), *Mothers, Sisters, Resisters*, 296–7.
27. Rose Meth's account in ibid. 299–305.
28. The difference in numbering relates to whether the original gas chamber in Auschwitz I is numbered as one, and the four new ones built in Birkenau are then sequentially numbered from two to five; or whether these four are numbered in a sequence of their own, as one to four. In either case, Roman numerals are conventionally used.
29. Garliński, *Fighting Auschwitz*, 239–40. See also the eyewitness account in Miklós Nyiszli, *I was Doctor Mengele's Assistant* (Oświęcim: Frap Books, 2001), 119–35; this account, while providing a vivid description of the frantic attempts at resistance and violent suppression of the revolt, provides details and figures that cannot be corroborated from other sources.
30. Rose Meth, in Gurewitsch (ed.), *Mothers, Sisters, Resisters*, 303.
31. See, e.g., Friedler et al (eds), *Zeugen aus der Todeszone*, 281.
32. Shelley (ed.), *Union Kommando in Auschwitz*, 142.
33. Heilman, *Never Far Away*, 135.
34. Lustiger (ed.), *Zum Kampf auf Leben und Tod!*, 221–2.
35. Both dates are mentioned in different accounts; possibly two women were hanged on the evening of one day and two on the morning of the following day, rather than on the morning and evening of the same day.
36. Shiber's account of her life in Shelley (ed.), *Union Kommando in Auschwitz*, 103–5.
37. Shiber's drawing and account of the execution in ibid. 124.
38. Ibid. 137.
39. Rose Ickowicz Rechnic, *Try to Survive . . . and Tell the World* ([USA]: Real Press, 2002), 98–102.
40. Heilman, *Never Far Away*, 140. A full account of the executions, written in 1993 in Ottowa, is given on pp. 138–41.
41. LVR, Klausa 400, Udo Klausa, 'Erlebt—Davongekommen. Erinnerungen'. vol. i. 'Erlebt—Überlebt, 1910–1948' (1980), 156.
42. ZSt, BArch, B 162/7723, fo. 212.
43. LVR, Klausa 400, 'Erlebt', 156.
44. ZSt, BArch, B 162/1608, fo. 19R.
45. Ibid., fos 19R–20.
46. Ibid., fo. 127.
47. Ibid., fo. 127.

48. Ibid., fo. 129.
49. Ibid., fo. 126.
50. ZSt, BArch, B 162/19657, fos 506, 517.
51. ZSt, BArch, B 162/1609.
52. ZSt, BArch, B 162/7711, fos 126–8.
53. ZSt, BArch, B 162/7723, fo. 53.
54. Ibid., fo. 45.
55. Ibid., fos 214–16.
56. Ekkehard Klausa states that his father in fact had few if any alternative options, and was almost entirely trapped in the system, the only acceptable option being the one he took: 'escape' to the army (personal communication, 6 Nov. 2011). But Udo Klausa certainly had far more by way of privileges and options than did the Jews whom he had helped to impoverish and imprison. It is the fact that so many Germans felt they had to go along with and implement whatever they were asked to do, and whatever their inner doubts, that made this system function in the way that it did.
57. Wiener Library, 068-WL-1631, Lichtenstein, 'Eighteen Months', p. 15.

CHAPTER 13. AFTERWARDS AND AFTER-WORDS

1. Letter from Alexandra to her mother, Crottorf, 29 Nov. 1948, private family archive.
2. On the post-war careers of members of the SS who were involved in the policies of 'Germanization', see, e.g., Isabel Heinemann, '*Rasse, Siedlung, deutsches Blut*': *Die Rasse- und Siedlungshauptamt der SS und die rassenpolitische Neuordnung Europas* (Göttingen: Wallstein Verlag, 2003), 'Nachkriegskarrieren', 585–8.
3. Arnold Shay, *From Bendzin to Auschwitz: A Journey to Hell* (Hanover, MA: Christopher Publishing House, 1996), 4. See also Donald Grey Brownlow and John Eleuthère du Pont, *Hell was my Home: Arnold Shay, Survivor of the Holocaust* (Hanover, MA: Christopher Publishing House, 1983).
4. Josef Baumgarten, USC VHA, Interview Code 10509. Born Będzin, 7 July 1925; interviewed San Diego, CA, USA, by John Kent, 22 Dec. 1995.
5. Yetta Kleiner, USC VHA, Interview Code 288. Born Będzin, 5 Mar. 1928; interviewed Toronto, Ontario, Canada, by Anita Jacobson, 28 Nov. 1994.
6. Milla Tenenbaum (née Mindzia Schickman, born in Chorzów; lived first in Dąbrowa then Będzin), USC VHA, Interview Code 33627. Born Chorzów, 28 Sept. 1932; interviewed Toronto, Ontario, Canada, by Fran Starr, 16 Sept. 1997.
7. LVR, Klausa 322, 'Reise nach Schlesien 1989', p. 3.
8. Basil Kerski and Joanna Skibińska (eds), *Ein jüdisches Leben im Zeitalter der Extreme: Gespräche mit Arno Lustiger* (Osnabrück: fibre Verlag, 2004), 104–7.
9. Gila Lustiger, *So sind wir* (Berlin: Berliner Taschenbuch Verlag, 2007).
10. These comments raise issues of far broader significance and scope than can be adequately considered here.

11. For illustrated pamphlets and more substantial publications produced or supported by the city authorities and municipal museums of Będzin and Sosnowiec, see, e.g.: Boresława Ciepieli, *Żydzi w Zagłębiu Dąbrowskim i Okolicy* (Będzin: Progres, 2004); Aleksandry Namysło (ed.), *Zagłada Żydów Zagłębiowskich* (Będzin: MAGIC, 2004); Aleksandry Namysło, *Zanim nadeszła Zagłada... Żydzi w Zagłębiu Dąbrowskim w okresie okupacji niemieckiej* (Sosnowiec: Muzeum w Sosnowcu, 2008); Adam Szydłowski, *Synagoga Mizrachi: The Synagogue of Mizrachi* (Będzin: MAGIC, 2005).
12. Szydłowski, *Synagoga Mizrachi*, 8.
13. Robert Garstka, interview, 10 Aug. 2008.
14. Robert Garstka, *Dom Wieczności* (Będzin: Via Arte, 2008).
15. Josef Baumgarten, USC VHA, interview.
16. Erin Einhorn, *The Pages in Between: A Holocaust Legacy of Two Families, One Home* (New York: Simon and Schuster, 2008).
17. Nor is this the appropriate place for discussion of this topic. But see further, e.g.: Robert Cherry and Annamaria Orla-Bukowska (eds), *Rethinking Poles and Jews: Troubled Past, Brighter Future* (Lanham, MD: Rowman and Little, 2007); Antony Polonsky (ed.), *My Brother's Keeper: Recent Polish Debates on the Holocaust* (London: Routledge, 1990).
18. See Bradley Smith and Agnes Peterson (eds), *Heinrich Himmler: Geheimreden 1933 bis 1945* (Berlin: Propyläen Verlag, 1974), 169.
19. LVR, Klausa 400, Udo Klausa, 'Erlebt—Davongekommen. Erinnerungen'. vol. i. 'Erlebt—Überlebt, 1910–1948' (1980), 146.
20. This is, of course, speculation, as Ekkehard Klausa points out (personal communication, 6 Nov. 2011); but I do know that my mother was explicitly frustrated by what she felt was a restriction in her friendship to discussion of largely social topics, such as updating news of family and friends, but never addressing difficult issues of politics and history in the way that she could with other former schoolfriends.
21. Ekkehard Klausa, personal communication, 21 Jan. 2012.
22. Ekkehard Klausa suggests that 'cowardice' is an inappropriate word, and that 'self-preservation' would be more appropriate, given that in practice Udo Klausa could not have achieved anything different at the time (personal communication, 6 Nov. 2011). This does not, however, deal with the question of prevarications, omissions, and apparent lack of remorse after 1945; Udo Klausa was never quite able to face up to admitting the full scope and implications of his role.
23. See further Mary Fulbrook, *Dissonant Lives: Generations and Violence through the German Dictatorships* (Oxford: Oxford University Press, 2011); Michael Wildt, *Generation des Unbedingten: Das Führungskorps des Reichssicherheitshauptamtes* (Hamburg: Hamburger Edition, 2002).
24. Ekkehard Klausa suggests that his father actually began to break with Nazism in the later 1930s, and that 1942 was in effect the final straw for him (personal communication, 21 Jan. 2012).

25. LVR, Klausa 400, 'Erlebt', 145.
26. On 'social death', see Marion Kaplan, *Between Dignity and Despair: Jewish Life in Nazi Germany* (Oxford: Oxford University Press, 1998).
27. There is an often-repeated family story, not corroborated as far as I know by any contemporary evidence, that, on being asked by a trainee nurse whether the Red Cross should also treat any Jews seeking medical assistance, Alexandra replied that the Red Cross had a commitment to treat everyone, regardless of race, religion, or social class (Ekkehard Klausa, personal communication, 2 Feb. 2012; see also LVR, Klausa 400, 'Erlebt', 153–4).
28. Anonymizing names, as is the convention with respect to those who were not 'persons of contemporary history' by virtue of their roles, clearly does not work in this particular case. There are growing exceptions to this rule—a rule that is so often emphasized by archivists in the course of research, with blacking-out of names on occasion making it very hard to make sense of documents—with a widening of the sphere of what is held to be permissible in historical writing. See, e.g., Gudrun Schwarz, *Eine Frau an seiner Seite: Ehefrauen in der 'SS-Sippengemeinschaft'* (Hamburg: Hamburger Edition, 1997).
29. Given my mother's deep commitment to Quaker principles, I suspect that she would have been determined to understand and achieve reconciliation; I think she would also have been shocked; but she would in all likelihood have retained a desire to feel accepted, and would therefore not have wanted to risk further exclusion from a friendship that mattered so much to her. However, all of this is again pure speculation.
30. See, e.g., the debates unleashed by Hannah Arendt's critique of the Jewish Councils in *Eichmann in Jerusalem* (London: Penguin, 2006; orig. 1963); see also Shmuel Ron's remarks on the atmosphere in post-war Israel, in *Die Erinnerungen haben mich nie losgelassen: Vom jüdischen Widerstand im besetzten Polen* (Frankfurt am Main: Verlag Neue Kritik, 1998).

Index

Bold entries refer to illustrations or maps.